Understanding Google Docs

2025 Edition

Kevin Wilson

Understanding Google Docs: 2025 Ed

Copyright © 2025 Elluminet Press

This work is subject to copyright. All rights are reserved by the Publisher, whether the whole or part of the material is concerned, specifically the rights of translation, reprinting, reuse of illustrations, recitation, broadcasting, reproduction on microfilms or in any other physical way, and transmission or information storage and retrieval, electronic adaptation, computer software, or by similar or dissimilar methodology now known or hereafter developed. Exempted from this legal reservation are brief excerpts in connection with reviews or scholarly analysis or material supplied specifically for the purpose of being entered and executed on a computer system, for exclusive use by the purchaser of the work. Duplication of this publication or parts thereof is permitted only under the provisions of the Copyright Law of the Publisher's location, in its current version, and permission for use must always be obtained from the Publisher. Permissions for use may be obtained through Rights Link at the Copyright Clearance Centre. Violations are liable to prosecution under the respective Copyright Law.

Trademarked names, logos, and images may appear in this book. Rather than use a trademark symbol with every occurrence of a trademarked name, logo, or image we use the names, logos, and images only in an editorial fashion and to the benefit of the trademark owner, with no intention of infringement of the trademark.

The use in this publication of trade names, trademarks, service marks, and similar terms, even if they are not identified as such, is not to be taken as an expression of opinion as to whether or not they are subject to proprietary rights.

While the advice and information in this book are believed to be true and accurate at the date of publication, neither the authors nor the editors nor the publisher can accept any legal responsibility for any errors or omissions that may be made. The publisher makes no warranty, express or implied, with respect to the material contained herein.

iStock.com/golibo, PeopleImages, ymgerman. Photo 130859010 © Kaspars Grinvalds - Dreamstime.com. Photo 103557713 © Konstantin Kolosov - Dreamstime.com. Yuri Arcurs via Getty Images, Cover Image by Chris Bardgett / Alamy Stock Photo, iStockPhoto elenabs

Publisher: Elluminet Press
Director: Kevin Wilson
Lead Editor: Steven Ashmore
Technical Reviewer: Mike Taylor, Robert Ashcroft
Copy Editors: Joanne Taylor, James Marsh
Proof Reader: Mike Taylor
Indexer: James Marsh
Cover Designer: Kevin Wilson

eBook versions and licenses are also available for most titles. Any source code or other supplementary materials referenced by the author in this text is available to readers at www.elluminetpress.com/resources

For detailed information about how to locate your book's resources, go to www.elluminetpress.com/resources

Table of Contents

About the Author 8

Acknowledgements 9

Introducing Google Docs 10
    Introduction 11
    Google Account Types 15
    Gemini 16
    Google One 17

Getting Started 18
    Creating a Google Account 19
    Sign In 20
    Get Started 21
        Menus & Toolbars 22
        Page Rulers 23
    Download Google Chrome 24

Building Documents 26
    Creating a New Document 27
    Entering Text 28
    Dictate Text 28
        Setup 28
        Voice Commands 30
    Selecting Text 31
    Text Justification 32
    Paragraph Indents 33
        Indenting a Line 33
        First Line Indent 33
        Hanging Indent 34
        Customize Indents with the Ruler 36
        Tab Stops 37
    Paragraph Spacing 39
    Line Spacing 40
    Cut, Copy & Paste 41
        Cut & Paste 41
        Copy & Paste 43
        Paste without Formatting 45
    Bold, Italic & Underlined 46

Superscript & Subscript	47
Highlighting Text	48
Text Color	49
Text Size	49
Change Font	50
Change Case	51
Paragraph Styles	52
Bullet Lists	53
Numbered Lists	53
Inserting Symbols	54
Hidden Characters	55
Hyper-links	57
Equations	58
Page & Section Breaks	61
Inserting Page Breaks	*61*
Inserting Section Breaks	*62*
Headers and Footers	63
Inserting Headers	*63*
Inserting Footers	*64*
Formatting Headers and Footers	*65*
Footnotes	67
Creating Columns	68
Contents Pages	69
Emojis	71
Document Tabs	72
Smart Canvas	73
Smart Chips	*73*
Smart Templates	*75*
Smart Checklists	*76*
Smart Tables	*77*
Automatic Document Generation	78

Adding Images & Graphics 80

Adding Images	81
From Google Drive	*81*
Google Photos	*82*
Upload from PC	*83*
Web Search	*84*
Camera on Laptop	*86*
Camera on Tablet/Phone	*87*
Resize Images	89
Rotate an Image	90
Cropping Images	91

Wrap Text around Images 93
Drawings 95
    WordArt 96
    Shapes 97
    Images 100
Generating Images with AI 102

Tables and Charts 104

Tables 105
    Inserting Tables 105
    Text Formatting 107
    Cell Color 107
    Borders 109
    Cell Padding 111
    Cell Alignment 112
    Split Cells 113
    Merge Cells 113
    Row Height 114
    Column Width 114
    Insert Row 115
    Insert Column 117
    Delete Column 118
    Delete Row 118
Adding Charts 119
Customise your Chart 121
    Chart Style 123
    Chart & Axis Titles 123
    Data Series 124
    Horizontal Axis 125
    Vertical Axis 125
    Gridlines and Ticks 126
Download & Publish Chart 127

Sharing and Collaboration 128

Sharing a Document 129
Accepting the Invitation to Collaborate 131
Editing Shared Documents 132
    Making Edits 132
    Chatting with Other Collaborators 132
    Making Comments 133
    Reply to Comment 134
    Resolve a Comment 134
    Making Suggestions 135

Sharing a Link 137
    Sharing a Link with Anyone 137
Restricted Links 139
People without Google Accounts 141
Stop Sharing a File 143
Integrated eSignatures 144
    Adding an eSignature 144
    Signing a Document 147
Document Approvals 148

Managing Documents 150

Opening Documents 151
Uploading Documents 153
Downloading & Converting Documents 155
Printing Documents 156
    Page Setup 156
    Print 159
Email as Attachment 163
Document Translation 165
Define & Lookup 166
Spelling & Grammar 167
AI Writing Tools 170
    Help Me Write 170
Add-ons 172
    Install 172
    Manage Add-ons 175
    Useful Add-ons 175

Using Tablets 176

Download Google Docs 177
Getting Started 178
Formatting Text 181
Paragraph Formatting 182
Insert Images 183
Resize Image 185
Insert Table 186
Insert Row 187
Insert Column 187
Format your Table 188

Using Google Drive 190

Opening Google Drive 191
    On the Web 191

  The App.. *191*
 Getting Around Google Drive...192
 Sync Files with your Computer 195
  Google Drive for Desktop *195*
  Backup and Sync.. *195*

Resources 200
 File Resources 201
 Video Resources 202
 Scanning the Codes 204
  iPhone *204*
  Android *205*

Index 206

About the Author

With over 20 years' experience in the computer industry, Kevin Wilson has made a career out of technology and showing others how to use it. After earning a master's degree in computer science, software engineering, and multimedia systems, Kevin has held various positions in the IT industry including graphic & web design, programming, building & managing corporate networks, and IT support.

He serves as senior writer and director at Elluminet Press Ltd, he periodically teaches computer science at college, and works as an IT trainer in England while researching for his PhD. His books have become a valuable resource among the students in England, South Africa, Canada, and in the United States.

Kevin's motto is clear: "If you can't explain something simply, then you haven't understood it well enough." To that end, he has created the Exploring Tech Computing series, in which he breaks down complex technological subjects into smaller, easy-to-follow steps that students and ordinary computer users can put into practice.

Acknowledgements

Thanks to all the staff at Luminescent Media & Elluminet Press for their passion, dedication and hard work in the preparation and production of this book.

To all my friends and family for their continued support and encouragement in all my writing projects.

To all my colleagues, students and testers who took the time to test procedures and offer feedback on the book

Finally thanks to you the reader for choosing this book. I hope it helps you to use Google Docs with greater understanding.

1 Introducing Google Docs

Google Docs began as a web-based word processor called Writely, created by a company called Upstartle. In March 2006, Google acquired Upstartle and its Writely platform, recognizing the potential for web-based collaboration tools. After the acquisition, Writely was merged into Google's new offering called Google Docs & Spreadsheets, which launched publicly in October 2006.

Following the launch, Google continued to enhance the platform by integrating it more tightly with other services and expanding its capabilities. Over time, Google Docs evolved from a simple online word processor into a fully featured collaboration tool, with real-time editing, commenting, version control, and seamless sharing across devices.

Today, it forms a central part of the Google Workspace suite, which is used by millions of users worldwide in education, business, and personal productivity.

Chapter 1: Introducing Google Docs

Introduction

Google Docs is a cloud-based word processor that allows you to create, edit, and share documents easily from any device with an internet connection. It is included as part of Google Workspace, along with other productivity tools such as Google Sheets, Google Slides, Google Forms, Google Drawings, and Google Sites. Users with a free Google Account have access to these core applications. Organizations can also subscribe to paid Google Workspace plans to access additional administrative controls, increased Google Drive storage, custom domains, and enhanced collaboration features.

You can use Google Docs on multiple platforms such as Windows, macOS, Linux, and Chromebooks. It runs in any modern web browser, although optimized for Google Chrome for best performance and access to all features. A Google Docs app is also available for iPhone, iPad, and Android devices, allowing you to access and edit documents while on the go. Additionally, Google Docs supports offline editing, allowing users to continue working on documents even when an internet connection is unavailable.

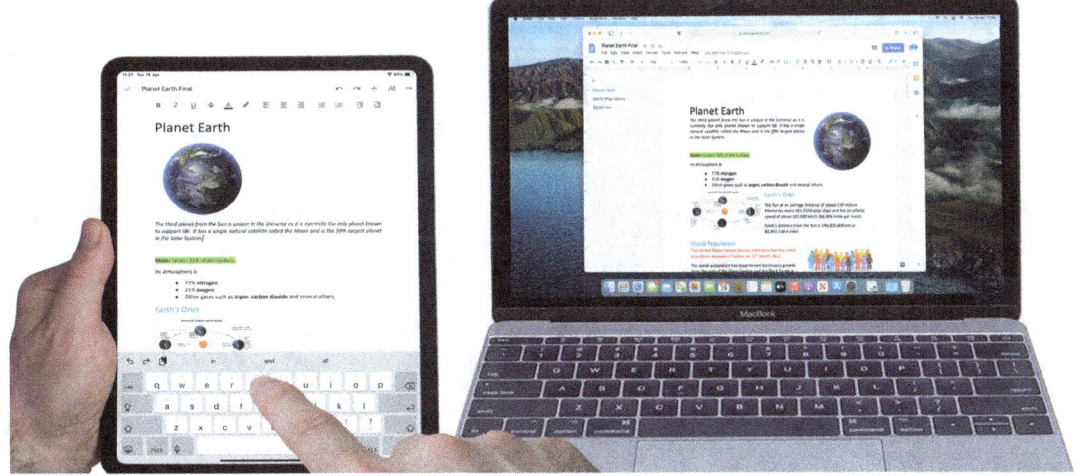

Chapter 1: Introducing Google Docs

Because Google Docs is a cloud-based application, you can access your documents from anywhere as long as you have an internet connection. If your computer is lost, damaged, or stolen, your documents are still safely stored online and can be accessed from another device simply by logging into your Google Account.

One of the biggest advantages of Google Docs is its support for real-time collaboration. Multiple people can work on the same document at the same time, with each user's changes appearing live on screen. Each editor's contributions are highlighted and tagged with their name, so you can easily see who made which changes. You can also add comments, suggest edits, and track revision history, making it easy for teams to collaborate efficiently no matter where they are located.

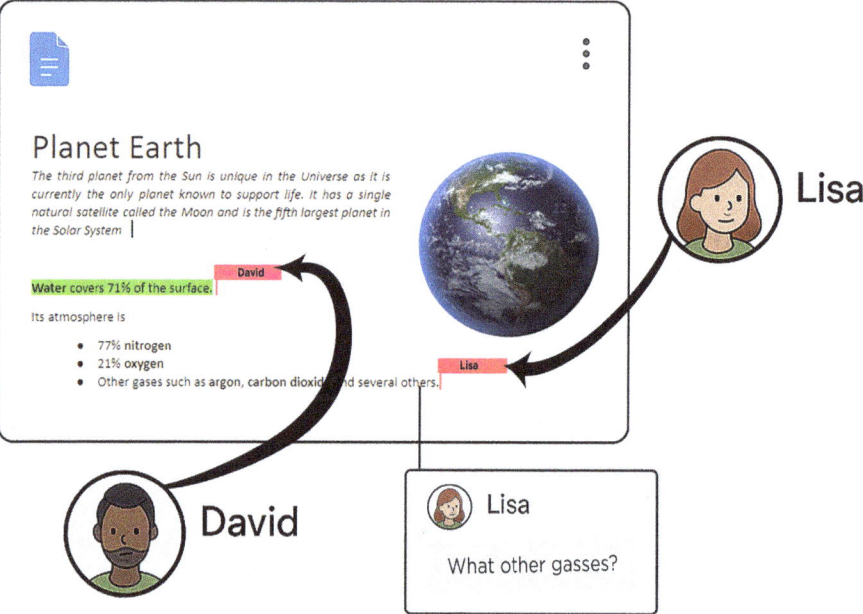

Google Docs also provides spelling and grammar checking tools that work as you type, helping you catch errors quickly.

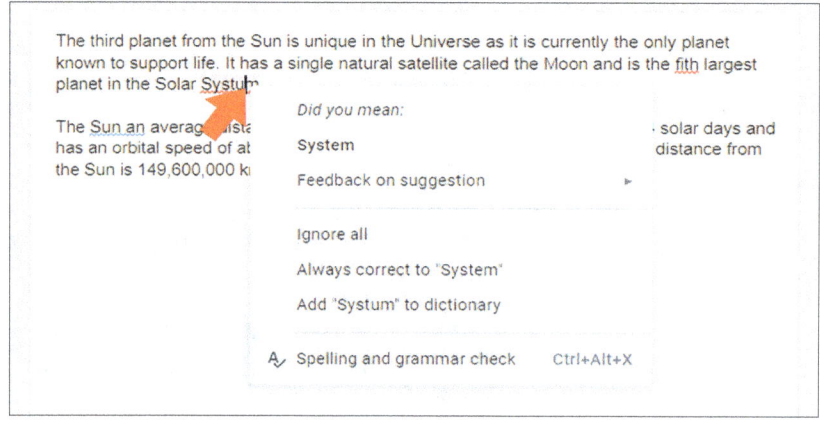

Chapter 1: Introducing Google Docs

As well as saving your documents on Google Drive, you can also export them in multiple formats. You can download your documents as Microsoft Word (.docx) files, OpenDocument (.odt) files, PDF files, Rich Text Format (.rtf) files, plain text (.txt), or EPUB files. This allows you to work with users who use other operating systems or office software. Google Docs can also import Word documents and other formats, converting them into the Google Docs format for editing.

Another helpful feature is the built-in document translation tool. With it, you can translate an entire document into a different language. However, because the translation is powered by machine learning and automated services, translations might not always be perfect and should be reviewed carefully, especially for professional or formal communications.

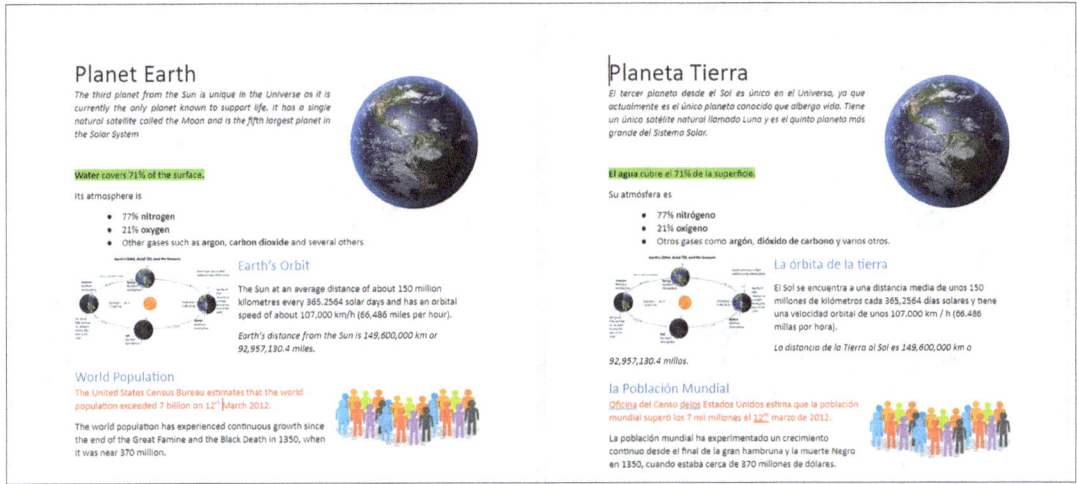

You can expand the functionality of Google Docs by installing add-ons, which are small software extensions created mostly by third-party developers. Add-ons can help you perform tasks like mail merges, advanced grammar checking, mathematical equation editing, and diagram creation. These add-ons can be installed from the Google Workspace Marketplace.

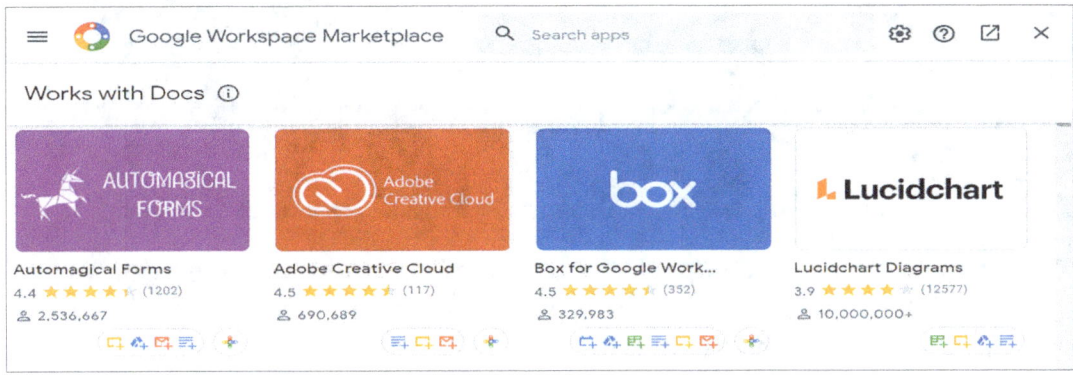

Chapter 1: Introducing Google Docs

Google operates a vast network of data centers strategically distributed across the world, including North America, Europe, Asia, and South America. This allows user requests to be routed to the nearest or most efficient facility, minimizing latency and ensuring fast document load and save times. The data centers consist of rows of cabinets, each populated with servers, storage devices, and networking equipment. These are carefully arranged to maximize space, efficiency and maintain proper airflow for cooling. In addition, digital load balancing software distributes computing workloads across servers to ensure optimal performance.

Every time you access Google Docs to edit a document or save a document to Google Drive, those actions are processed and stored securely within this global data center infrastructure.

Chapter 1: Introducing Google Docs

Google Account Types

A free Google Account is a personal account that gives individual users access to Google's core services, including Gmail, Google Docs, Google Sheets, Google Slides, Google Photos, Google Calendar, and Google Meet, along with 15 GB of storage shared across Gmail, Google Drive, and Google Photos. Anyone can sign up for a Google Account at no cost using a personal email address, typically ending in `@gmail.com`.

A Google Workspace account is part of a paid subscription service designed for businesses, educational institutions, nonprofits, and other organizations. Previously known as G Suite, Google Workspace includes the same core applications as a free account but adds advanced administrative controls, enhanced security features, greater storage options, and premium collaboration tools.

One of the major differences is in account management and domain ownership. Free Google Accounts are tied to Google-managed `@gmail.com` addresses, whereas Google Workspace accounts typically use custom domain names such as `@yourcompany.com` or `@yourschool.edu`, providing professional branding and centralized control for organizations. This means Workspace administrators can manage user accounts, enforce security policies, set up multi-factor authentication, monitor usage, and control sharing permissions across the organization.

Google Workspace users also have access to a range of premium features. These include AI-powered writing tools such as "Help Me Write" and "Help Me Refine," integrated electronic signature workflows within Google Docs, advanced Smart Canvas collaboration enhancements, and Timeline View for visualizing document version history. Access to AI-powered features may depend on the organization's specific Workspace edition and whether Google Gemini for Google Workspace is enabled.

In addition, Workspace users benefit from larger Google Drive storage, starting at 30 GB per user with the Business Starter plan, scaling to 2 TB per user with Business Standard, 5 TB per user with Business Plus, and higher or capacities with Enterprise plans depending on the organization's subscription. Additionally, Shared Drives (or Team Drives) are available in the Business Standard and higher-tier plans, which provide a centralized space where teams can store, access, and collaborate on files.

Pricing for Google Workspace varies depending on the subscription plan selected, and each tier unlocks additional features, greater storage limits, and higher service-level agreements (SLAs) for uptime and support.

Chapter 1: Introducing Google Docs

Gemini

Google Gemini is Google's family of advanced artificial intelligence models, developed by Google DeepMind. These models are designed to perform a wide range of complex generative and analytical tasks, including text generation, code completion, image understanding, audio interpretation, video analysis, and logical reasoning across multiple modalities.

Personal Google accounts can access Gemini via the free Gemini web app at `gemini.google.com` with more advanced features available through Gemini Advanced, which is included in the Google One AI Premium Plan subscription. This plan provides access to Google's most capable Gemini models and includes additional benefits such as increased cloud storage.

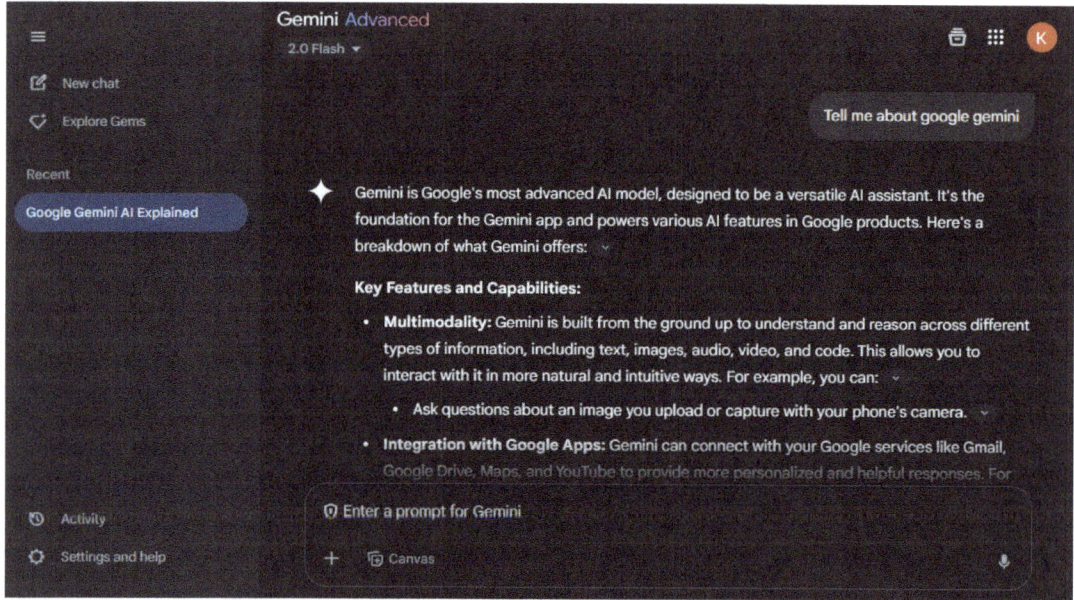

Google Workspace users can access Gemini features integrated into core apps—such as Gmail, Docs, Sheets, Slides, and Drive—with eligible Workspace plans. Additional Gemini capabilities may be available through Workspace add-ons depending on the subscription tier.

Gemini can integrate with various Google services—such as Gmail, Google Drive, and Google Maps. For example, Gemini can summarize emails or extract specific information from your inbox, help plan trips using data from Google Maps and Google Flights, brainstorm ideas, generate, debug, and explain programming code, simplify complex topics into more understandable explanations, and summarize documents, presentations, and websites.

Chapter 1: Introducing Google Docs

Google One

Google One is a subscription-based service developed by Google, launched in May 2018, that provides expanded cloud storage and additional benefits across Google services such as Drive, Gmail, and Photos. It serves as an upgrade to the 15 GB of free storage included with every Google Account, offering various paid tiers to accommodate different storage needs and user preferences. You can access Google One from the following website.

```
one.google.com
```

Subscribers also gain access to enhanced photo editing tools within Google Photos. These include advanced features such as Magic Eraser, which allows users to remove unwanted elements from images, and Portrait Light, which improves lighting on faces. These AI-powered tools offer capabilities comparable to premium photo editing software. Availability may vary depending on the user's device, operating system, or subscription tier—some features are exclusive to Pixel devices or the Google One AI Premium Plan.

Google One also includes a dark web monitoring feature that scans the dark web for exposed personal data, such as email addresses, names, and phone numbers linked to your Google Account. If a match is found, users are notified and provided with actionable steps to secure their accounts or mitigate risks. Note that this feature is currently available in select regions and may not be globally accessible.

Plans are available in a range of storage capacities, from 100 GB up to 30 TB, allowing users to choose a tier that suits their needs. Each plan includes the option to share storage with up to five additional family members, making it a practical and cost-effective solution for households. Every user on a shared plan retains their own private space, while drawing from the shared storage pool.. Below are the Google One plans as of 2025.

Plan	Storage	Key Benefits
Basic	100 GB	Entry-level storage, family sharing
Standard	200 GB	More storage, extra support
Premium	2 TB	VPN, enhanced security features
AI Premium	2 TB + Gemini Advanced	Full access to Google's most advanced AI tools

2 Getting Started

In this chapter we'll take a look at getting started with Google Docs using a web browser such as Google Chrome. You can also use Microsoft Edge if you're on a PC or Safari if you're on a Mac.

- Creating a Google Account
- How to Sign In
- Tour of the main screen
- Menus
- Toolbars
- Page Rulers
- Download Google Chrome

Have a look at the video resources section. Open your web browser and navigate to the following website.

`elluminetpress.com/starting-googledocs`

Chapter 2: Getting Started

Creating a Google Account

If you use Gmail you will already have a Google Account. If this is the case, you don't need to create a new Google Account so you can skip this step.

If you don't have an account, you can create one online before you start. To do this, open your web browser and browse to the following page.

`accounts.google.com/signup`

Fill in your name in the first two fields, then under 'username', type in the name you want to appear in your email address. This can be a nickname or your full name. The name must be unique, so if someone else has already taken the name, you'll need to choose a new one or add a couple of numbers. Google will tell you if the username you entered has already been used.

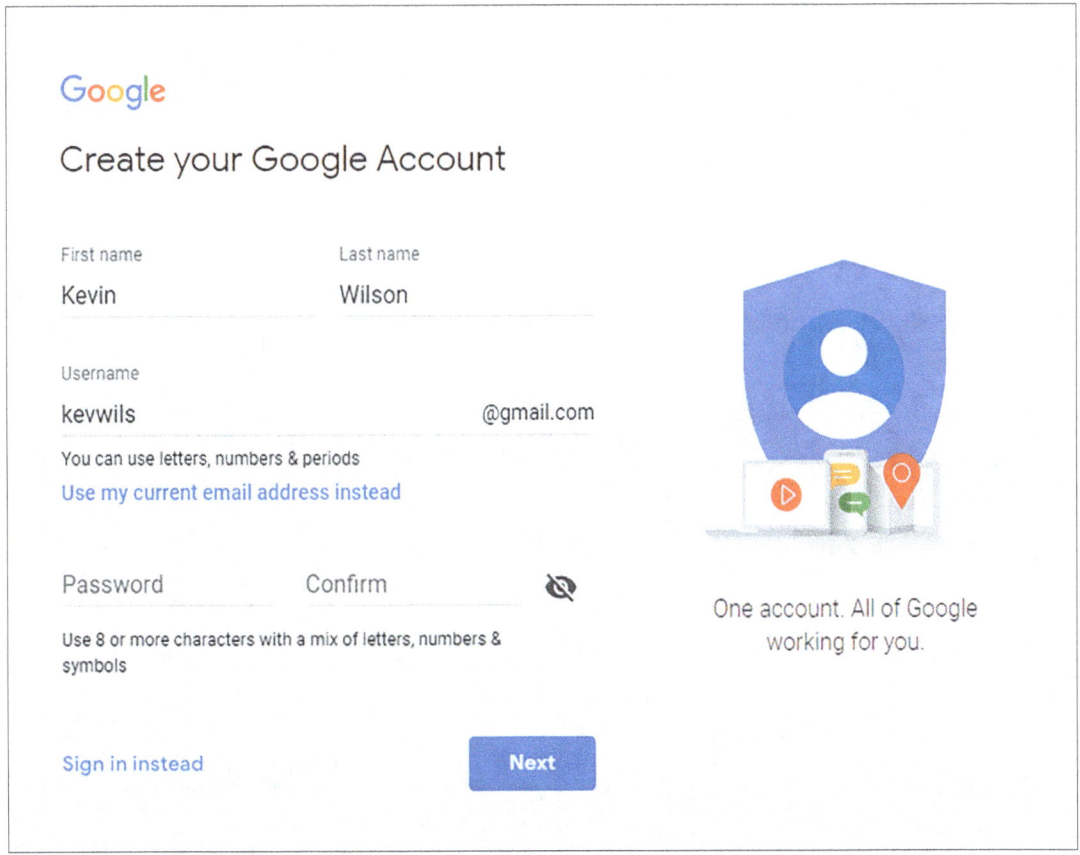

Enter the password you want to use in the 'password' field, then type it again to confirm it in the 'confirm' field.

Click 'next'.

Chapter 2: Getting Started

Sign In

Once you have your Google Account, you can sign in. Google docs will run in any web browser, however Google recommend using their own Chrome browser. To start Google Docs, go to the following website:

`docs.google.com`

Sign in with your Google Account email address and password.

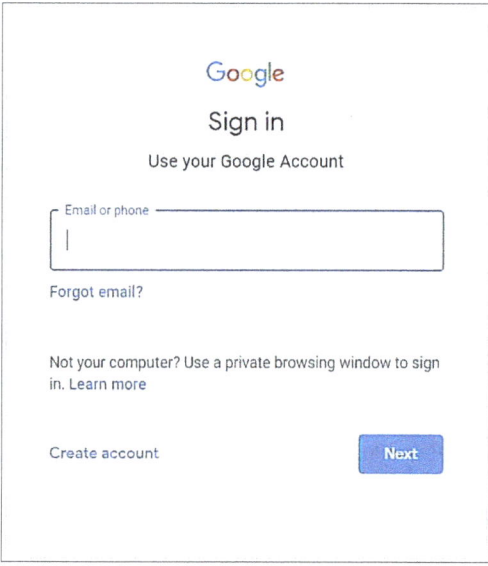

Once you sign in, you'll land on the Google Docs start or home screen.

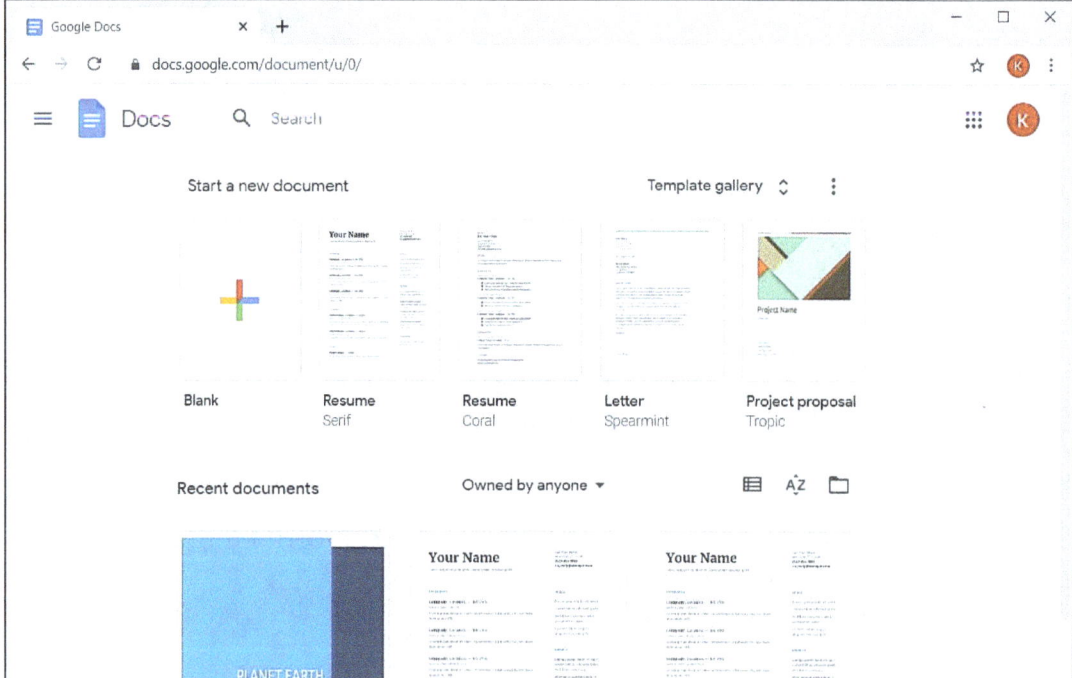

Chapter 2: Getting Started

Get Started

Let's take a closer look at the start screen.

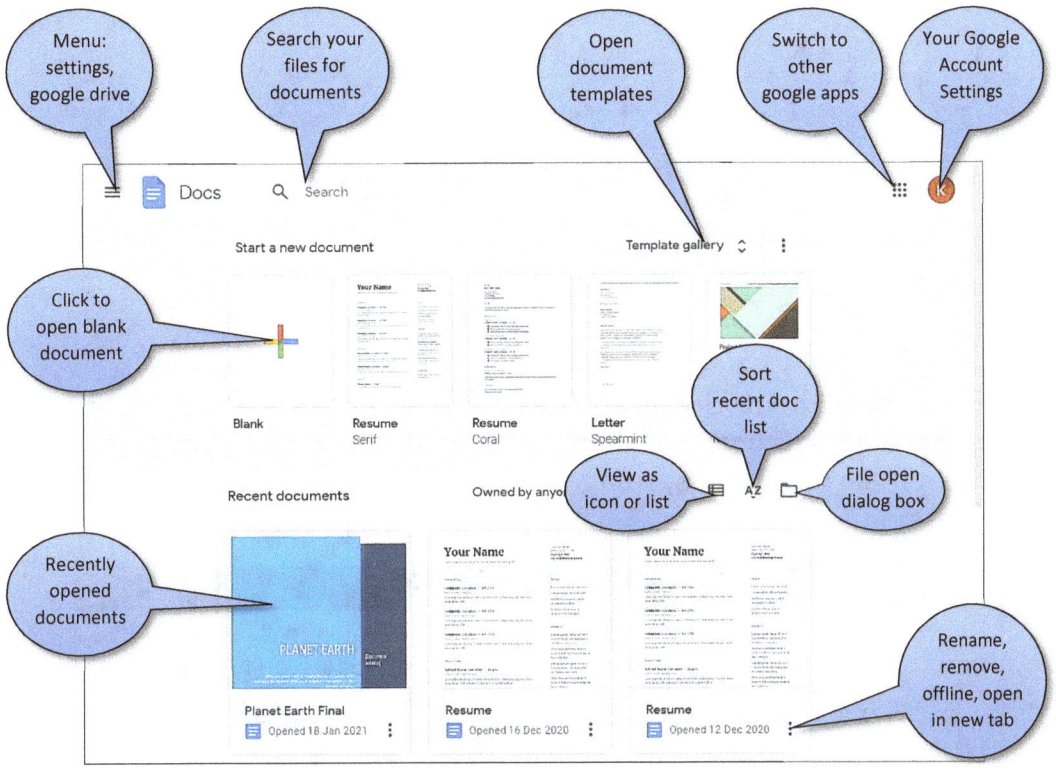

From here, you can create a new document. You can do this by selecting a blank document.

You can select a template from the pre-designed documents if you want to create a letter, report, or resume/cv. To do this click 'template gallery', then click on a template.

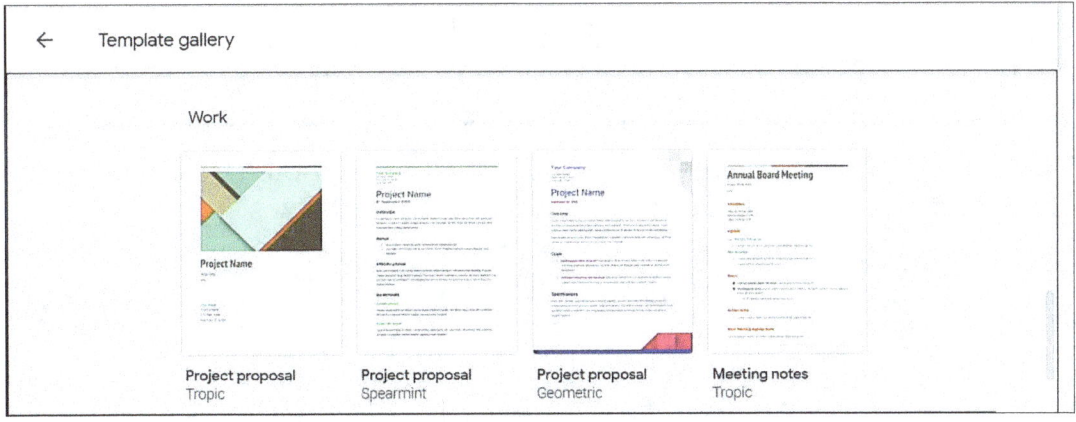

In this example, we're going to start a document from scratch, so select 'blank'

Chapter 2: Getting Started

Menus & Toolbars

When you open a new document, you'll see a menu along the top of the screen

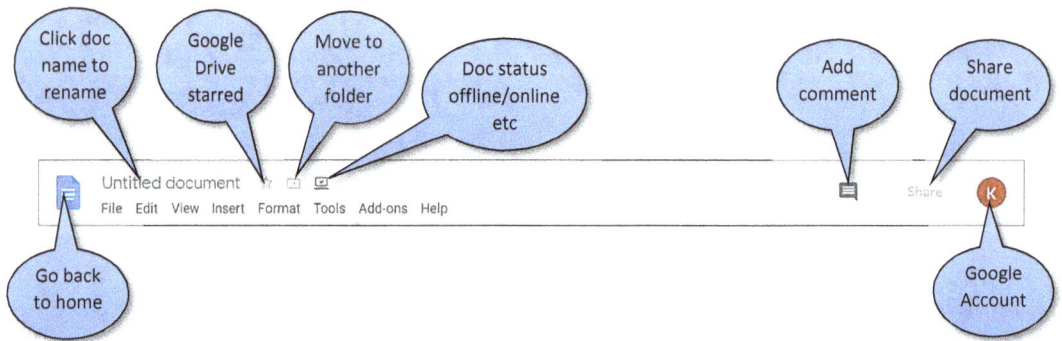

Under the document title there are pull-down menus. You will find various commands here for dealing with files, editing your document, as well as inserting tables, images, tools for grammar and spelling and so on.

Menu	Commands
File	Share document, create new document, open, make a copy. Email, download a copy, offline. Move, rename, publish on web, page setup, print.
Edit	Copy, paste, cut. Find, replace, select all.
View	Show ruler, view mode. Ruler, doc outline, equation, section breaks, full screen.
Insert	Image, table, drawing, chart, line, footnote. Special characters, equations. Headers, footers, link, comment. Table of contents
Format	Text, paragraph styles, alignment, indents, line spacing. Columns, bullets, numbering. Headers & footers, page numbers, page orientation, format image, format table.
Tools	Spelling, grammar, word count, review suggested edits, citations, dictionary, voice typing, preferences.

Underneath the menus along the top, you'll see a toolbar. This is where you'll find your formatting tools, font colours and sizes.

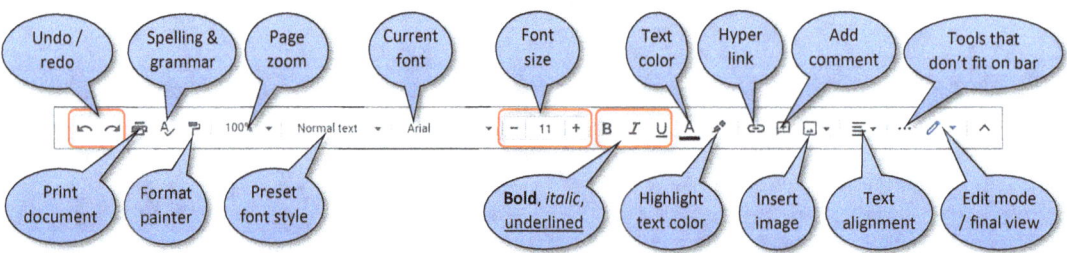

Chapter 2: Getting Started

Page Rulers

The page ruler runs across the top of your page and is useful for setting your margins, paragraph indentations, and tab stops.

On the top left, you'll see three markers. The small rectangular one at the top is your first line indent - this indents the first line of the selected text. The small triangular one is the left indent - this indents all the selected text. The last marker is hidden by the other two, but if you move the markers out the way, you'll see the point where the ruler turns from white to grey. This is the left margin.

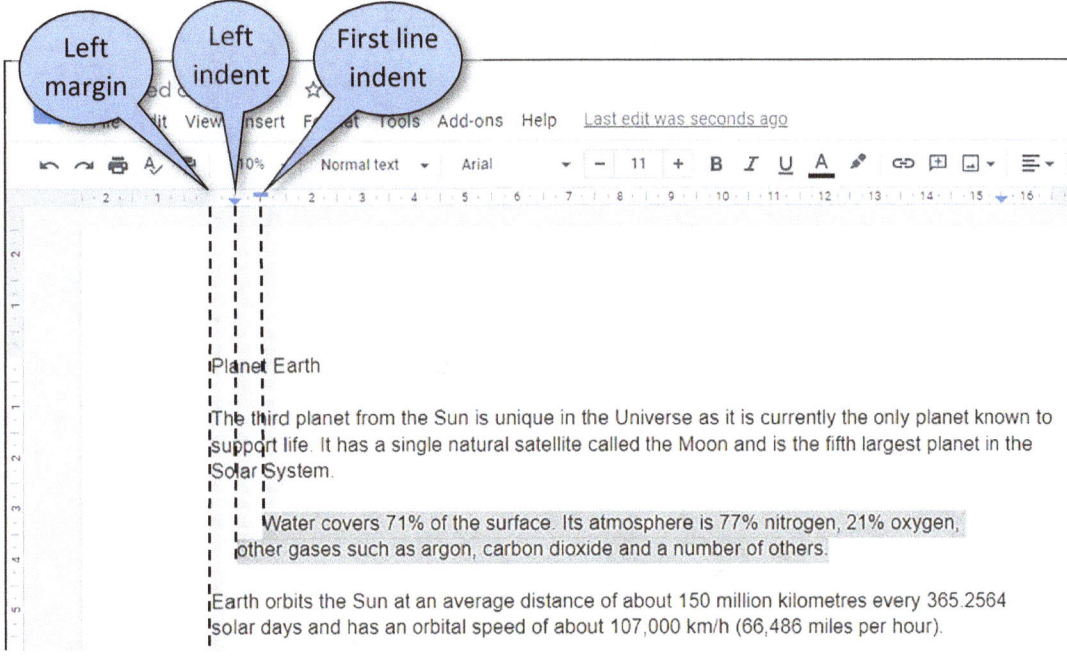

It's the same on the right hand side, you have a right indent and a right margin, but no first line indent.

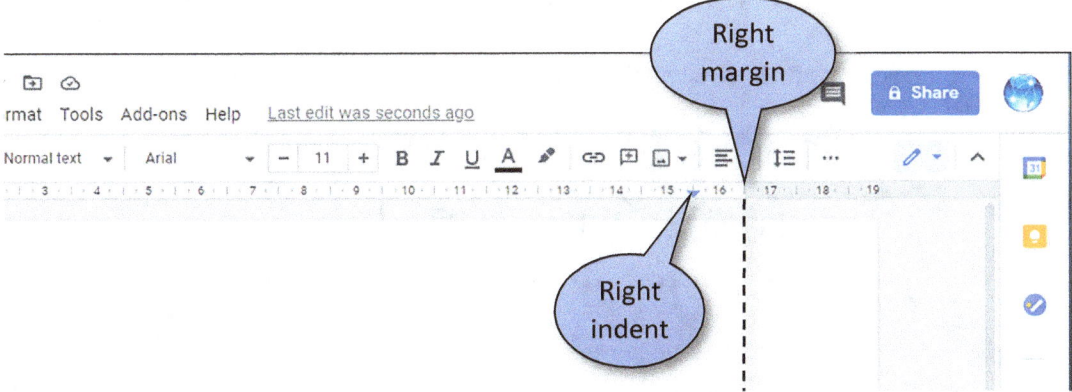

There is also a ruler that runs down the left hand side.

23

Chapter 2: Getting Started

Download Google Chrome

Google Chrome is a fast and streamlined browser that is a good alternative to Microsoft Edge. To use Google Chrome, you'll first need to download it.

Open your current web browser and navigate to the following website. You can download Google Chrome from here.

`www.google.com/chrome`

Click the blue 'download chrome' button on the web page.

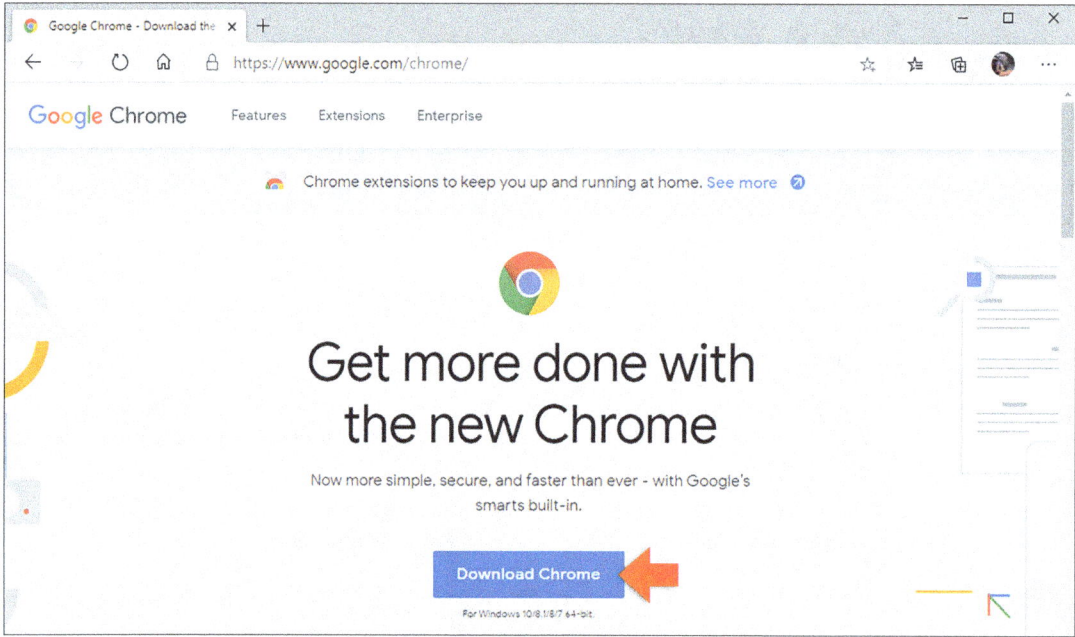

Click 'open' when prompted by your browser then follow the on screen instructions to install Chrome.

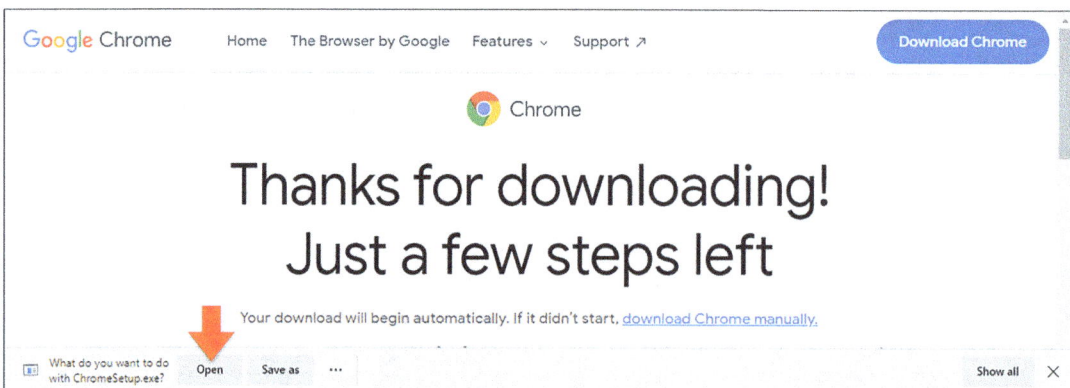

If you don't see the prompt, go to your downloads folder and double click 'chromesetup.exe'.

Chapter 2: Getting Started

You'll find Chrome on your start menu and on your desktop. Click the chrome icon to start.

Once you open Chrome, sign in with your Google Account email address and password. Click the profile icon on the top right. Then click 'turn on sync.

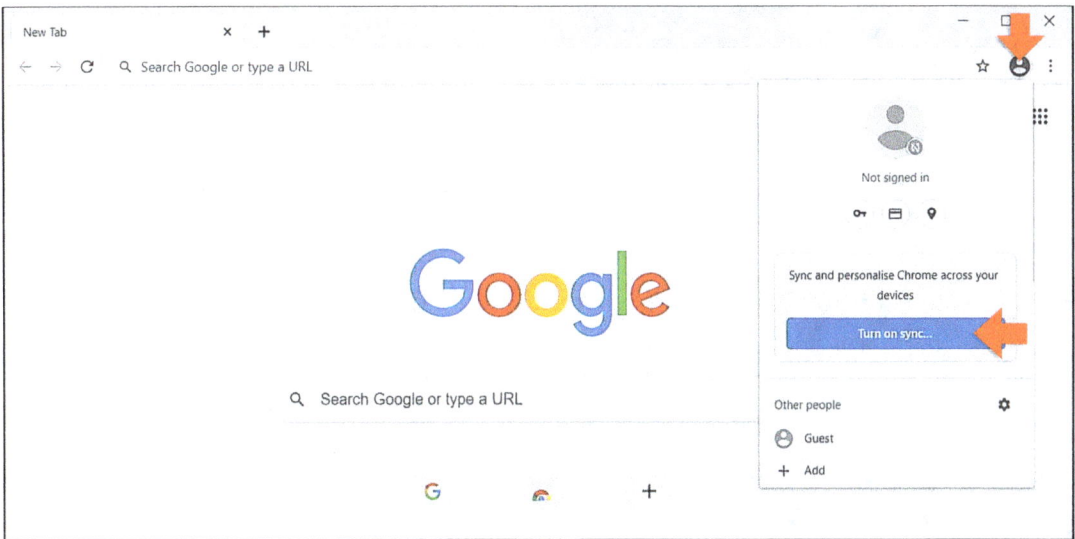

Enter your Google Account email address and password when prompted. Click 'next'.

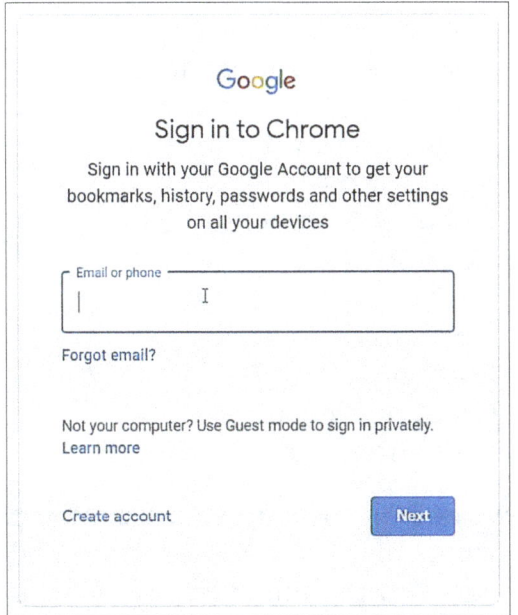
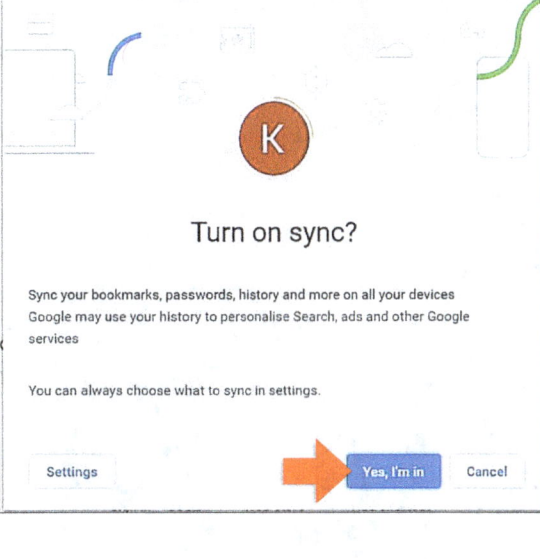

Click 'yes I'm in' to synchronise your data across all your devices. This is useful if you use your account on your iPad, tablet, phone, Chromebook, as well as on Windows 10/11 or Mac.

3 Building Documents

In this section, we're going to take a look at how to build a document using the various tools and features offered by Google Docs.

We'll go through creating a new document, entering or dictating text, as well as formatting text.

- Creating a New Document
- Entering Text
- Text Justification
- Paragraph Indents & Spacing
- Line Spacing
- Cut, Copy & Paste
- Bold, Italic, Underlined, Superscript & Subscript
- Text Color, and Size
- Paragraph Styles
- Bullet & Numbered Lists
- Equations
- Page & Section Breaks
- Headers & Footers
- Footnotes
- Creating Columns
- Contents Pages

Have a look at the video resources section. Open your web browser and navigate to the following website.

elluminetpress.com/building-googledocs

Chapter 3: Building Documents

Creating a New Document

To create a new document, select 'blank' from the Google Docs home page.

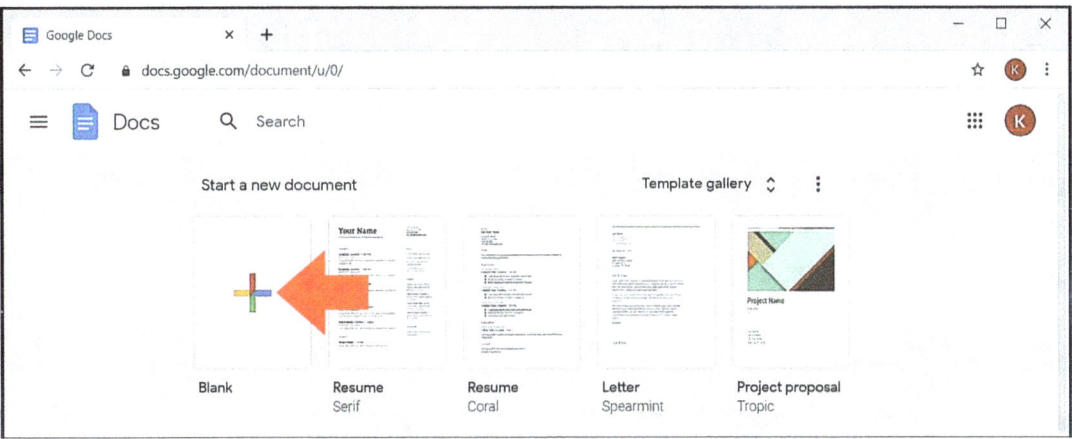

To get to the home page, click the 'docs' icon on the top left, or navigate to the following website:

`docs.google.com`

You can also select a template from the template gallery, if you want to write a letter or a report. To do this, click 'template gallery', then select a template.

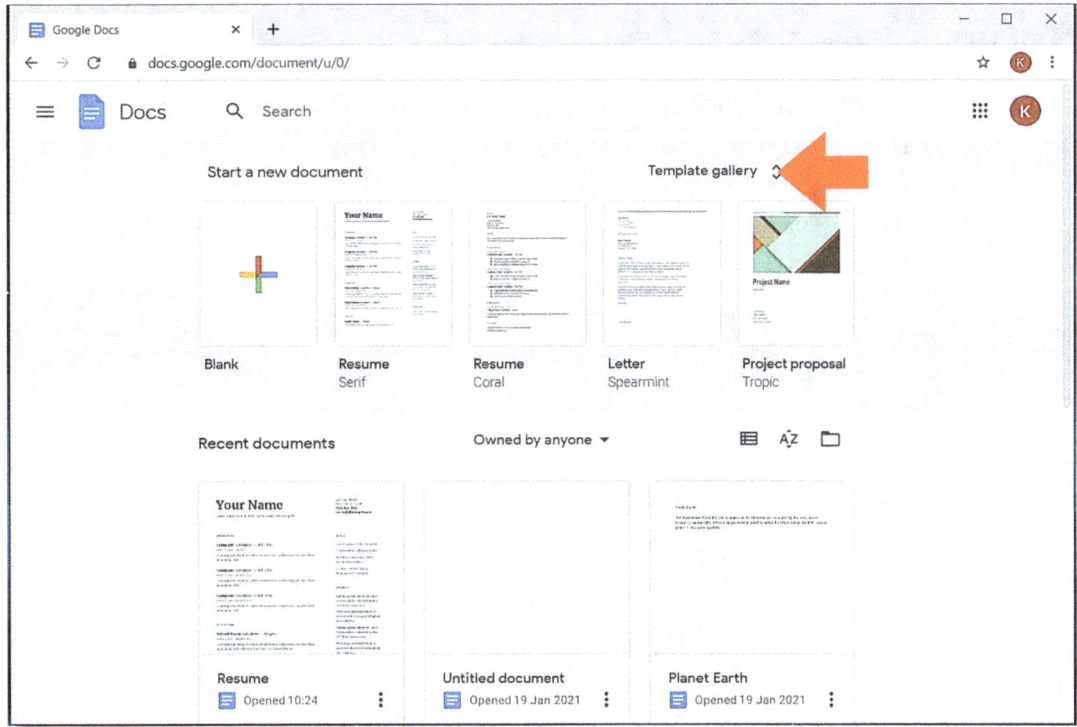

27

Chapter 3: Building Documents

Entering Text

Use your keyboard to type in your text. You'll see a small flashing bar called a cursor (shown below). This tells you were the text will appear when you type.

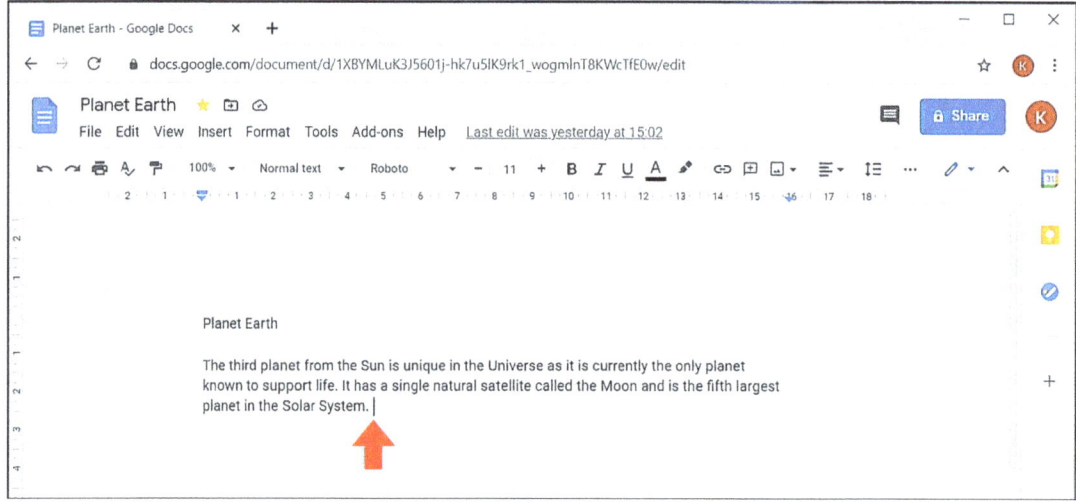

Dictate Text

If typing isn't your thing, you can dictate your text using the voice typing feature.

Setup

To do this, click the position in your document you want the text to start, then from the 'tools' menu, click 'voice typing'.

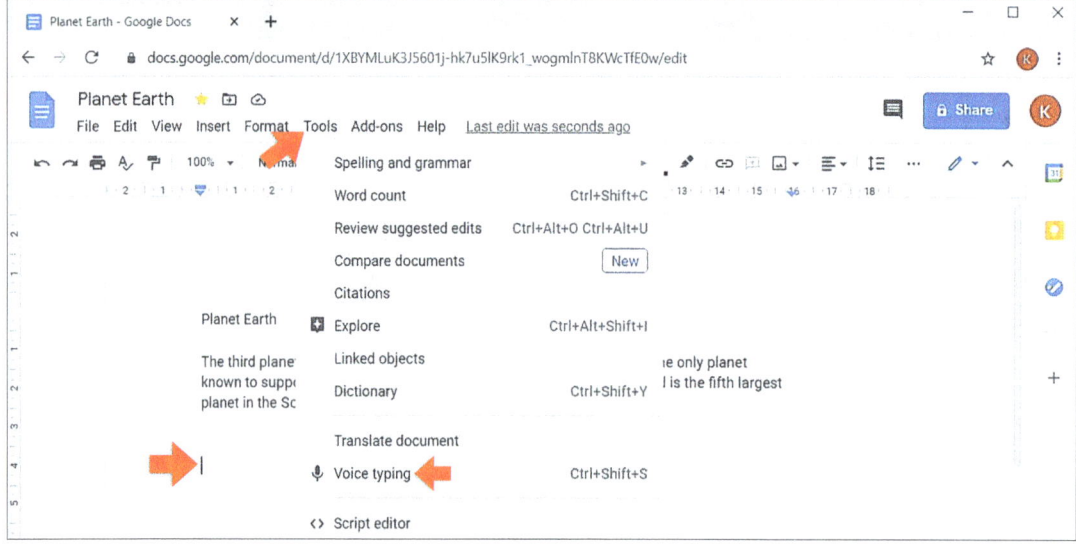

Chapter 3: Building Documents

You'll see a mic icon appear on the left hand side of your screen. Click the icon to start.

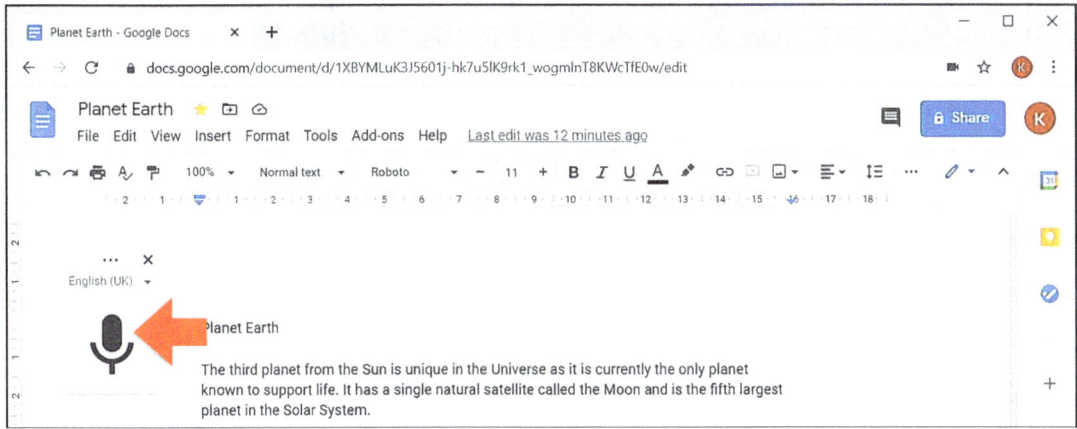

If you see a security prompt asking to use your microphone, click 'allow'.

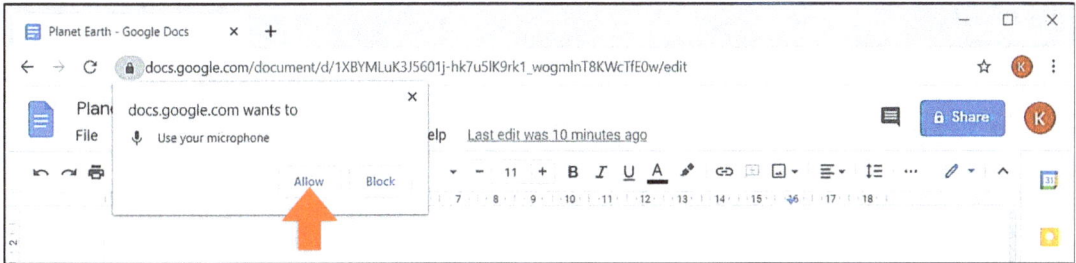

Now, you can dictate your text using your microphone.

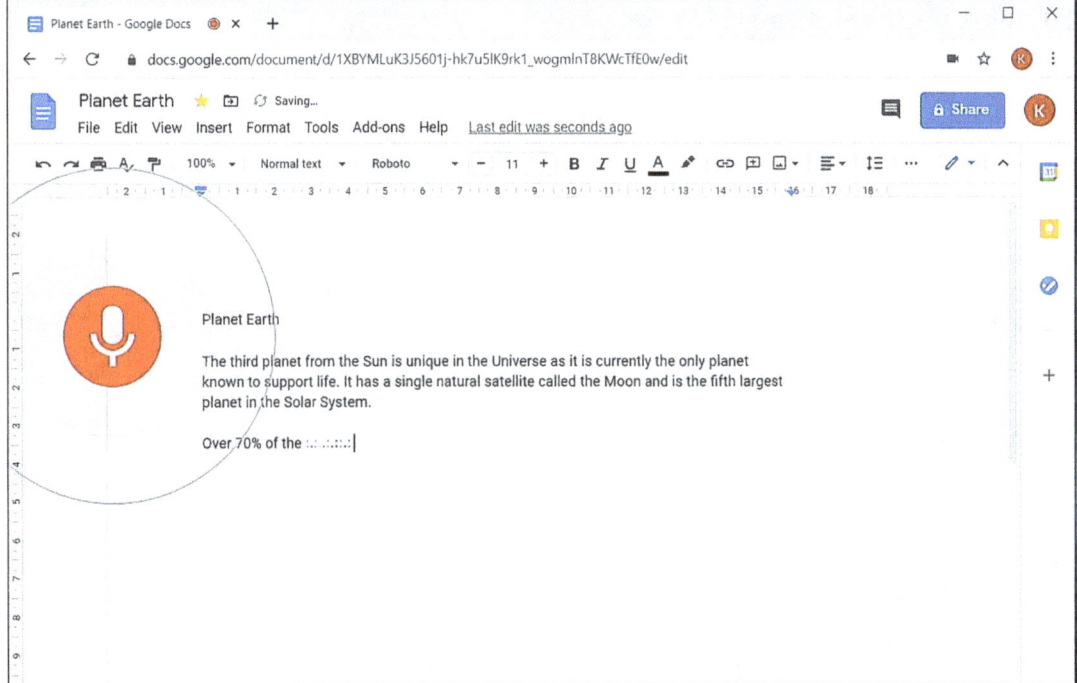

Chapter 3: Building Documents

Voice Commands

Use the following phrases to add punctuation to your text. Make sure you pause before and after each command to differentiate it from an actual word.

```
Comma
Period
New line
New paragraph
Question mark
Exclamation point
```

To format your text use the following commands.

```
Bold
Italic
Subscript
Superscript
Underline
All caps
Decrease font size
Increase font size
Font size [6-400]
Create bulleted list
Create numbered list
```

To align your text use

```
Align center
Align justified
Align left
Align right
```

To select a word or paragraph use

```
Select all
Select line
Select paragraph
Select word
Unselect
Select none
Delete last word
Delete sentence
Go to start of line
Go to next paragraph
```

Chapter 3: Building Documents

Selecting Text

To select text, click and drag your mouse over the text you want to select. The selected text with be highlighted in grey.

> Planet Earth
>
> The third planet from the Sun is unique in the Universe as it is currently the only planet known to support life. It has a single natural satellite called the Moon and is the fifth largest planet in the Solar System.
>
> Water covers 71% of the surface. Its atmosphere is 77% nitrogen, 21% oxygen, other gases such as argon, carbon dioxide and a number of others.
>
> Earth orbits the Sun at an average distance of about 150 million kilometres every 365.2564 solar days and has an orbital speed of about 107,000 km/h (66,486 miles per hour).

To quickly select a paragraph, triple click on any word in the paragraph.

> Planet Earth
>
> The third planet from the Sun is unique in the Universe as it is currently the only planet known to support life. It has a single natural satellite called the Moon and is the fifth largest planet in the Solar System.
>
> Water covers 71% of the surface. Its atmosphere is 77% nitrogen, 21% oxygen, other gases such as argon, carbon dioxide and a number of others.
>
> Earth orbits the Sun at an average distance of about 150 million kilometres every 365.2564 solar days and has an orbital speed of about 107,000 km/h (66,486 miles per hour).

To quickly select a word, double click on it.

> Planet Earth
>
> The third planet from the Sun is unique in the Universe as it is currently the only planet known to support life. It has a single natural satellite called the Moon and is the fifth largest planet in the Solar System.
>
> Water covers 71% of the surface. Its atmosphere is 77% nitrogen, 21% oxygen, other gases such as argon, carbon dioxide and a number of others.
>
> Earth orbits the Sun at an average distance of about 150 million kilometres every 365.2564 solar days and has an orbital speed of about 107,000 km/h (66,486 miles per hour).

Chapter 3: Building Documents

Text Justification

You can justify your text to align it to the left or right margins. You can fully justify your text, meaning it is aligned with the left and right margins.

> The third planet from the Sun is unique in the Universe as it is currently the only planet known to support life. It has a single natural satellite called the Moon and is the fifth largest planet in the Solar System.

You can align the text to the right margin...

> Water covers 71% of the surface. Its atmosphere is 77% nitrogen, 21% oxygen, other gases such as argon, carbon dioxide and a number of others.

...you can align text to the centre of the page...

> Earth orbits the Sun at an average distance of about 150 million kilometres every 365.2564 solar days and has an orbital speed of about 107,000 km/h (66,486 miles per hour).

...or to the left margin.

> The United States Census Bureau estimates that the world population exceeded 7 billion on 12th March 2012. The world population has experienced continuous growth since the end of the Great Famine and the Black Death in 1350, when it was near 370 million.

To align text, first select it with your mouse, then click the alignment icon on the toolbar.

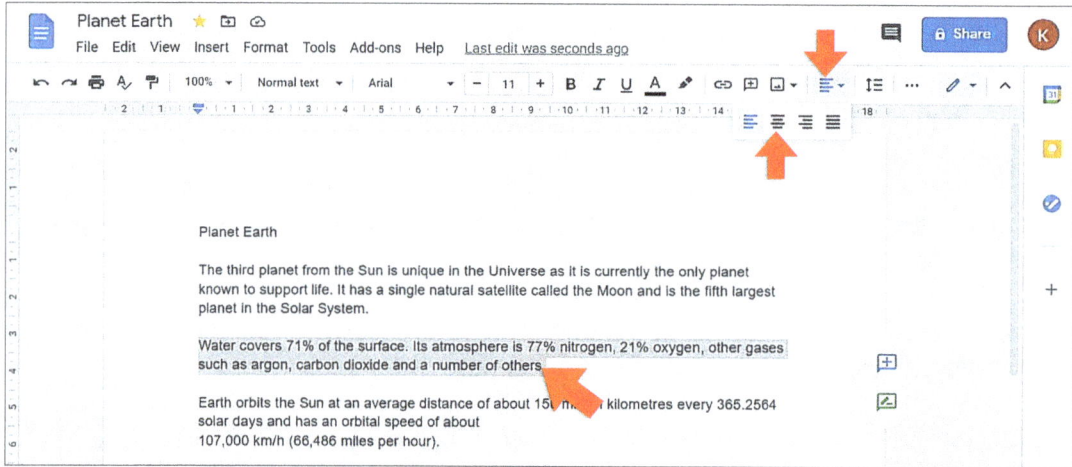

Select an alignment (left, centre, right, full justification).

Paragraph Indents

To increase the indent of a paragraph, select the text with your mouse so it's highlighted.

Indenting a Line

You can indent lines, paragraphs or lists to help separate them from the rest of your document. This can make documents easier to read. To indent text, select it with your mouse, then select the increase indent icon from the toolbar. *If the icon isn't there, click the three dots icon.*

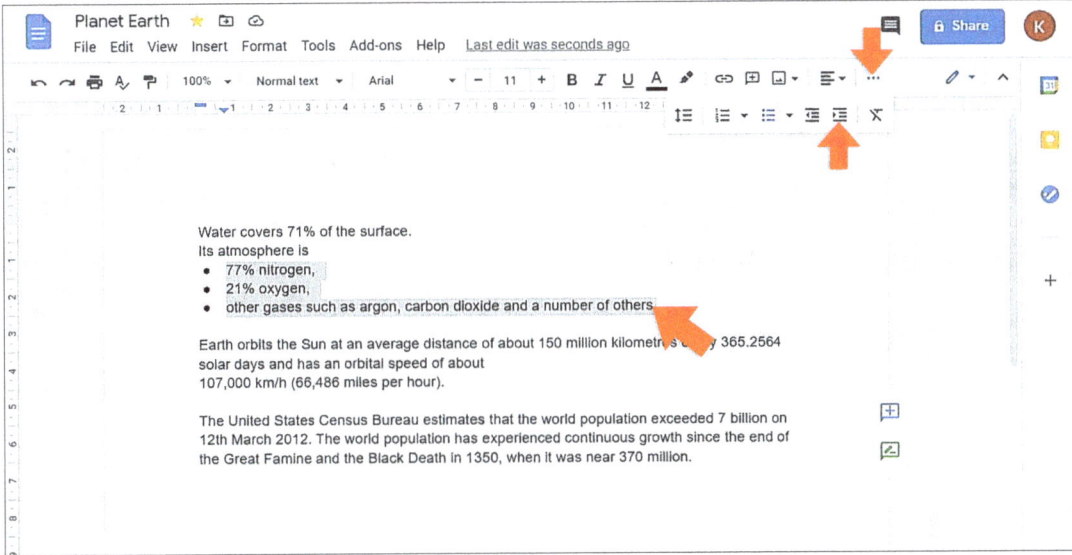

To decrease the indent, just select the decrease indent icon on the toolbar.

First Line Indent

The first line indent is a good way to begin paragraphs. This helps the reader to process the information and to identify sections in your text.

First select the text you want to indent, highlighting it with your mouse as shown below.

Chapter 3: Building Documents

From the 'format' menu, select 'align and indent'. Click 'indentation options' on the slideout menu.

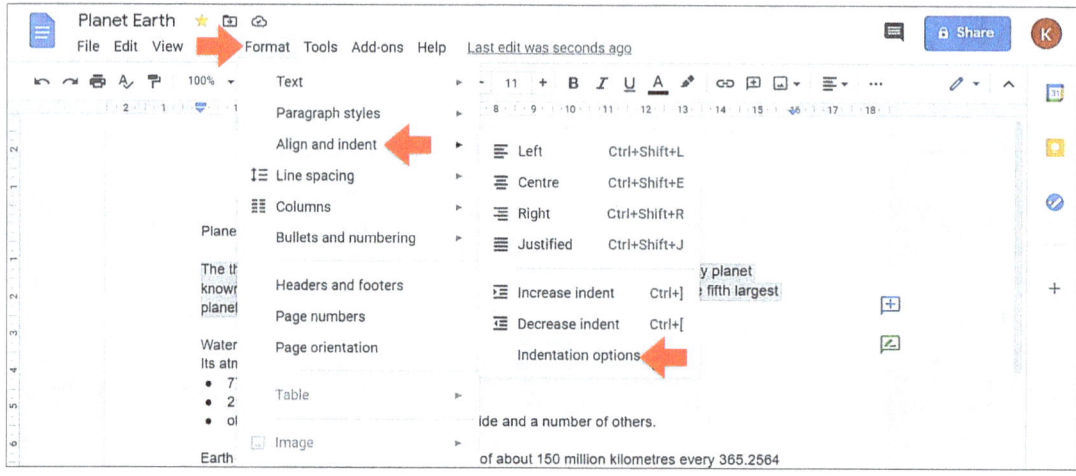

Under 'special indent' and select 'first line'. Set distance if required.

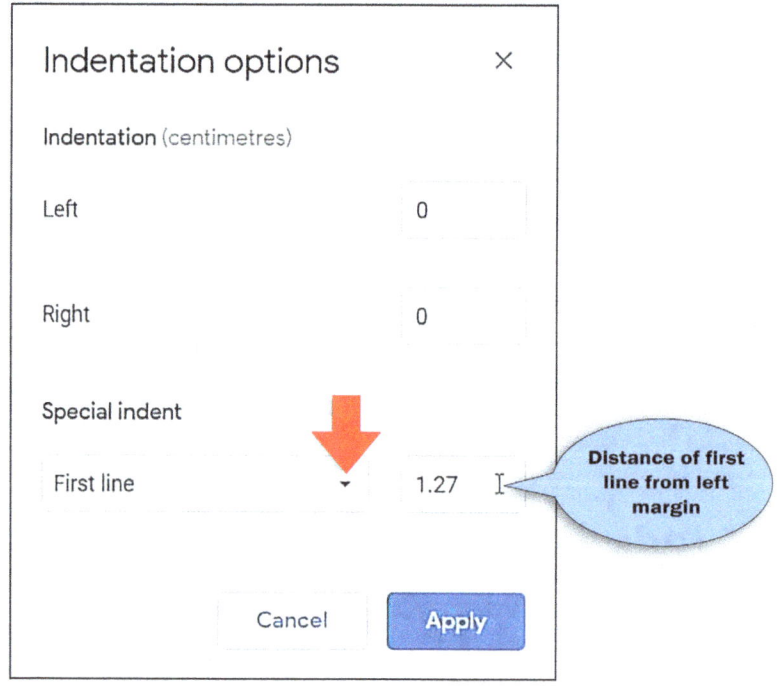

Hanging Indent

A hanging indent, indents all the lines except the first one. These indents are usually used with lists, bullet points or bibliographies.

Wilson. K (2016, March 4). Using Microsoft Office 2016: *Getting Started With Word, p34, Chapter 4.* Retrieved from http://www.elluminetpress.com

Chapter 3: Building Documents

First select the text you want to indent, highlighting it with your mouse as shown below.

> Planet Earth
>
> The third planet from the Sun is unique in the Universe as it is currently the only planet known to support life. It has a single natural satellite called the Moon and is the fifth largest planet in the Solar System.

From the 'format' menu, select 'align and indent'. Click 'indentation options' on the slideout menu.

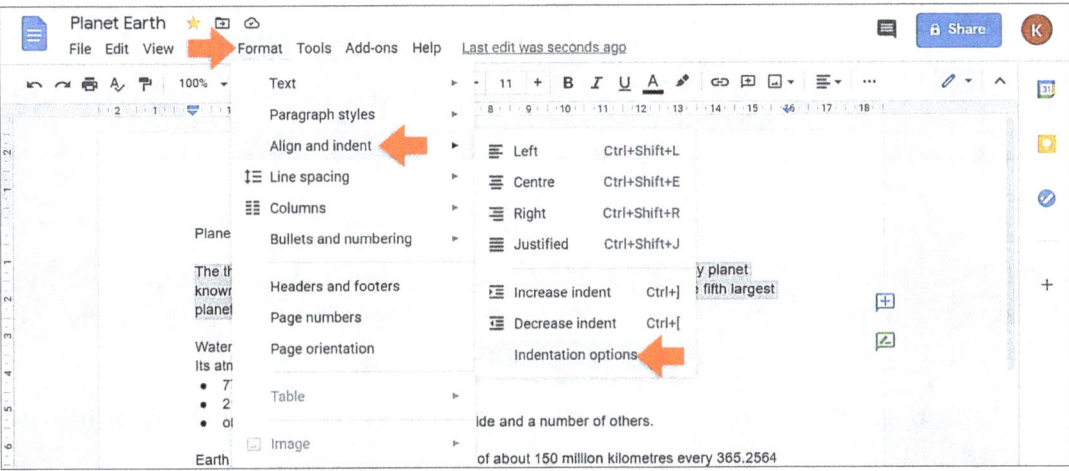

Under 'special indent', select 'hanging'. Set distance if required.

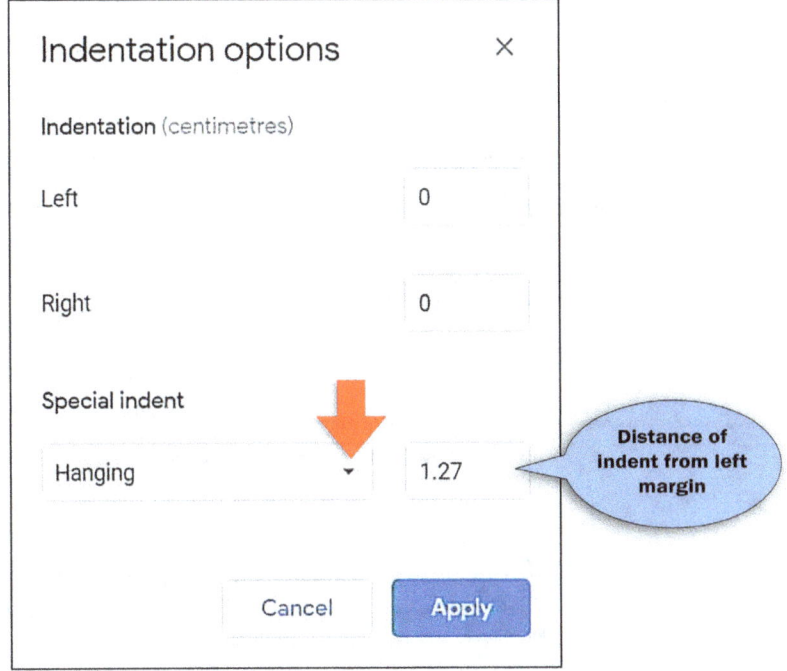

35

Chapter 3: Building Documents

Customize Indents with the Ruler

If you look closely at the ruler. On the left hand side, you'll see two markers.

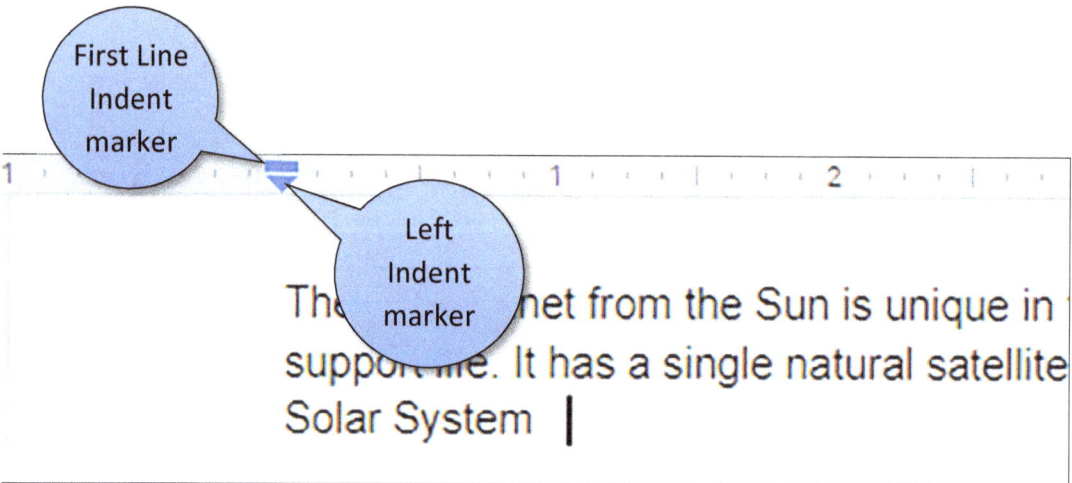

First line indent marker, adjusts the first-line indent of the selected paragraph. The left indent marker, moves in unison with the first line indent marker and indents all the lines in the paragraph.

You can click and drag these markers to adjust the paragraph and line indentation. Click and drag the first line indent marker.

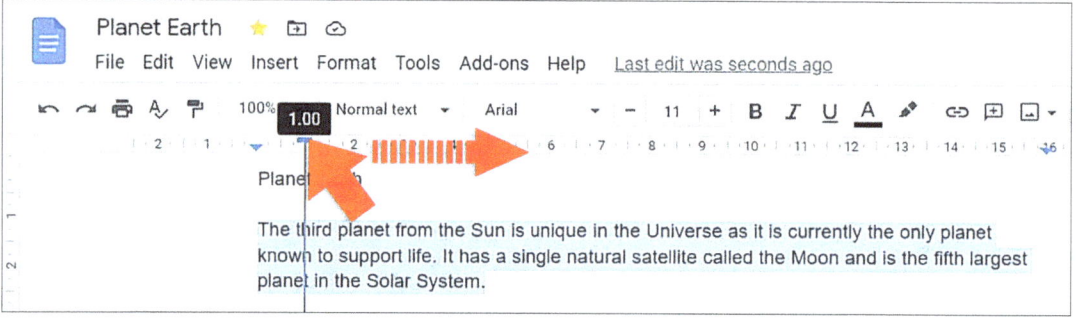

Once you release your mouse, the first line will indent.

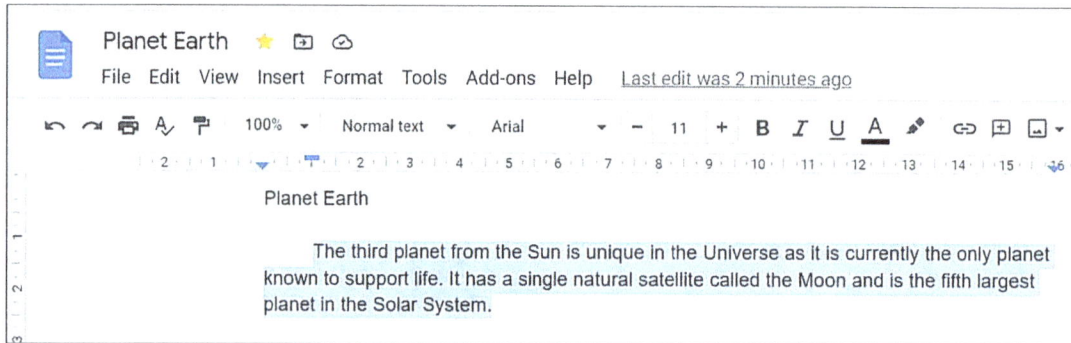

Chapter 3: Building Documents

You can also indent the right hand side. To do this, drag the right indent marker as shown below.

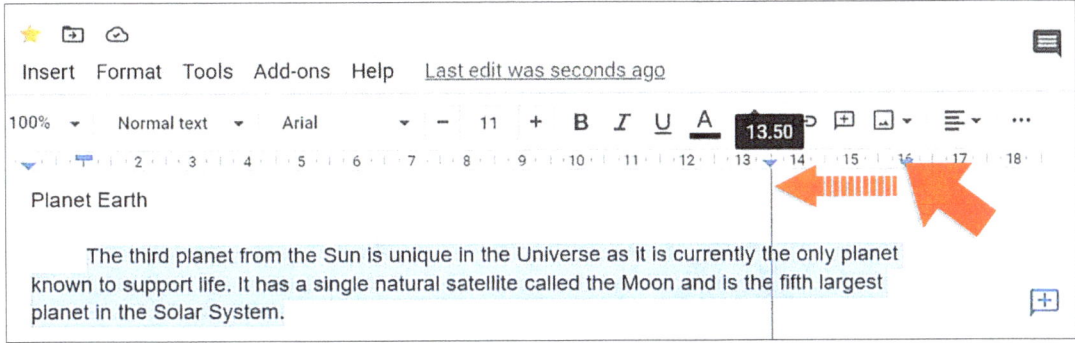

Tab Stops

Tab stops give you more control over the placement of your text. This allows you to tab out your text using the tab key on your keyboard. For example, tab out the following information.

> Water covers 71% of the surface. Its atmosphere is
>
> 77% nitrogen,
> 21% oxygen,
> 2% other gases such as argon and carbon dioxide.

To add a tab stop, select the text you want to tab. Right-click the location for the tab stop on the ruler along the top of your document. Eg 3cm.

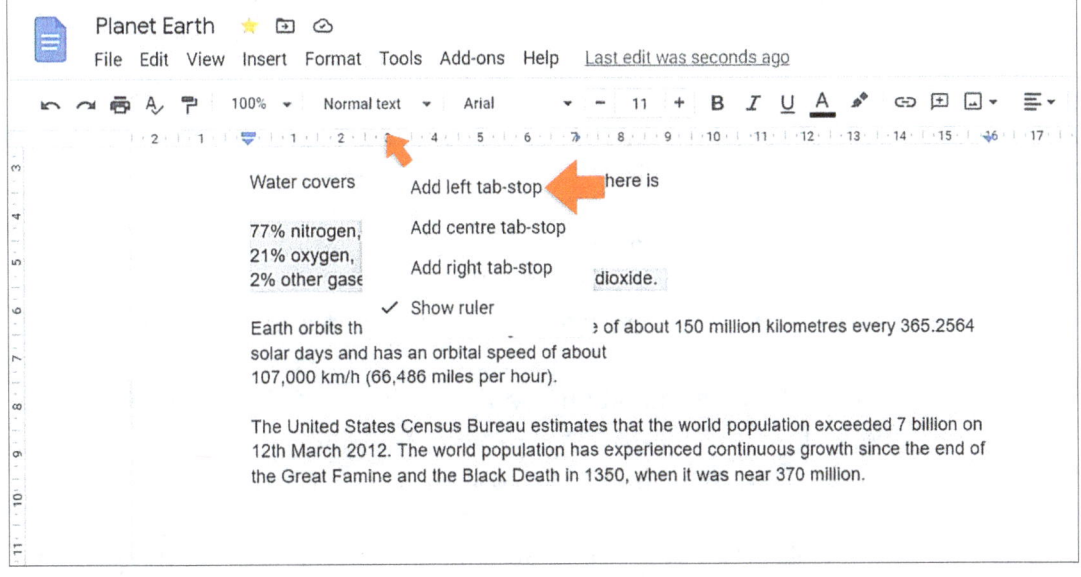

Select 'add left tab stop'.

Chapter 3: Building Documents

Now you can space out the data using the tab key. For example, if I want to tab the first line, eg separate "77%" and "nitrogen", click between the two and press the tab key on your keyboard.

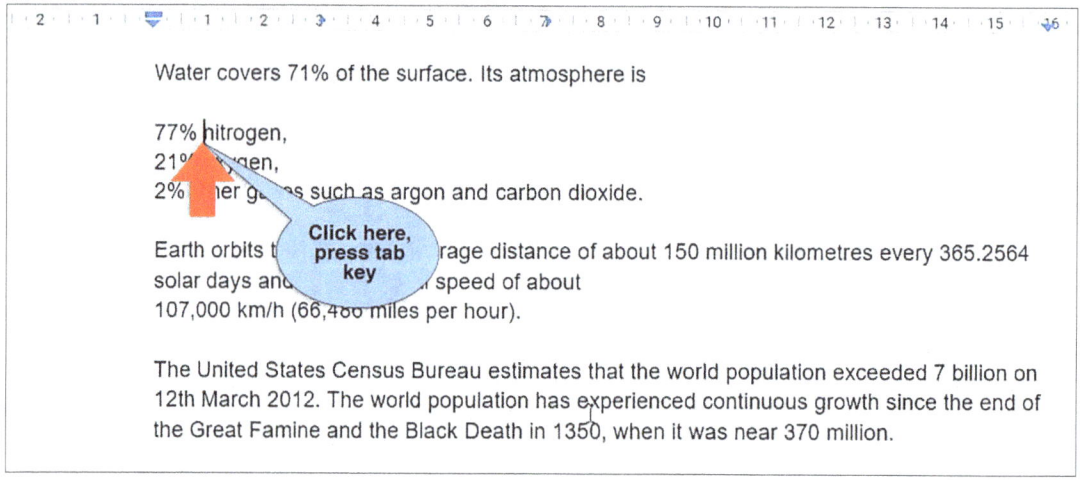

Do the same for the rest...

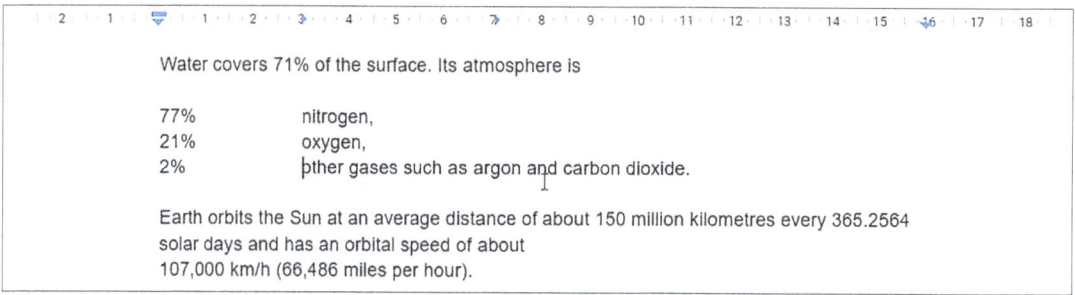

To remove a tab stop, just click on the marker on the ruler and drag it downwards.

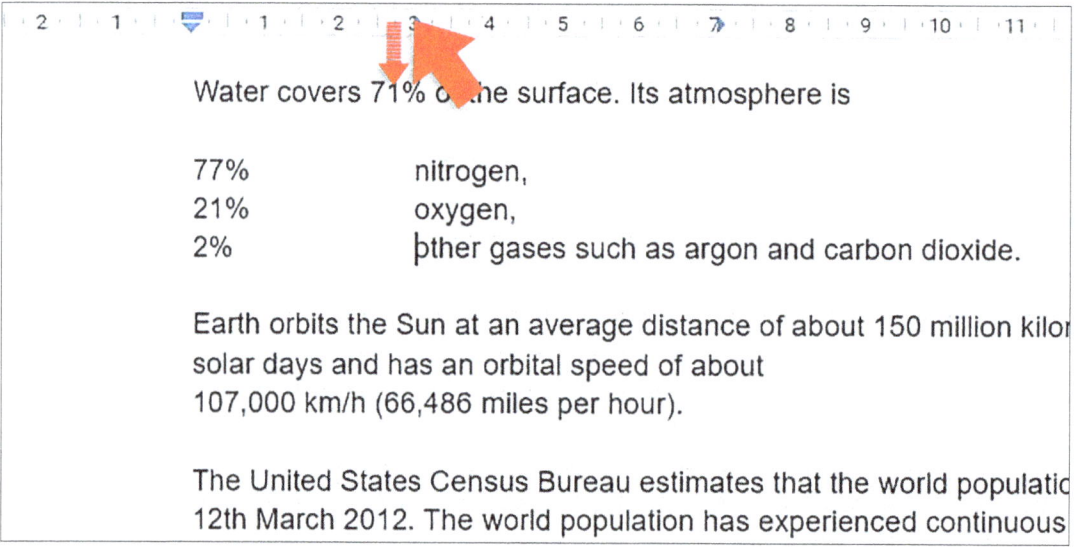

Chapter 3: Building Documents

Paragraph Spacing

You can add space before and after a paragraph to help separate your paragraphs on the page.

> **Space before paragraph**
> The third planet from the Sun is unique in the Universe as it is currently the only planet known to support life. It has a single natural satellite called the Moon and is the fifth largest planet in the Solar System.
> **Space after paragraph**

To adjust the spacing, select the paragraph or paragraphs you want to adjust. From the 'format' menu, select 'line & paragraph spacing'. Click 'add space after paragraph'. *To add a custom spacing - select 'custom spacing' from the slideout... then enter the spacing in the 'paragraph spacing' section of the dialog box that appears.*

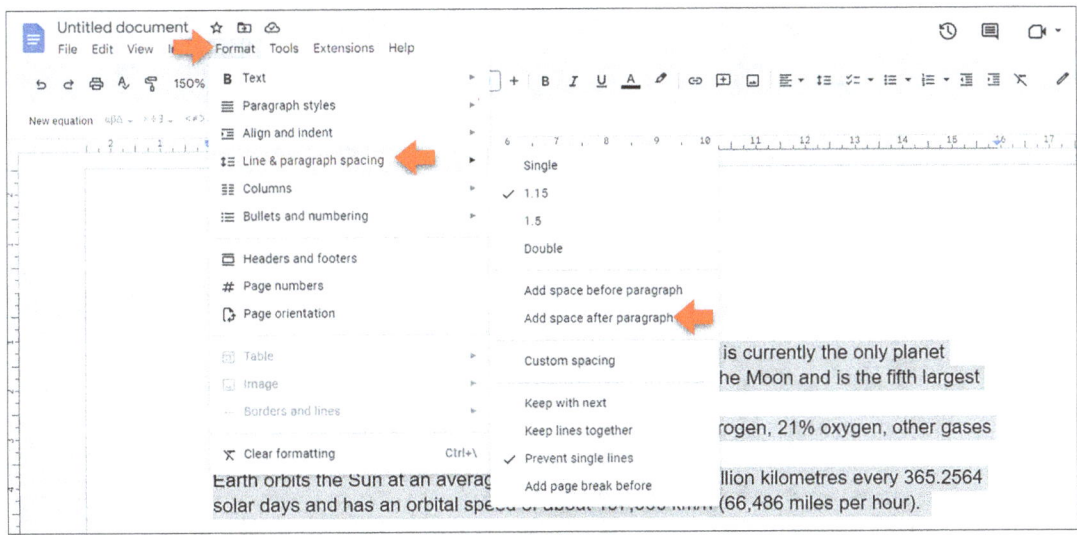

You'll see a space after each paragraph.

> The third planet from the Sun is unique in the Universe as it is currently the only planet known to support life. It has a single natural satellite called the Moon and is the fifth largest planet in the Solar System.
>
> Water covers 71% of the surface. Its atmosphere is 77% nitrogen, 21% oxygen, other gases such as argon, carbon dioxide and a number of others.
>
> Earth orbits the Sun at an average distance of about 150 million kilometres every 365.2564 solar days and has an orbital speed of about 107,000 km/h (66,486 miles per hour).
>
> The United States Census Bureau estimates that the world population exceeded 7 billion on 12th March 2012. The world population has experienced continuous growth since the end of the Great Famine and the Black Death in 1350, when it was near 370 million.

39

Chapter 3: Building Documents

Line Spacing

Line spacing, as its name suggests, adjusts the spacing between the lines of text on your page.

> The third planet from the Sun is unique in the Universe as it is currently the only planet
>
> known to support life. It has a single natural satellite called the Moon and is the fifth largest
>
> planet in the Solar System.

First, select the text you want to adjust, then from the 'format' menu, select 'line & paragraph spacing'. Click one of the options circled below.

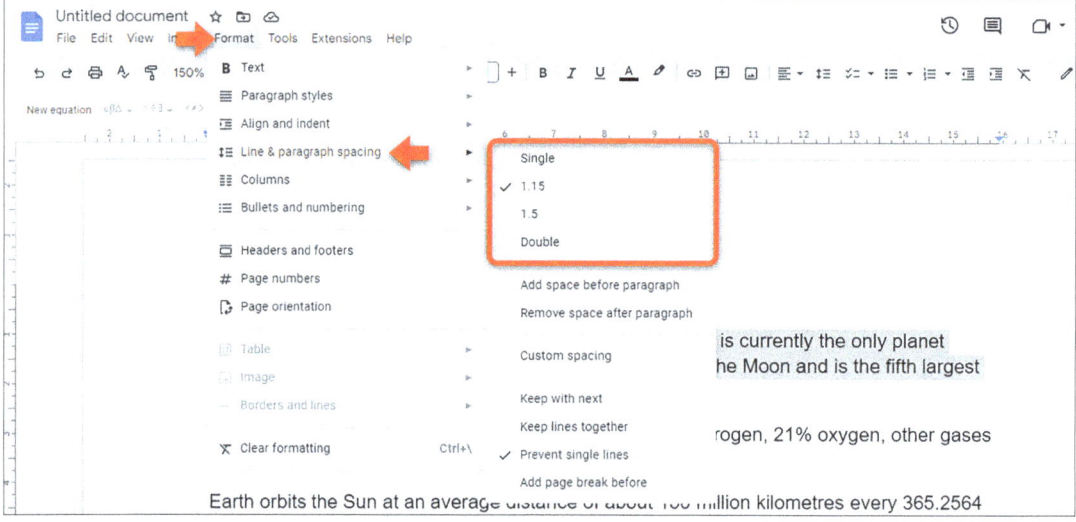

To add a custom spacing - select 'custom spacing' from the slideout... then enter the spacing in the 'line spacing' section of the dialog box that appears.

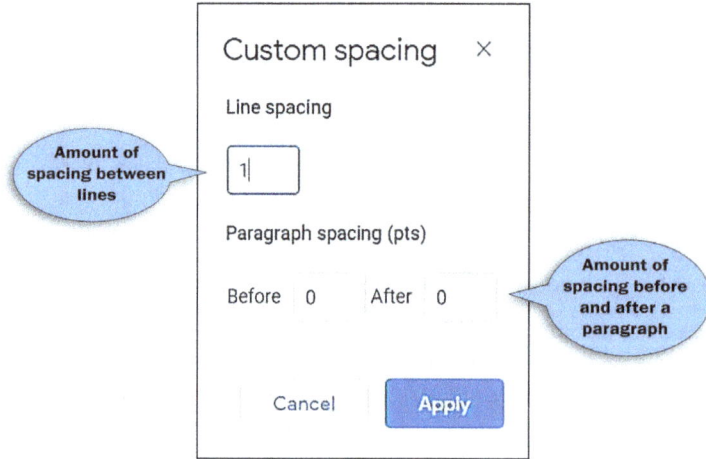

Chapter 3: Building Documents

Cut, Copy & Paste

To ease editing documents, you can use copy, cut and paste to move paragraphs or pictures around on different parts of your document.

'Cut' moves the selected text from its original location, while 'copy' creates a duplicate of the selected text and leaving the original text in place.

Cut & Paste

First select the paragraph below with your mouse. To do this click before the word 'Earth', then drag your mouse across the line towards the end, as shown below.

> The third planet from the Sun is unique in the Universe as it is currently the only planet known to support life. It has a single natural satellite called the Moon and is the fifth largest planet in the Solar System. Earth's distance from the sun is 149,600,000 km.
>
> *Click & drag across text to highlight*

Once you have done that, select the 'edit' menu. From the drop down, click on 'cut'.

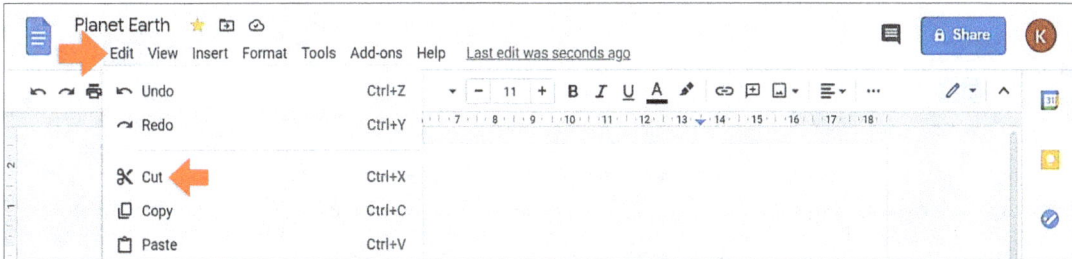

Now click on the position in the document you want the paragraph you just cut out to be inserted.

> Earth orbits the Sun at an average distance of about 150 million kilometres every 365.2564 solar days and has an orbital speed of about 107,000 km/h (66,486 miles per hour).
>
> The United States Census Bureau estimates that the world population exceeded 7 billion on 12th March 2012. The world population has experienced continuous growth since the end of the Great Famine and the Black Death in 1350, when it was near 370 million.

Chapter 3: Building Documents

Once you have done that, go back to the 'edit' menu and select 'paste'.

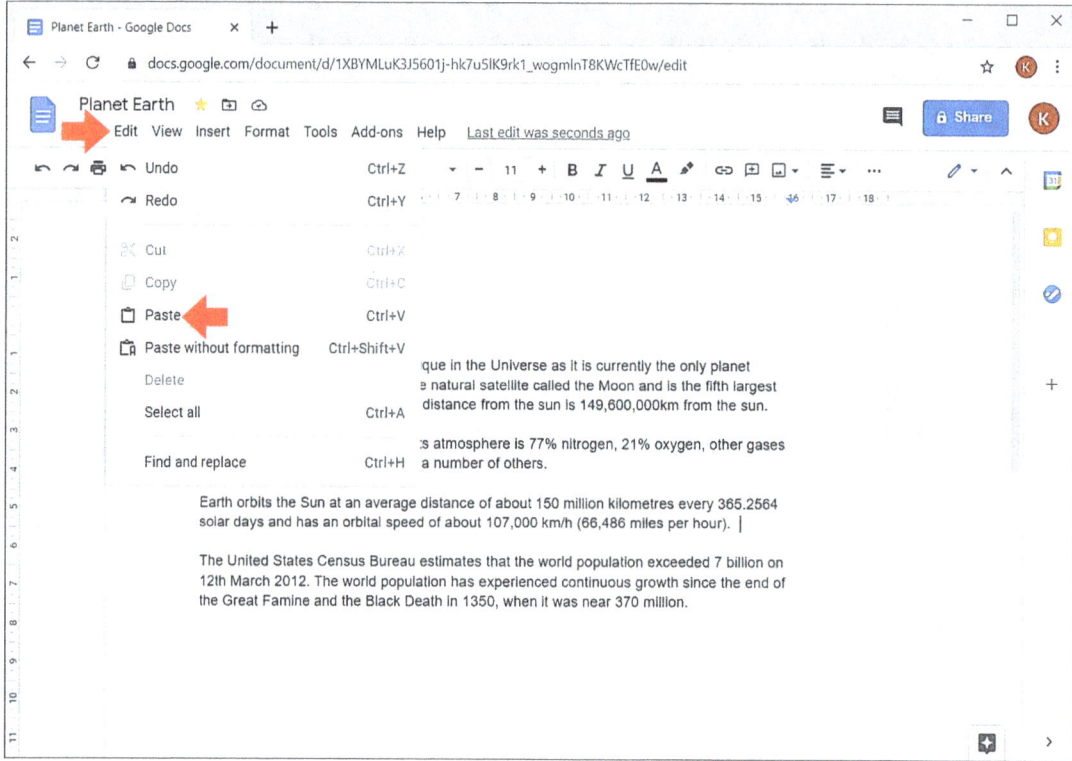

Here, we can see the sentence we cut out earlier has been pasted into position

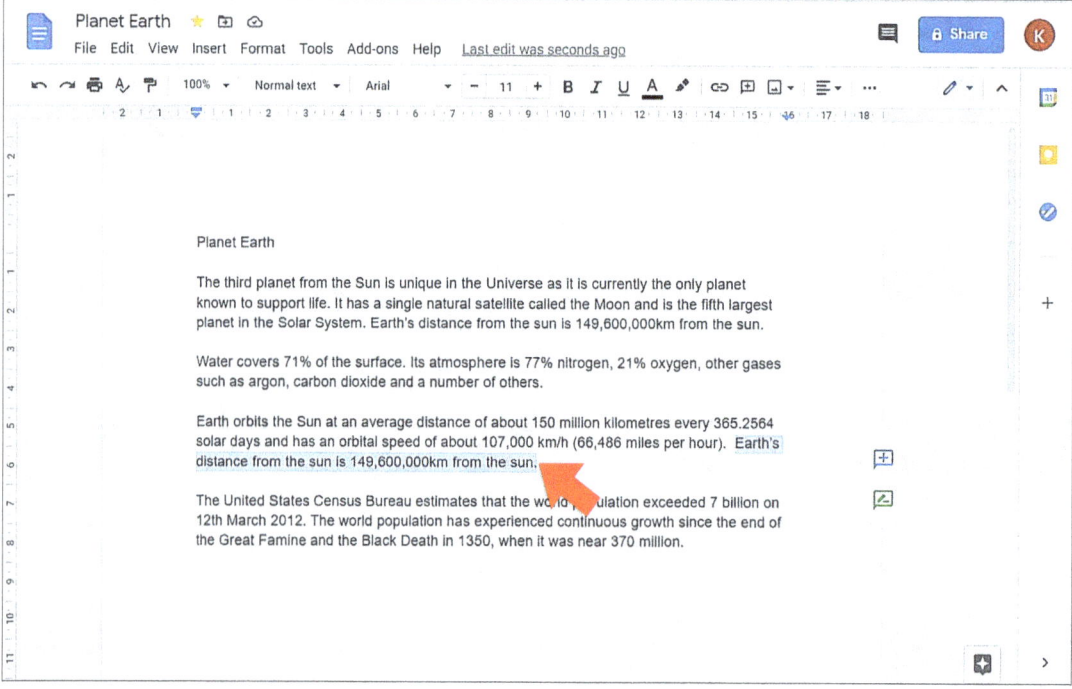

Chapter 3: Building Documents

Copy & Paste

If you wanted to copy something ie make a duplicate of the text, then use the same procedure except click 'copy' instead of 'cut'.

First select the paragraph below with your mouse. To do this click before the word 'Earth', then drag your mouse across the line towards the end, as shown below.

> The third planet from the Sun is unique in the Universe as it is currently the only planet known to support life. It has a single natural satellite called the Moon and is the fifth largest planet in the Solar System. Earth's distance from the sun is 149,600,000 km.
>
> Click & drag across text to highlight

Once you have done that, select the 'edit' menu. From the drop down, click on 'cut'.

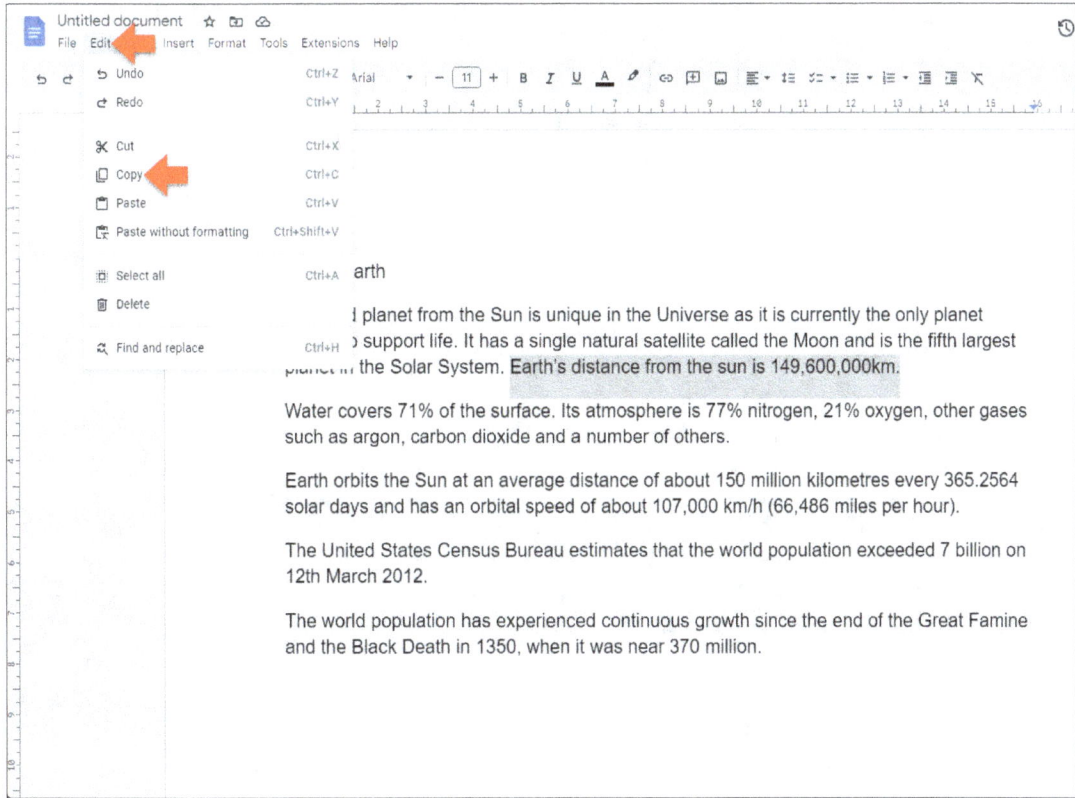

43

Chapter 3: Building Documents

Now click on the position in the document you want the paragraph you just cut out to be inserted.

> The third planet from the Sun is unique in the Universe as it is currently the only planet known to support life. It has a single natural satellite called the Moon and is the fifth largest planet in the Solar System.
>
> Water covers 71% of the surface. Its atmosphere is 77% nitrogen, 21% oxygen, other gases such as argon, carbon dioxide and a number of others.
>
> Earth orbits the Sun at an average distance of about 150 million kilometres every 365.2564 solar days and has an orbital speed of about 107,000 km/h (66,486 miles per hour). |
>
> The United States Census Bureau estimates that the world population exceeded 7 billion on 12th March 2012. The world population has experienced continuous growth since the end of the Great Famine and the Black Death in 1350, when it was near 370 million.

Once you have done that, go back to the 'edit' menu and select 'paste'.

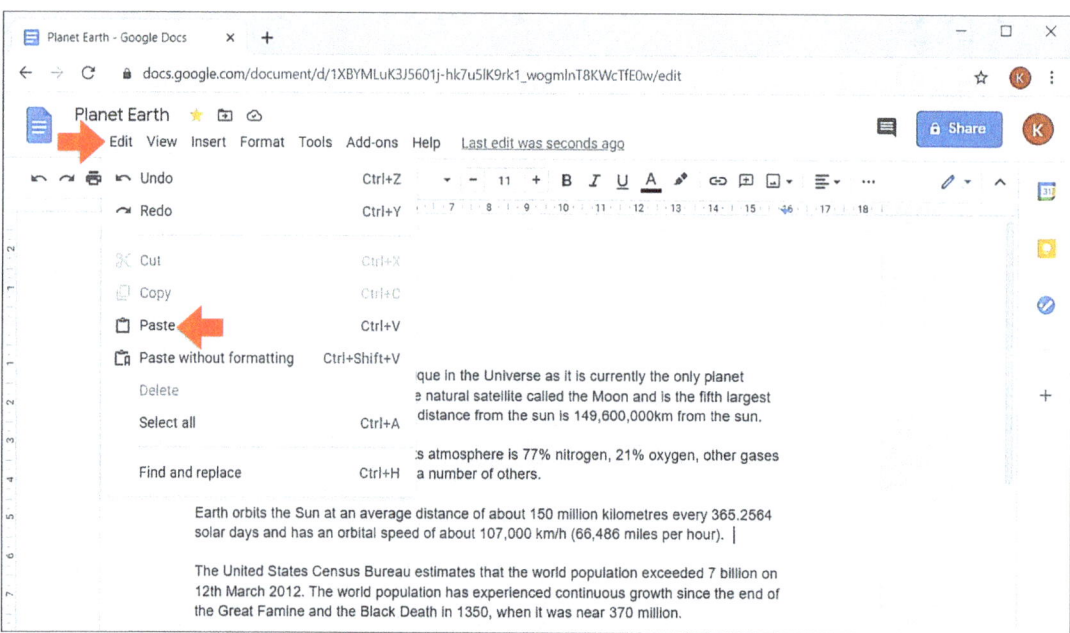

Here, you can see that we've copied the text.

> The third planet from the Sun is unique in the Universe as it is currently the only planet known to support life. It has a single natural satellite called the Moon and is the fifth largest planet in the Solar System. Earth's distance from the sun is 149,600,000km.
>
> Water covers 71% of the surface. Its atmosphere is 77% nitrogen, 21% oxygen, other gases such as argon, carbon dioxide and a number of others.
>
> Earth orbits the Sun at an average distance of about 150 million kilometres every 365.2564 solar days and has an orbital speed of about 107,000 km/h (66,486 miles per hour). Earth's distance from the sun is 149,600,000km.
>
> The United States Census Bureau estimates that the world population exceeded 7 billion on 12th March 2012.

Chapter 3: Building Documents

Paste without Formatting

Paste without formatting is a command that is used to paste text without carrying over any formatting from the source text. This is useful when you want to paste text without altering the formatting of the document you are pasting into.

For example, when you copy text from a web page, another document, or any source that contains formatting information, that formatting information is also copied along with the text. This means that when you paste the text into a new location, it retains the formatting from the source.

The formatting is usually different to what you've got in your Google Docs page. You can use 'paste without formatting' to paste in the text with no original formatting so it will match the formatting in your document.

If we copy the text from the web page shown below, we just want the text, not the font, text size, or text color. Highlight the text on the webpage, then press control C on your keyboard to copy.

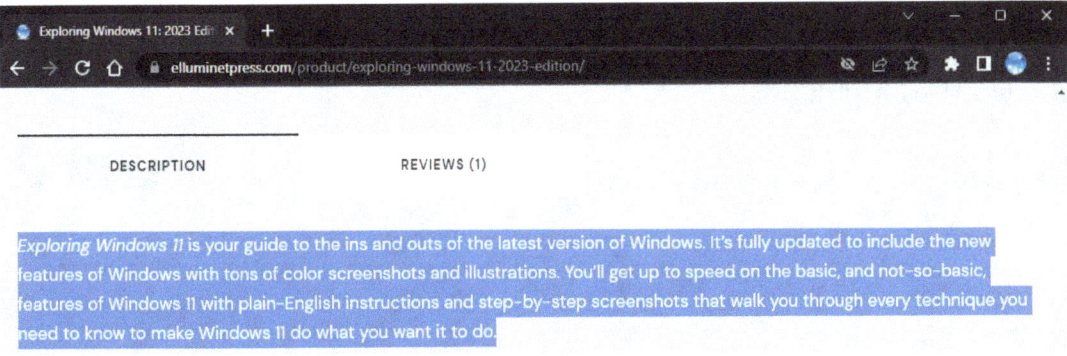

To paste this into our document, go up to the edit menu, then select 'paste without formatting'.

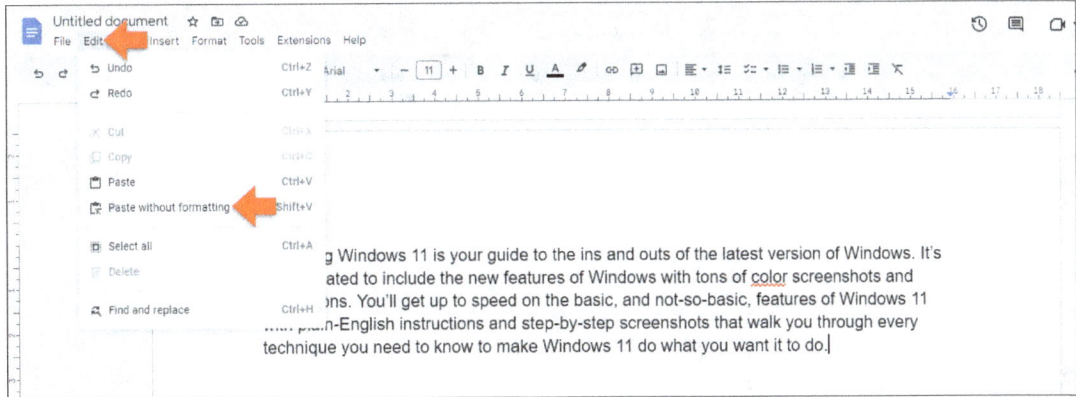

45

Chapter 3: Building Documents

Bold, Italic & Underlined

You can use **bold**, *italic* or <u>underlined</u> text to emphasise certain words or paragraphs.

To do this, select the text you want to apply formatting to, then from the toolbar along the top of the screen, select one of the icons: **bold**, *italic* or <u>underlined</u>.

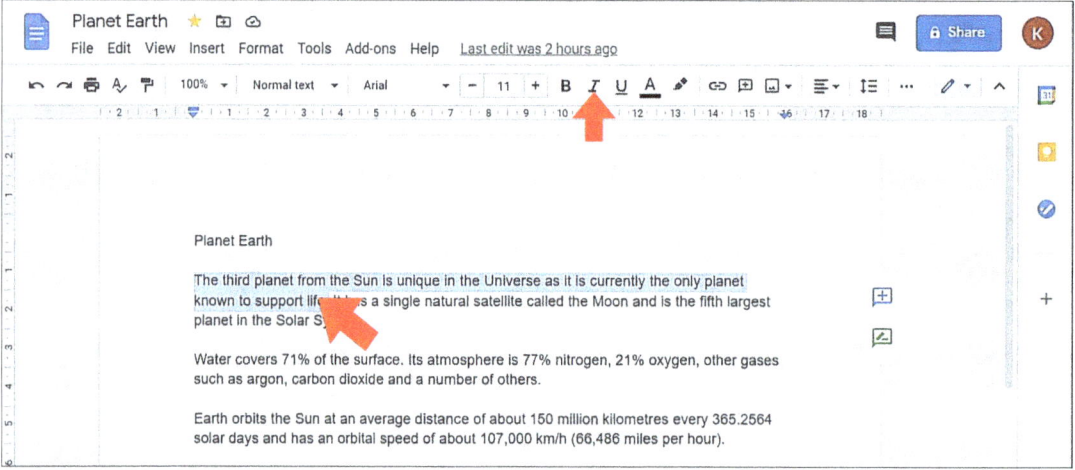

To make the text "water", "nitrogen" and "oxygen" bold, double click on the word to highlight it.

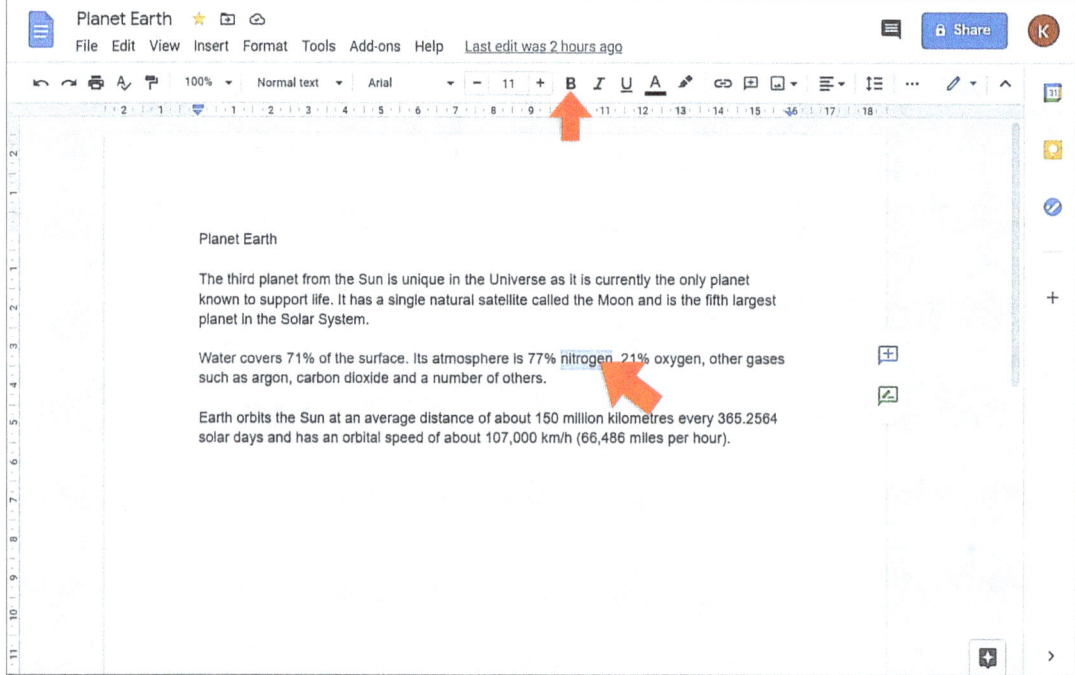

Select the bold icon from the toolbar.

Chapter 3: Building Documents

Superscript & Subscript

Subscripts appear below the text line, and are used primarily in mathematical formulas to express chemical compounds or footnotes.

For example.

H_2O or CO_2

You can add subscripts to your text. To do this, first highlight the character you want to make into a subscript. In this example, I want to select the '2' in H2O. From the 'format menu' select 'text', then click 'subscript' on the slideout menu.

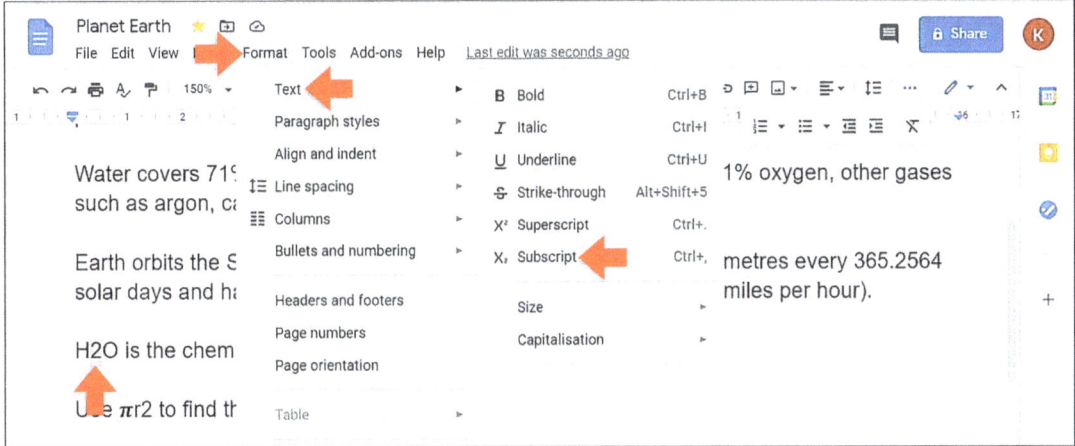

Superscripts appear at the top of the text line and are used primarily in mathematical formulas, such as the area of the circle is = πr^2

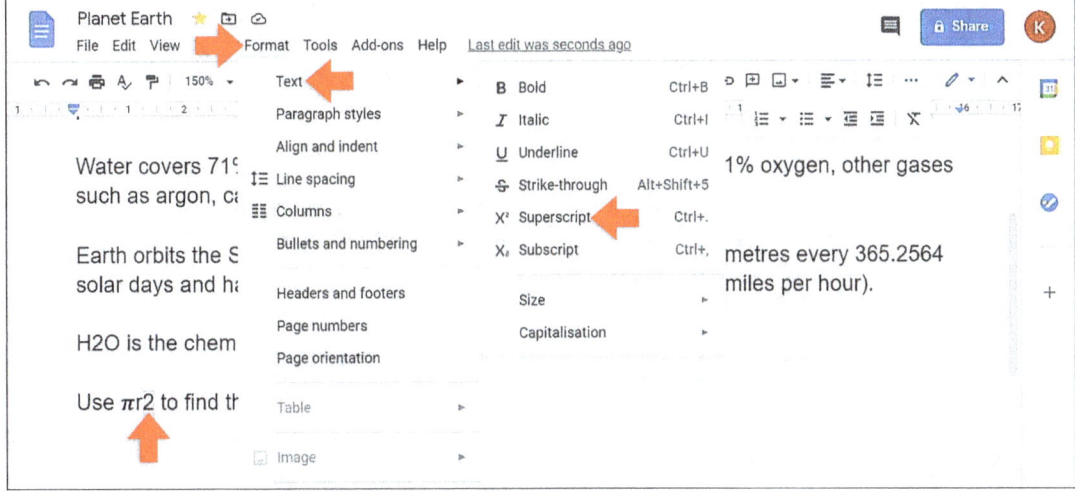

Select the '2' from the formula πr2. From the 'format menu' select 'text', then click 'subscript' from the slideout menu.

47

Chapter 3: Building Documents

Highlighting Text

You can highlight words, sentences and paragraphs to make important information stand out. To do this, first select the text with your mouse.

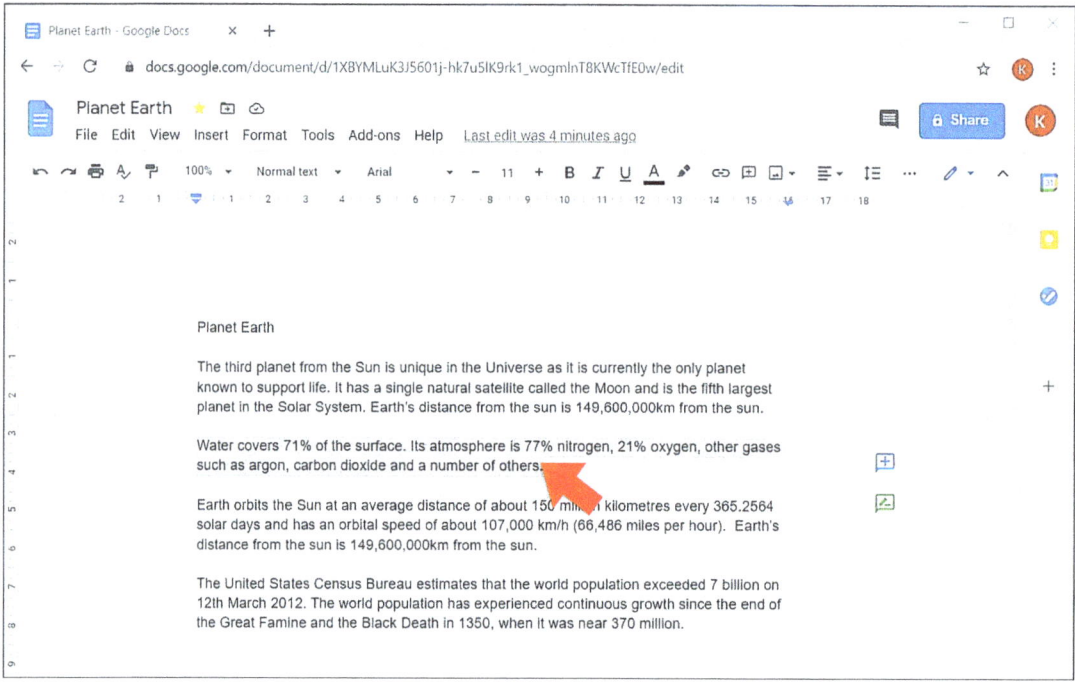

Click the highlight icon on the toolbar, then select a color from the palette.

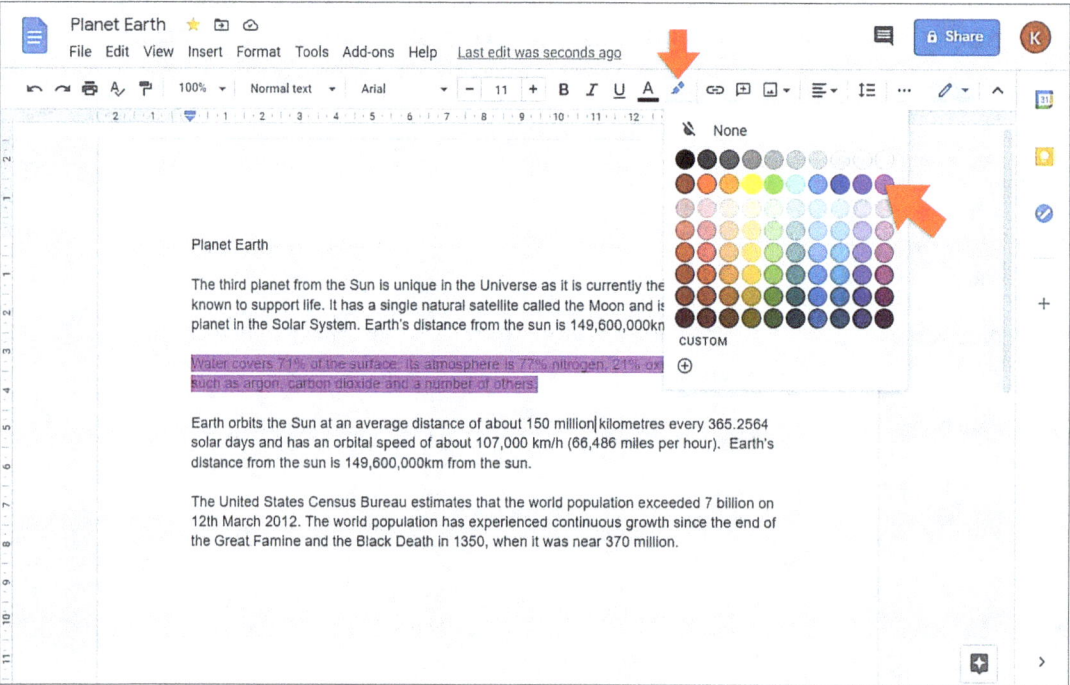

48

Chapter 3: Building Documents

Text Color

To change the color of the text, first highlight it with your mouse. In the example below, I want to change the text color of the first paragraph. To do this, click before the word 'the' and drag your mouse across the paragraph, to the end after 'March 2012', to highlight it.

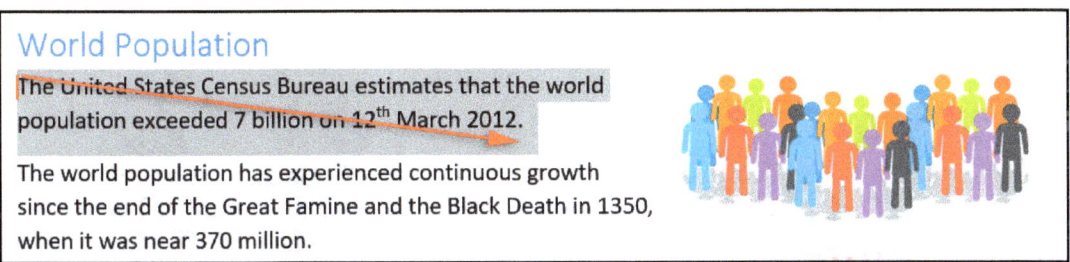

Click the text color icon on the toolbar, then select a color from the palette.

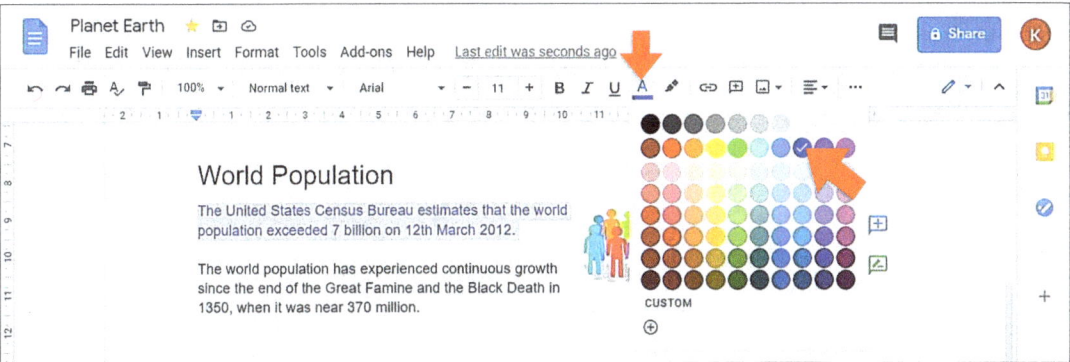

Text Size

To change the size of the text, select it with your mouse, then use the font size controls on the toolbar.

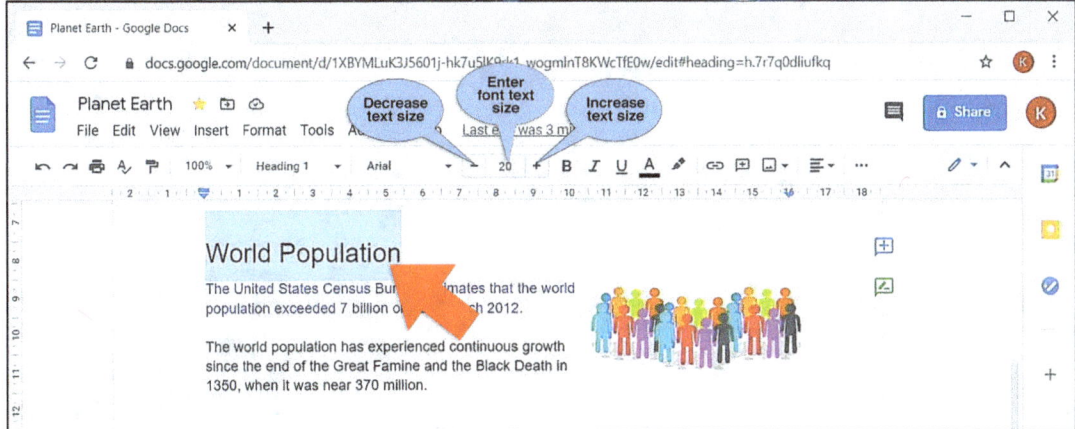

49

Chapter 3: Building Documents

Change Font

To change the font, select it the text with your mouse.

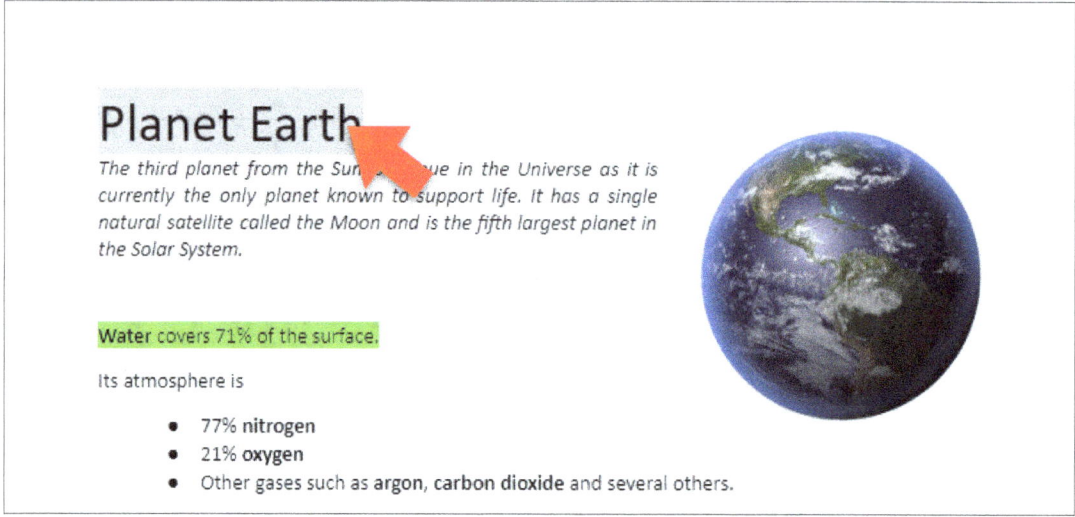

From the toolbar, click on the typeface drop down menu, then select a font from the list.

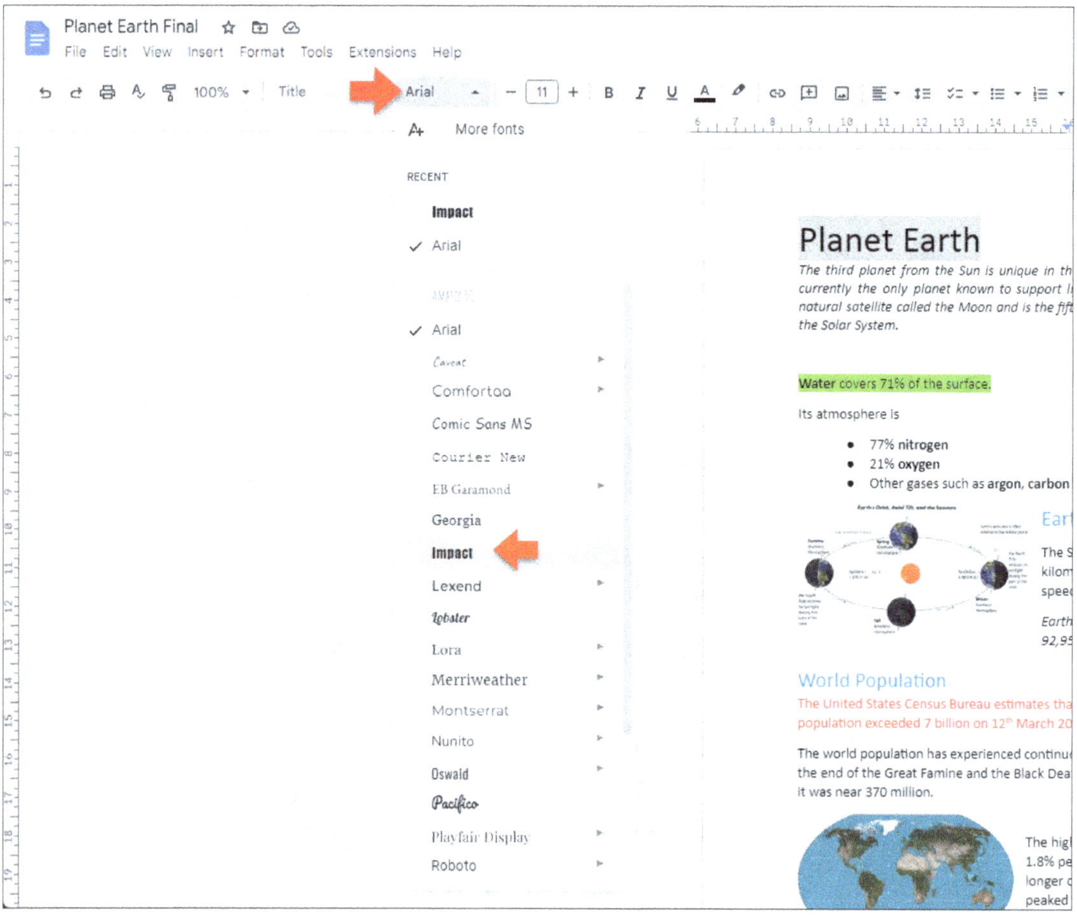

Chapter 3: Building Documents

Change Case

You can change the case of a word or sentence using the change case feature. You can use:

> lowercase text
>
> UPPERCASE TEXT
>
> Title Case, Capitalises First Letter Of Each Word

To change the case of a word or sentence, first highlight it with your mouse.

> Planet earth
>
> The third planet from the Sun is unique in the Universe as it is currently the only planet known to support life. It has a single natural satellite called the Moon and is the fifth largest planet in the Solar System.
>
> Water covers 71% of the surface. Its atmosphere is 77% nitrogen, 21% oxygen, other gases such as argon, carbon dioxide and a number of others.
>
> Earth orbits the Sun at an average distance of about 150 million kilometres every 365.2564 solar days and has an orbital speed of about 107,000 km/h (66,486 miles per hour).

From the 'format' menu, go down to 'text', select 'capitalisations' from the slideout menu.

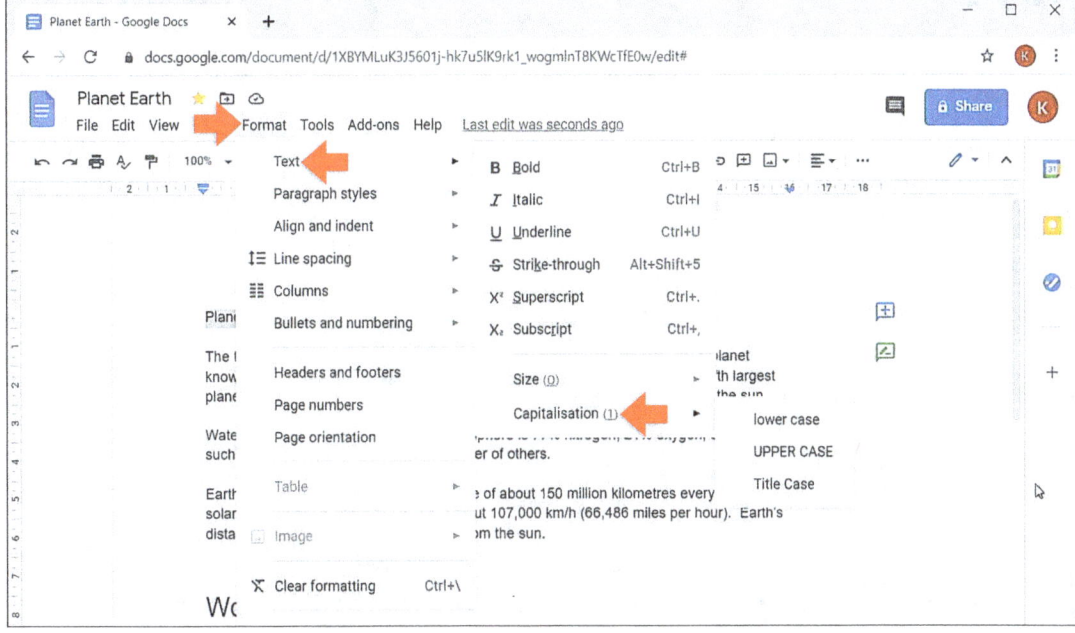

Select either 'lower case', 'UPPER CASE' or 'Title Case'.

51

Chapter 3: Building Documents

Paragraph Styles

Docs has numerous paragraph styles that are useful for keeping your formatting consistent. The idea is to format all your headings with 'title', 'heading 1', 'heading 2', 'heading 3', your main text as 'normal', and so on. This makes it easier to format your document so you don't have to apply the same font style, size and color manually every time you want a heading.

To apply the styles to a heading or paragraph, highlight it with your mouse as shown below.

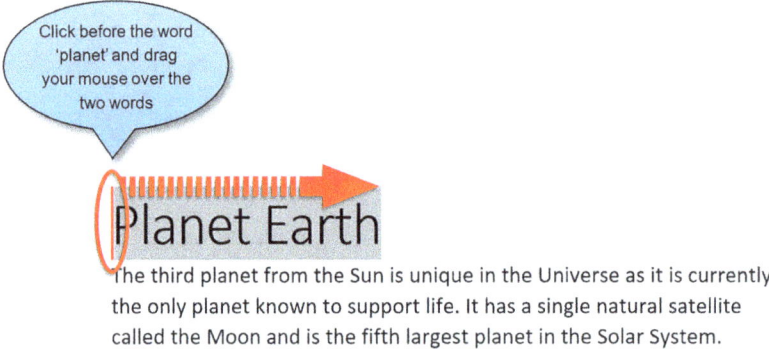

Select a style from the styles drop down box on the toolbar.

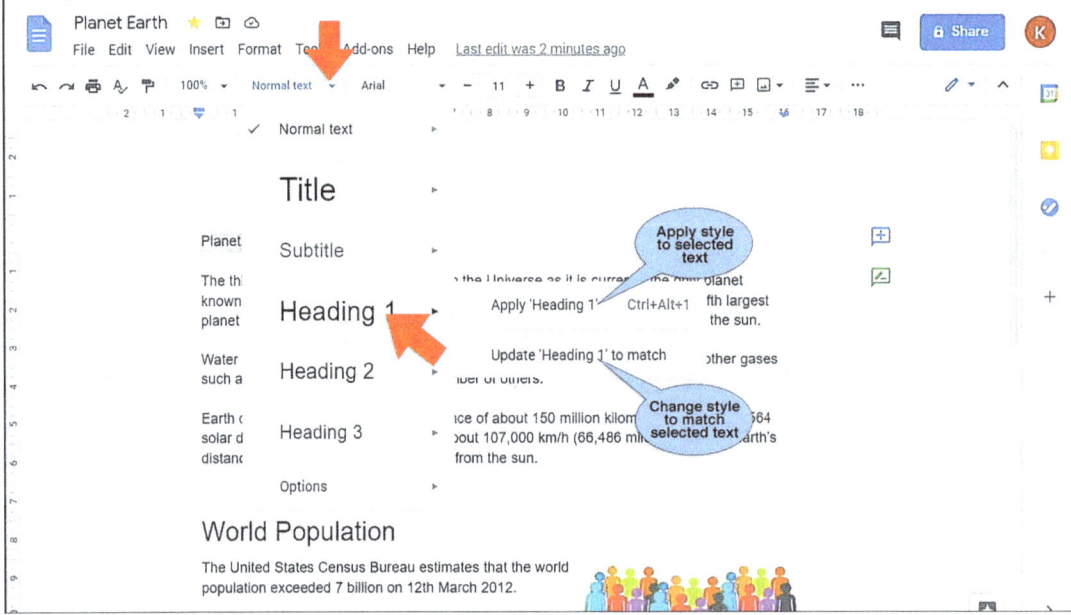

Click on a style to apply it to the selected text. Click the small to the right and select 'update to match' if you want to assign the current text formatting to the style.

Chapter 3: Building Documents

Bullet Lists

We can edit the document and change the sentence explaining atmospheric composition to a bullet point list. First, select the text using your mouse as shown below.

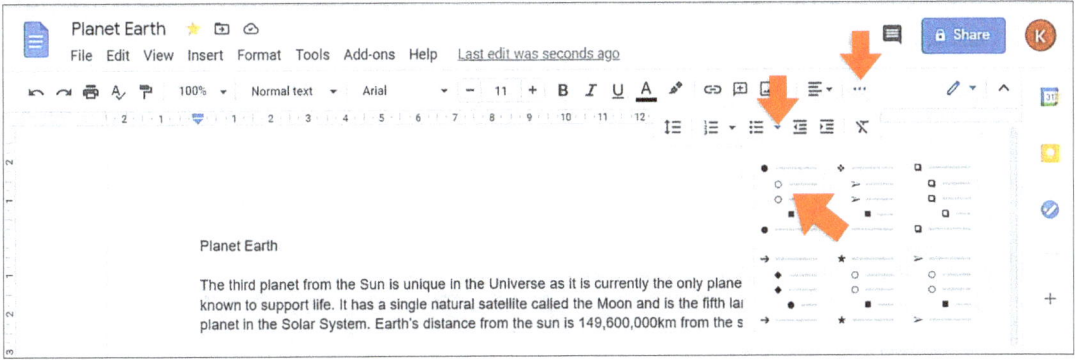

From the toolbar click the small down arrow next to the bullet list icon. If the icon isn't there, click the three dots icon on the right hand side of the toolbar.

From the drop down menu, select a bullet style.

Numbered Lists

We can edit the document and change the sentence explaining atmospheric composition to a numbered point list. Select the text using your mouse as shown below.

Chapter 3: Building Documents

From the toolbar click the small down arrow next to the numbered list icon. If the icon isn't there, click the three dots icon on the right hand side of the toolbar.

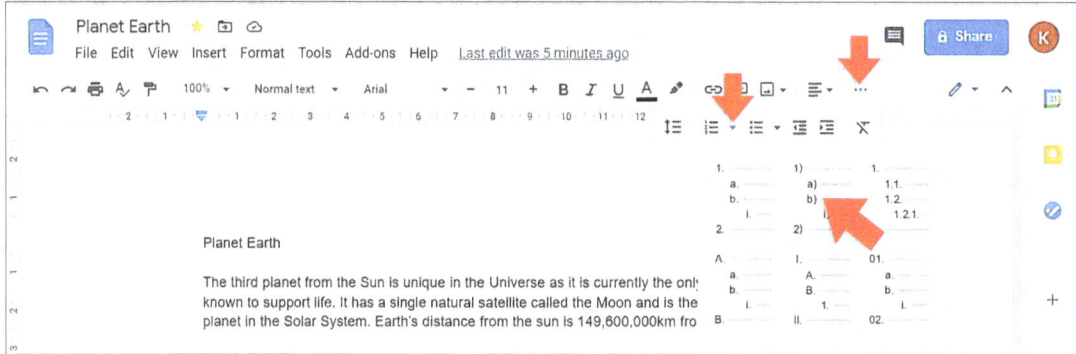

From the drop down menu, select a numbered list style.

Inserting Symbols

You can insert special symbols for mathematics, emojis, and special punctuation characters.

In the example sentence below, I want to insert the degree symbol after the number 40.

Last summer we saw temperatures of up to 40

To insert a symbol, go to the 'insert' menu then select 'special character'.

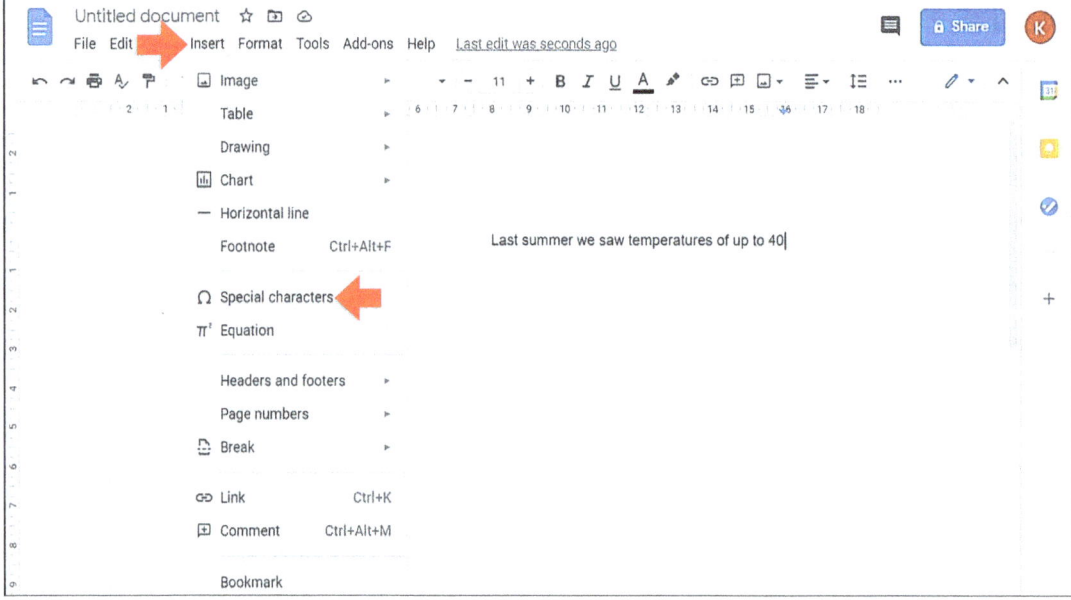

Chapter 3: Building Documents

Select the character from the dialog box. If you can't find it, try searching for it using the search field on the right hand side.

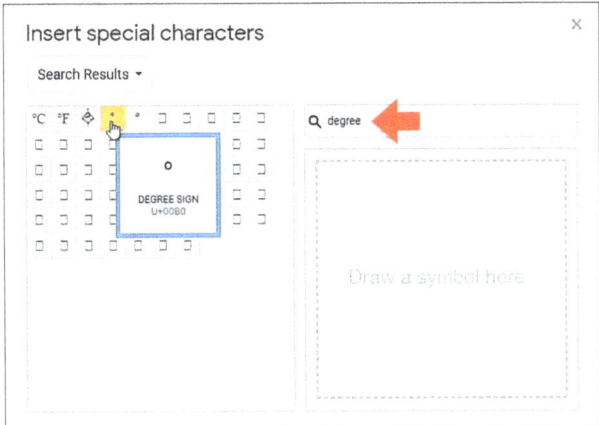

Click on the one you want to add.

Last summer we saw temperatures of up to 40°|

Hidden Characters

Google Docs inserts formatting characters such as carriage returns, spaces, tab characters that are hidden by default, to make editing your document easier for you.

To see these characters, you'll first need to install an add-on. Go to the 'add-ons' menu, then select 'get add-ons'. Type show into the search field.

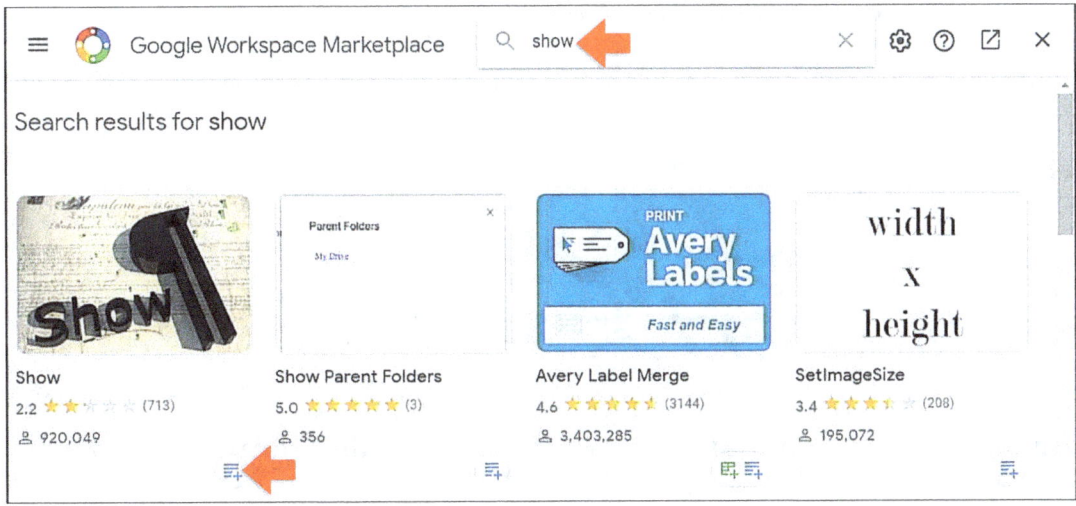

Click the small 'add' icon underneath the add-on's thumbnail icon.

55

Chapter 3: Building Documents

Click the 'install' button. You may be prompted to enter your Google Account email address and password.

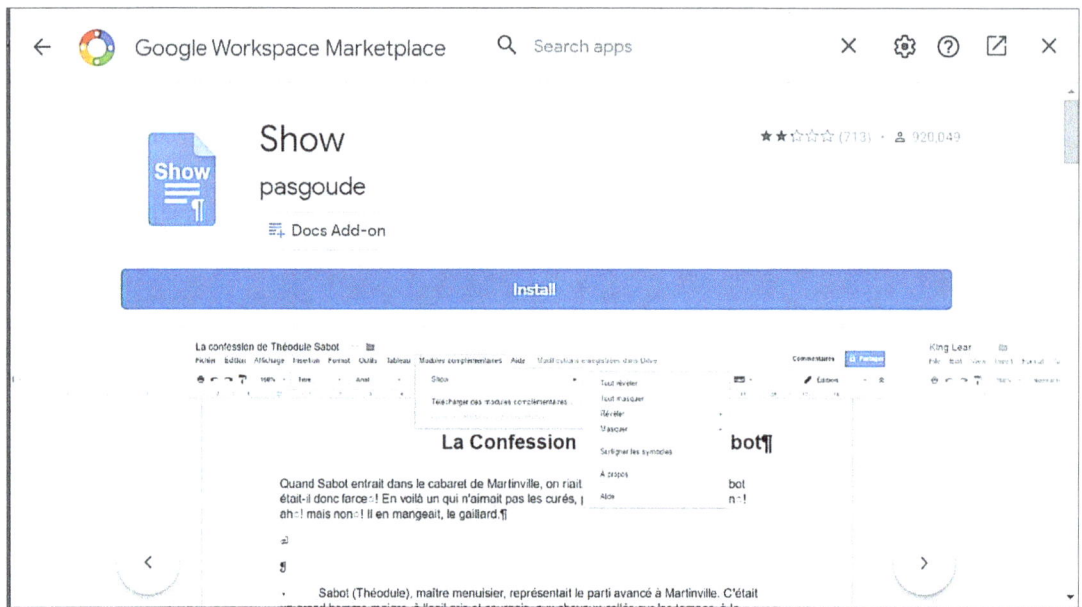

Once the add-on is installed, go to the 'add-ons' menu, go down to 'show', then select 'show all' from the slideout menu.

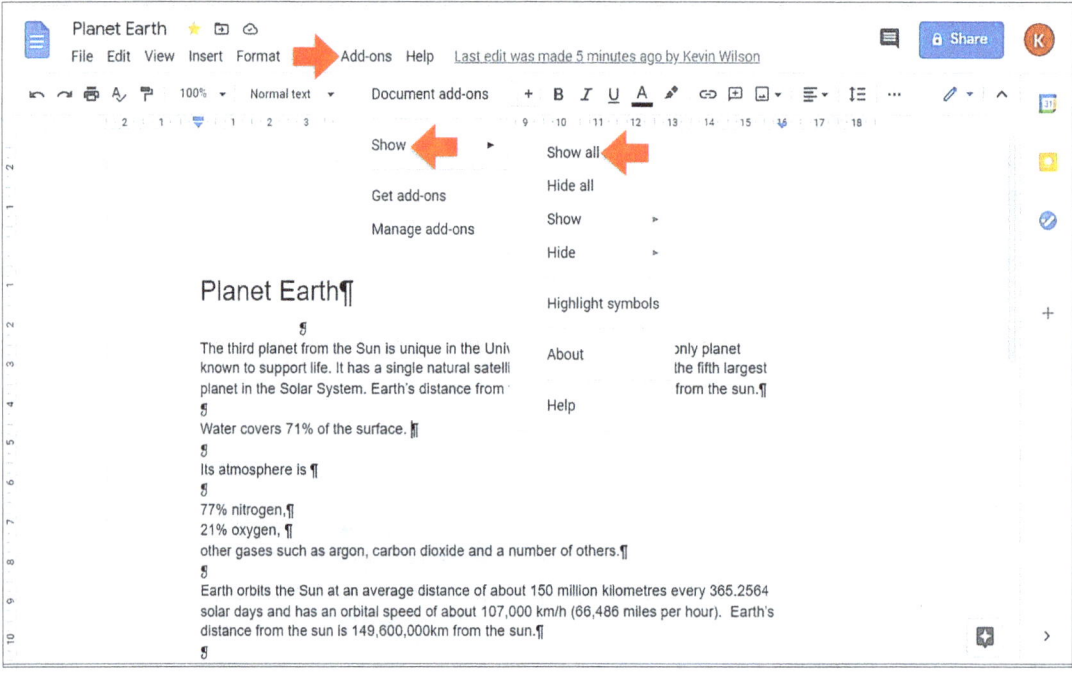

You'll see all the formatting markers for carriage return, line breaks and section breaks appear.

To remove the formatting markers, just select 'hide all' from the menu.

Chapter 3: Building Documents

Hyper-links

Google Docs automatically creates hyper-links for email addresses and website URLs.

For more go to www.elluminetpress.com or email office@elluminetpress.com

To insert a hyper-link for anything else, first select the word or text with your mouse.

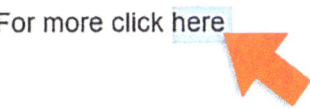

Right click on your selection, then select 'link' from the popup menu.

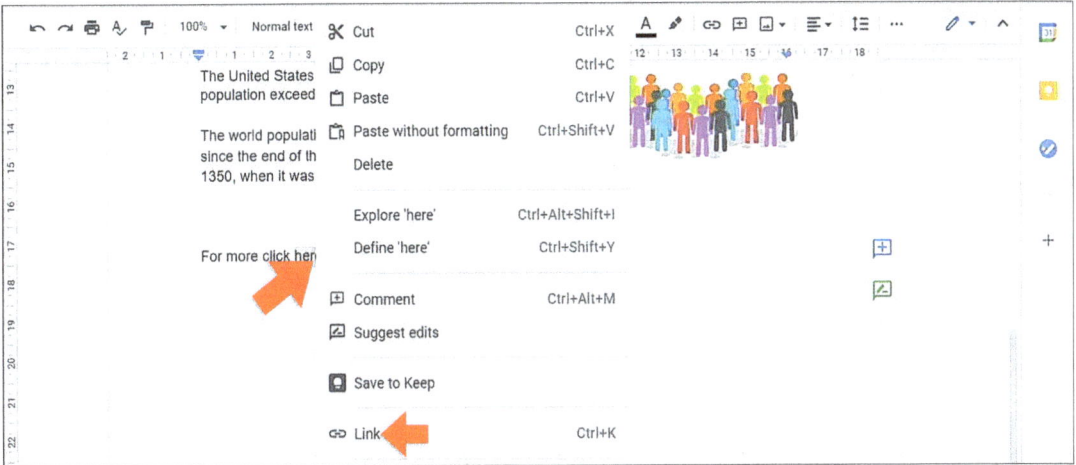

Enter the URL of the website you want to link to, then click 'apply'.

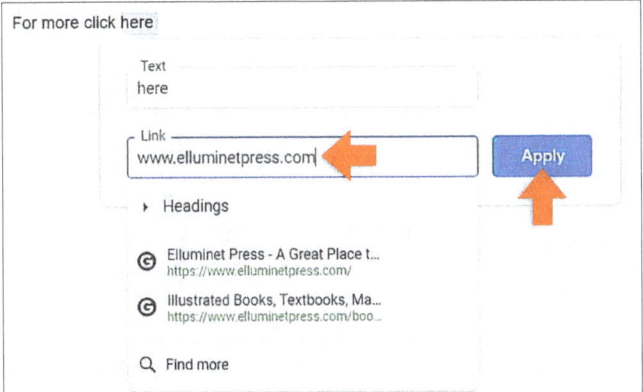

To remove a hyper-link, just right click on it, then select 'remove link' from the popup menu.

57

Chapter 3: Building Documents

Equations

Google Docs includes a feature for displaying equations correctly and has some very common ones built in.

$$Speed = \frac{Distance}{Time}$$

$$Volume = \frac{4}{3}\pi r^3$$

To build an equation, go to your insert menu and select 'equation'.

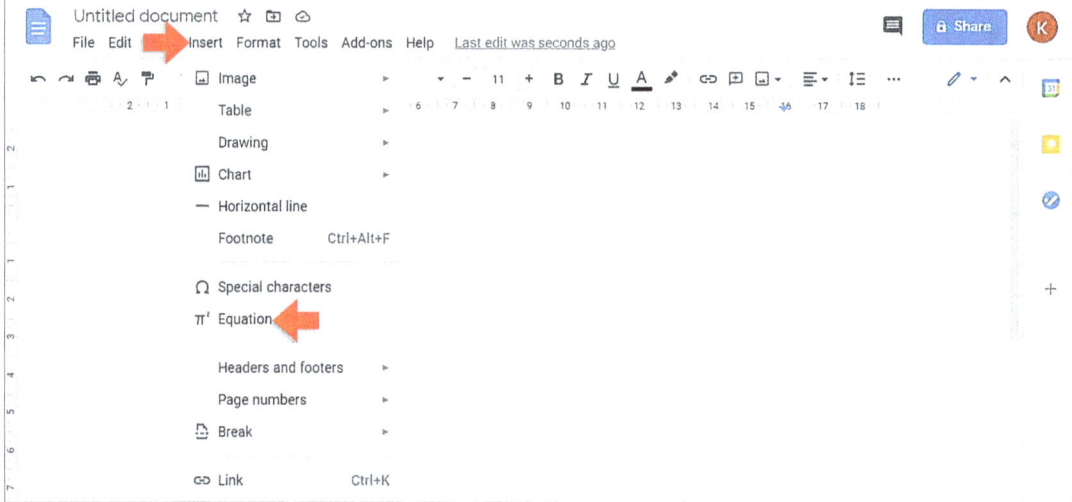

An equation toolbar will appear. Here, you'll find five groups of symbols you can use to create your equations.

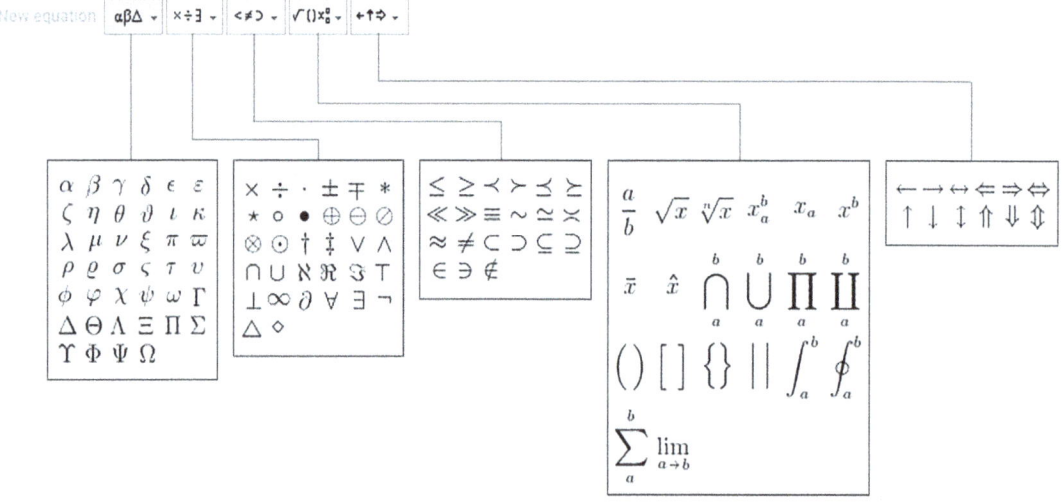

Chapter 3: Building Documents

We can start building our equation. In this example, we're creating the formula for calculating the volume of a sphere. First type

```
volume =
```

Then we need to insert a fraction, so from the equation templates, select the 'mathematical operators' group, then click 'a/b'.

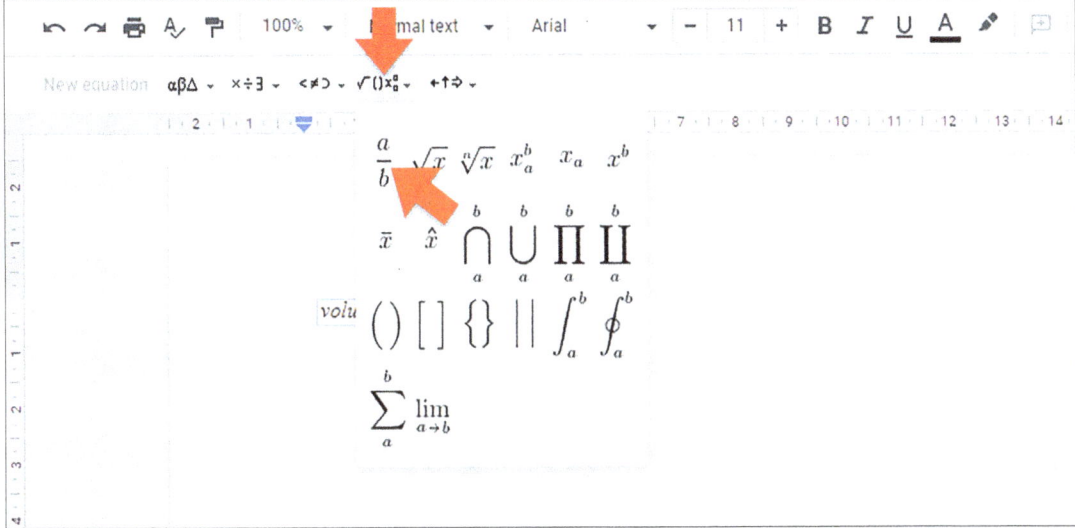

Then type 4 at the top, press the tab key on your keyboard, they type 3 at the bottom. Press the tab key again to move on.

Now we need to insert a symbol for Pi. So from the Greek letters group select Pi (π).

59

Chapter 3: Building Documents

Next, we need to enter r^3. To do this, select the 'mathematical operator' group on the equation toolbar, then click x^b.

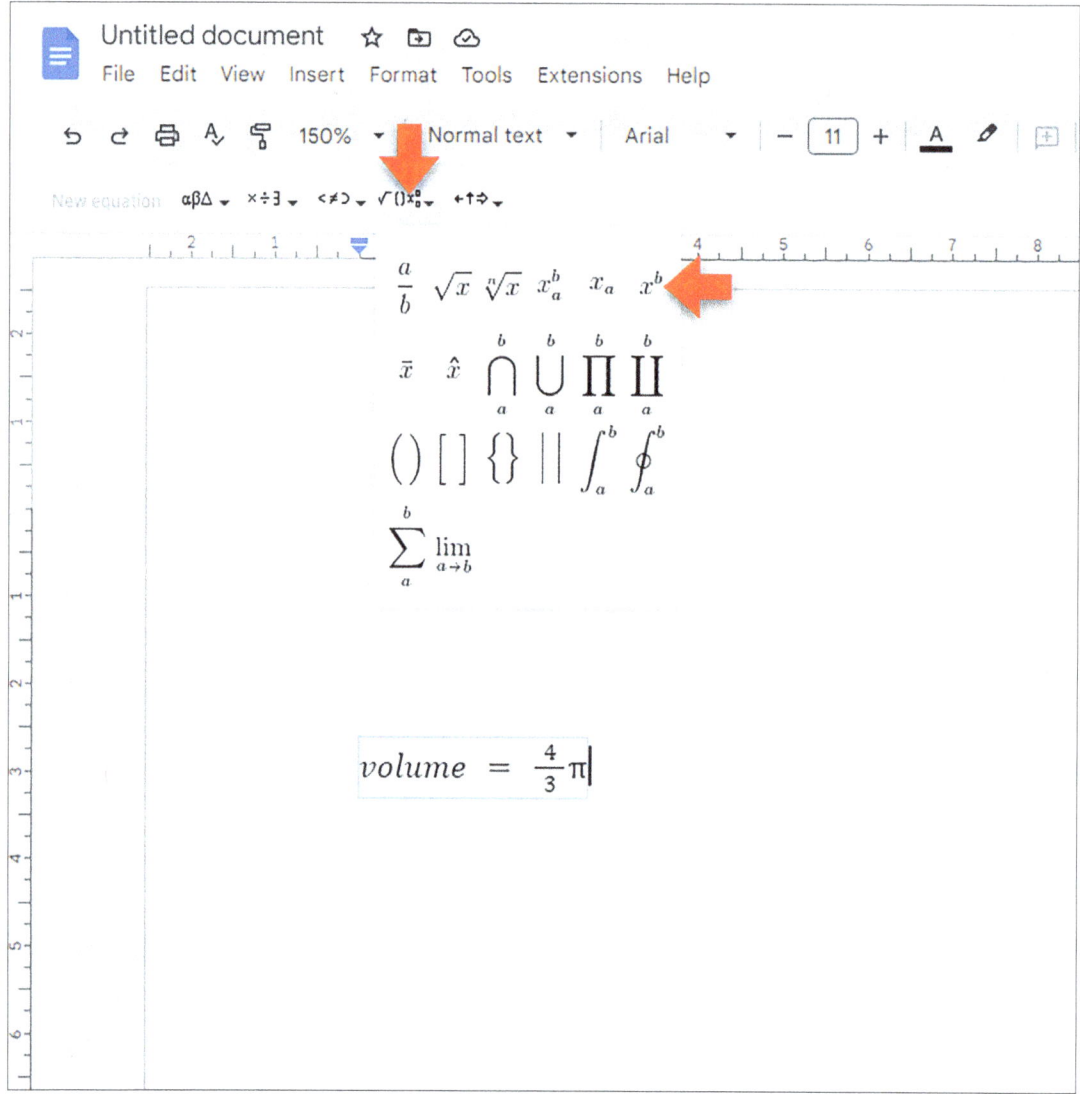

Type in r, press tab, then type in 3.

$$volume = \frac{4}{3}\pi r$$

You'll end up with your equation.

$$volume = \frac{4}{3}\pi r^3$$

This is a very simple example to demonstrate the feature.

Chapter 3: Building Documents

Page & Section Breaks

There are two types of breaks: a page break and a section break. A page break, breaks the body text of the document onto a new page.

A section break, breaks the body text and creates a new section in the document with different formatting, page orientation, margins, headers & footers, and page numbering.

There may be occasions where you need to force a new page. Perhaps you are writing a report and you need to start a new chapter. Instead of pressing the return key until a new page is created, you should insert a page break.

You may need to insert a section break if, for example, you are writing a report and want to add a section for the contents pages and front matter. The reason you'd insert a section break, is so you can apply page numbering or formatting that is different to the rest of the report - perhaps Roman numeral page numbers instead of regular page numbers.

Inserting Page Breaks

To insert a page break, first click on the line in your document where you want the break.

> Total annual births were highest in the late 1980s at about 139 million and is now expected to remain essentially constant at their 2011 level of 135 million, while deaths number 56 million per year, and are expected to increase to 80 million per year by 2040.

Select the 'insert' menu.

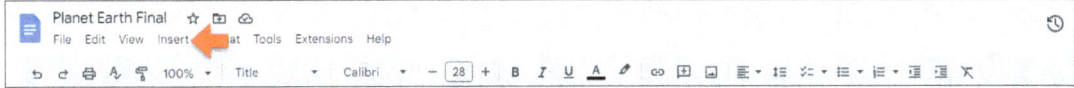

Go down to 'break', then from the slideout menu select 'page break'.

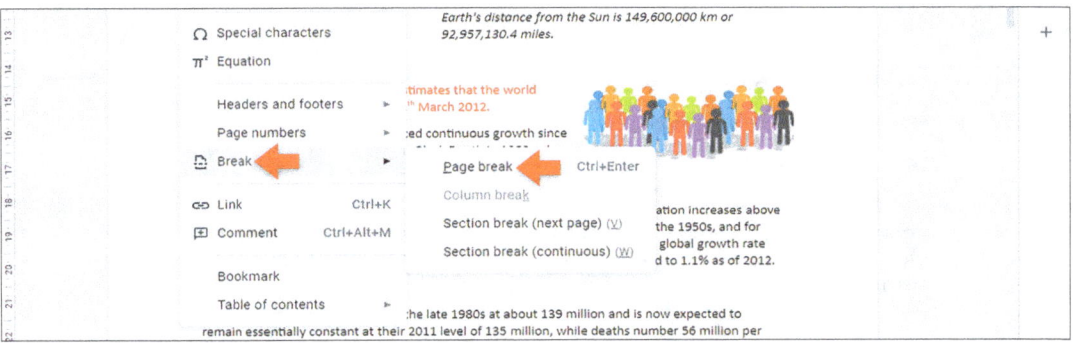

61

Chapter 3: Building Documents

Inserting Section Breaks

To insert a section break, first click on the line in your document where you want the break.

> Total annual births were highest in the late 1980s at about 139 million and is now expected to remain essentially constant at their 2011 level of 135 million, while deaths number 56 million per year, and are expected to increase to 80 million per year by 2040.

Select the 'insert' menu. Go down to 'break', then from the slideout menu select 'section break (next page)' or section break (continuous).

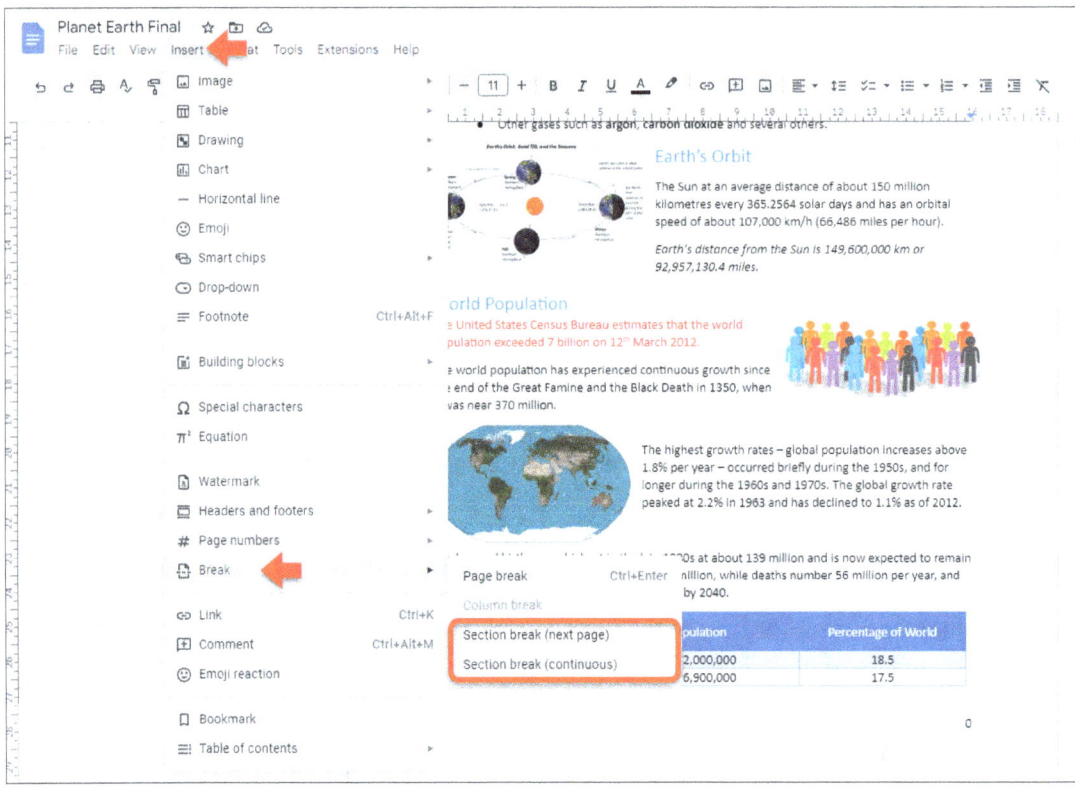

What's the difference? Well, a 'continuous section break' starts the new section on the same page. A 'next page section break', starts the new section on a new page. In this example, I selected 'section break (next page)'.

> Total annual births were highest in the late 1980s at about 139 million and is now expected to remain essentially constant at their 2011 level of 135 million, while deaths number 56 million per year, and are expected to increase to 80 million per year by 2040.

Chapter 3: Building Documents

Headers and Footers

Headers and footers appear at the top and bottom of a page. For example, the header on this page is "Chapter 3: Building Documents" and the footer is a page number on the bottom right.

Inserting Headers

To insert a header, select the 'insert' menu, go down to 'headers and footers', then click 'header' on the slideout menu.

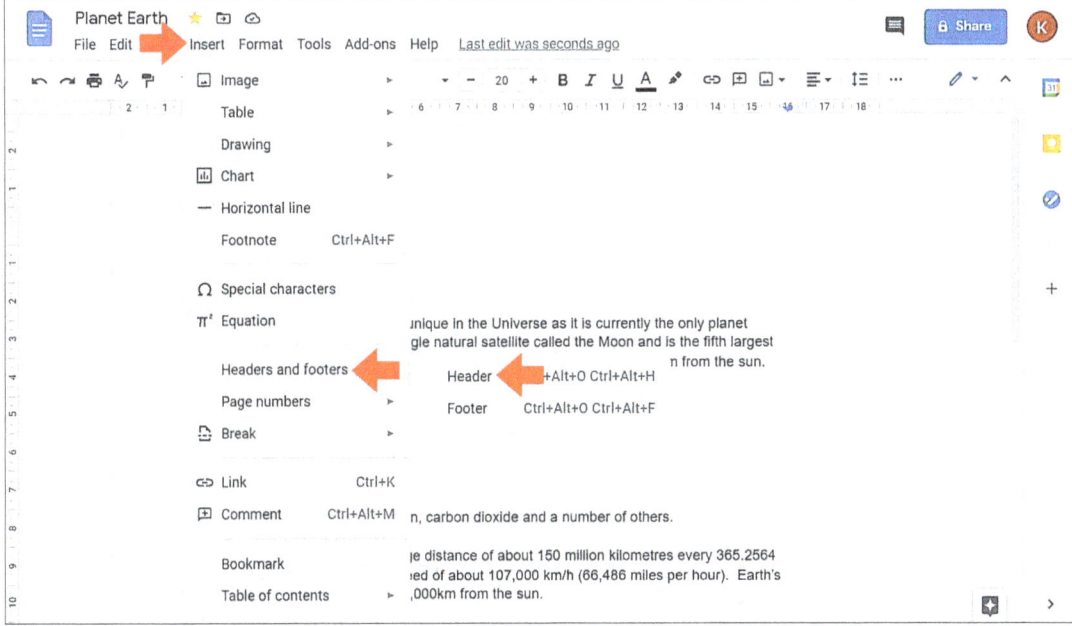

Add your page header in the top section of the screen.

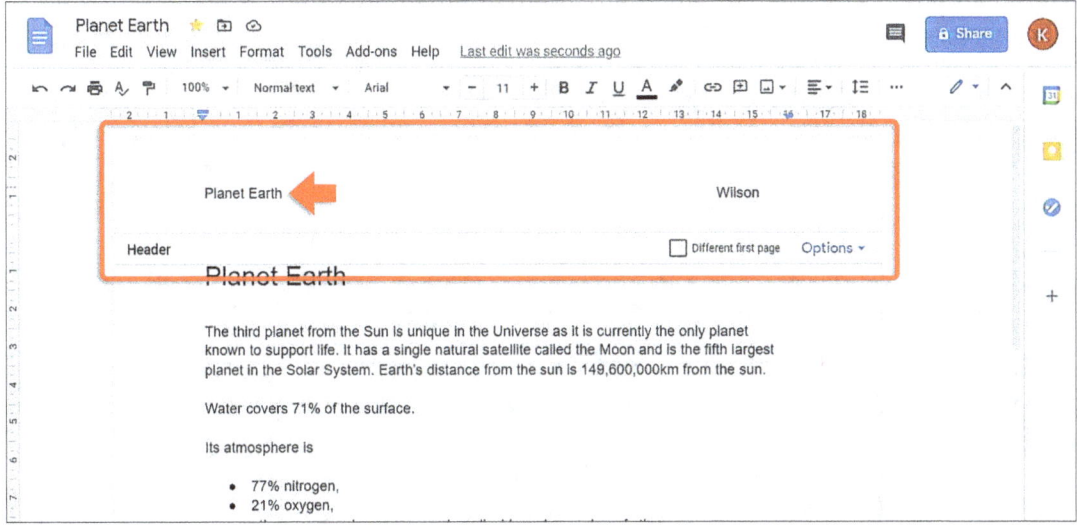

Chapter 3: Building Documents

Inserting Footers

To insert a footer, select the 'insert' menu, go down the 'headers and footers', then click 'footer' on the slideout menu.

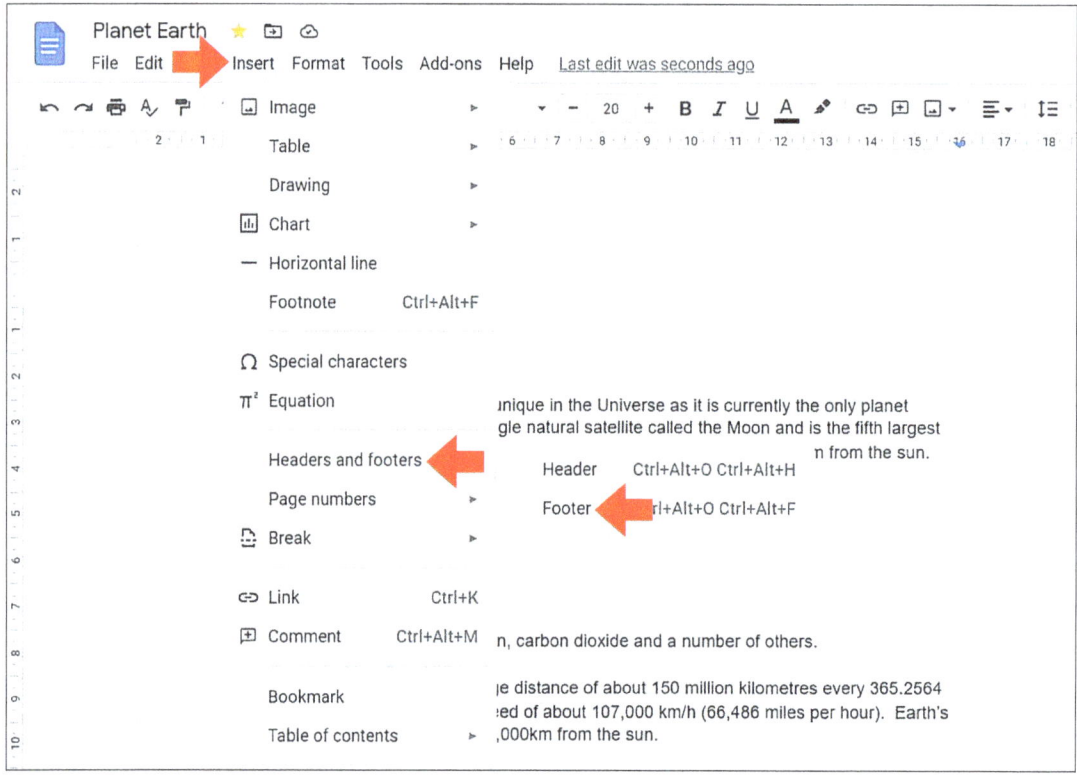

Here, you can type in your footer information in the footer section shown at the bottom of the document.

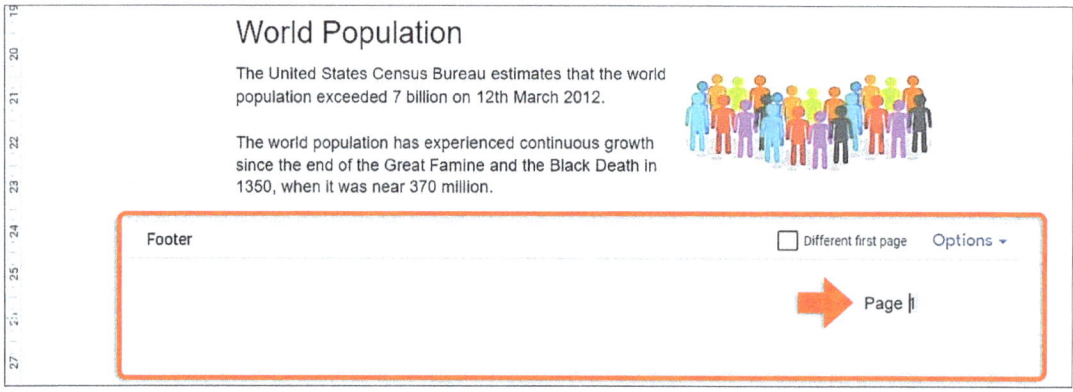

To add page numbers, click 'options', then select 'page numbers' from the popup menu.

Use the text alignment (left, centre, right), to move the footer to the left, middle, or right hand side of the page.

64

Chapter 3: Building Documents

Formatting Headers and Footers

To format your headers or footers, first select the header or footer, then click on the 'options' menu that appears on the right hand side. From the drop down click 'format header', or 'format footer'.

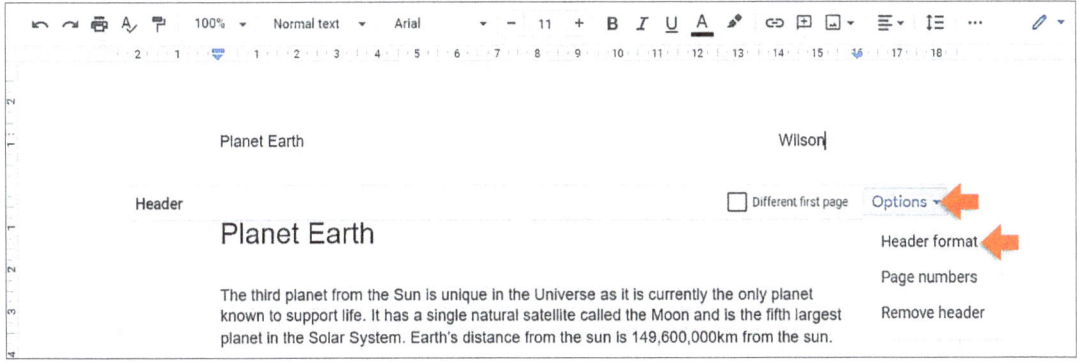

Here you can change the distance of the header from the top of the page, as well as the distance of the footer from the bottom of the page.

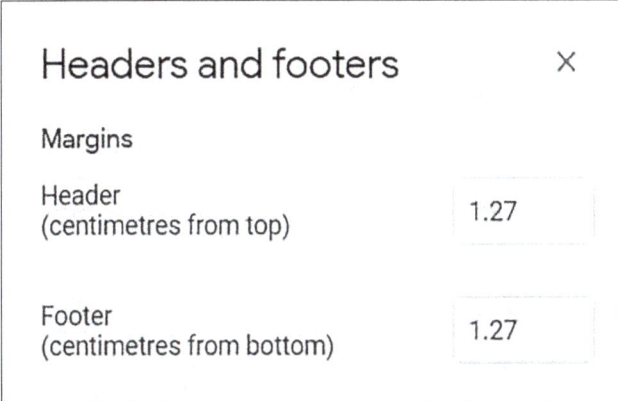

In the layout section of the dialog box, you can allow a different header for the first page of your document - useful if you have a title page that doesn't have a header or footer.

Chapter 3: Building Documents

Or you can create a different header and footer on odd or even pages of your document - eg if you wanted the page number on the left on the odd pages, and on the right on the even pages.

This is useful if you're printing booklets. Here's a booklet printout with a separate header on the left for odd pages (1, 3, 5, 7, 9...)

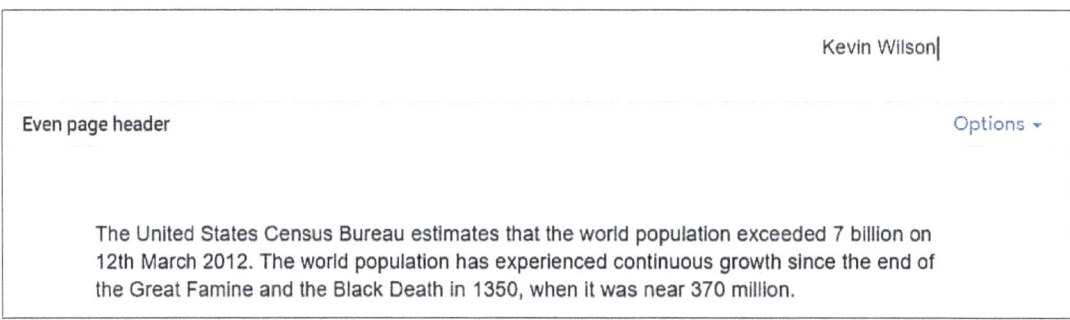

And a different header on the right for even pages (2, 4, 6, 8...)

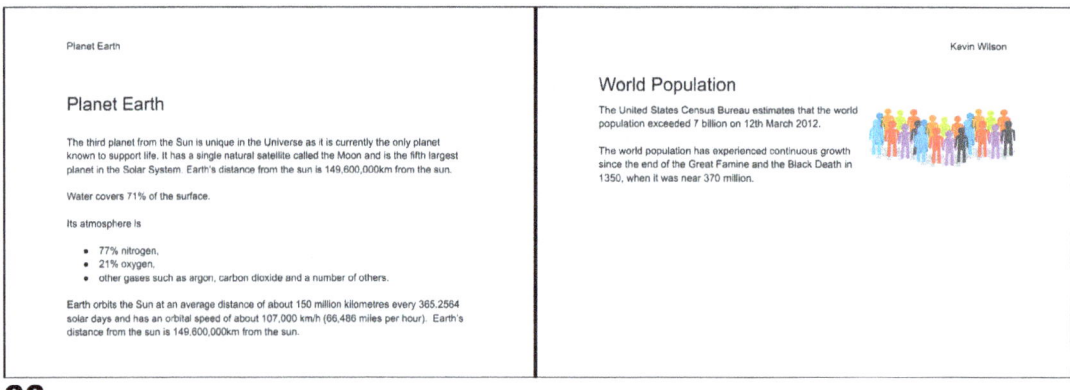

Click 'apply' on the dialog box to apply any changes to your document. Here below on the left, is an odd page (page 1) and on the right, an even page (page 2). Notice where the headers are.

Chapter 3: Building Documents

Footnotes

Click the position in the document where you want to insert a footnote.

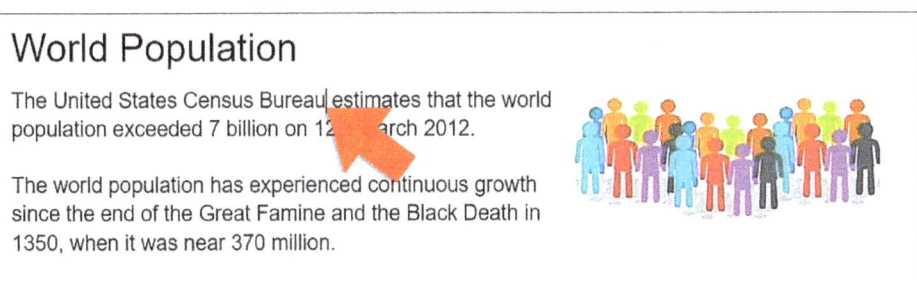

Click the 'insert' menu, then select 'footnote'.

In the section that appears at the bottom of your document, type your footnote.

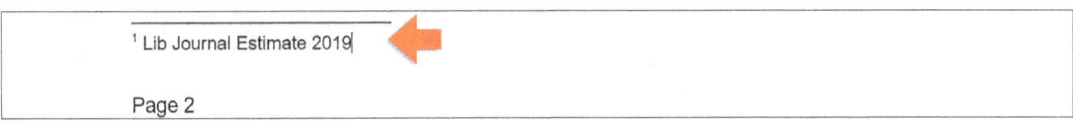

Here, you can see the footnote added to the bottom of the page.

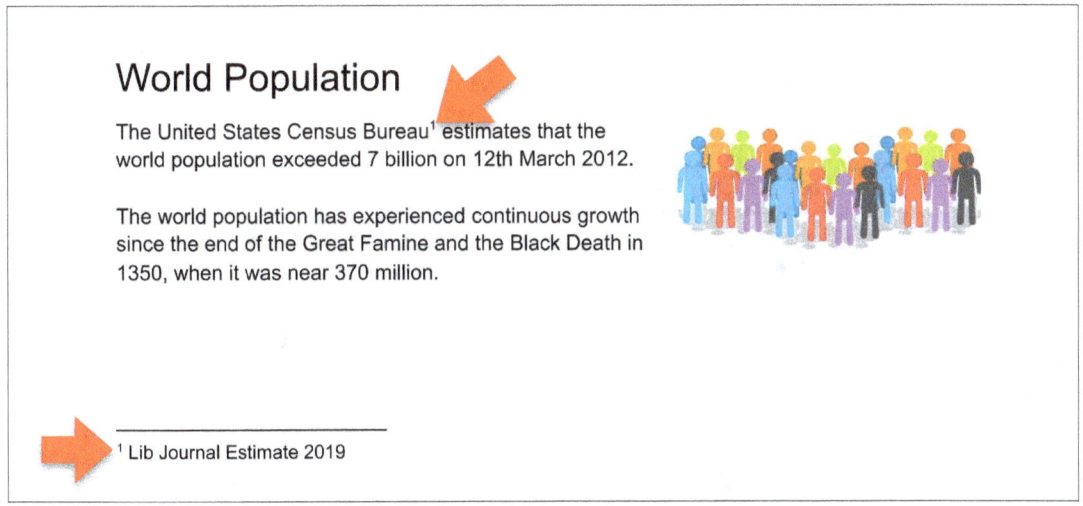

Chapter 3: Building Documents

Creating Columns

Adding columns to your document arranges your text in a similar fashion to a newspaper. To add columns, click on the 'format' menu, then go down to columns. Select a pre-set from the slideout menu

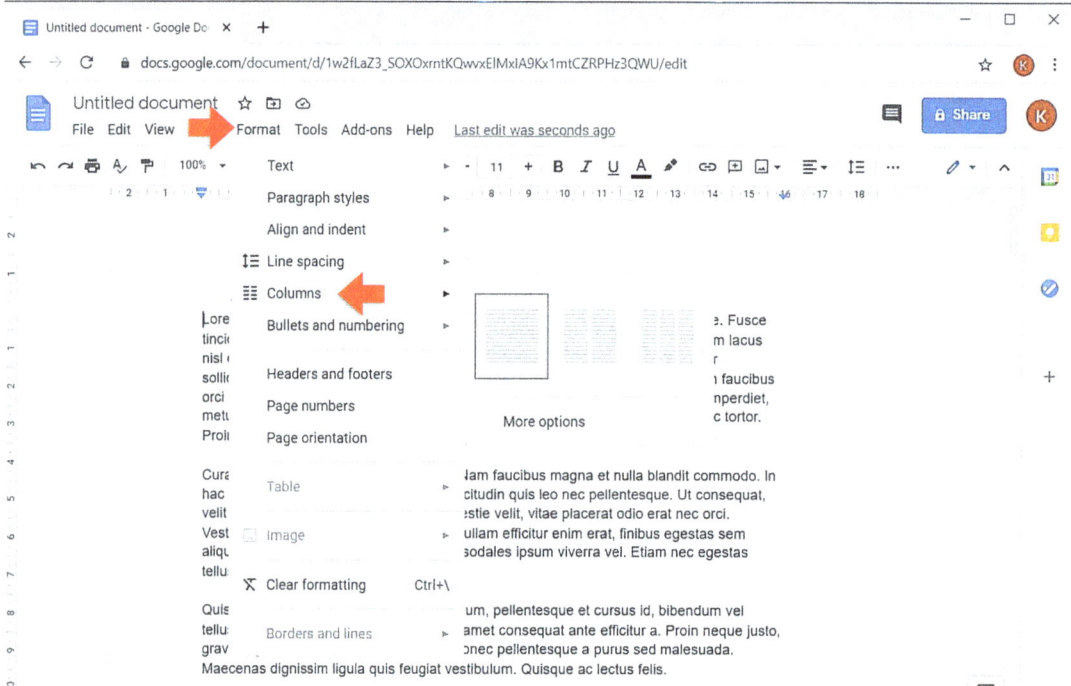

If you want to create custom columns, click 'more options'. In the 'column options' dialog box, enter the number of columns (1, 2 or 3), set the size of the gap between the columns in 'spacing', then select whether you want to add a line between the columns or not.

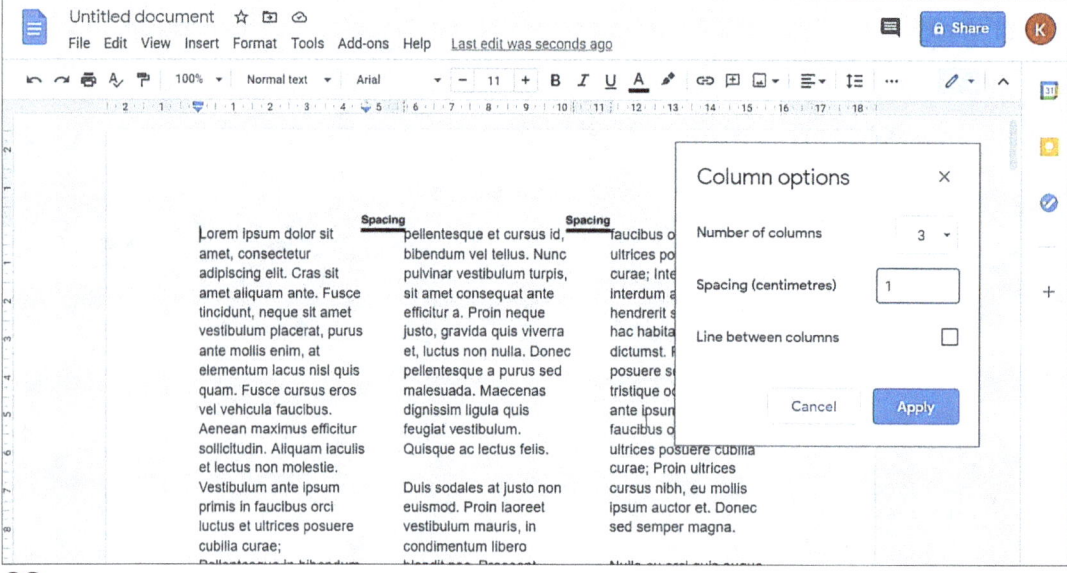

Chapter 3: Building Documents

Contents Pages

The contents tool works by scanning your document for heading styles. For example, Title, Heading 1, Heading 2, Heading 3 and so on. So in the example below we see 'planet earth' is marked as 'heading 1', 'earth's orbit' is marked as 'heading 2'.

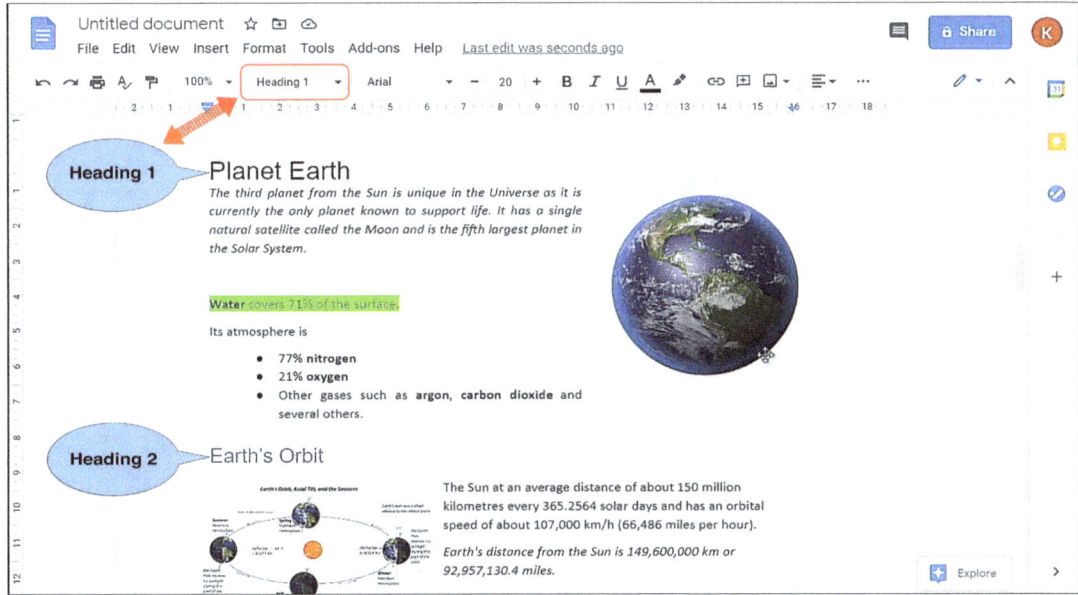

To create a table of contents, create a blank page at the start of the document - to do this, go to the top of the page and insert a page break. Add the title 'contents' to the page. Next, click the 'insert' menu, go down to 'table of contents'. Select either contents with page numbers, or contents without page numbers.

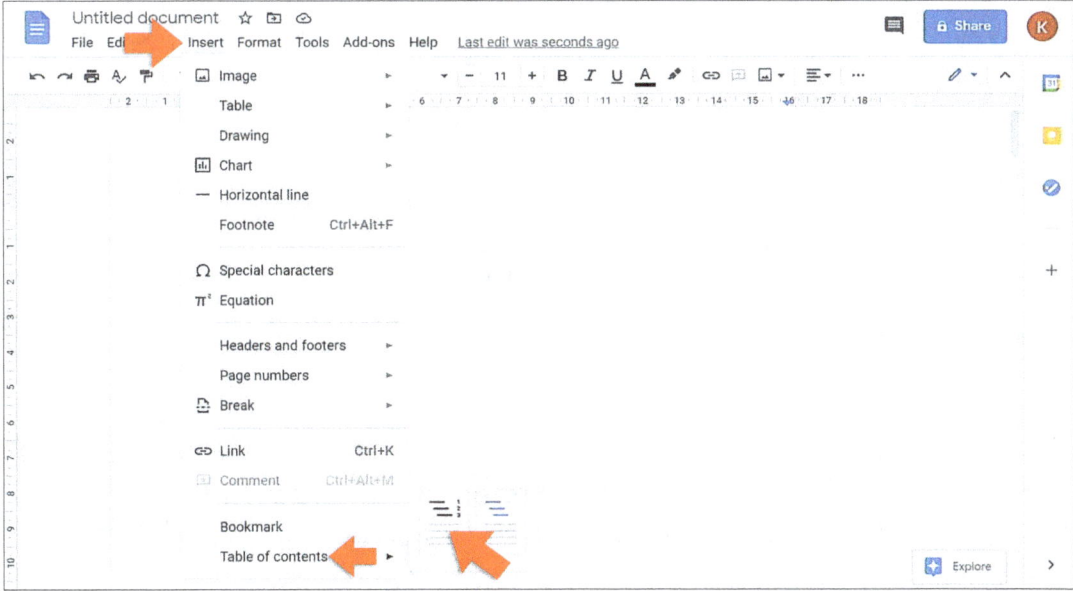

69

Chapter 3: Building Documents

Once the table of contents has been generated, it will appear below your title

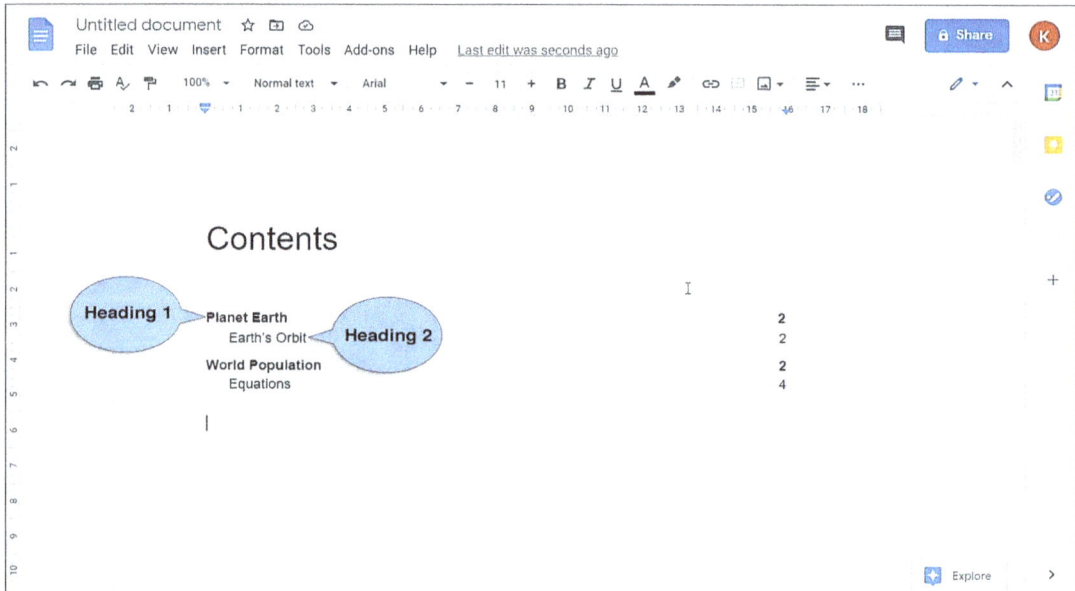

You can click on the links in the table of contents to edit the link or font.

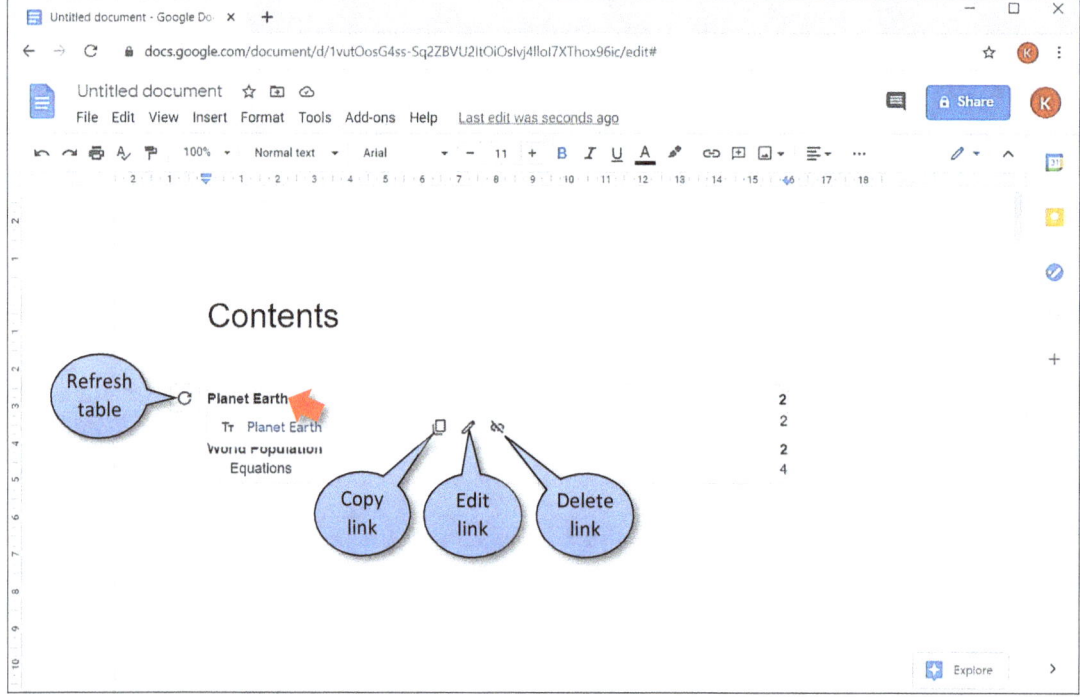

Here, you can refresh the table of contents - if you've added pages or edited your document. You can also copy a link, edit and delete links to pages.

Chapter 3: Building Documents

Emojis

An emoji is a small digital image or icon that represents an idea, emotion, or concept. Emojis are often used in electronic communication, such as text messages, social media posts, and email, to convey feelings or emotions that might be difficult to express in words alone.

To insert an emoji, place your cursor where you want to insert the emoji in your document. Go to the 'insert' menu then select 'emoji'.

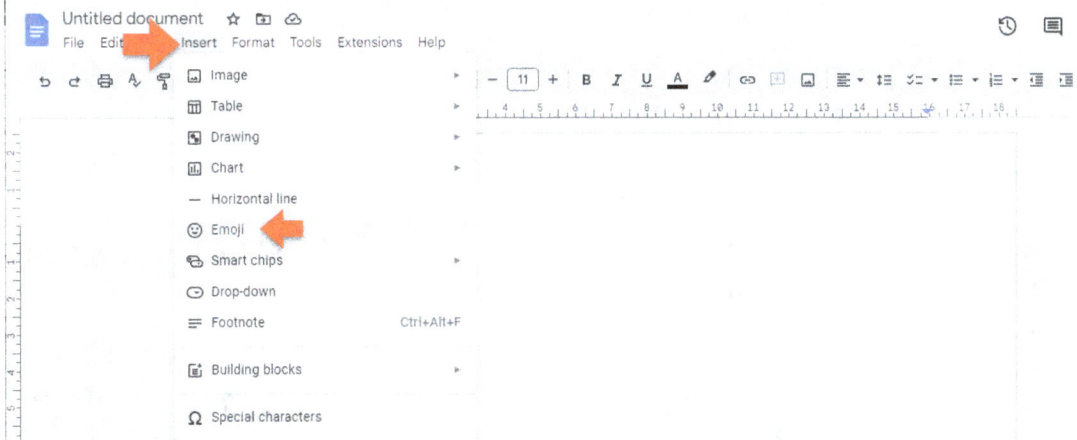

From the popup window, select the 'emoji' category from the drop-down menu. Then click on the emoji you want to insert.

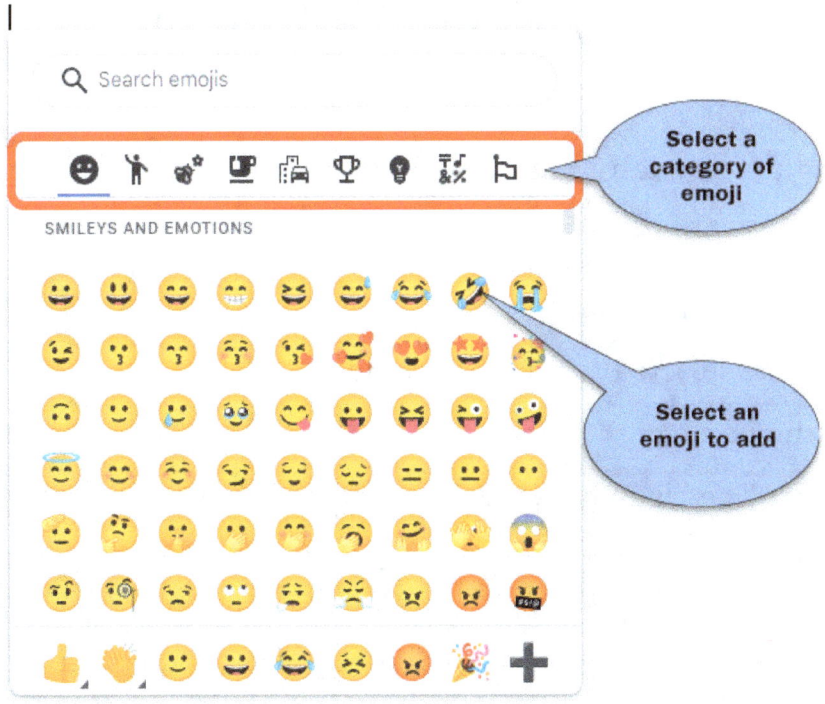

Chapter 3: Building Documents

Document Tabs

This is a feature in Google Docs that allow you to create and manage multiple related documents within a single Google Doc file using a tabbed interface. Instead of opening and managing separate files for closely connected content — such as different chapters of a report, sections of a project, or multiple meeting notes — you can organize them as distinct tabs inside one master document. Each tab acts like a mini-document with its own headings, content, and structure, but all tabs are stored together in a single file, making navigation, editing, sharing, and version control much easier.

To use document tabs, on the left hand side of the screen, you'll see a document tab side bar. If you don't see it, go to the 'view' menu and select 'view tabs and outlines sidebar'.

You'll see any document tabs in your document listed here, select any of these to go to the tab in the document. Click the '+' icon on the top right of the sidebar to create a new tab.

To the right of the tab name, you'll see a three-dot menu. From here you can:

Add subtab. This create a subtab beneath the current main tab, allowing hierarchical organization.

Duplicate the selected tab and its content.

Rename the name of the tab.

Choose emoji to visually represent or label the tab.

Copy link to generate a direct link to the specific tab within the document.

Hide outline to hide the document's structural outline, typically showing headings.

Chapter 3: Building Documents

Smart Canvas

Smart Canvas is a collection of features designed to make documents more flexible, structured, and collaborative. You can insert Smart Chips, Smart Templates, Smart Checklists, and Smart Tables directly into documents. For example you can insert interactive elements such as people, dates, files, and events, organize project information using templates, assign tasks with checklists, and build lightweight tables for managing tasks or project timelines. Some advanced Smart Canvas features may require a Google Workspace account, but many core elements are available to all users.

Smart Chips

A Smart Chip is an interactive tag that displays additional information about a specific person, document, or topic. They make it really easy to reference other people, files, dates, or calendar events. This allows you to add context to your document by mentioning other people, files, and topics from within your document.

To use Smart Chips in Google Docs, you can simply type "@" followed by the name of a person or a file, and Google Docs will suggest relevant matches from your Google Drive or Google Contacts. You can then select the desired match, and Google Docs will automatically create a link to that person or file, which can be clicked on to access more information.

For example, in the following document, Claire and I are collaborating on a document. Lets say I want to reference another document that contains a chart for this section.

Total annual births were highest in the late 1980s at about 139 million and is now expected to remain essentially constant at their 2011 level of 135 million, while deaths number 56 million per year, and are expected to increase to 80 million per year by 2040.

Country	Population	Percentage of World
China	1,372,000,000	18.5
India	1,276,900,000	17.5
USA	321,793,000	4.35
Indonesia	252,164,800	3.35
Brazil	204,878,000	2.77

Chapter 3: Building Documents

To reference the document, first type in an at sign @. You'll see a popup menu appear.

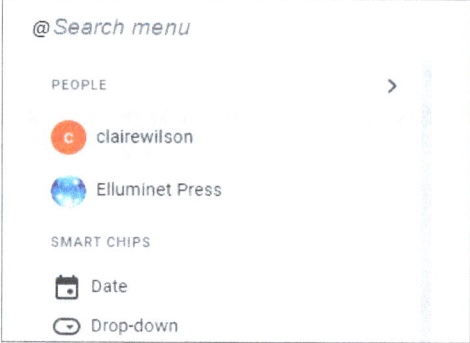

You can also go up to the 'insert' menu and select 'smart chips'.

Then type in the name of the document. Keep in mind that the document will need to be saved to your Google Drive. Select the document.

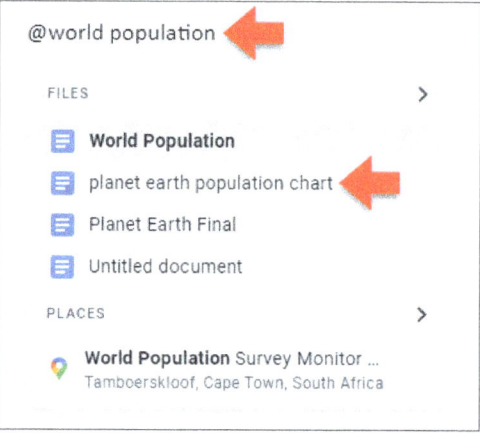

Now when your collaborators hover their mouse pointer over the smart chip, they'll see a link to the file, to which they can request access.

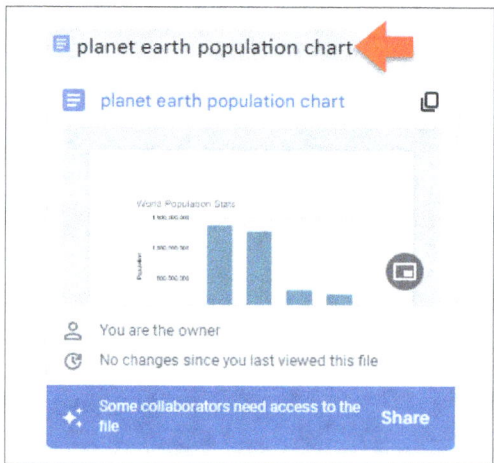

Chapter 3: Building Documents

You can also add people, dates, and places.

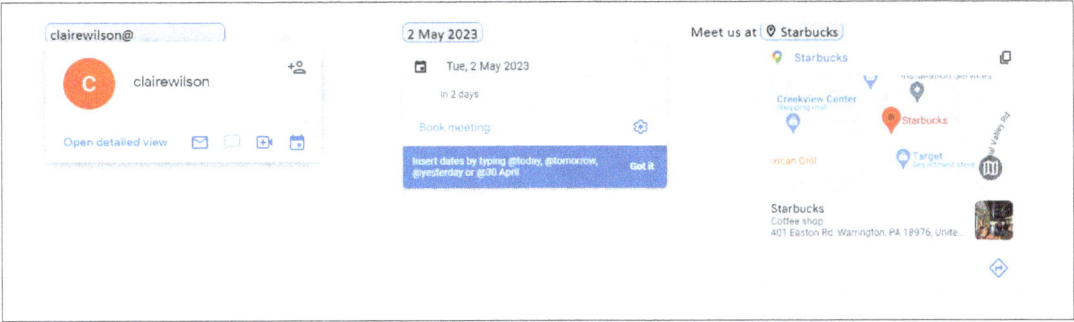

Smart chips are a useful tool to save time and improve collaboration, allowing users to easily reference and share relevant information from other apps without having to switch between different tabs or applications.

Smart Templates

These are pre-built, interactive document components called building blocks which are designed to streamline common workflows such as meeting documentation and project planning. Rather than starting from a blank page, you can insert these templates with a single click to instantly structure a documents with headings, tables, and smart chips.

To use smart templates, place your cursor where you want to insert the template, then go up to the 'insert' menu, then select 'building blocks'.

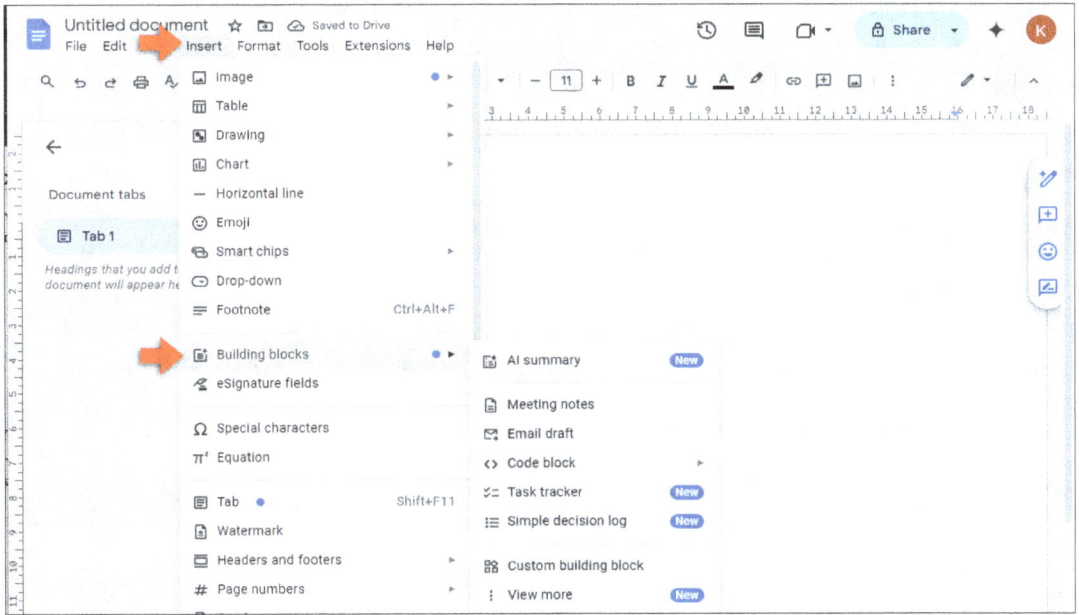

Chapter 3: Building Documents

Choose one of the available Smart Templates from the menu, or select 'view more' to open the sidebar. For example, here I want to add a summary to the end of my document. I can use the 'summary' building block to do this.

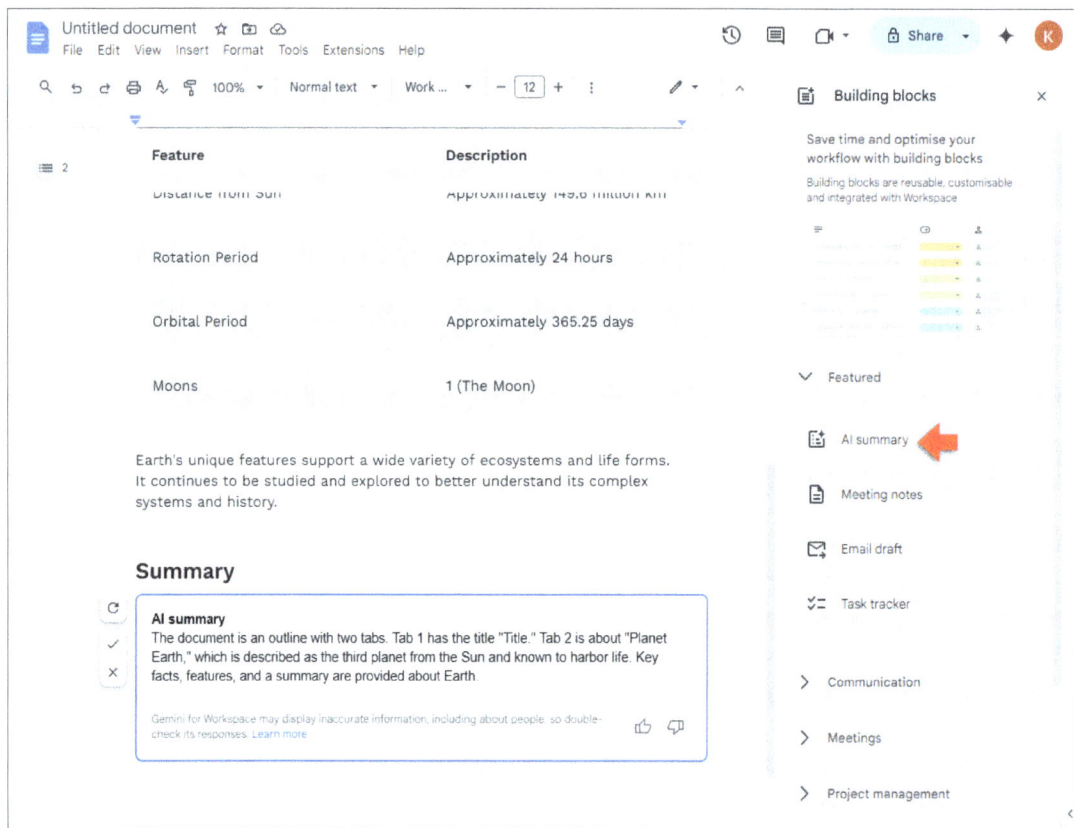

Note that some of these building blocks are only available in Google Workspace accounts, particularly those with business or education plans.

Smart Checklists

Smart Checklists allow you to insert interactive checkboxes into your documents. These are ideal for to-do lists, task management, or tracking items in shared documents. Each checkbox can be ticked or unticked, and changes are synced across collaborators in real time.

Type [] followed by a space to insert a checklist item. Once you press space, this will convert into a checklist item.

Chapter 3: Building Documents

Type in the item. Once you press enter on your keyboard, another checklist item will appear. To close the checklist press enter on your keyboard twice.

- ☑ ~~Write first draft of blog post~~
- ☑ ~~Review draft with editor~~
- ☐ Add final graphics and images

You can click the checkbox to mark the item as complete.

Smart Tables

Smart Tables are interactive, pre-formatted tables in Google Docs that include dynamic elements—such as dropdown menus, people, and date pickers—that enable real-time collaboration and status tracking directly within the document.

Click where you want to insert the table. There are various pre-formatted smart tables you can use such as project trackers, decision logs, contact lists and so on.

Template Name	Description	What to Type
Launch Content Tracker	Track articles, blog posts, or media for launches, including status and due dates.	@Launch content tracker
Project Assets	Keep an inventory of project-related files or assets with links and owners.	@Project assets
Review Tracker	Coordinate and monitor document or process reviews with assigned reviewers.	@Review tracker
Product Roadmap	Visualize upcoming product features, phases, and responsible leads.	@Product roadmap
Task Tracker	Assign tasks, set due dates, and track completion status.	@Task tracker
Team Directory	List team members, roles, contact info, and responsibilities.	@Team directory
Project Assignments	Assign project roles and responsibilities to team members.	@Project assignments
Simple Decision Log	Record quick decisions with context, outcomes, and dates.	@Simple decision log
Detailed Decision Log	Document decisions in greater detail, including pros, cons, and rationale.	@Detailed decision log

Chapter 3: Building Documents

So, if I wanted to create a table of members of my team, I'd type in

`@Team Directory`

You'll see a blank smart table appear. Here, you can edit dynamic fields such as select a person from your contact list, insert their location from Google Maps and so on.

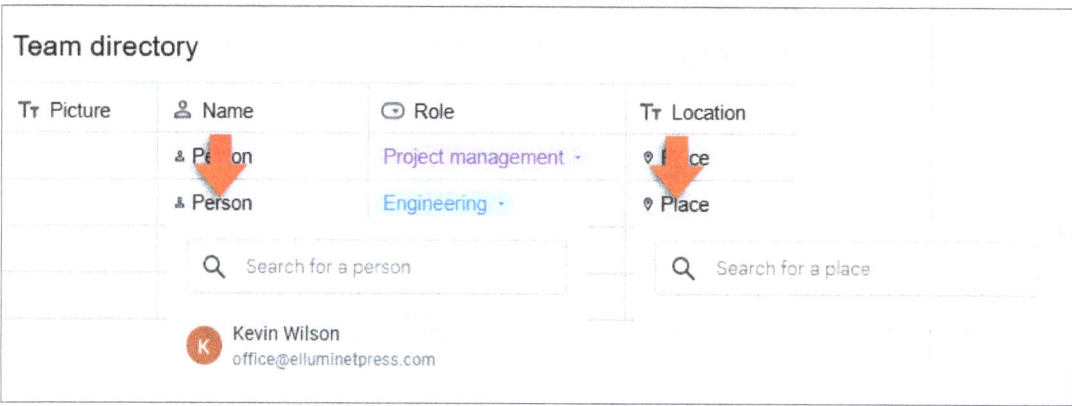

Automatic Document Generation

The Document Generation feature in Google Docs automatically creates entire document drafts based on a user prompt, and is available only to users with active subscriptions to Gemini for Google Workspace, or the Google One AI Premium Plan. Workspace users must have an eligible plan, such as Gemini Business or Gemini Enterprise, added to their standard Workspace subscription to access this functionality. Personal Google account holders can access the feature if they subscribe to the Google One AI Premium Plan, which includes Gemini Advanced capabilities. Free Google accounts without a paid AI plan, as well as standard Google Workspace accounts without Gemini upgrades, do not have access to the Generate Document feature.

You'll find this feature on the 'file' menu in Google Docs. Go to 'new', then select 'help me create'.

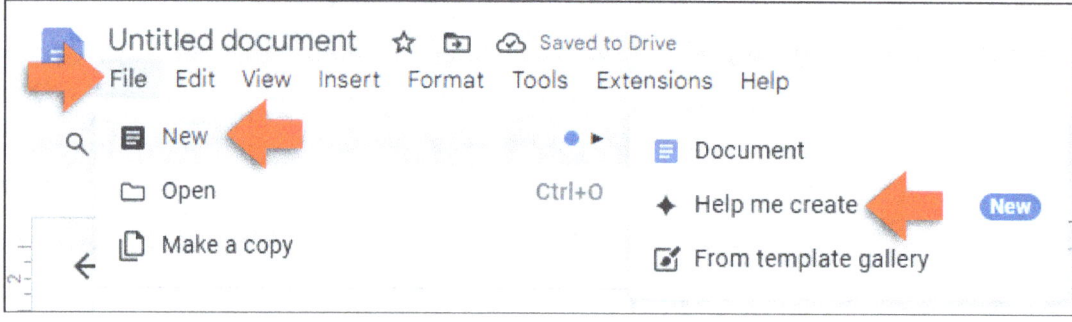

Chapter 3: Building Documents

Type a description of the document you want to create in the field at the bottom of the window.

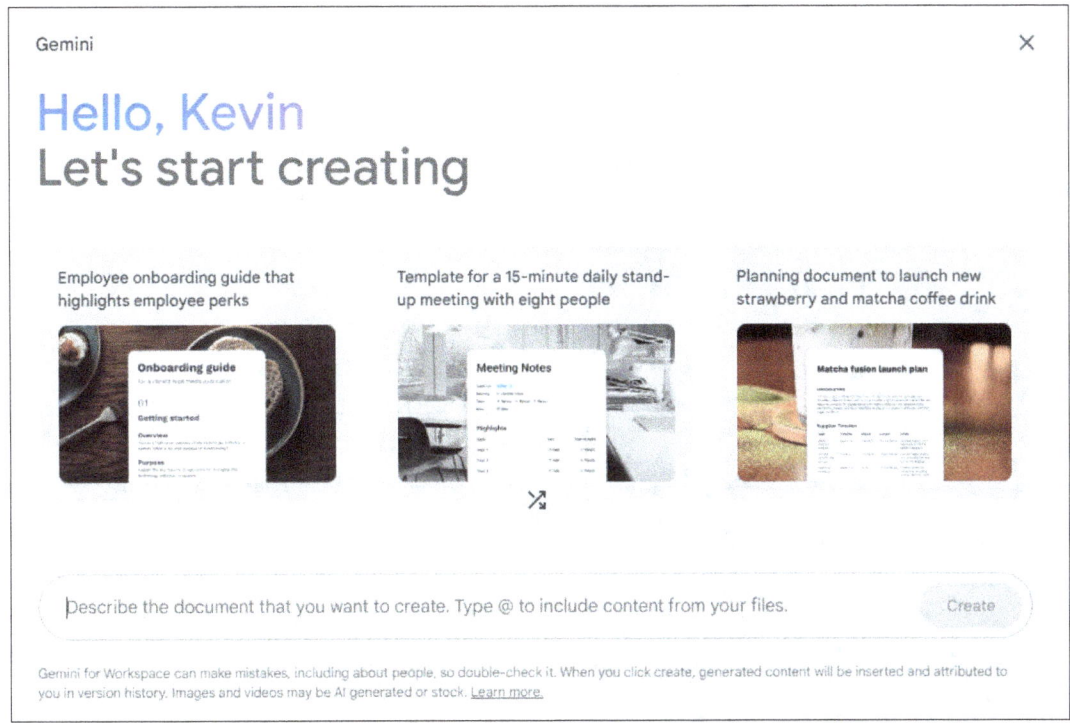

You'll see your document appear in the main window, were you can edit it.

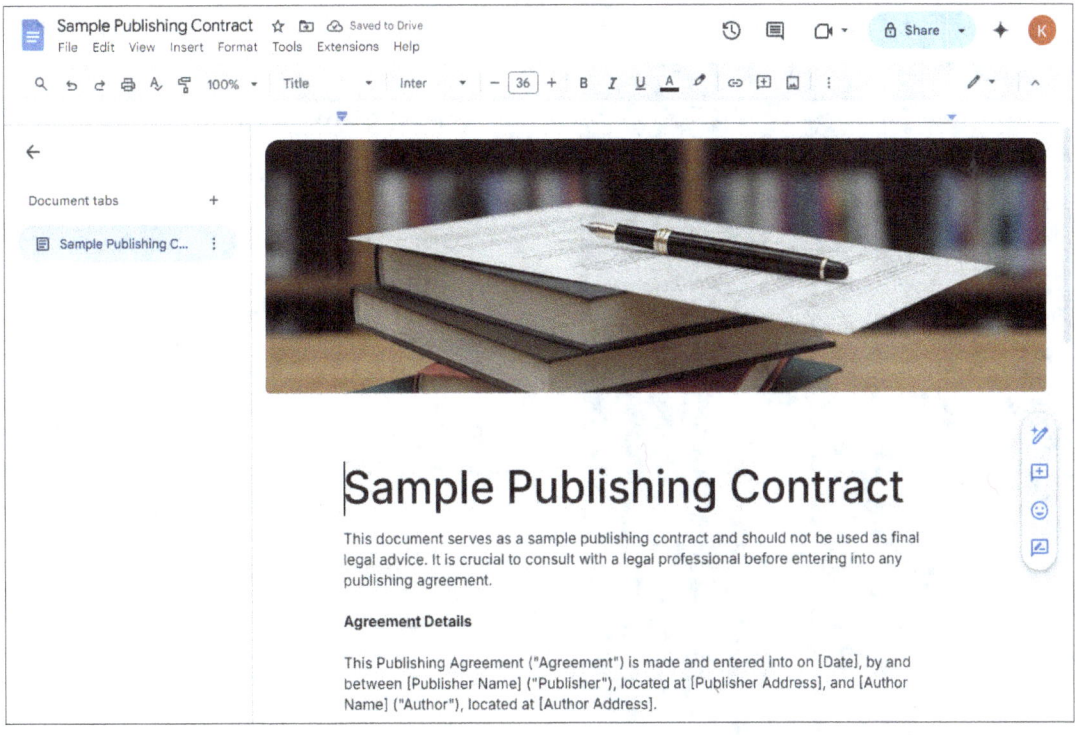

Adding Images & Graphics

With Google Docs, you can add pictures from Google Drive, your device, directly from your camera if you're using a tablet, phone or laptop, the web, and by URL.

In this section we'll take a look at adding graphics to your documents - how to upload and insert from various sources.

We'll also take a look at formatting, resizing and cropping images, as well as adjusting the text wrap.

We'll go through adding drawings, diagrams and WordArt.

- Adding & Resizing Images
- Rotate an Image
- Cropping Images
- Wrap Text around Images
- Drawings

Have a look at the video resources section. Open your web browser and navigate to the following website.

elluminetpress.com/images-googledocs

Chapter 4: Adding Images & Graphics

Adding Images

Adding images to your document is easy. There are six ways you can add photos:

- Your Google Drive - any photos you've uploaded or saved to Google Drive
- Your Google Photos - any photos you've taken on your phone or laptop that have been saved into the Google Photos App
- By URL - a link to an image on a website
- Search the web - using Google Image Search
- Upload from your computer - upload a photo saved on your device.
- Camera - taken directly from the camera on your phone or tablet.

From Google Drive

To add an image from your Google Drive, click the 'insert' menu

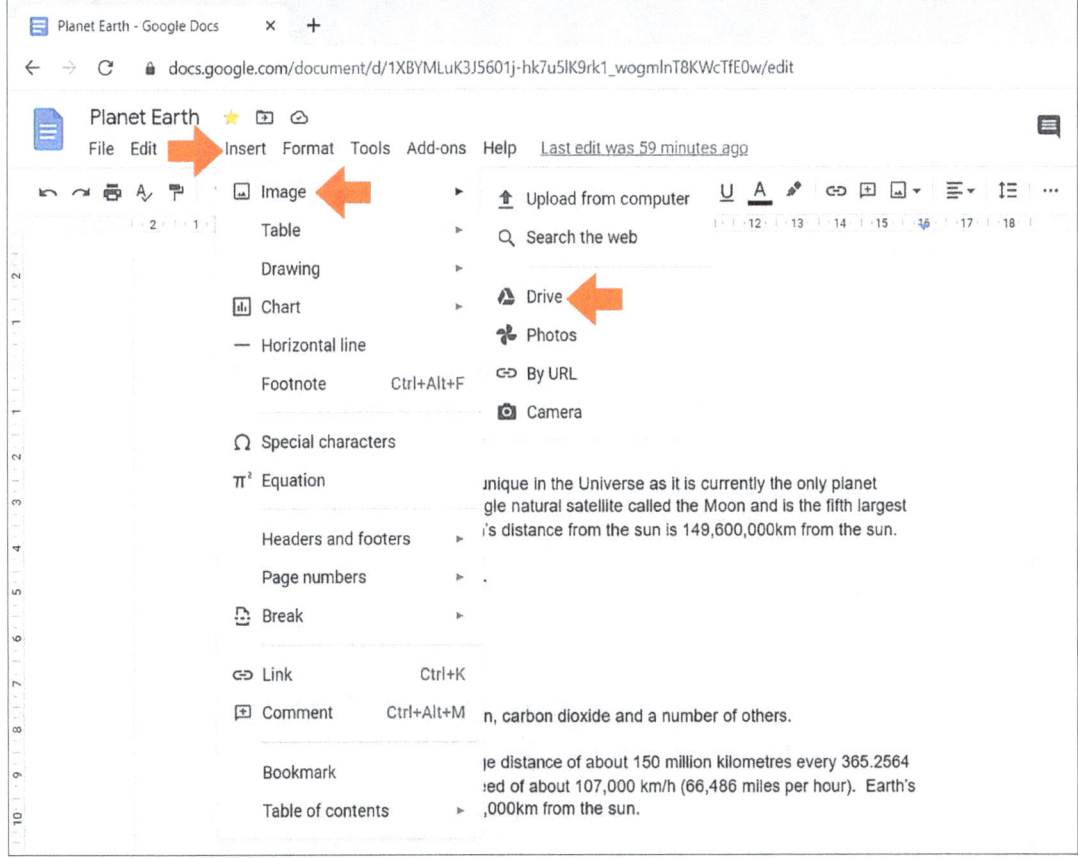

Go down to 'image', then select 'drive' from the slideout menu.

81

Chapter 4: Adding Images & Graphics

From the Google Drive panel on the right hand side, click 'my drive', then navigate to and select the image you want. Click 'insert'.

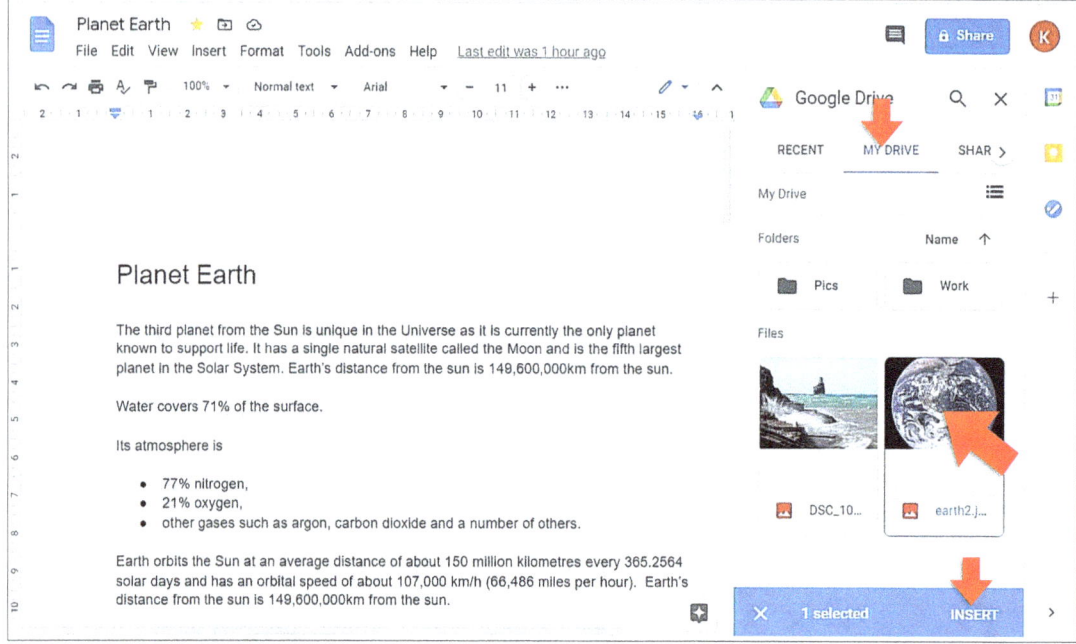

Google Photos

To add an image from your Google Photos, click the 'insert' menu.

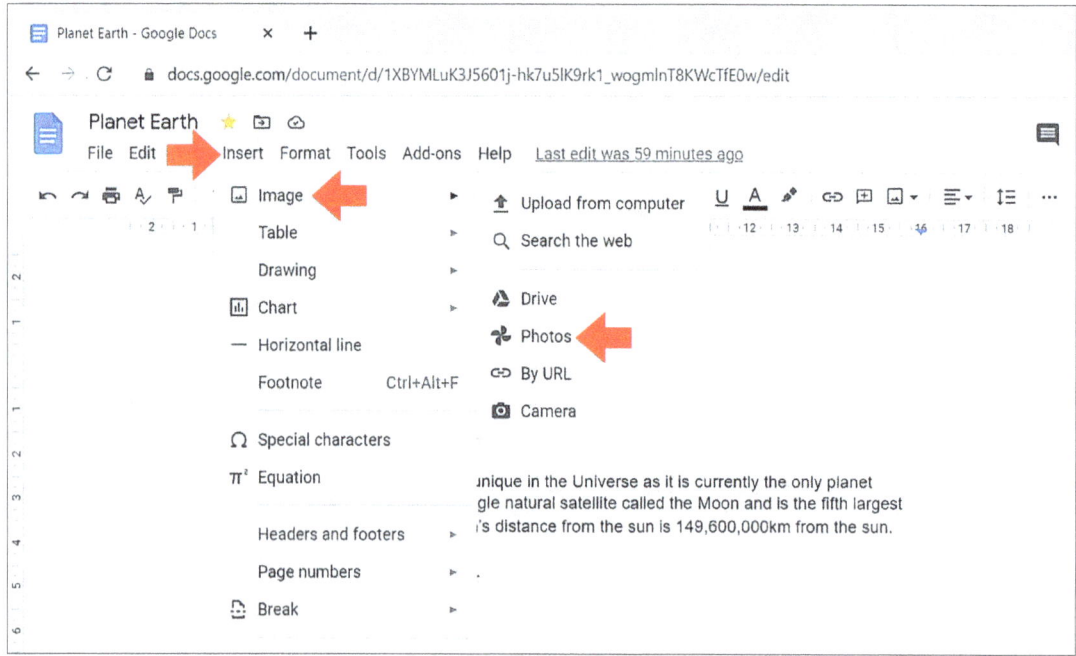

Go down to 'image', then select 'photos' from the slideout menu.

Chapter 4: Adding Images & Graphics

Browse through your photos or albums in the panel on the right hand side, click on the photo you want to add, then click 'insert'.

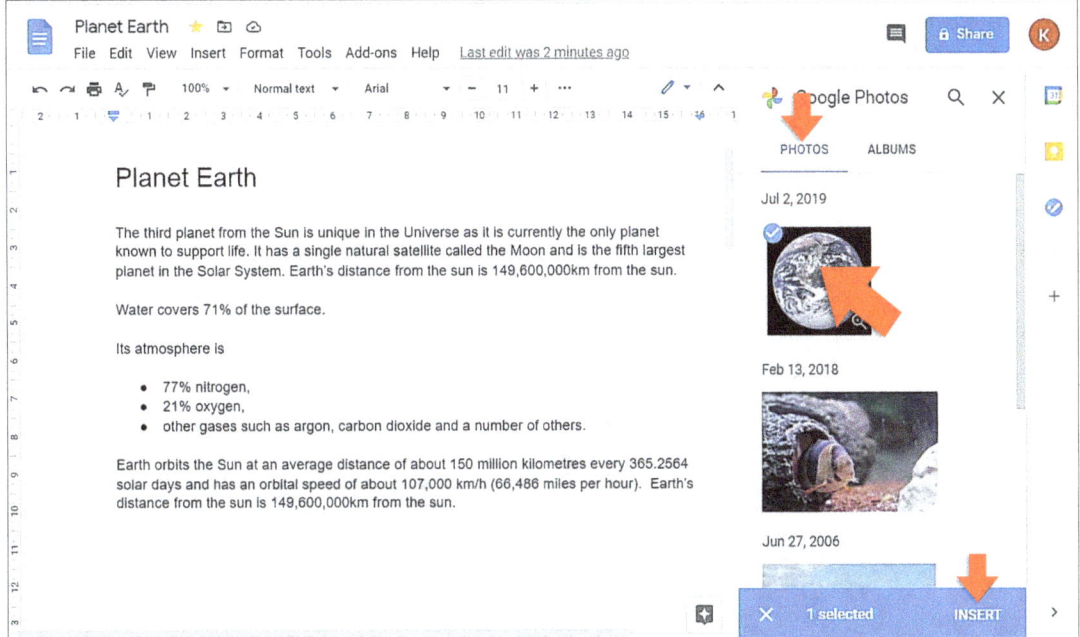

Upload from PC

If you have a photo on your Mac, PC or laptop, you can upload and insert it into your document. To do this, click the 'insert' menu, go down to 'images', select 'upload from computer' in the slideout menu.

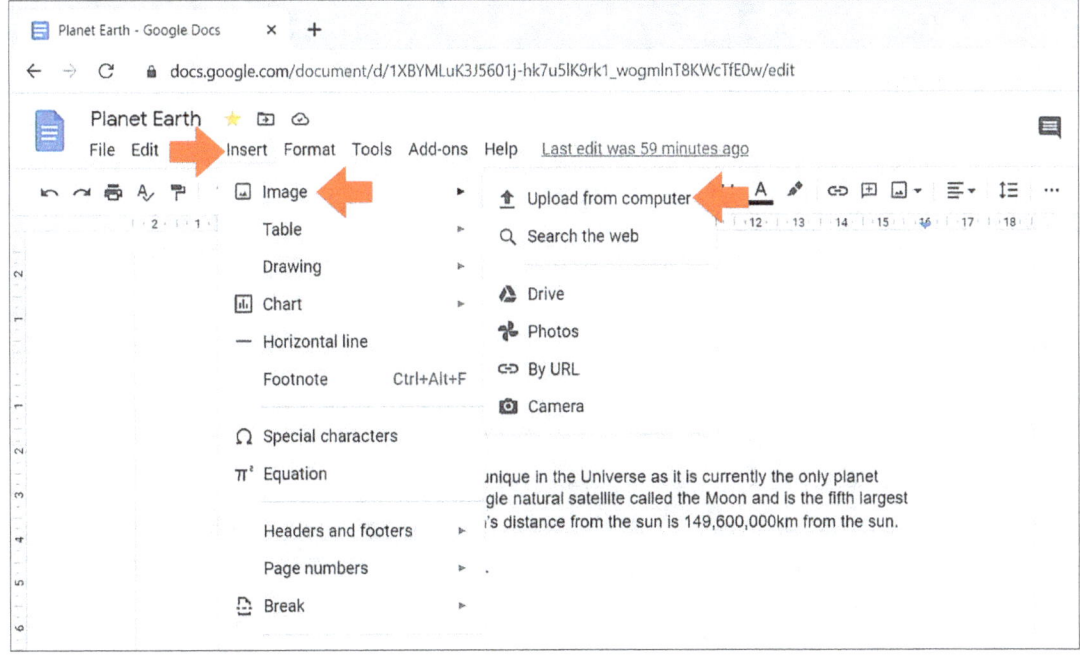

Chapter 4: Adding Images & Graphics

In the dialog box that appears, navigate to and select the photo you want to upload and insert. Then click 'open'.

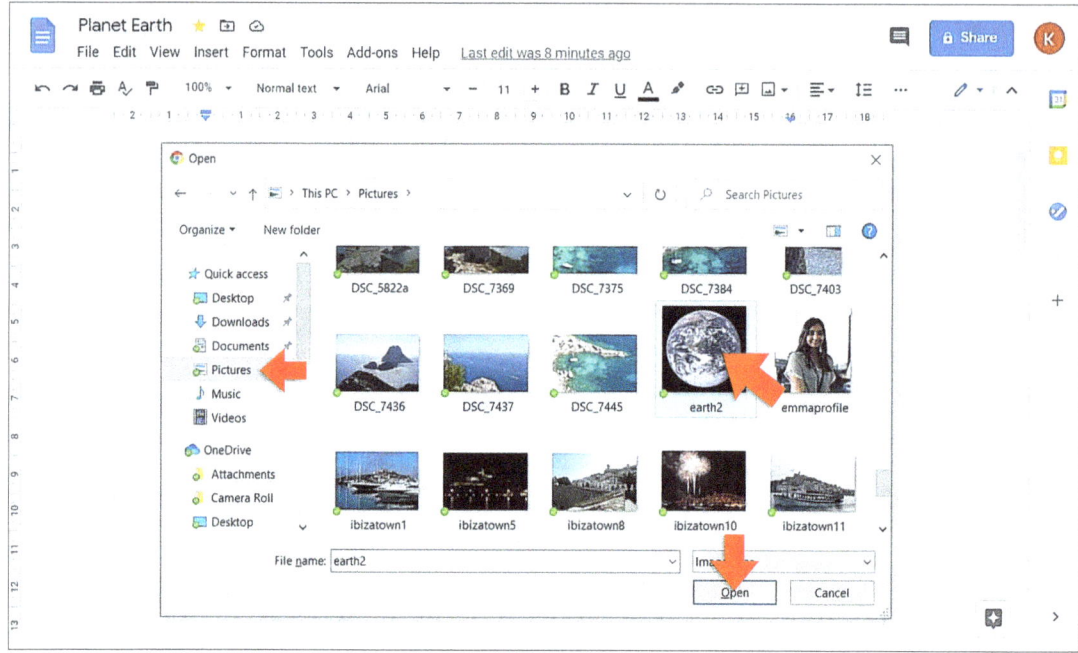

Web Search

You can search for images using Google Image Search. To do this, click the 'insert' menu, go down to 'images', select 'search the web' in the slideout menu.

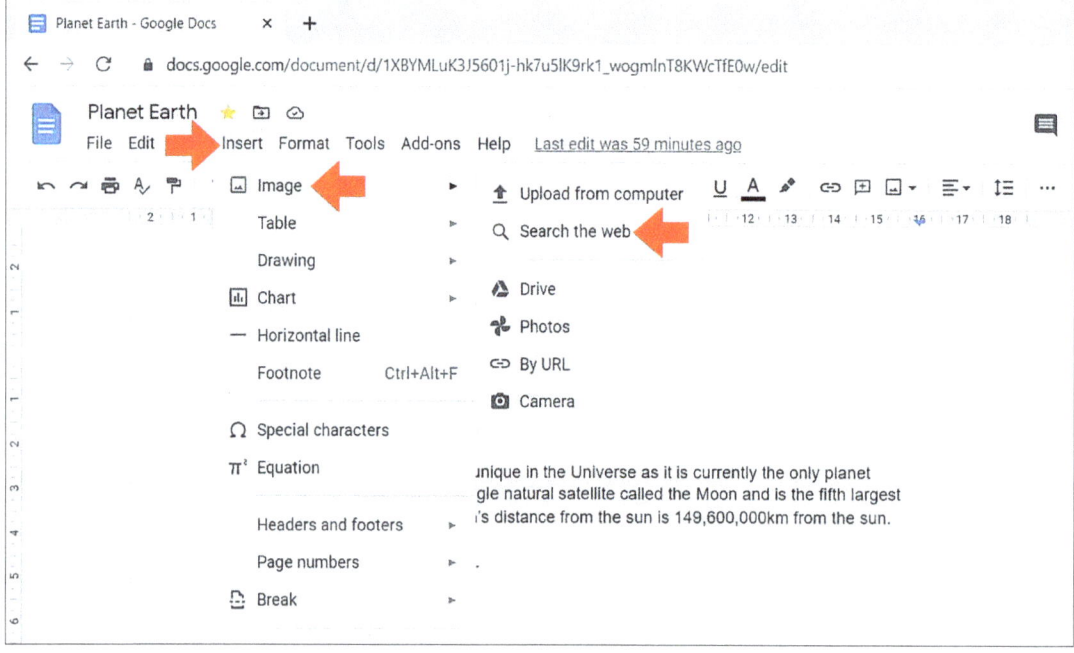

Chapter 4: Adding Images & Graphics

In the panel on the right hand side, enter your Google search in the search field at the top

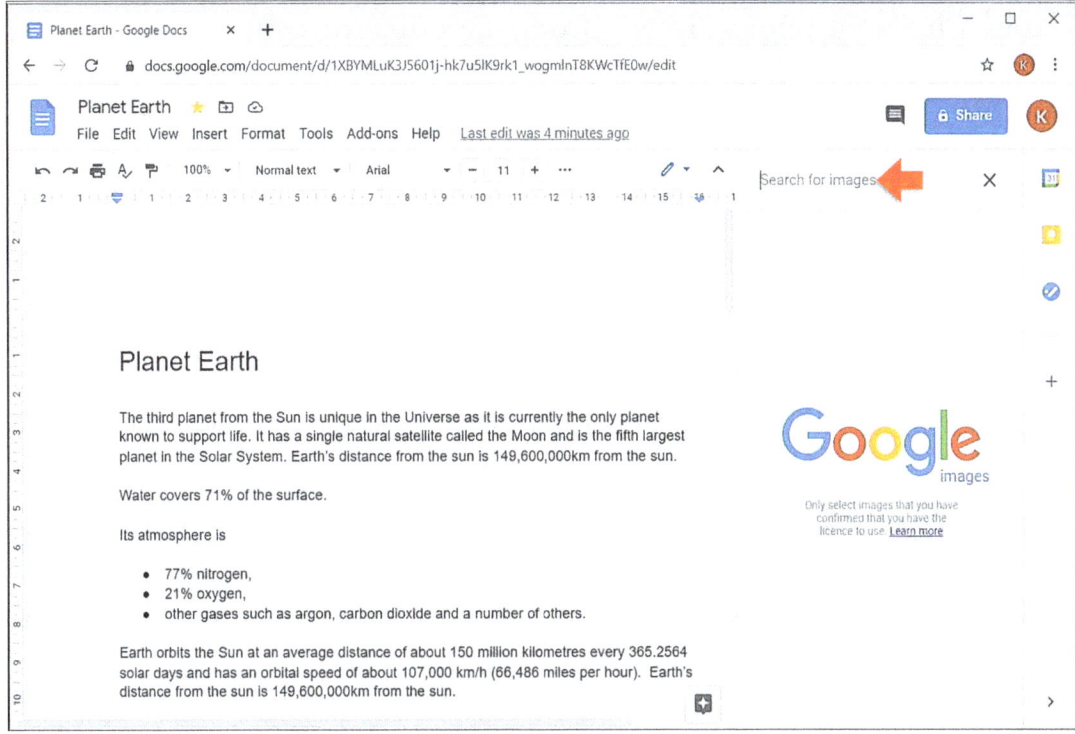

Select an image from the search results, then click 'insert'.

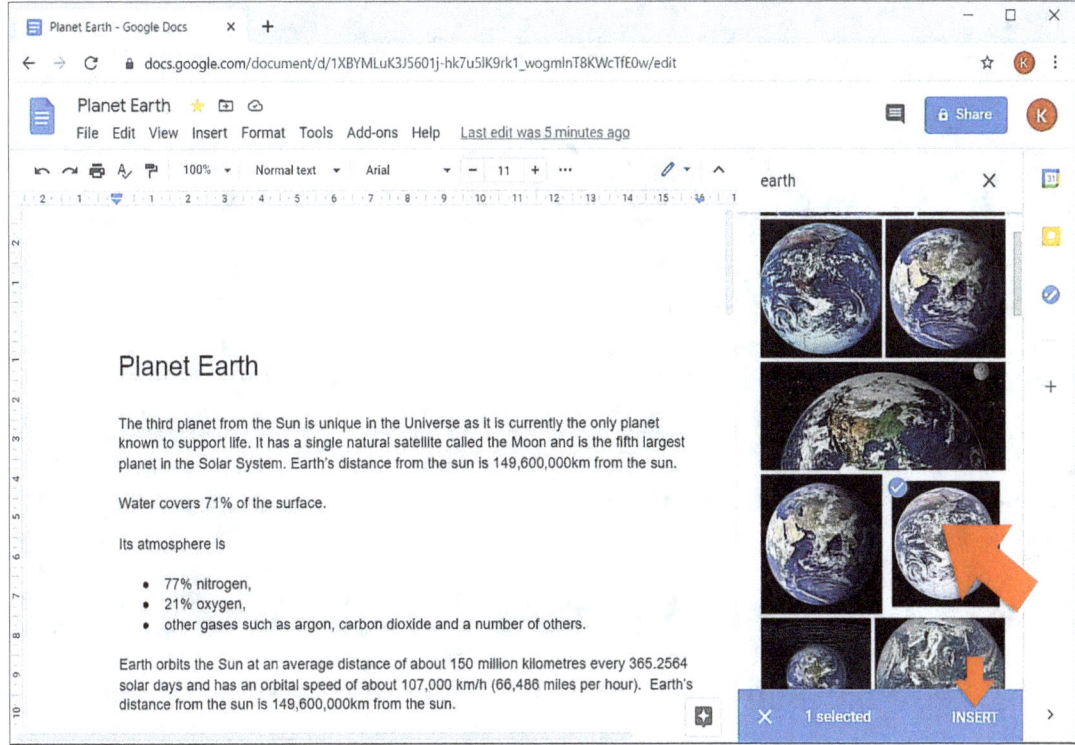

85

Chapter 4: Adding Images & Graphics

Camera on Laptop

If you are using Google Docs on a laptop/chromebook with a camera, you can insert a photo directly from the onboard camera. To do this, click the 'insert' menu, go down to 'images', select 'camera' from the slideout menu. Click 'allow' to allow access to your camera if prompted by your browser.

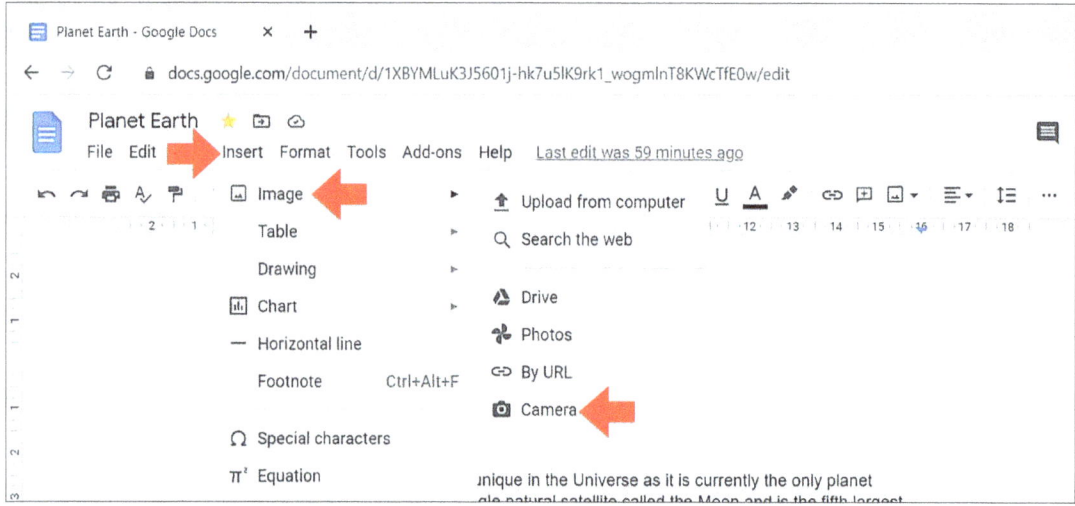

In the window that appears, line up the subject in the frame, then click the yellow capture icon at the bottom.

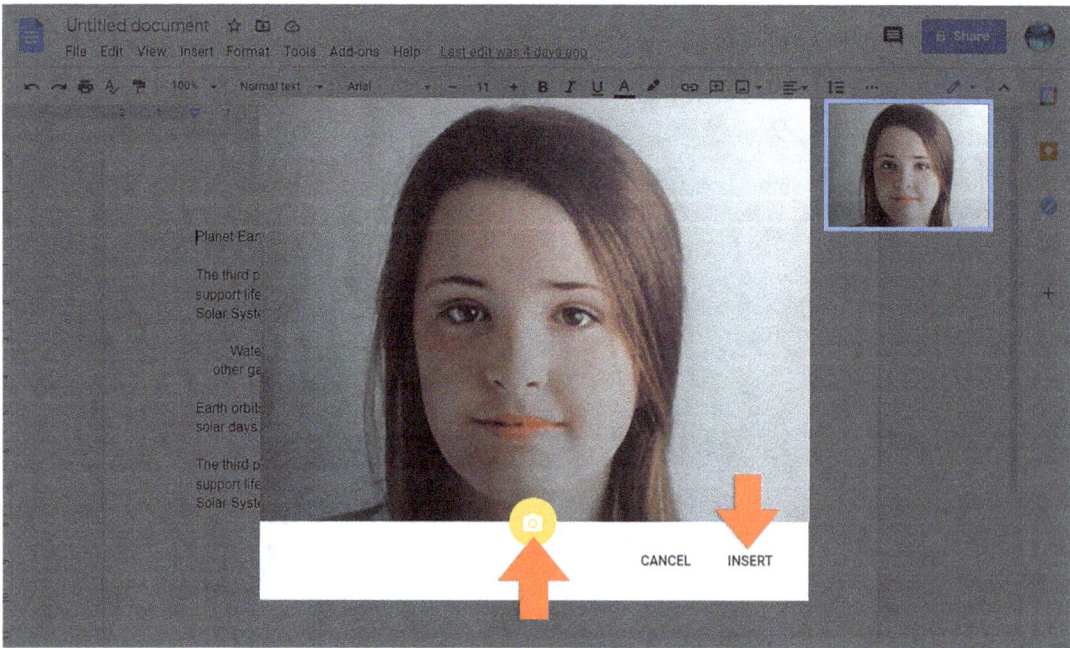

Select a photo from the right if you've taken more than one, then click 'insert'.

Chapter 4: Adding Images & Graphics

Camera on Tablet/Phone

If you are using Google Docs on a tablet (eg iPad) or phone, select the + icon on the top right. Go down to 'image', then tap 'from camera'. Tap 'allow' on any security prompts that may appear.

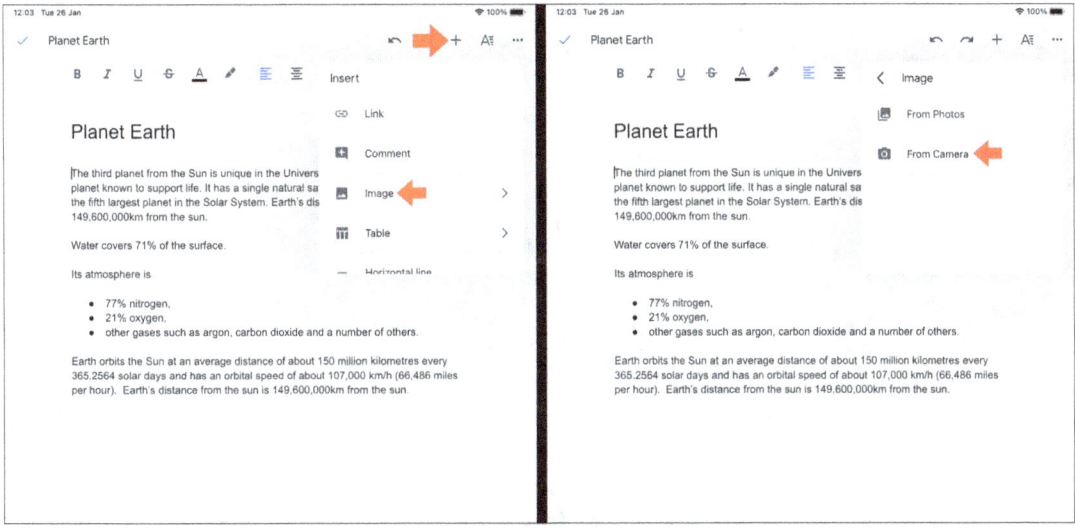

Take the photo with your camera.

Chapter 4: Adding Images & Graphics

Tap 'use photo' on the bottom right to insert the photo into your document.

The photo will appear in your document.

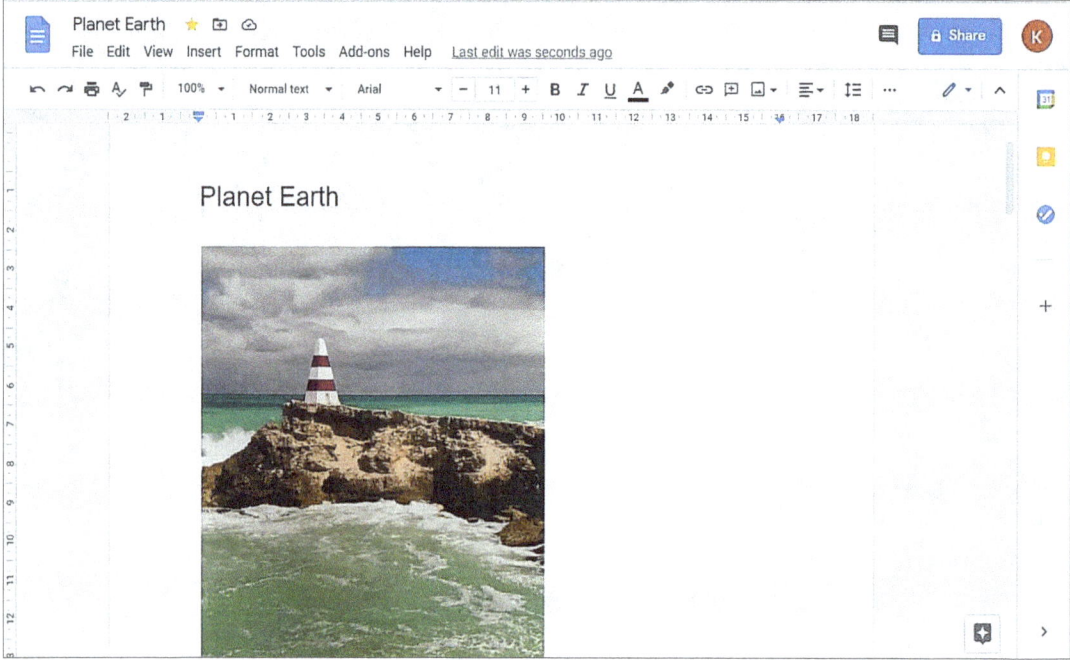

Chapter 4: Adding Images & Graphics

Resize Images

If you've inserted an image, you may need to resize it. See adding images on page 81. To resize, click on the image. Around the edges of the image, you'll see some resize handles.

To resize the image, click and drag these handles. The best way is to click and drag one of the corner handles to resize the image.

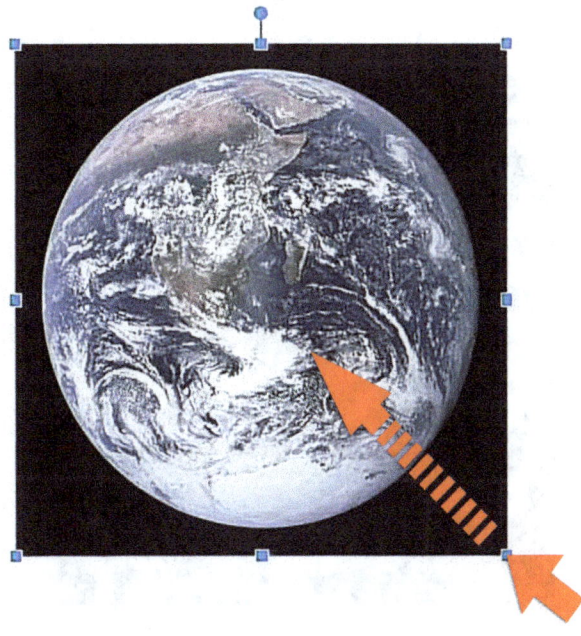

This will help prevent the image from becoming squashed or stretched

Chapter 4: Adding Images & Graphics

Rotate an Image

To do this, click on the image. At the top of the image, you'll see a rotate handle.

To rotate the image, click and drag the rotate handle to the right to rotate clockwise, drag left to rotate counter-clockwise..

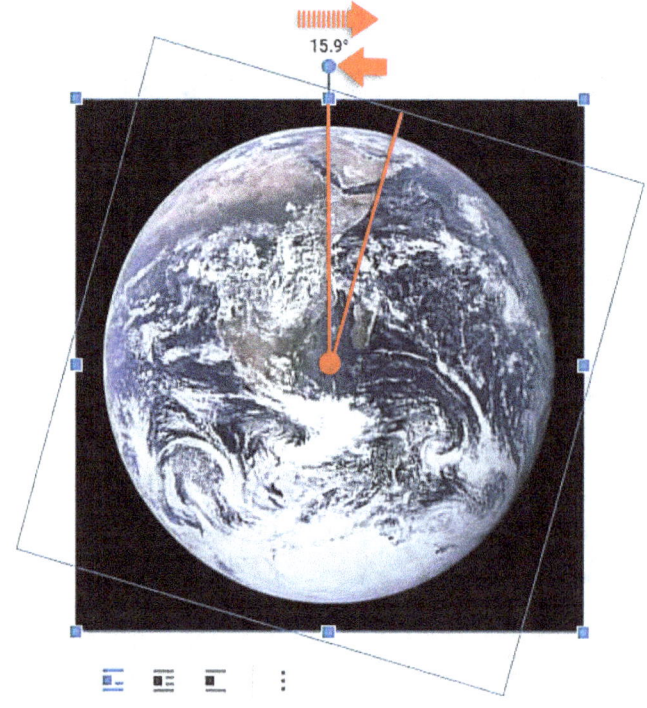

Chapter 4: Adding Images & Graphics

Cropping Images

If you insert an image into your document, and it has unwanted parts, or you want to concentrate on one particular piece of the picture, you can crop the image. First, insert an image into your document. See adding images on page 81.

To crop, click on the image, then select the 'crop' icon from the toolbar.

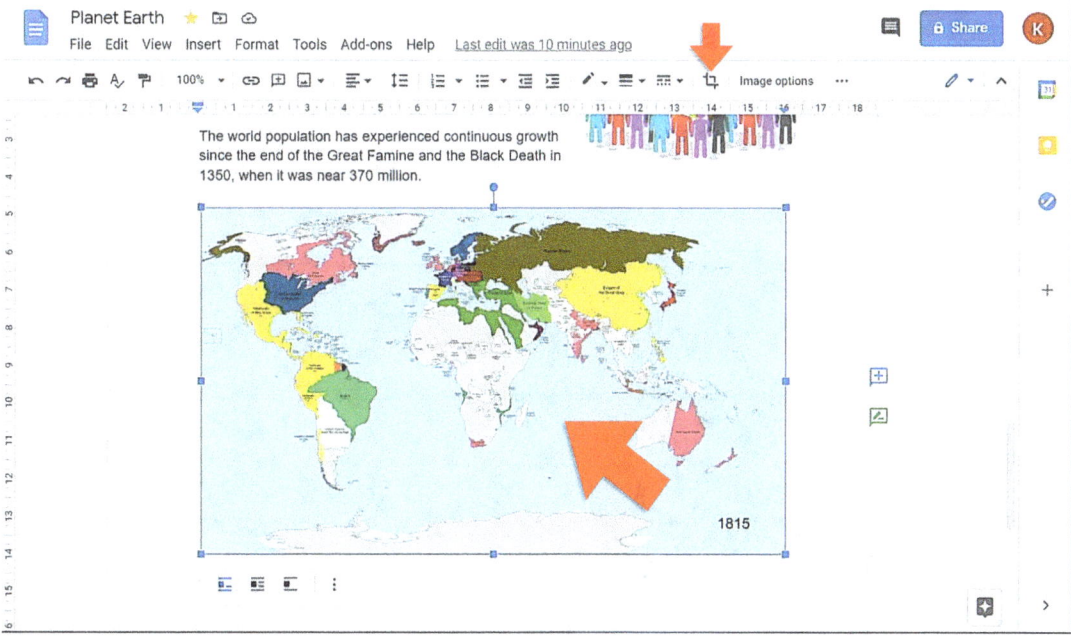

If you look closely at your image, you will see crop handles around the edges, circled below.

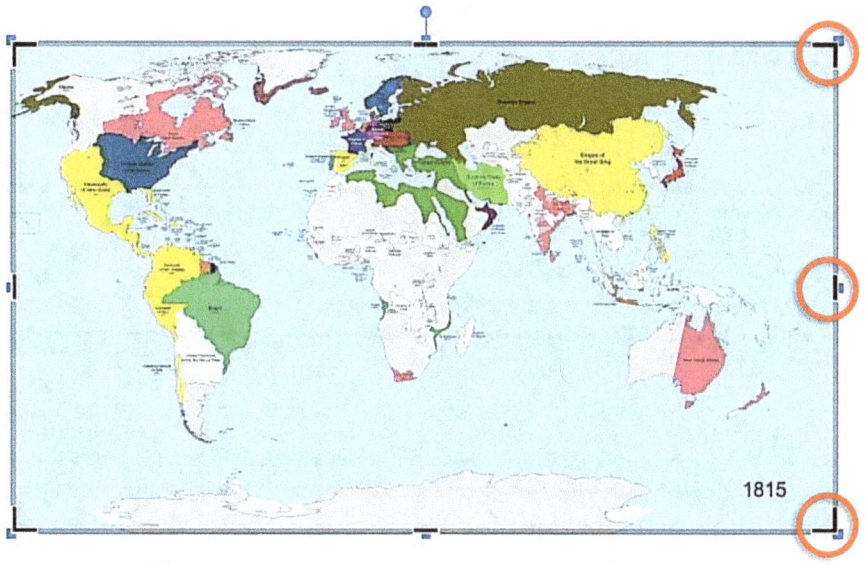

91

Chapter 4: Adding Images & Graphics

Click and drag these handles around the part of the image you want to keep. Eg, I just want to show Africa in the image. Start with the bottom right.

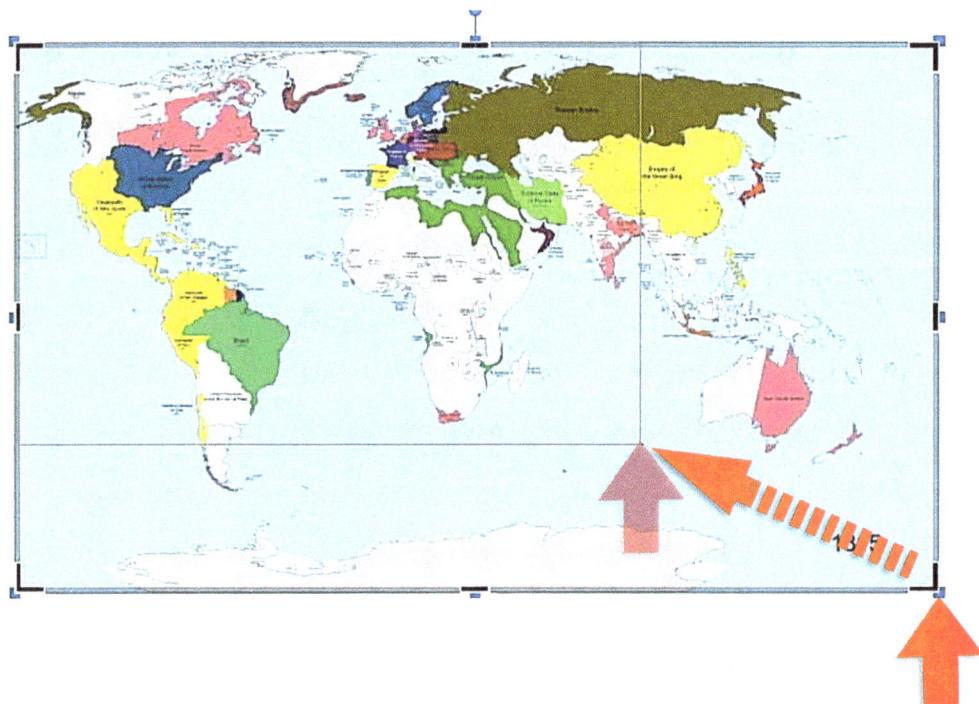

Do the same with the top left.

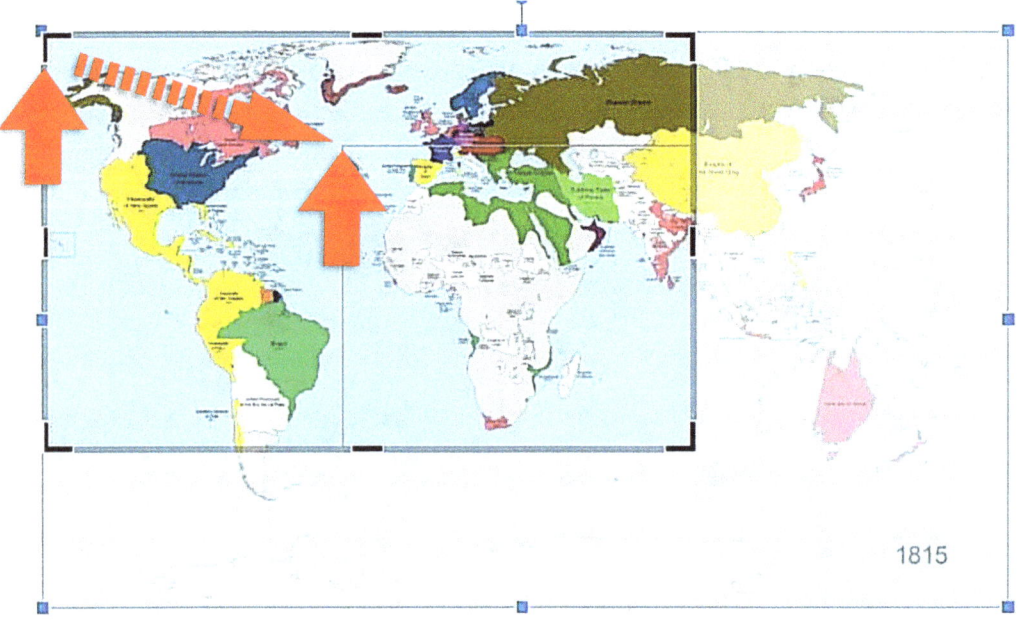

The light grey bits will be removed to leave the bit of the image inside the crop square. Press enter on your keyboard to execute the crop.

Chapter 4: Adding Images & Graphics

Wrap Text around Images

When you insert an image, the image will be inserted in-line with the text, meaning the image is on a line of text, as you can see below.

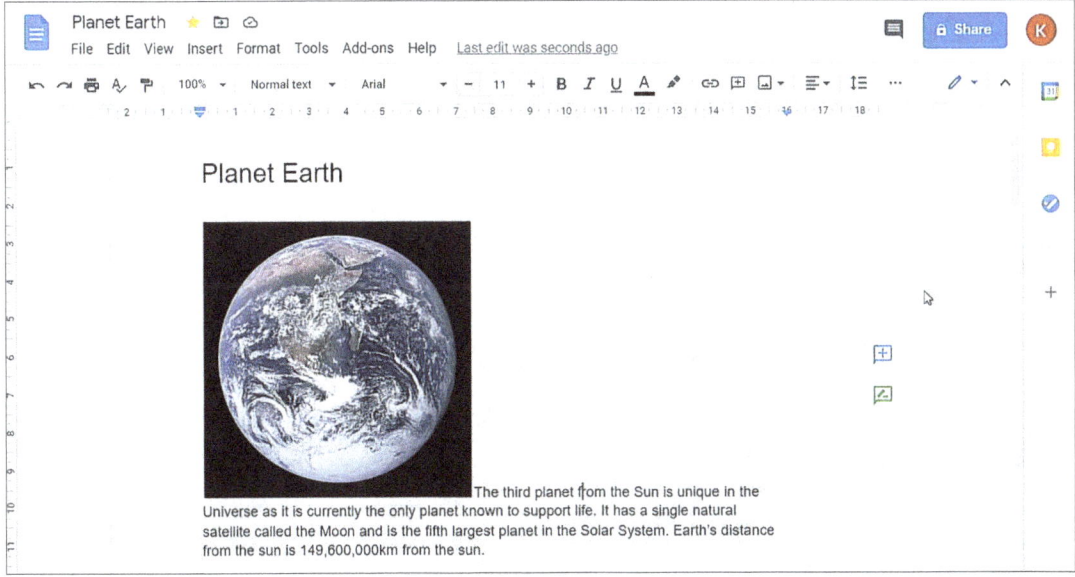

The document would flow much better if you wrapped the relevant text around the image. To change the text wrap, click on the image. You'll see icons appear along the bottom left

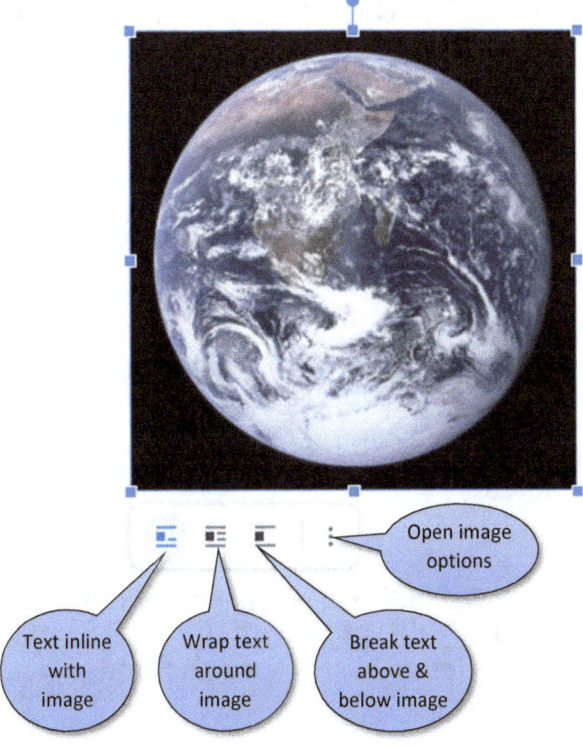

Chapter 4: Adding Images & Graphics

To wrap the text around the image, select the wrap text icon.

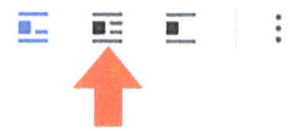

Set the margins - the gap around the top, right, bottom and left sides of the image.

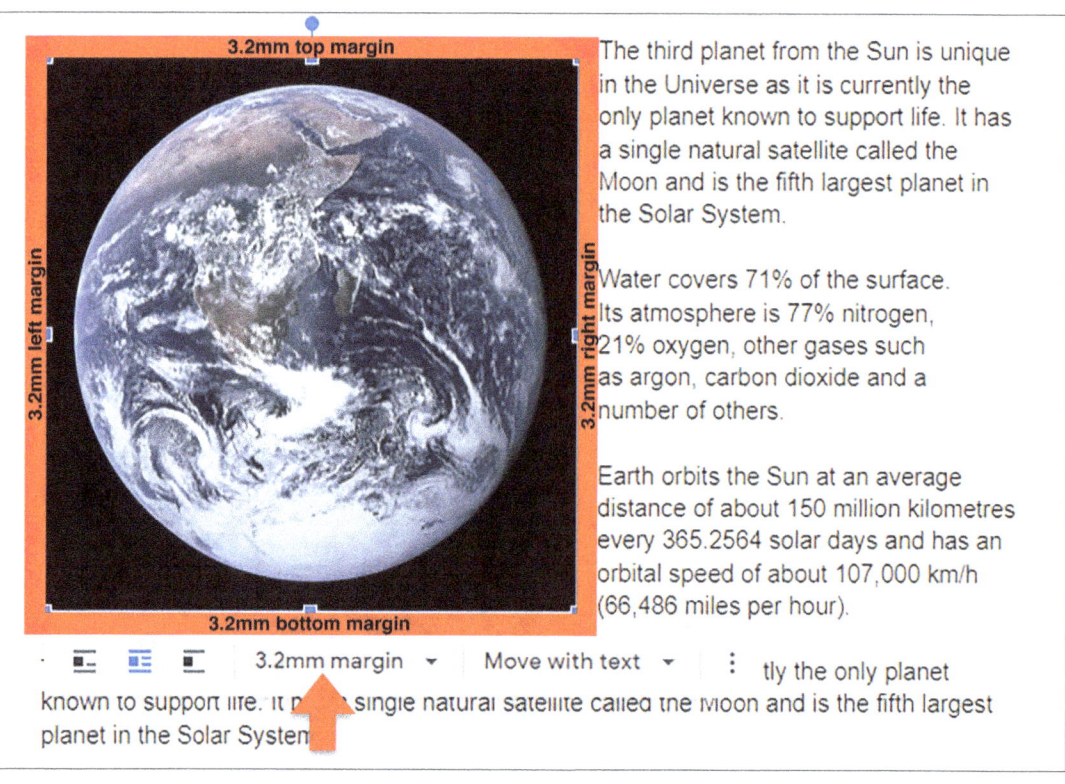

In the position options, you can choose between 'move with text' and 'fixed position on page'.

'Move with Text' means the image will move up or down with the paragraph it is aligned to if you add or delete text above the image.

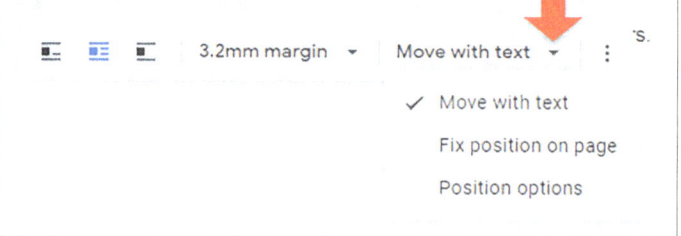

'Fix Position on Page' means any text added won't affect the position of the image, the image will remain in the position it was inserted, regardless if you add or delete text above the image.

Chapter 4: Adding Images & Graphics

Drawings

Drawings is a diagramming tool that allows you to import images, insert shapes, arrows, scribbles, text and wordart from pre-designed templates. To insert a drawing, select the 'insert' menu, then go down to drawings. Select 'new' from the slideout menu.

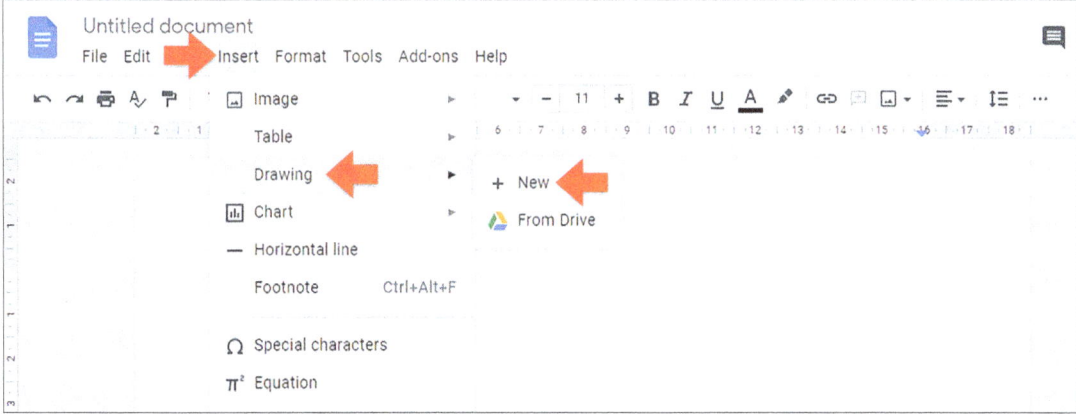

You'll see the drawing canvas window appear. Here you can create your drawings. Along the top of the window, you'll see some controls. Lets take a look at what they do.

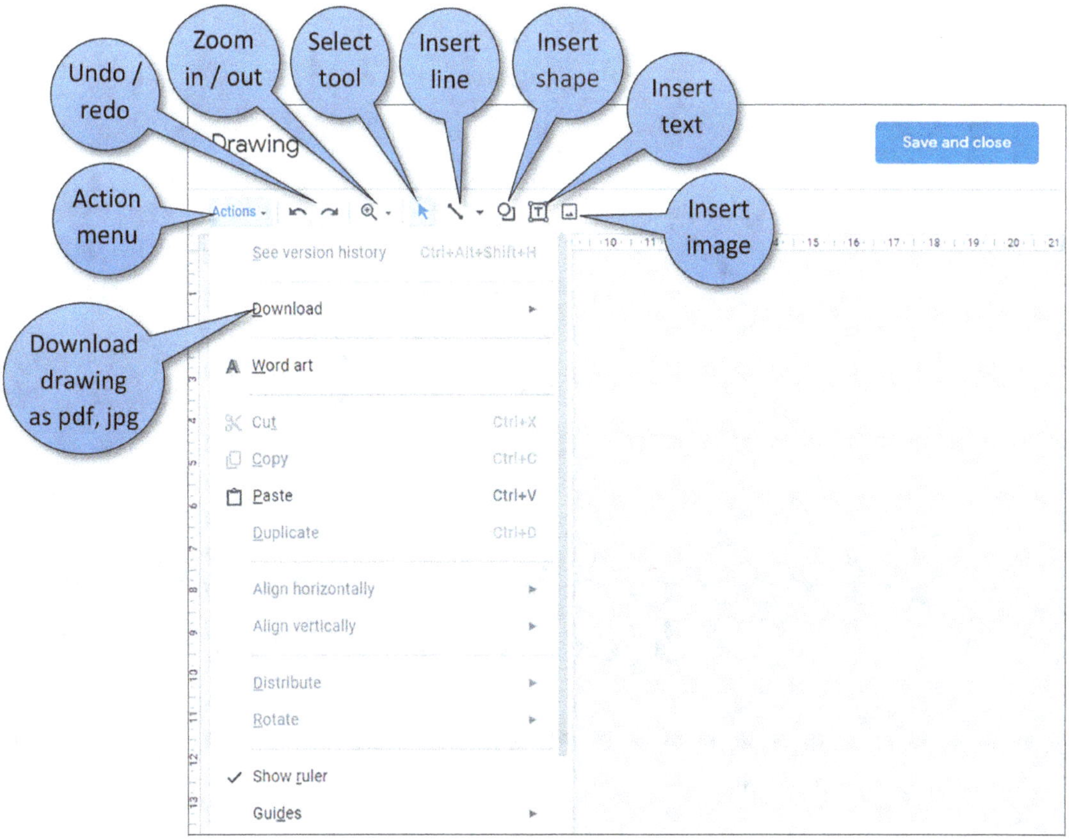

95

Chapter 4: Adding Images & Graphics

WordArt

WordArt is useful for creating titles. First open a new drawing as shown on page 95 if you haven't already done so. Click on the 'action menu', then select 'wordart'. In the field that appears, type in your title.

Click on your wordart to select it.

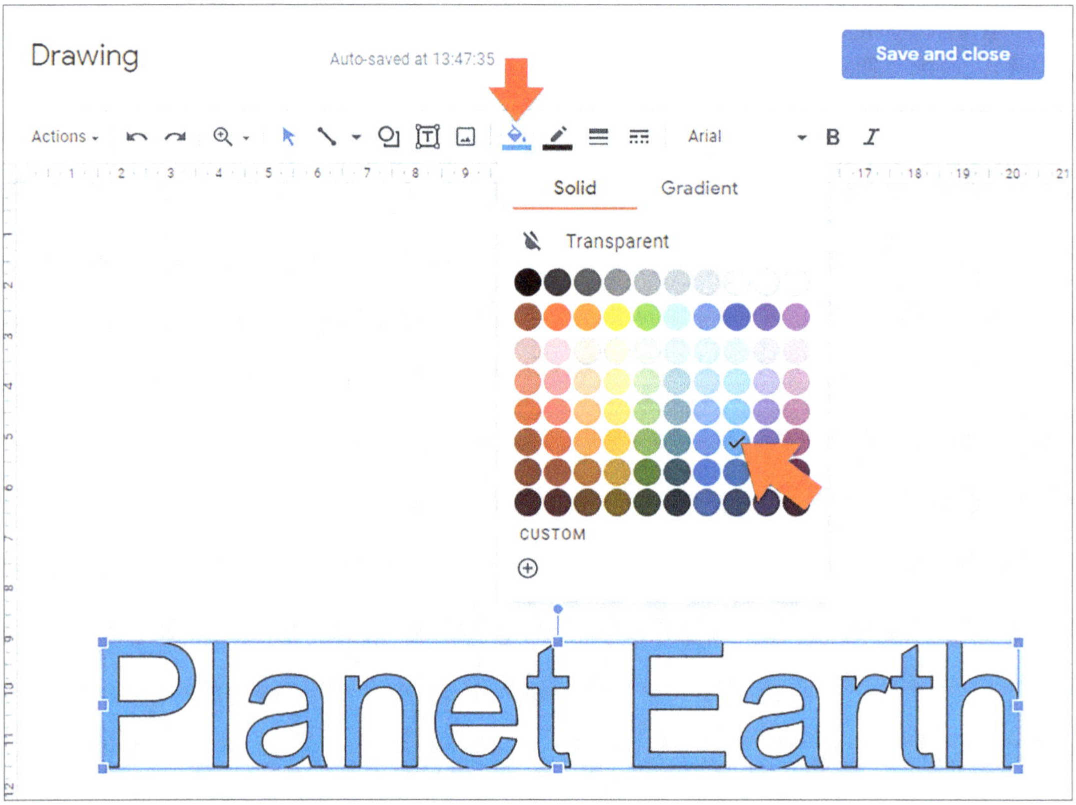

To change the colour, select the 'fill colour' icon from the toolbar. Click on a colour on the palette.

Chapter 4: Adding Images & Graphics

To change the outline, select the 'border colour' icon from the toolbar

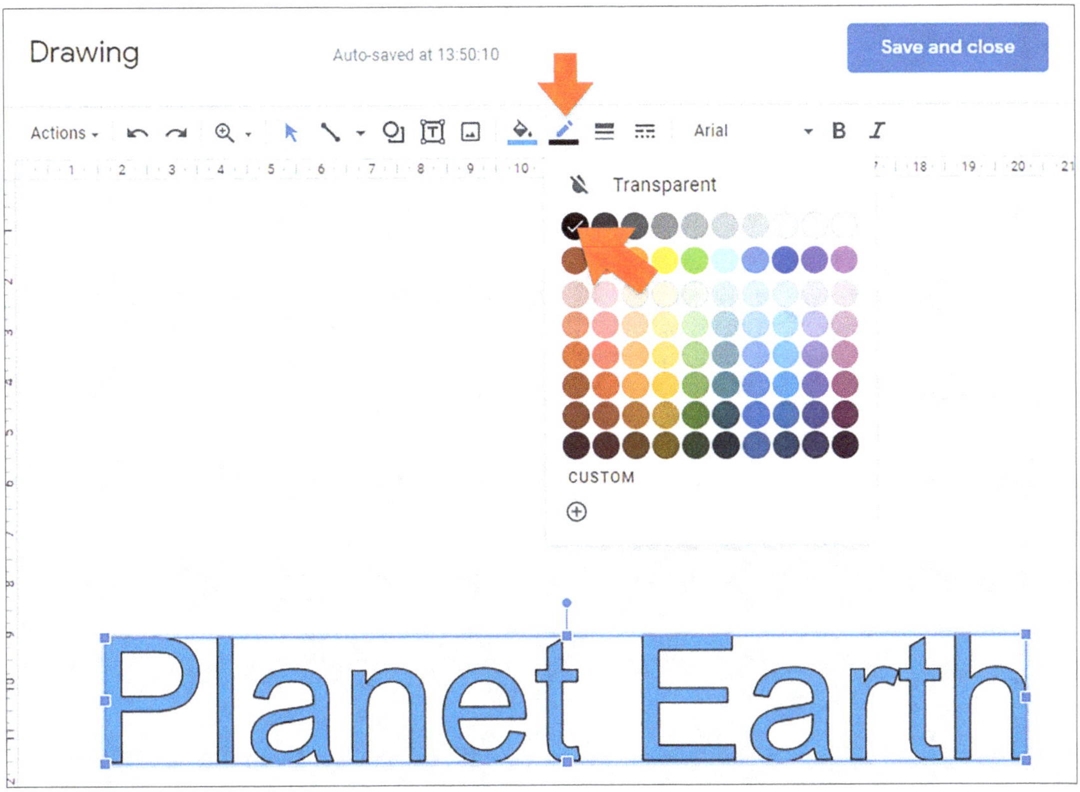

Click and drag your wordart to the top of the canvas.

Shapes

To add a shape, first open a new drawing as shown on page 95 if you haven't already done so. Select the 'shapes' icon from the toolbar, go down to 'shapes', 'arrows' or 'call outs', then select a shape you want to add from the slideout menu.

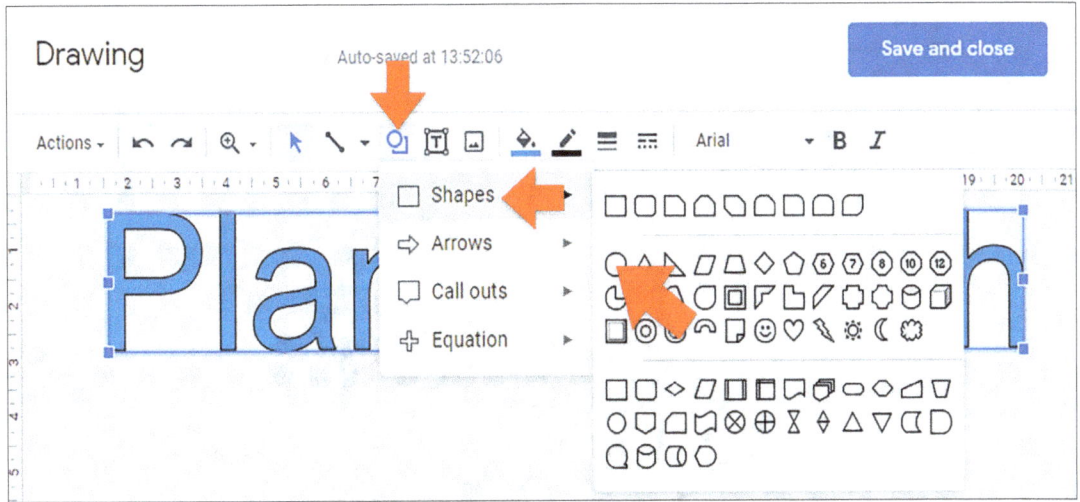

Chapter 4: Adding Images & Graphics

Click and drag the shape onto the canvas to set the size. To make a perfect circle or square, hold down the shift key.

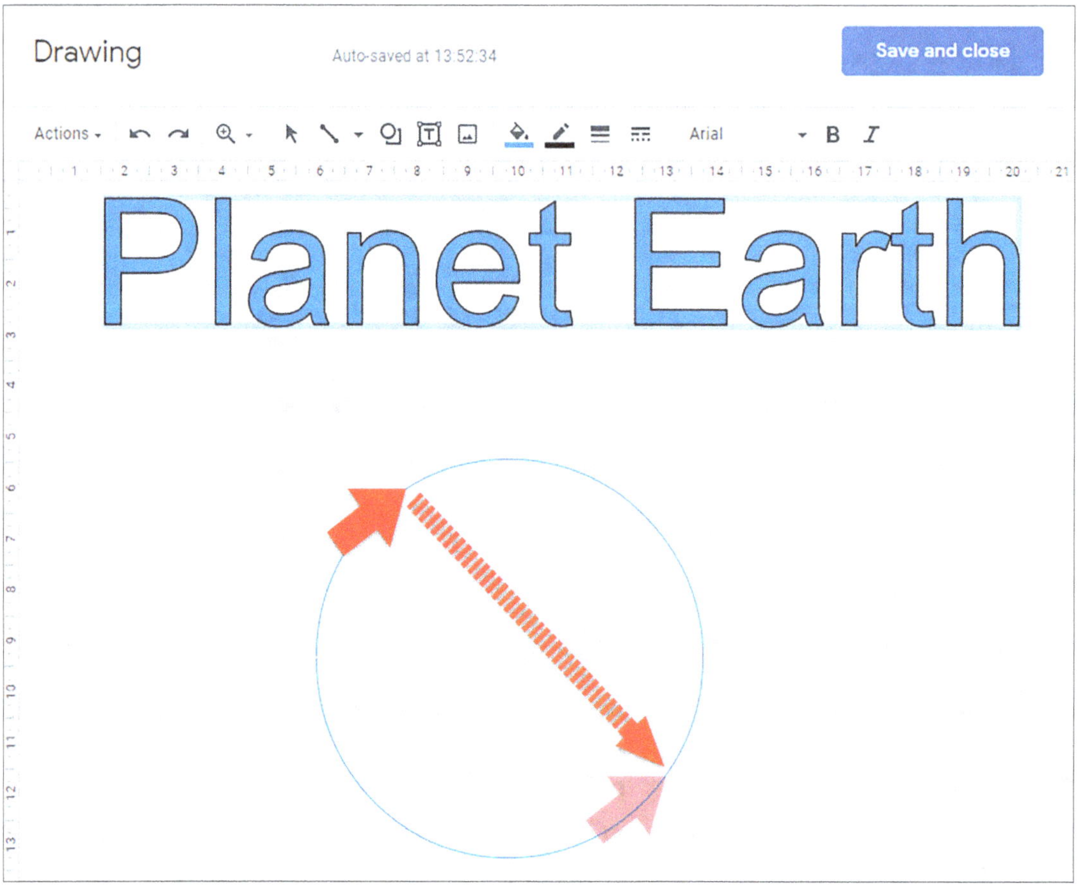

To change the fill colour, click the 'fill colour' icon, then select a colour.

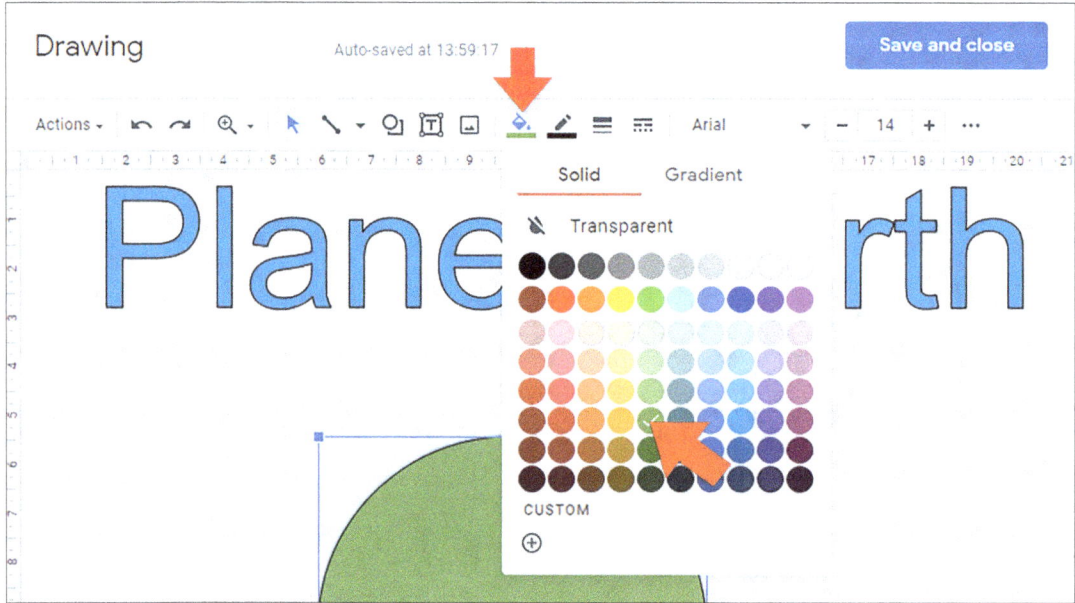

Chapter 4: Adding Images & Graphics

To change the border colour, click the 'border colour' icon, then select a colour

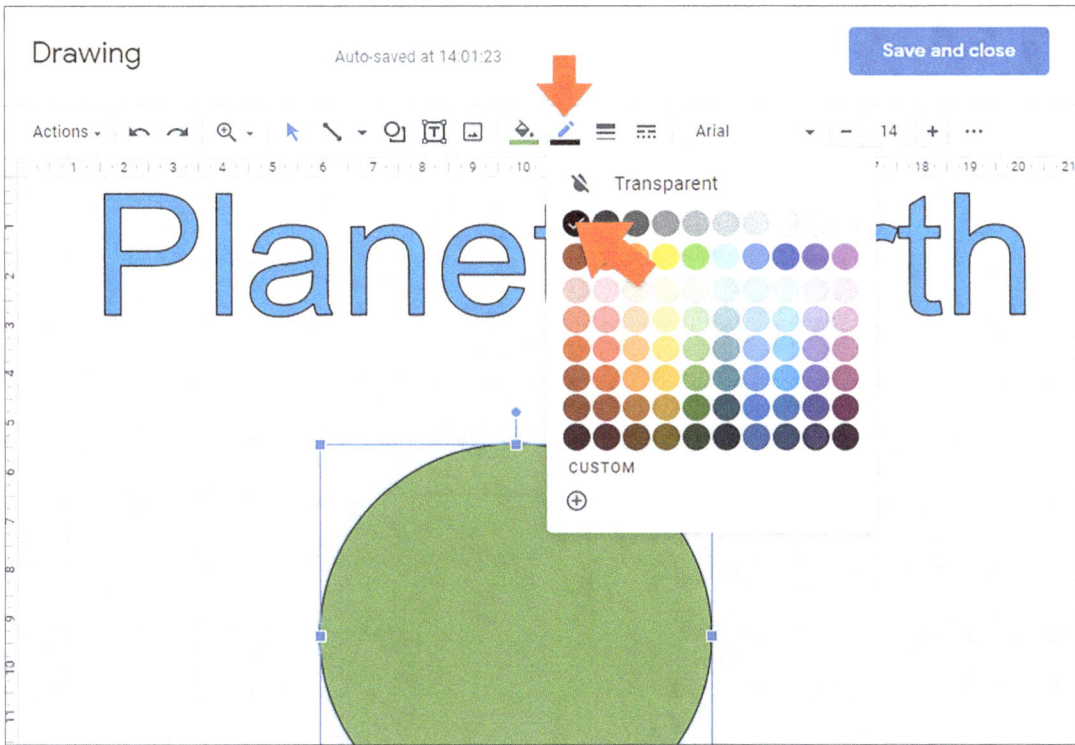

If you want to change the border thickness, click the 'borders' icon, then select a thickness from the slideout menu.

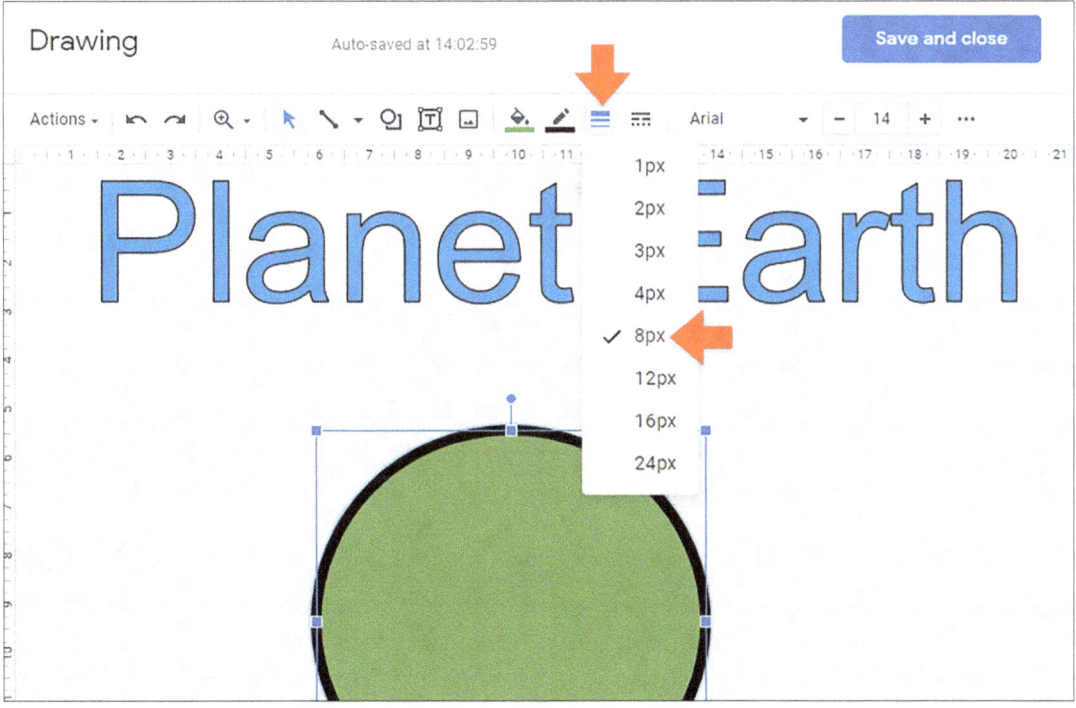

Chapter 4: Adding Images & Graphics

Images

You can insert images and photos into your drawings. To add an image, first open a new drawing as shown on page 95 if you haven't already done so. Select the image icon from the toolbar.

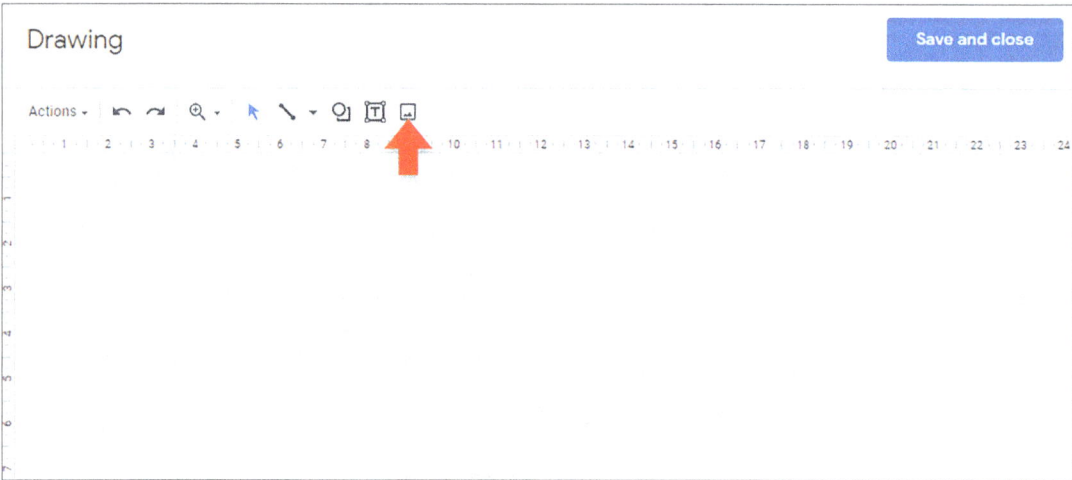

From the four tabs along the top of the screen, select where your image is stored.

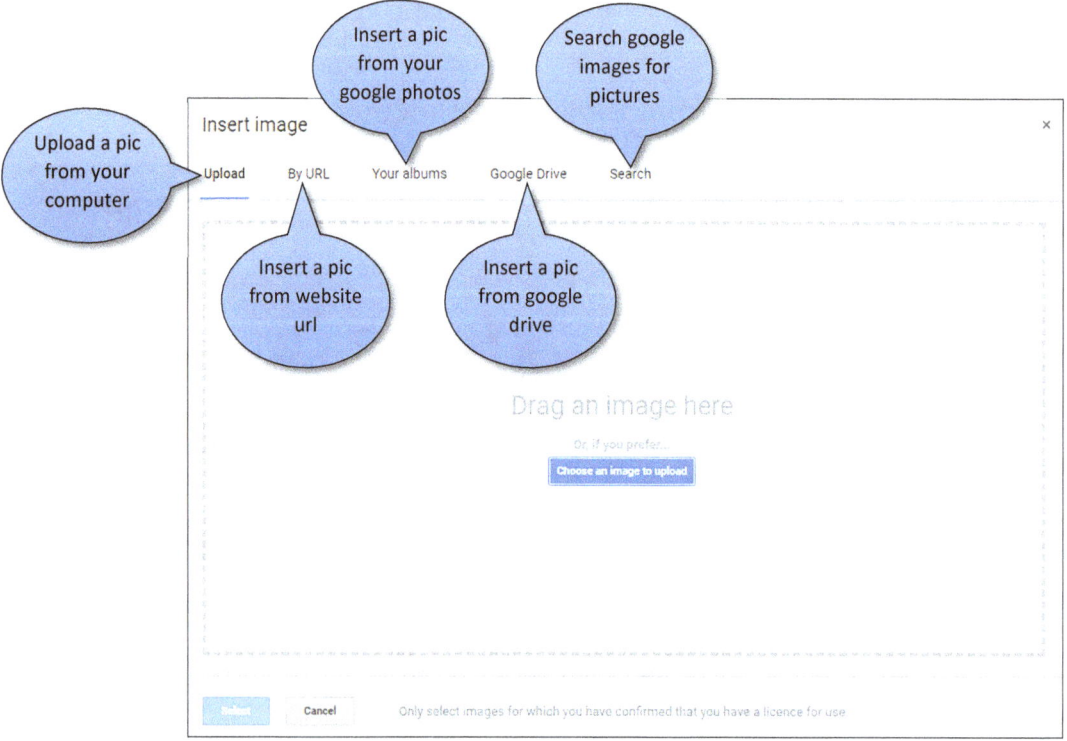

In this example, I'm going to upload the pic from my computer, so I'm going to select 'upload'. Then click 'choose an image to upload'.

Chapter 4: Adding Images & Graphics

Browse to and select the image you want to insert.

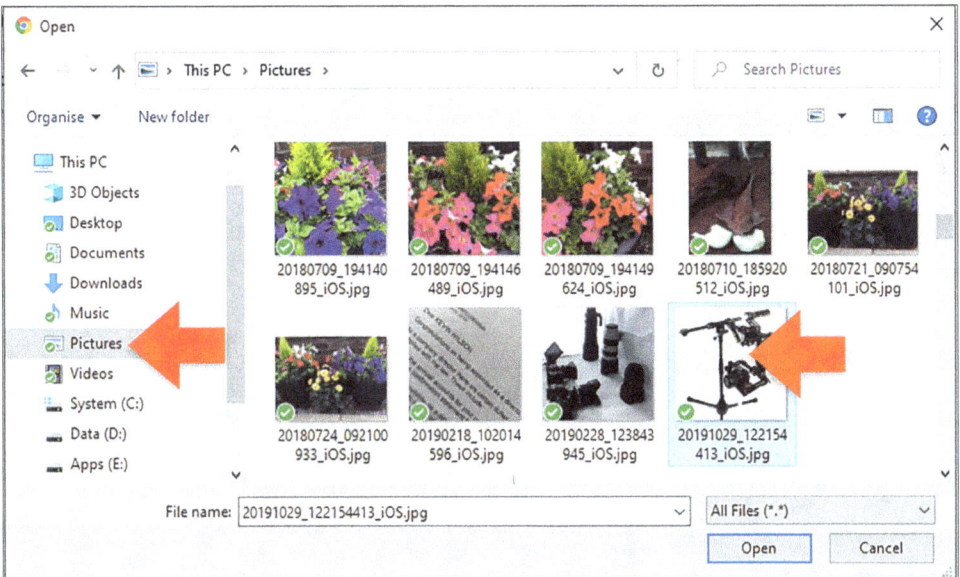

Now, you can insert shapes and other objects. For example, below, I've added a callout bubble to label the camera and stand. To learn how to insert shapes see page 97.

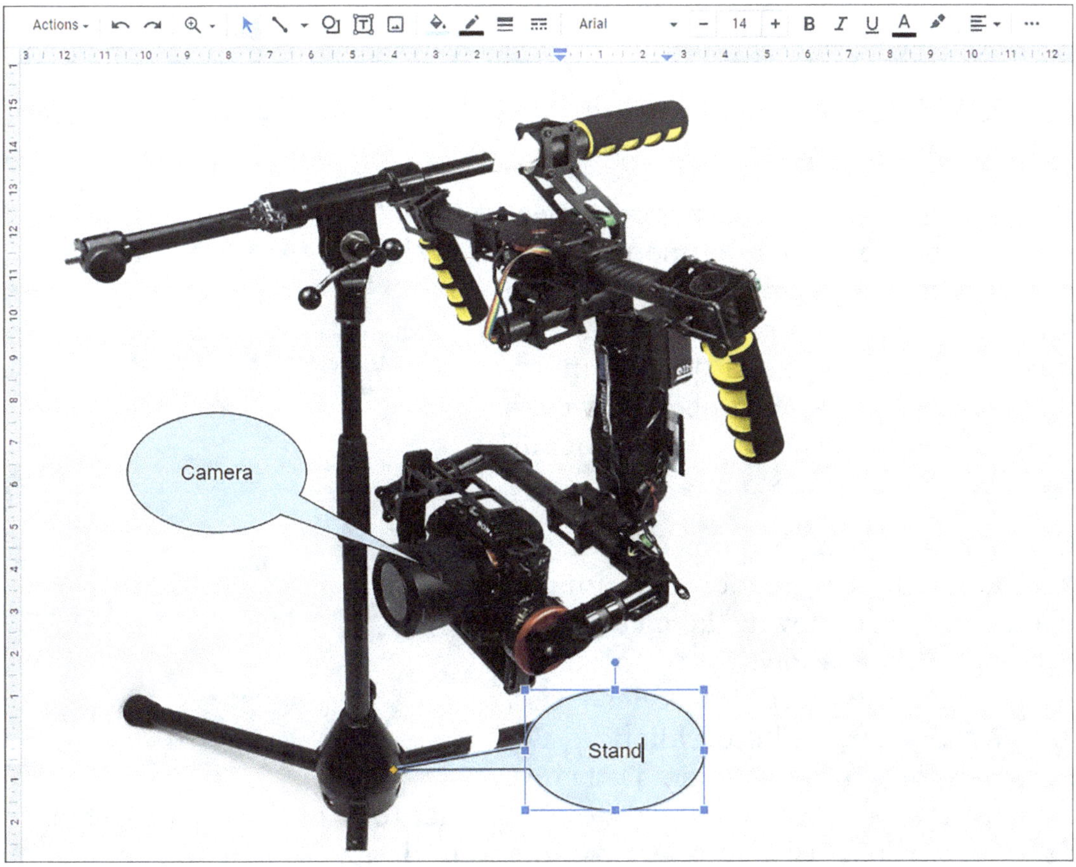

Chapter 4: Adding Images & Graphics

Generating Images with AI

The "Generate an Image" feature in Google Docs enables users to create custom images by providing a descriptive text prompt. This feature is available to Google Workspace users with Gemini as well as to Google One AI Premium subscribers.

Go up to the 'insert' menu, select 'image', then click on 'generate an image'.

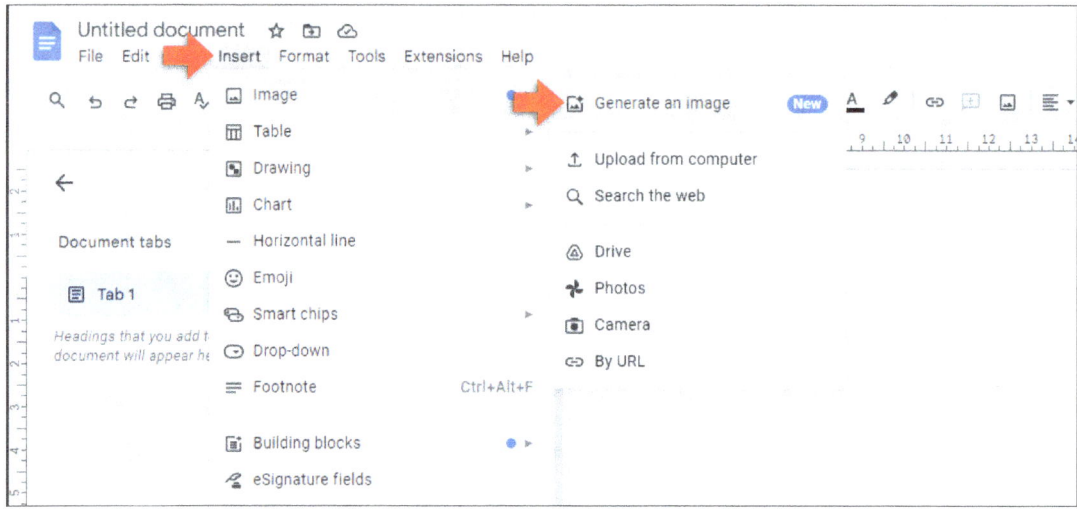

In text field at the top of the right hand side panel, type in a description of the image you want.

Next, select the desired image aspect ratio to match your document layout or use case. A **Square** image is suitable for in-line illustrations or document inserts. **Wide** is ideal for banners, slide decks, or panoramic. Tall works best posters, cover art, or vertically stacked infographics.

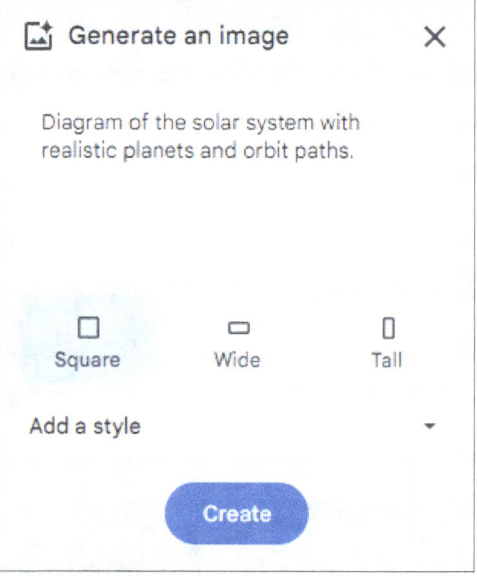

If you'd like to apply a specific visual aesthetic to the generated image, click the dropdown labeled "Add a style." This allows you to select from predefined artistic styles such as Watercolor, Photorealistic, 3D Illustration, Flat Art, Line Drawing, and Fantasy Art. Each style alters the visual tone of the image to better fit your purpose. Click 'create' when you're done.

Chapter 4: Adding Images & Graphics

Select from the generated images at the bottom of the right hand side panel.

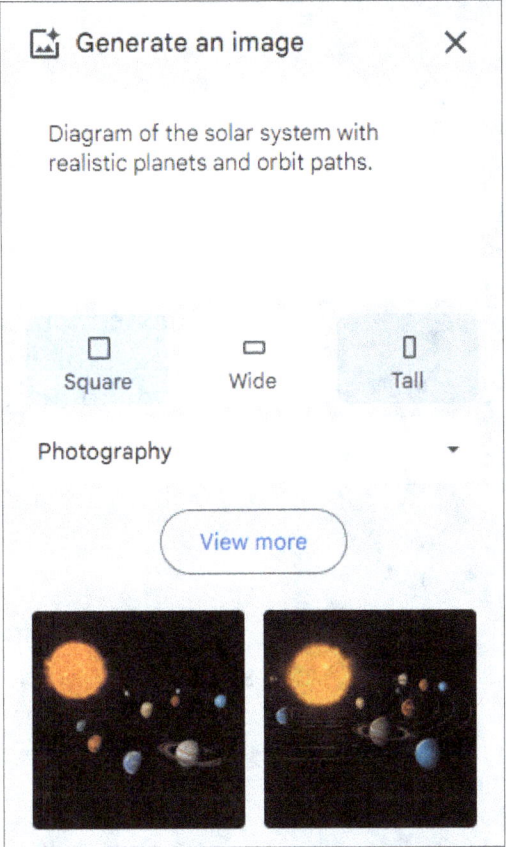

You'll see your selection appear in the document. From here you can resize or move the image as required.

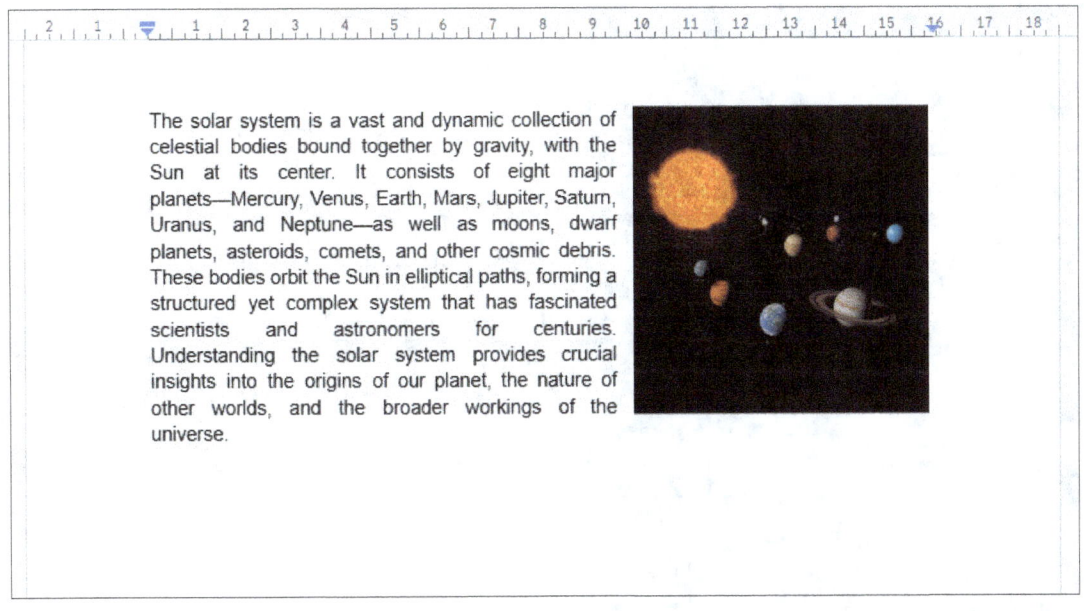

5

Tables and Charts

In this section, we'll take a look at creating tables and adding charts to our documents.

We'll go through inserting tables, as well as formatting and laying out a table.

We'll also take a look at inserting various types of charts to illustrate statistics and data in your documents. You can add pie charts, line graphs, and bar or column charts.

- Adding Tables
- Formatting Tables
- Borders, Cell Shading
- Split and Merge Cells
- Adding Charts
- Formatting Charts
- Customising Chart

Have a look at the video resources section. Open your web browser and navigate to the following website.

elluminetpress.com/charts-googledocs

Chapter 5: Tables and Charts

Tables

We have added some more text about world population to our document. Now we want to add a table to illustrate our text.

Inserting Tables

To insert a table, click on your document where you want the table to appear. In this example, I want it to appear just below world population paragraph.

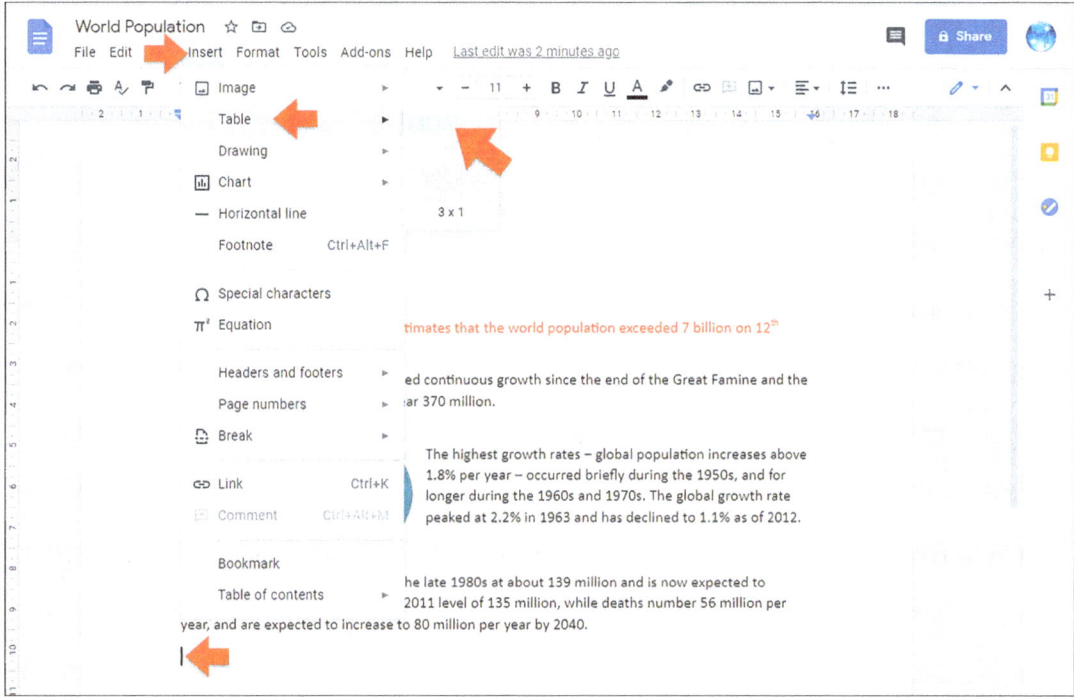

Click on the 'insert' menu, go down to 'table'. From the slideout, select the number of rows and columns you want in your table using the grid. Here, in the example below, I've selected a table with 3 columns and 4 rows.

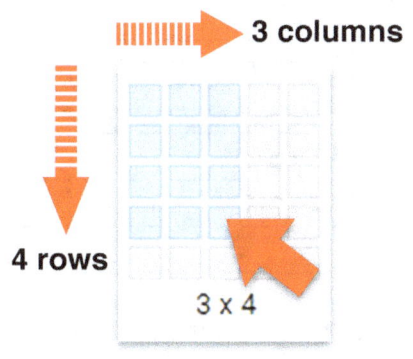

105

Chapter 5: Tables and Charts

You can now enter the data into your table. Press tab to move to the next cell, or click in the cell you want.

World Population

The United States Census Bureau estimates that the world population exceeded 7 billion on 12th March 2012.

The world population has experienced continuous growth since the end of the Great Famine and the Black Death in 1350, when it was near 370 million.

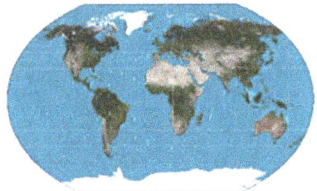

The highest growth rates – global population increases above 1.8% per year – occurred briefly during the 1950s, and for longer during the 1960s and 1970s. The global growth rate peaked at 2.2% in 1963 and has declined to 1.1% as of 2012.

Total annual births were highest in the late 1980s at about 139 million and is now expected to remain essentially constant at their 2011 level of 135 million, while deaths number 56 million per year, and are expected to increase to 80 million per year by 2040.

Country	Population	Percentage of World
China	1,372,000,000	18.5
India	1,276,900,000	17.5
USA	312,793,000	4.35

If you run out of rows, select the last cell on the bottom right, then press the tab key on your keyboard.

Country	Population	Percentage of World
China	1,372,000,000	18.5
India	1,276,900,000	17.5
USA	312,793,000	4.35 ←

A new row will be inserted at the end.

Country	Population	Percentage of World
China	1,372,000,000	18.5
India	1,276,900,000	17.5
USA	312,793,000	4.35

You can continue to enter the data into the table.

Chapter 5: Tables and Charts

Text Formatting

You can format your text in the same way as any other text in your document. For example, in this table I want to make the top row bold to indicate a column heading. To do this, first select the cells

Country	Population	Percentage of World
China	1,372,000,000	18.5
India	1,276,900,000	17.5
USA	312,793,000	4.35
Indonesia	252,164,000	3.35

Select the bold icon from the toolbar.

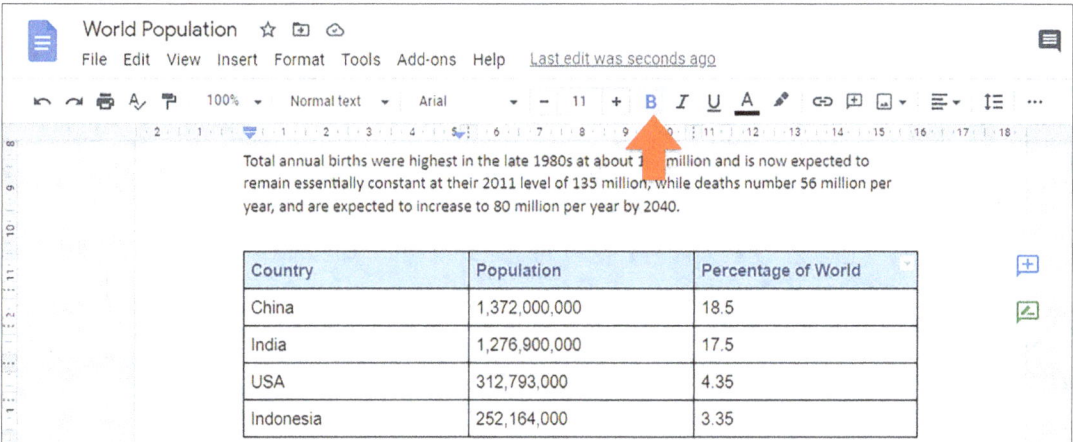

Cell Color

You can change the cell colors of any cells, rows, or columns on the table. For example, lets change the color of the cells on the top row to separate it from the rest of the table. This makes a good heading row.

First select the cells you want to format.

Country	Population	Percentage of World
China	1,372,000,000	18.5
India	1,276,900,000	17.5
USA	312,793,000	4.35
Indonesia	252,164,000	3.35

107

Chapter 5: Tables and Charts

Click on the 'format' menu, then go down to 'table'. Select 'table properties' from the slideout menu

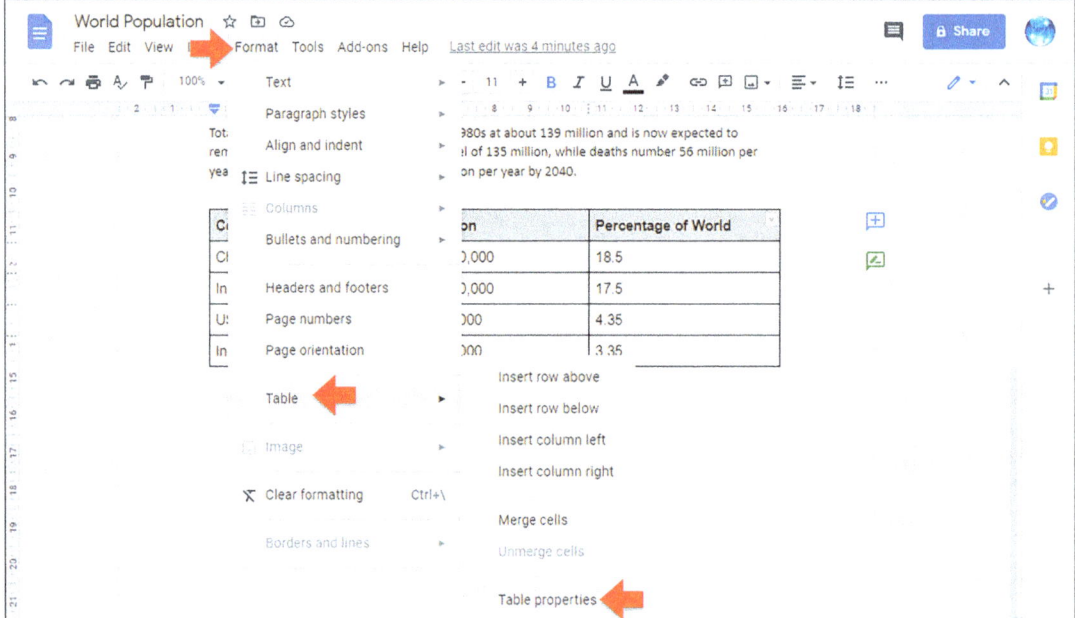

On the right hand side of the screen, select the 'color' tab. Select 'cell background color', then choose a color from the palette.

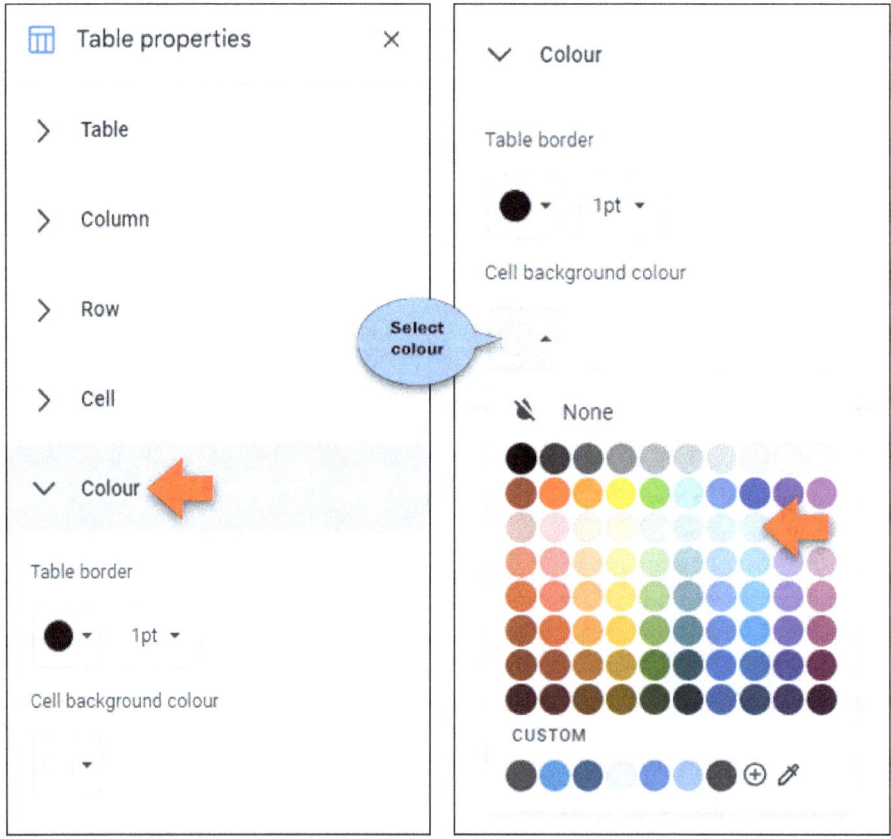

Chapter 5: Tables and Charts

Borders

To change the borders of the whole table, select the table, then click the 'format' menu, go down to table, then click 'table properties'.

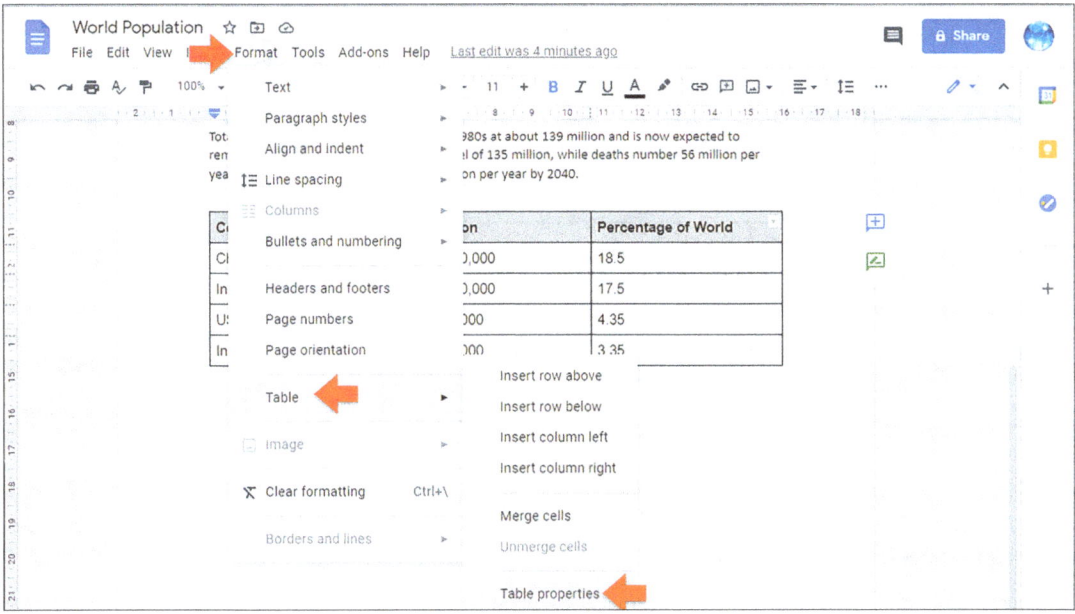

From panel on the right hand side of the screen, select the 'color' tab. Under 'table border', select a color from the left hand drop down box, then select a thickness from the drop down next to it.

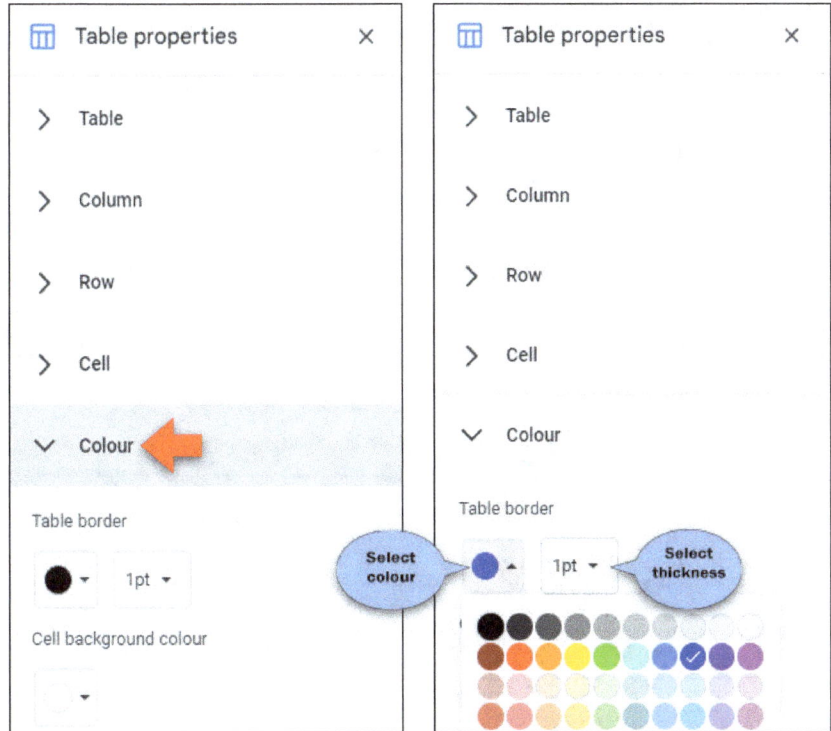

109

Chapter 5: Tables and Charts

To change individual borders, click on the borders on the table you want to change. If you're changing more than one border, hold down the shift key as you click each border you want to change.

For example, if I wanted to apply a thicker border to the outline of the table, I'd hold down shift, then click each of the borders on the outside of the table all the way around.

Country	Population	Percentage of World
China	1,372,000,000	18.5
India	1,276,900,000	17.5
USA	312,793,000	4.35
Indonesia	252,164,000	3.35

From the toolbar, click the border thickness icon. Select a thickness from the drop down menu.

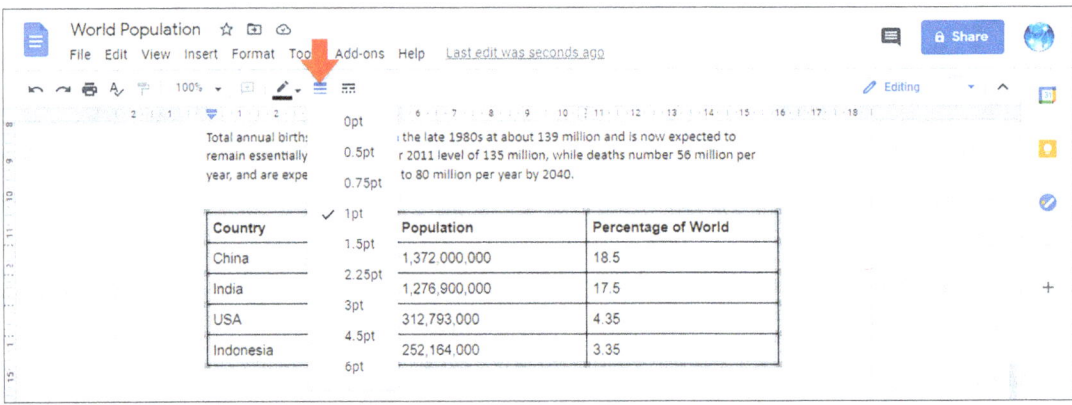

If you want to change the color, click the color icon, then select a color.

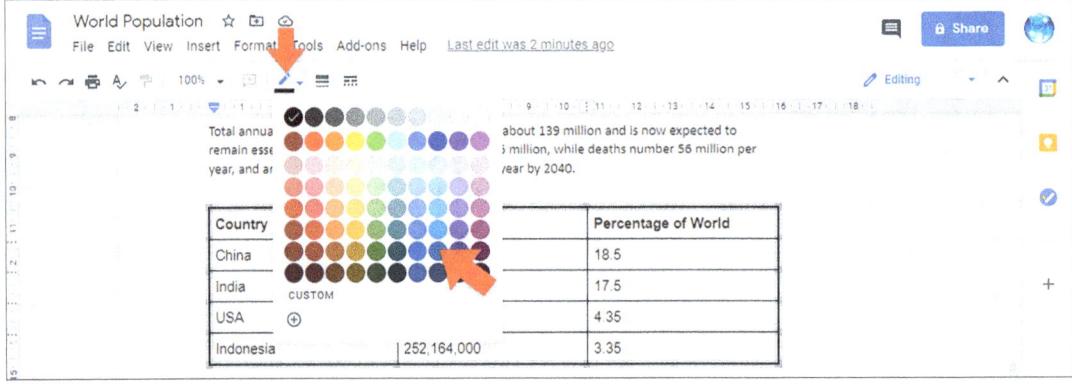

Chapter 5: Tables and Charts

Cell Padding

Cell padding is the space between the content of a table cell and its border. It refers to the amount of space that is added within the cell, between the content and the cell's edges.

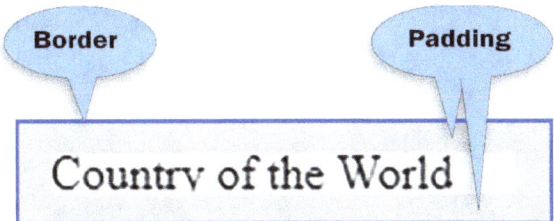

By default, a table cell in Google Docs has 0.176cm of padding, meaning that the content of the cell is 0.176 from the cell's border.

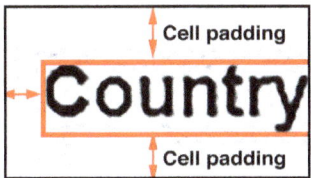

To adjust the cell padding, select the table or cells you want to format, then click the 'format' menu, go down to table, then click 'table properties'.

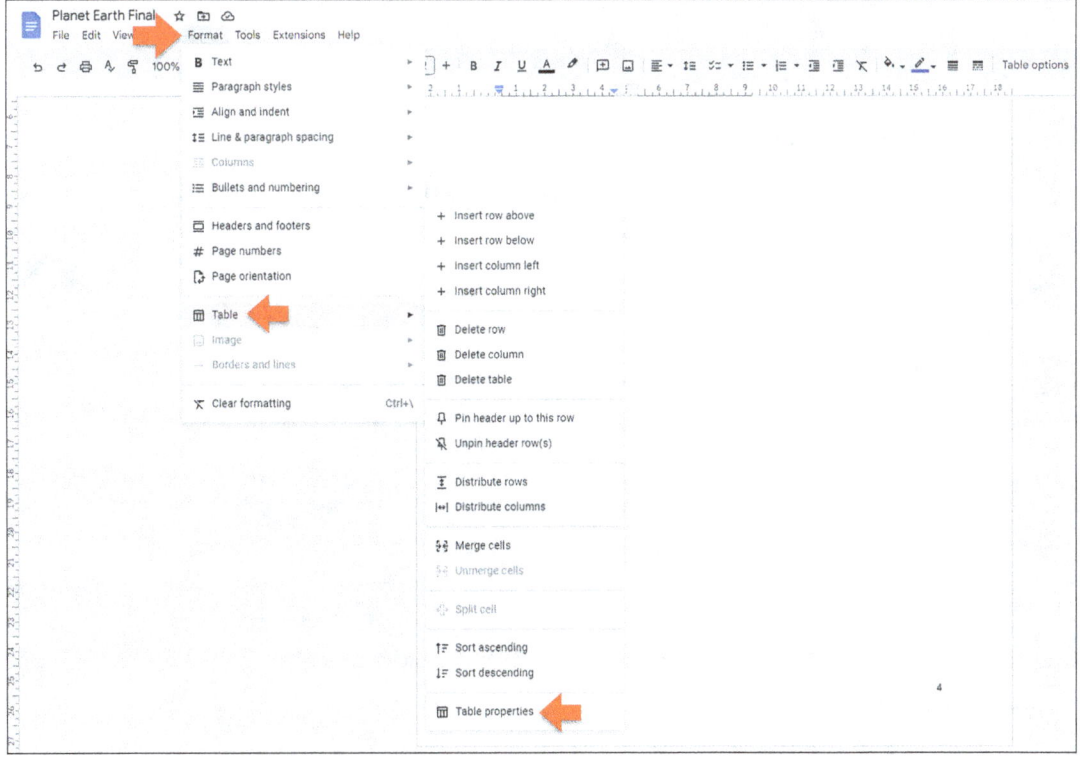

111

Chapter 5: Tables and Charts

From the panel on the right hand side, select 'cell'. Adjust the 'cell padding'.

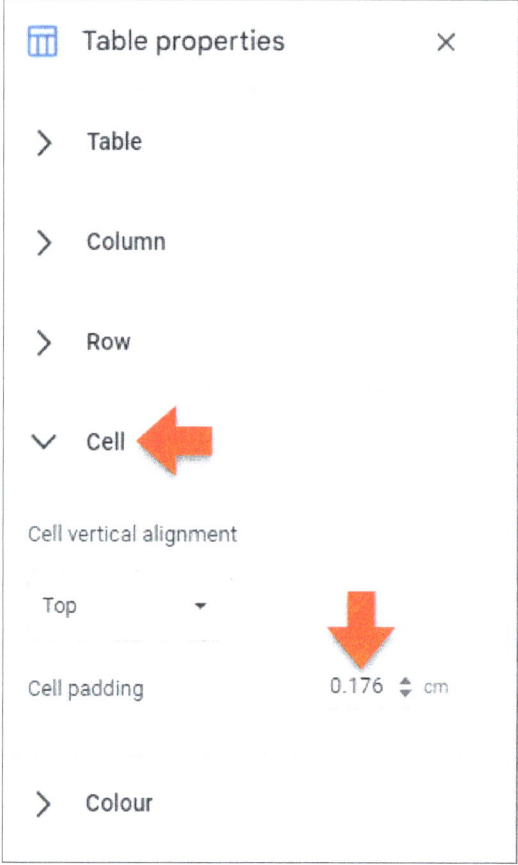

Cell Alignment

Select the data in the table, or click the cell you want to align.

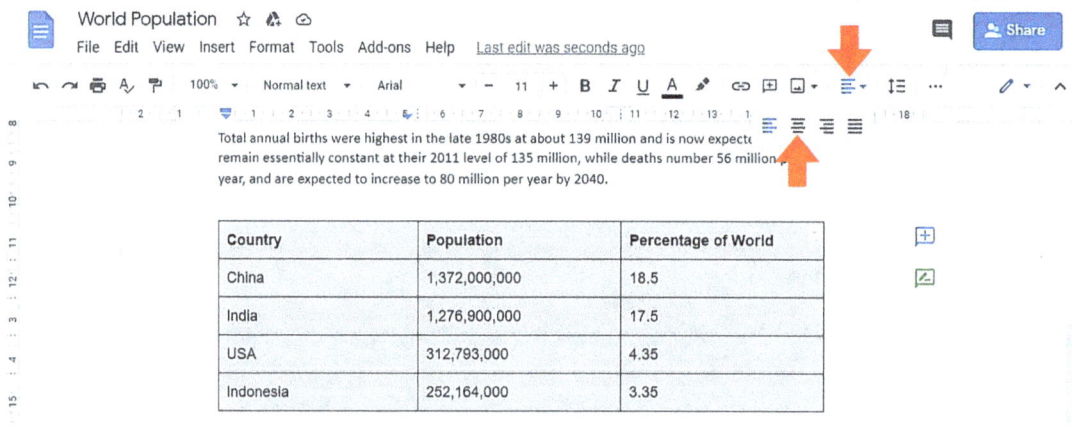

From the toolbar, select the alignment icon (left, center, right).

Chapter 5: Tables and Charts

Split Cells

Select the cell or cells that you want to split. Right click on the cell, then select 'split cell' from the popup menu.

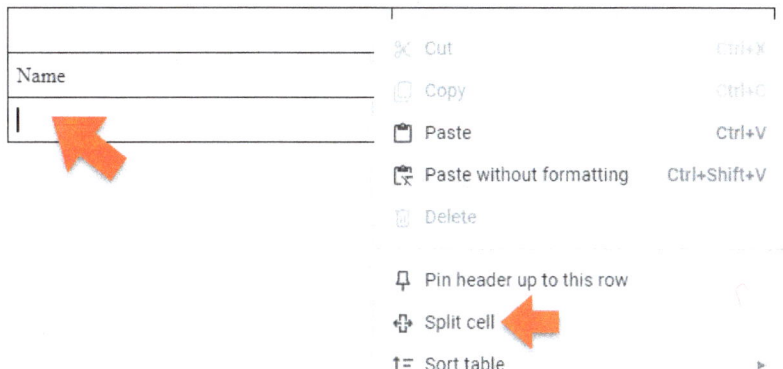

In the Split cell dialog box, choose the number of rows and columns you want to create, and click 'ok'.

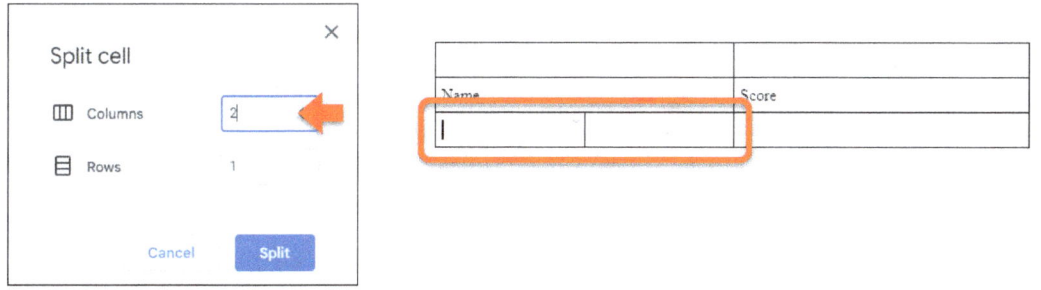

Merge Cells

Select the cells you want to merge. Right click on the selection, then select 'merge cells' from the popup menu.

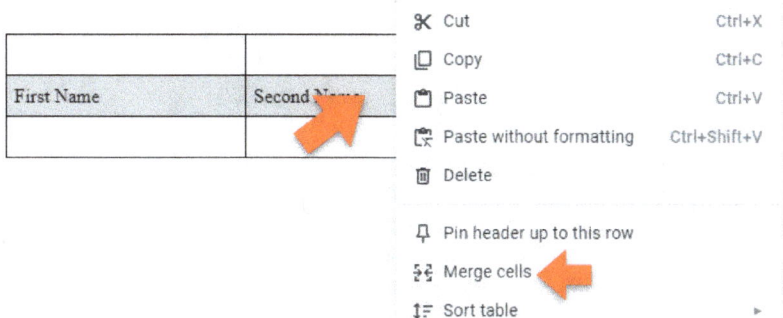

The selected cells will be merged into a single cell, and the content will be centered within the new merged cell.

113

Chapter 5: Tables and Charts

Row Height

To adjust a row height, click and drag one of the row dividing lines to the up or down.

Country	Population	Percentage of World
China	1,372,000,000	18.5
India	1,276,900,000	17.5
USA	312,793,000	4.35
Indonesia	252,164,000	3.35

Column Width

To adjust a column width, click and drag one of the column dividing lines to the left or right.

Country	Population	Percentage of World
China	000,000	18.5
India	1,276,900,000	17.5
USA	312,793,000	4.35
Indonesia	252,164,000	3.35

You can also adjust all the column and row heights together using the table properties. Select all the data in the table, click the 'format' menu, go down to 'table', click on 'table properties'.

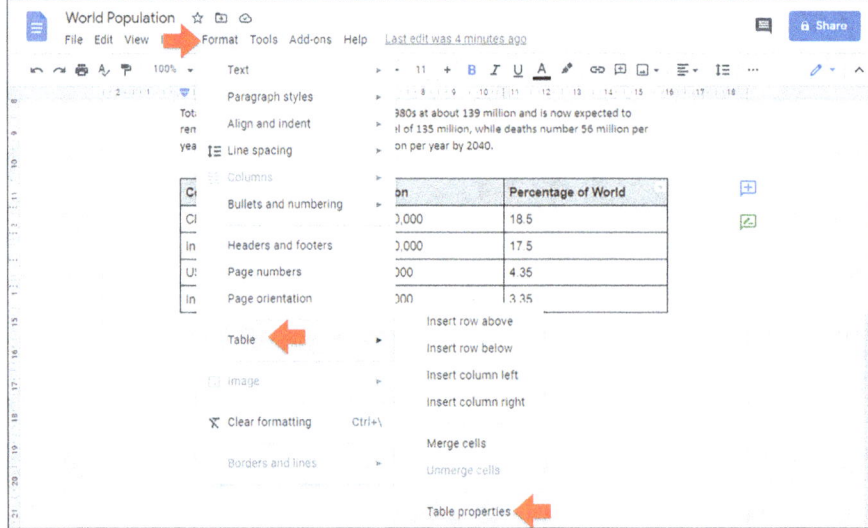

114

Chapter 5: Tables and Charts

From the panel on the right hand side, open up the row and column tabs. Enter the row height and column widths into the fields shown below.

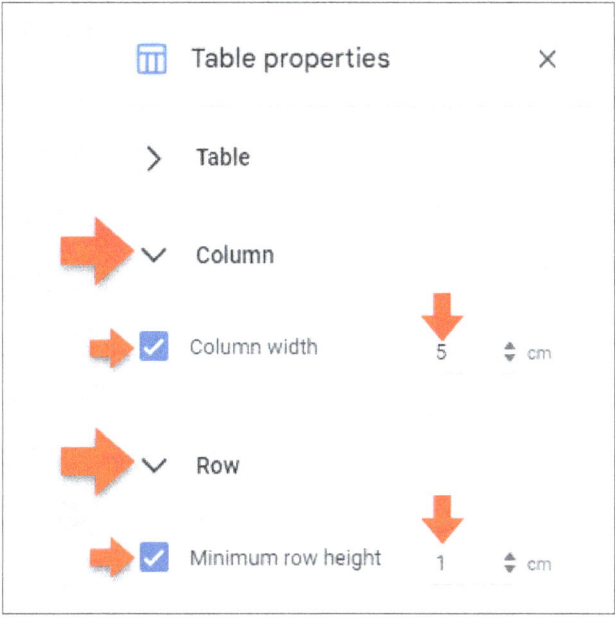

In this example, our columns are set to 5cm and the row height is 1cm.

Country	Population	Percentage of World
China	1,372,000,000	18.5
India	1,276,900,000	17.5
USA	312,793,000	4.35
Indonesia	252,164,000	3.35

Insert Row

In our table, lets add a row between 'india' and 'USA'.

Country	Population	Percentage of World
China	1,372,000,000	18.5
India	1,276,900,000	17.5
USA	312,793,000	4.35
Indonesia	252,164,000	3.35

115

Chapter 5: Tables and Charts

To do this, right click in the row 'india' is in. From the popup menu, select 'insert row below'.

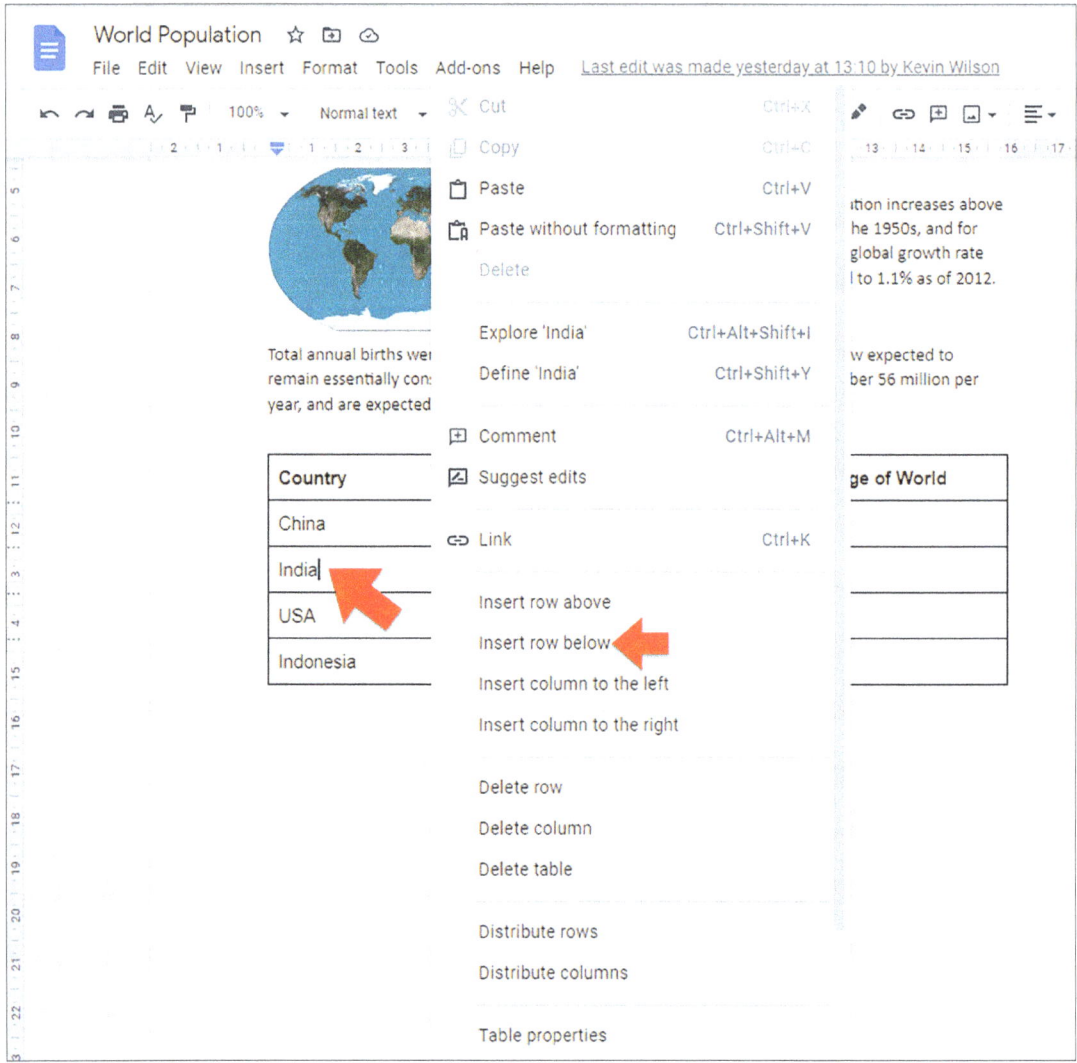

This will insert a row below the row 'india' is in - as you can see here below.

Country	Population	Percentage of World
China	1,372,000,000	18.5
India	1,276,900,000	17.5
USA	312,793,000	4.35
Indonesia	252,164,000	3.35

Chapter 5: Tables and Charts

Insert Column

In our table, lets add a column between 'population' and 'percentage of world'.

Country	Population	Percentage of World
China	1,372,000,000	18.5
India	1,276,900,000	17.5
USA	312,793,000	4.35
Indonesia	252,164,000	3.35

To do this, right click in the column 'percentage of world' is in.

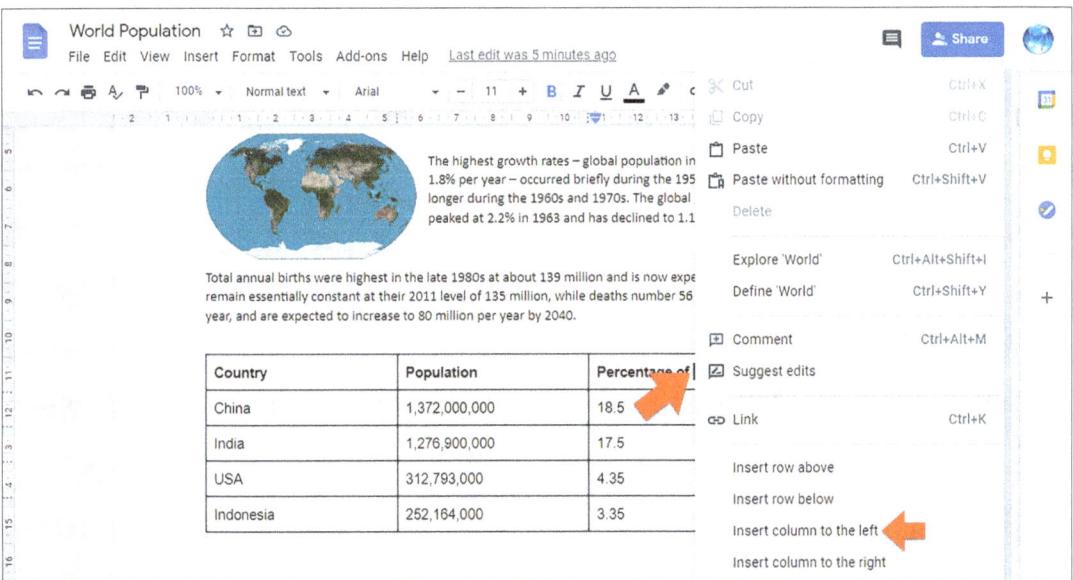

From the popup menu, select 'insert column to the left'. This will insert a column next to the column 'percentage of world' is in - as you can see here below.

Country	Population		Percentage of World
China	1,372,000,000		18.5
India	1,276,900,000		17.5
USA	312,793,000		4.35
Indonesia	252,164,000		3.35

If you wanted the column on the end, click 'insert column to the right' instead.

117

Chapter 5: Tables and Charts

Delete Column

To delete a column, right click in the column you want to remove, then select 'delete column'.

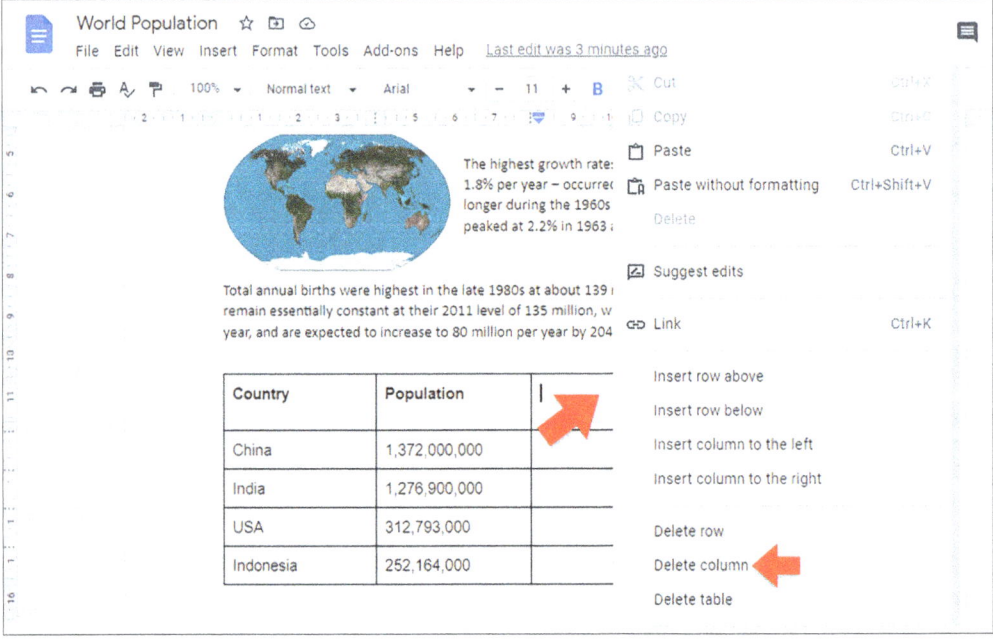

Delete Row

To delete a row, right click in the row you want to remove, then select 'delete row'.

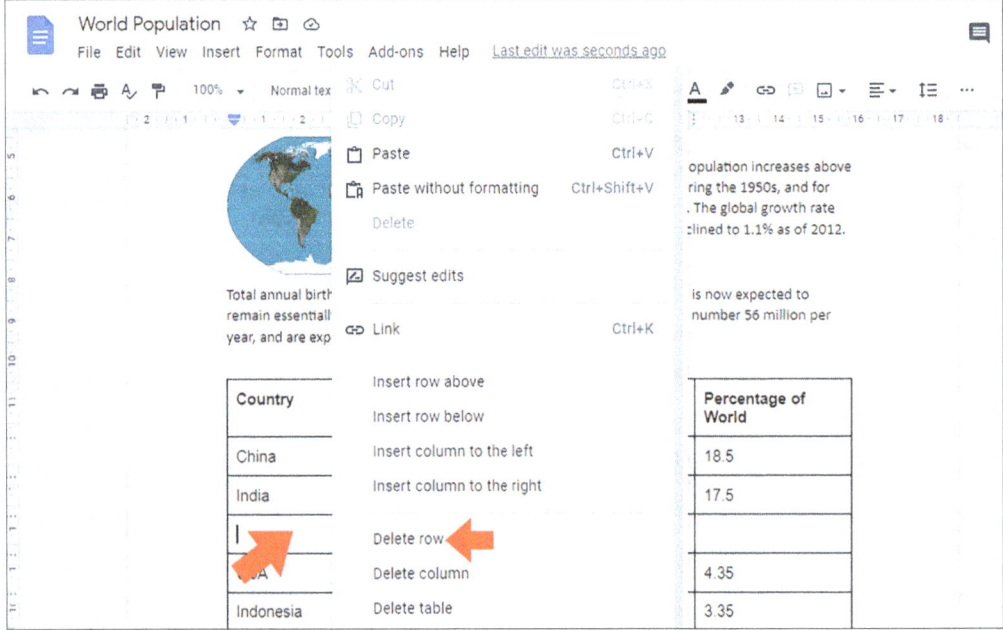

Chapter 5: Tables and Charts

Adding Charts

You can add various charts to your documents to represent data. You can add a bar or column chart, a line graph, or a pie chart.

To add a chart, click on the location in the document you want the chart to appear, then select the 'insert' menu. Go down to chart, then select a chart type from the slidout. In this example, I'm going to add a column chart.

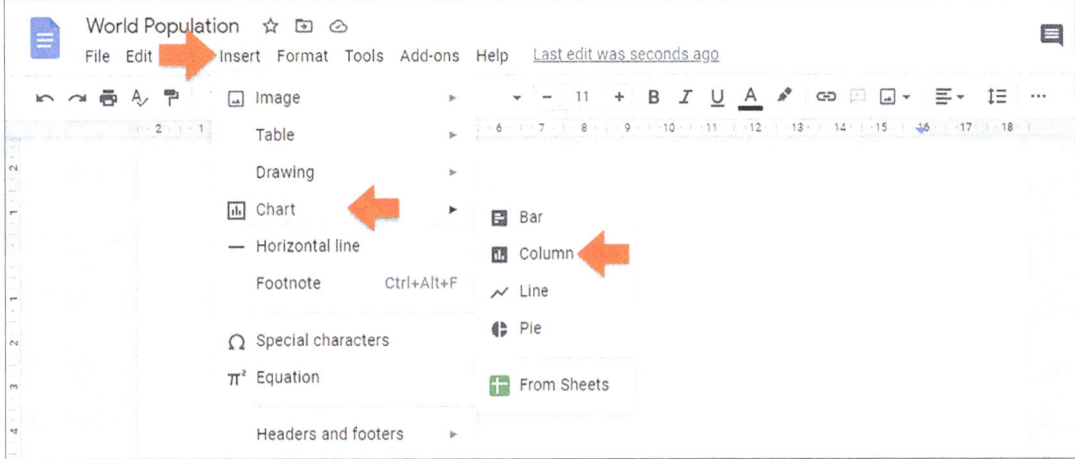

Now to enter the data, click on your chart to select it, then click the small 'link' icon on the top right.

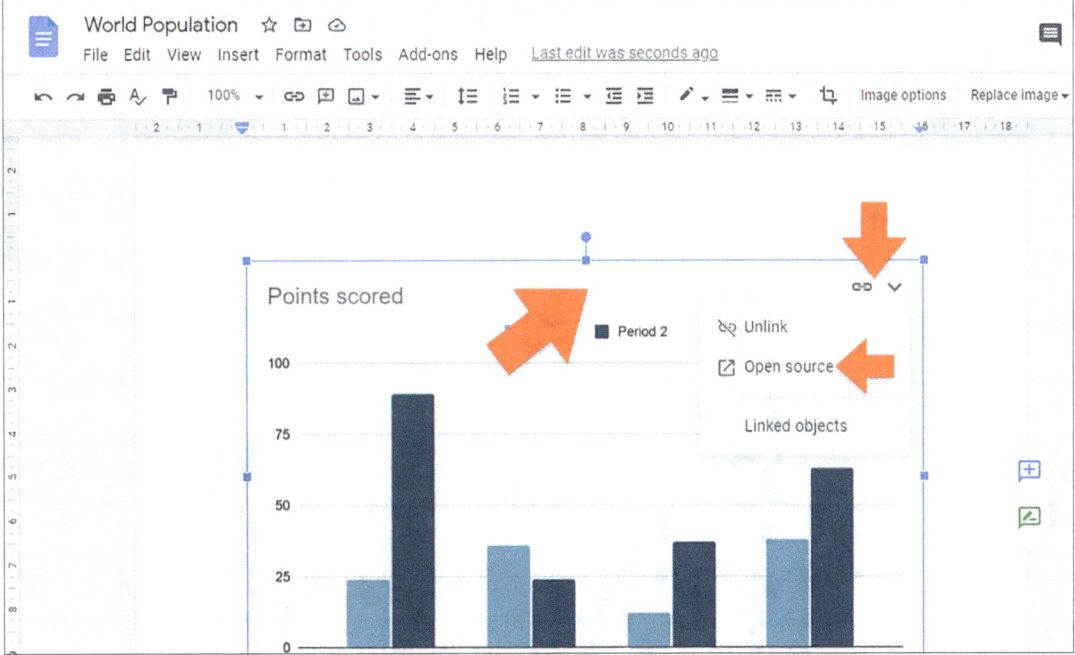

From the popup menu, select 'open source'.

119

Chapter 5: Tables and Charts

A spreadsheet will open up for you to enter your data. Column A is the x axis, and column B is the y axis

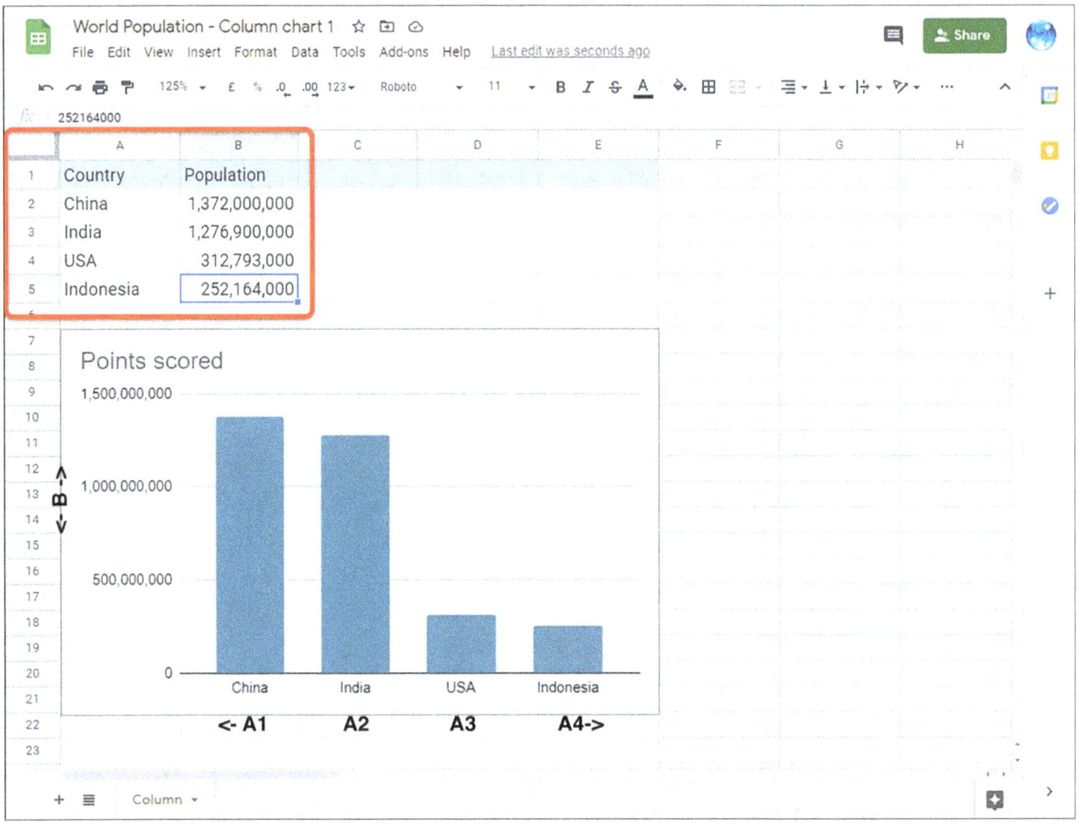

Once you've done that, make sure the spreadsheet is saved, then close the window. Go back to your document, click 'update' on your chart if it doesn't automatically update.

Chapter 5: Tables and Charts

Customise your Chart

To customise your chart, click on your chart to select it, then click the small 'link' icon on the top right. Select 'open source' from the popup menu.

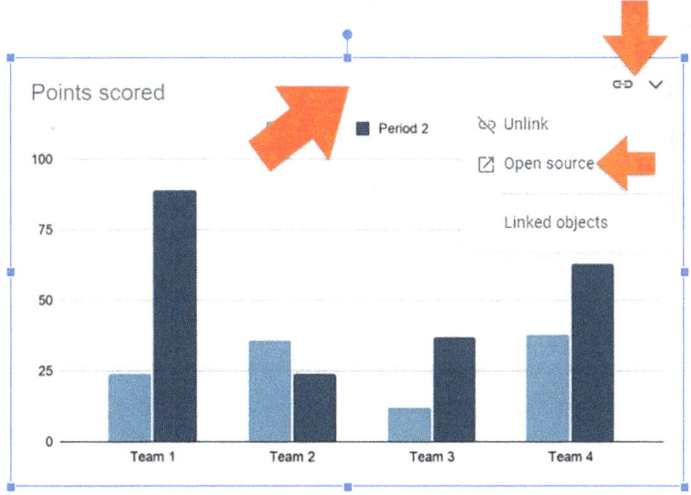

Your chart will open up in a spreadsheet. Click on your chart to select it, then click the three dots icon on the top right.

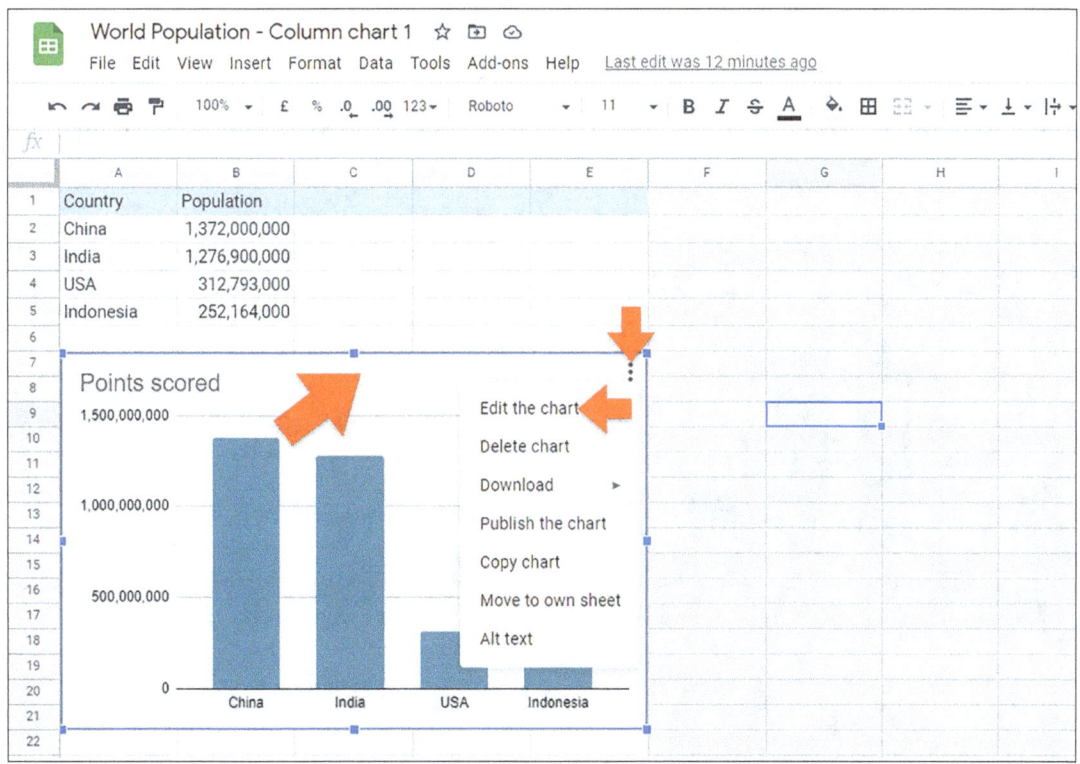

Select 'edit the chart'.

121

Chapter 5: Tables and Charts

You'll see the chart editor panel appear on the right hand side.

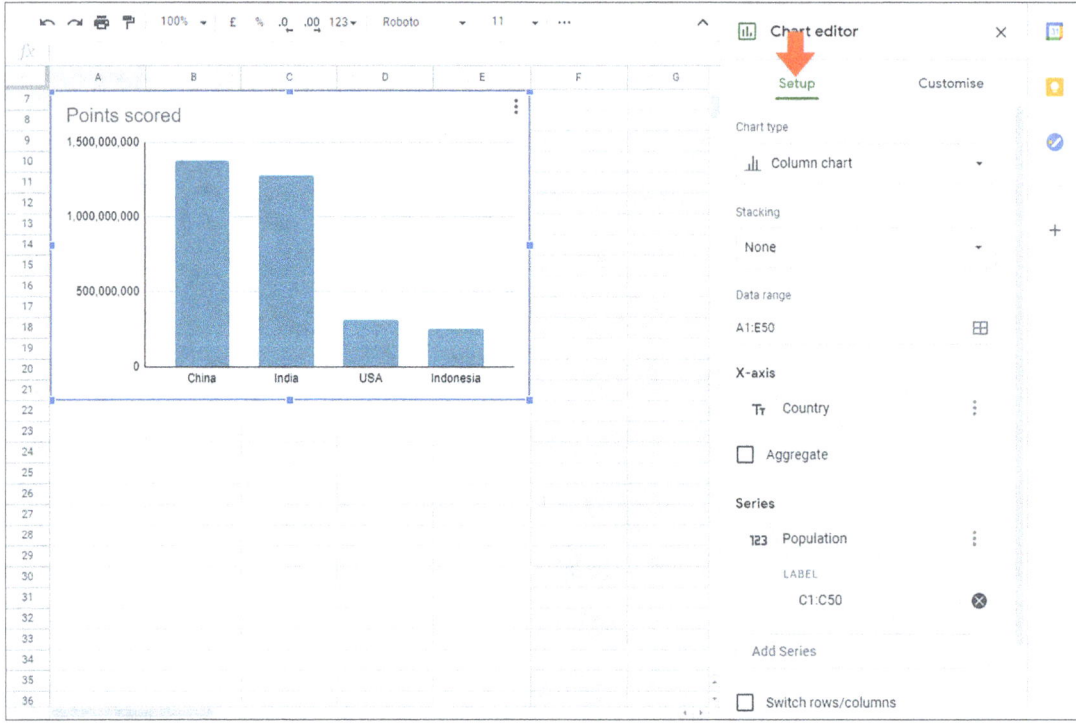

Here, you can start to customise your chart. From the 'setup' tab you can change the chart type (pie chart, column chart, line chart, etc). You can also add a data series and range for your chart.

From the 'customise' tab you can change the look and feel of your chart.

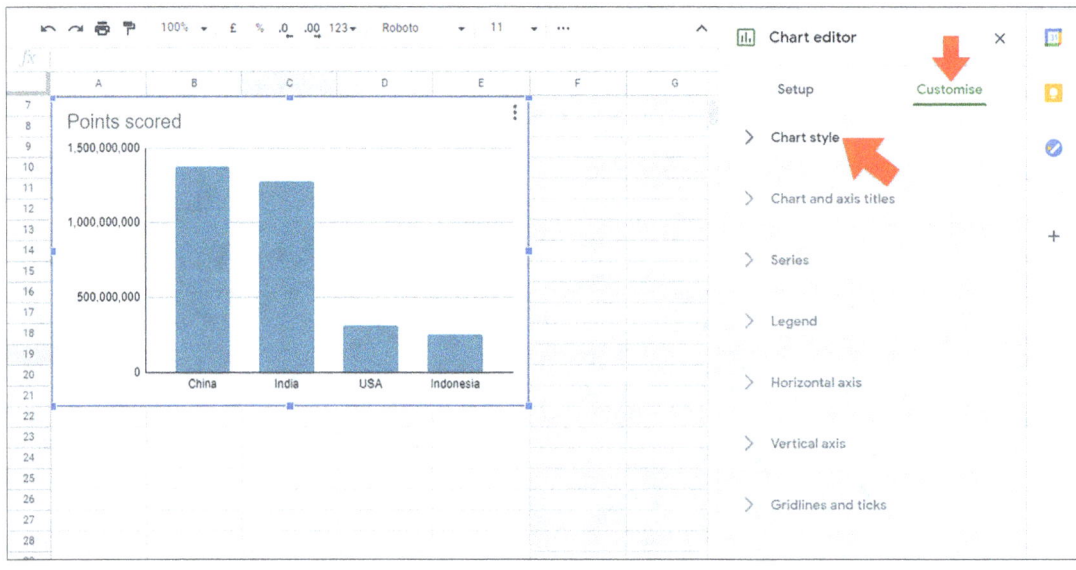

To do this, select one of the sections from the 'customise' tab to expand the customisation options.

Chapter 5: Tables and Charts

Chart Style

You can change the chart style - background color, border color, 3D effect, and font.

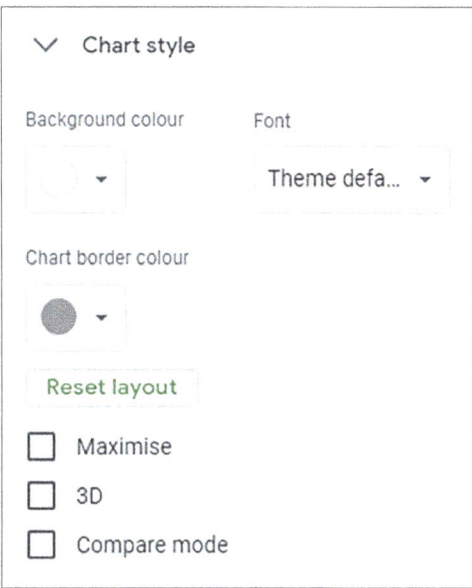

Chart & Axis Titles

You can change the chart title, as well as the horizontal and vertical axis labels - just use the 'chart title' drop down menu.

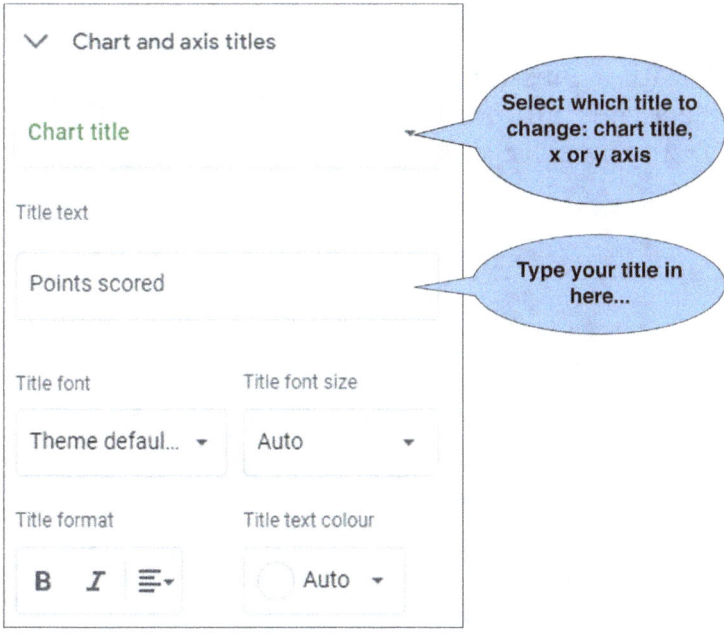

Here, you can also change the font and text color using the controls at the bottom of the section.

123

Chapter 5: Tables and Charts

Data Series

In the 'series' section, you can change the bar colors, as well as add data labels to the bars on your chart or add a trend line

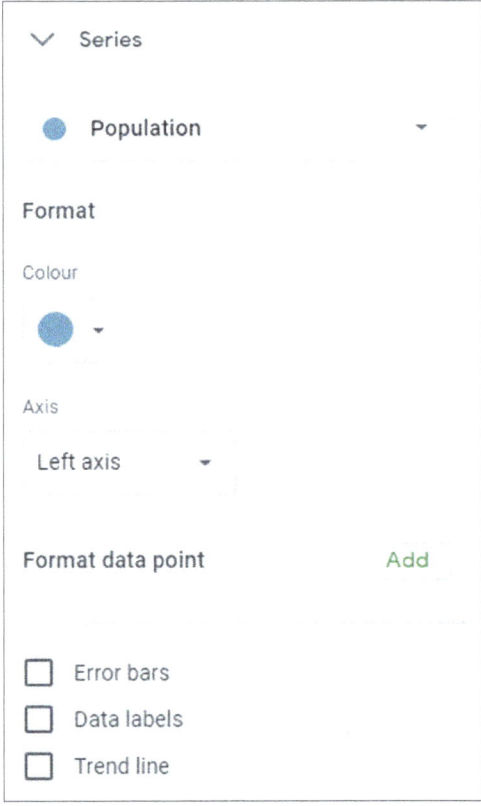

To format individual bars (or data points), click 'add' next to 'format data point', select the data point (or bar on your chart) you want, then select a color from the color palette.

In the 'legend' section, you can add and format your chart legend.

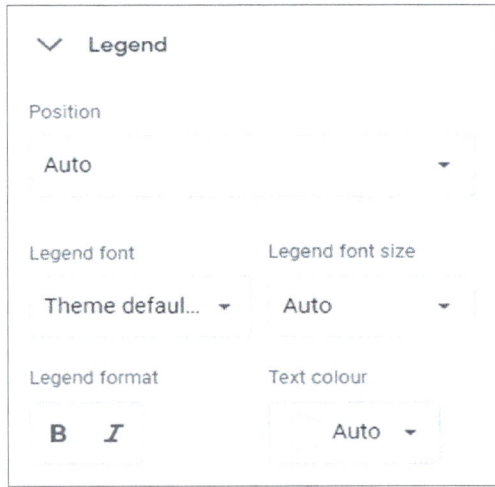

Chapter 5: Tables and Charts

Horizontal Axis

In the 'horizontal axis' section, you can format your horizontal axis labels, etc.

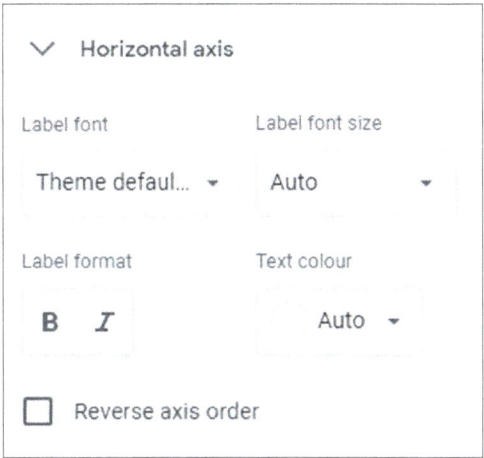

Vertical Axis

In the 'vertical axis' section, you can format your vertical axis labels, etc.

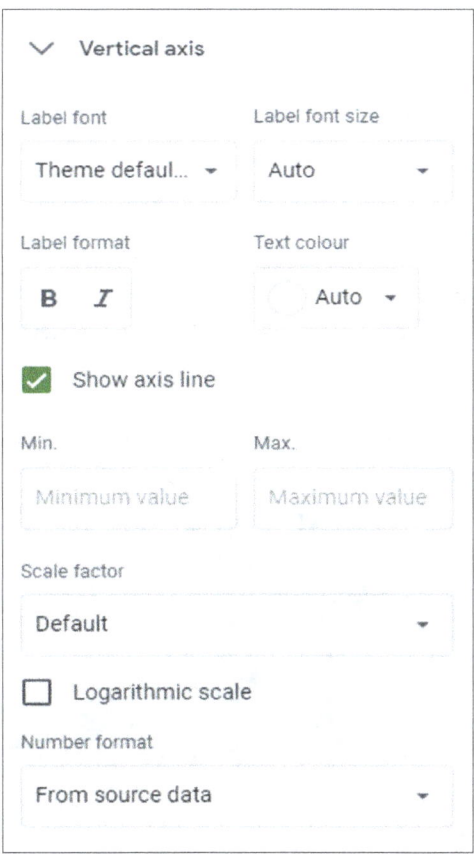

125

Chapter 5: Tables and Charts

Gridlines and Ticks

In the 'gridlines and ticks' section, you can adjust the scales and spacing for each axis. As well as add gridlines to make your chart easier to read.

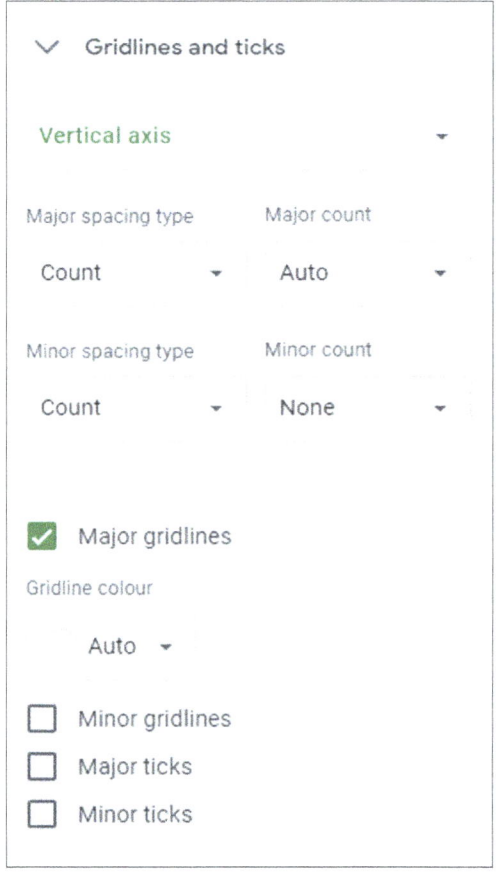

Using the sections described above, experiment with some of these settings and see what your chart looks like. Here, I've added a chart title, added labels to the x and y axis, and changed the color of the chart.

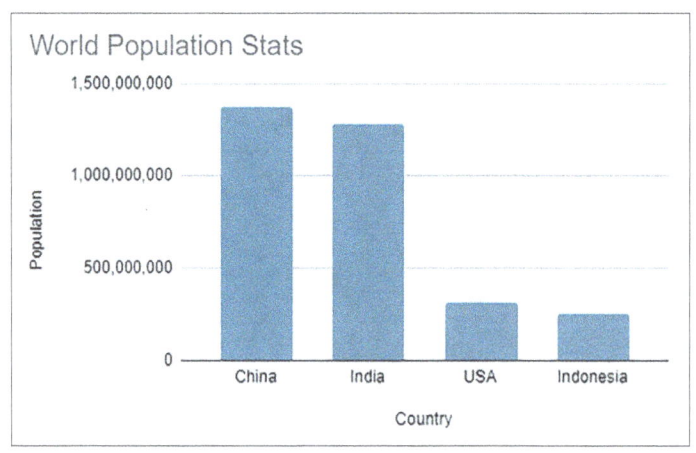

Chapter 5: Tables and Charts

Download & Publish Chart

You can download a chart as a PNG or PDF. To do this click on your chart to select it, then click the small 'link' icon on the top right. Select 'open source' from the popup menu.

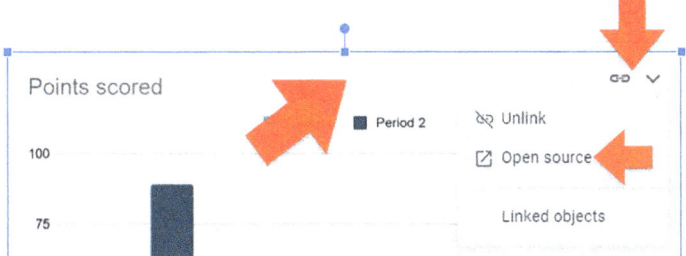

Your chart will open up in a spreadsheet. Click on your chart to select it, then click the three dots icon on the top right. To download the chart, go down to 'download', then select PNG to download the chart as an image.

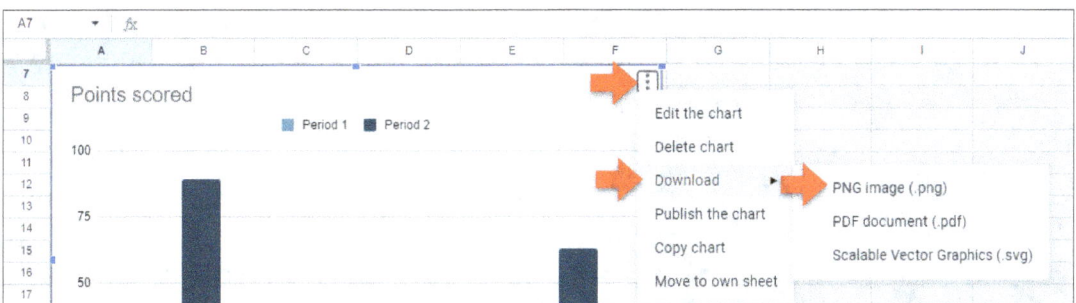

If you want to publish the chart to the web - ie create a link to send to other people, click the three dots icon on the top right of the chart, select 'publish the chart'. Click 'publish'.

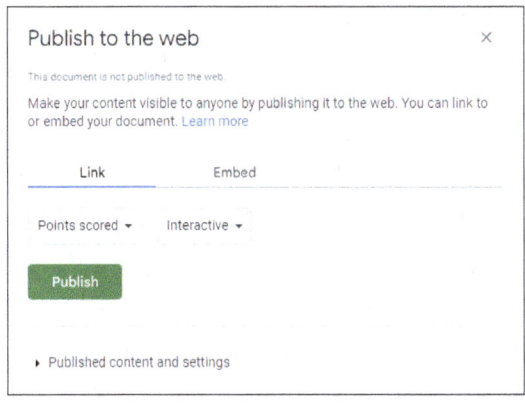 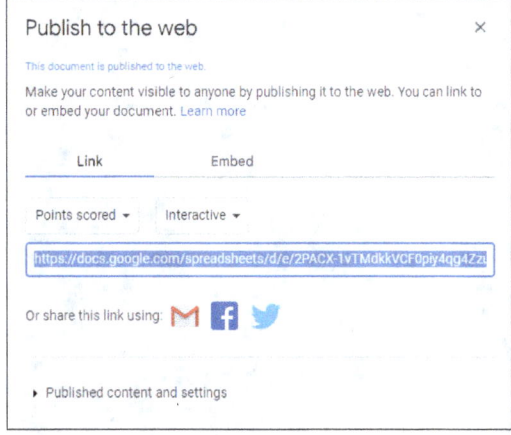

You can copy and paste the highlighted link into an email or message.

127

6 Sharing and Collaboration

One of Google Docs main advantages is it's sharing and real-time collaboration features.

This means you can share a file with others allowing them to edit the document and add to the project.

You can also communicate with your co-editors, see which changes have been made, and add comments.

In this section, we'll go through document collaboration. We'll find out how to share a document with other users, how to comment, edit, and work on a document with other people.

- Sharing a Document
- Accepting the Invitation to Collaborate
- Editing Shared Documents
- Sharing a Link
- Restricted Links
- People without Google Accounts
- Stop Sharing a File

Have a look at the video resources section. Open your web browser and navigate to the following website.

elluminetpress.com/sharing-googledocs

Chapter 6: Sharing & Collaboration

Sharing a Document

In this demo, lets share a document with two other users who will be collaborating on it. The setup is as follows. I will be sharing a document from my laptop with Sophie on her chromebook and Claire on her tablet.

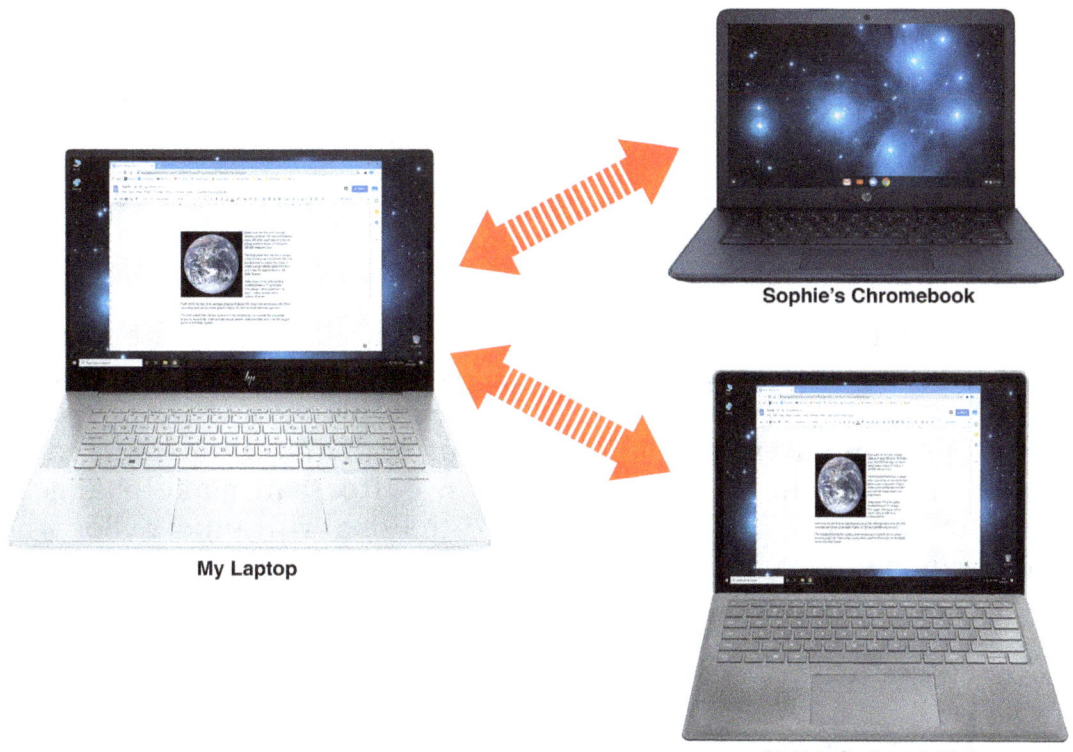

These devices could be anywhere in the world that has an internet connection.

To share a document, first open the one you want to share, then click the 'share' icon on the top right.

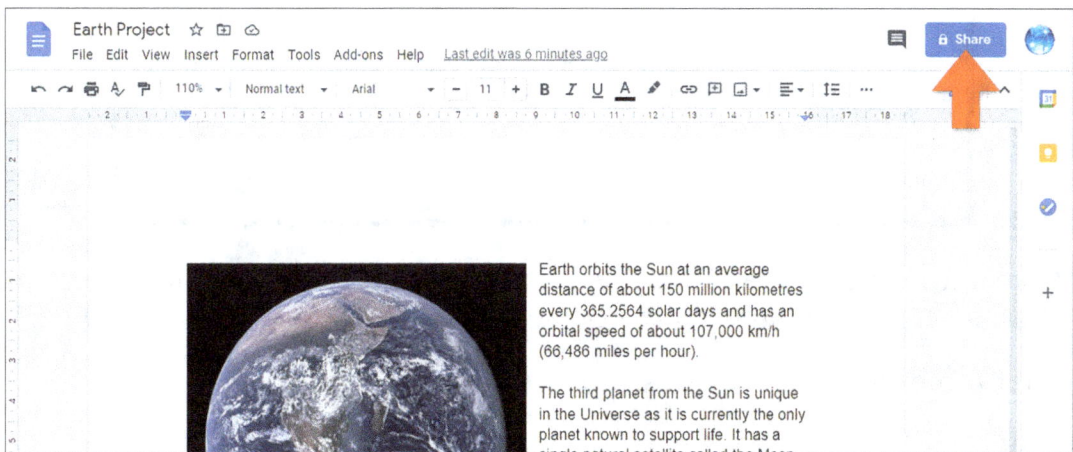

129

Chapter 6: Sharing & Collaboration

In the field at the top of the window, enter the email addresses of the people you want to share the document with. In this demo, I'm sharing my doc with Claire and Sophie, so I'd type in their email addresses.

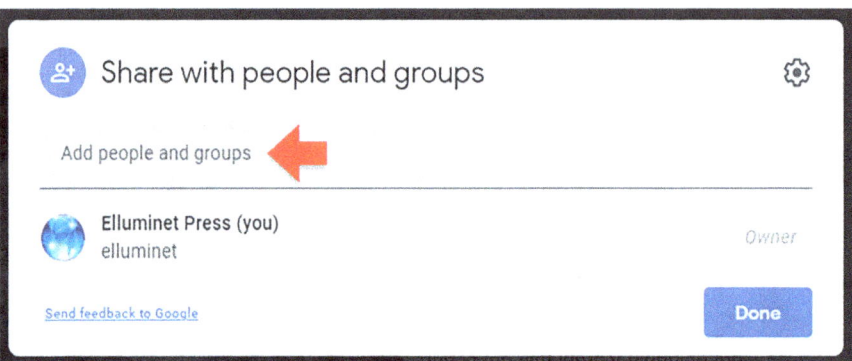

Now set what you want to allow people to do, click the 'editor' drop-down box on the top right. Select a permission from the drop down box. A **viewer** can view the doc, but can't make changes or share it with others. A **commenter** can make comments and suggestions, but can't change or share the doc with others. An **editor** can make changes, accept or reject suggestions, and share the doc with others. For full collaboration set it to 'editor'.

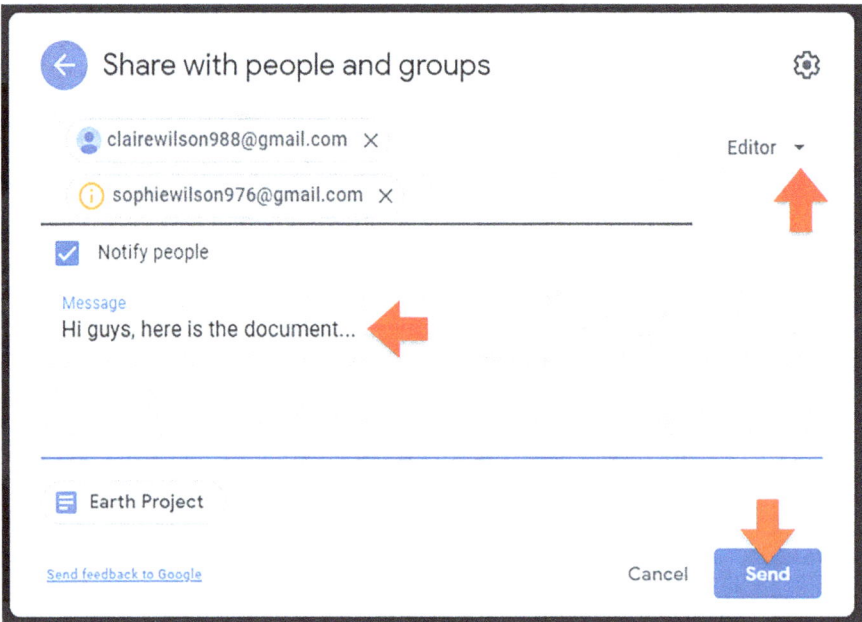

Make sure 'notify people' is ticked. If you enable 'notify people', all email address will be included in the message.

Enter a message, in the 'message' field.

Click 'send'.

Chapter 6: Sharing & Collaboration

Accepting the Invitation to Collaborate

If someone has shared a document with you in Google Docs, go to your email and open the invitation. Here on Claire's surface tablet, is the invitation to the document that was shared with her from my laptop in the previous section. Just click on the 'open in docs' button. This will open the shared document.

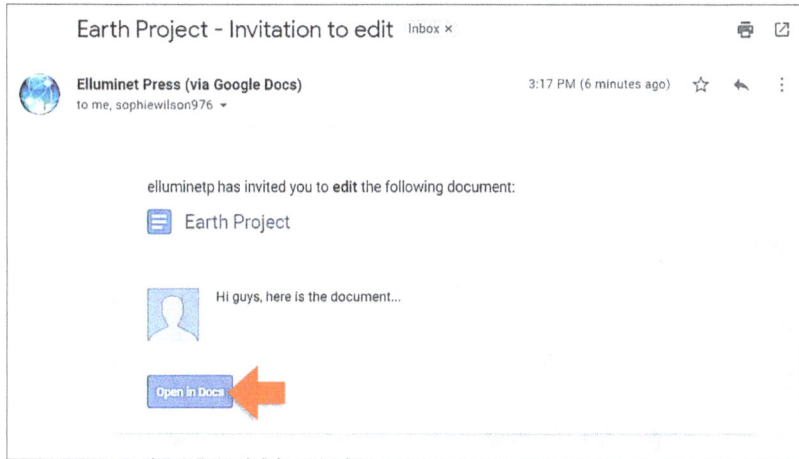

The document will open in Google Docs were you can edit the document, or write comments and chat with other users.

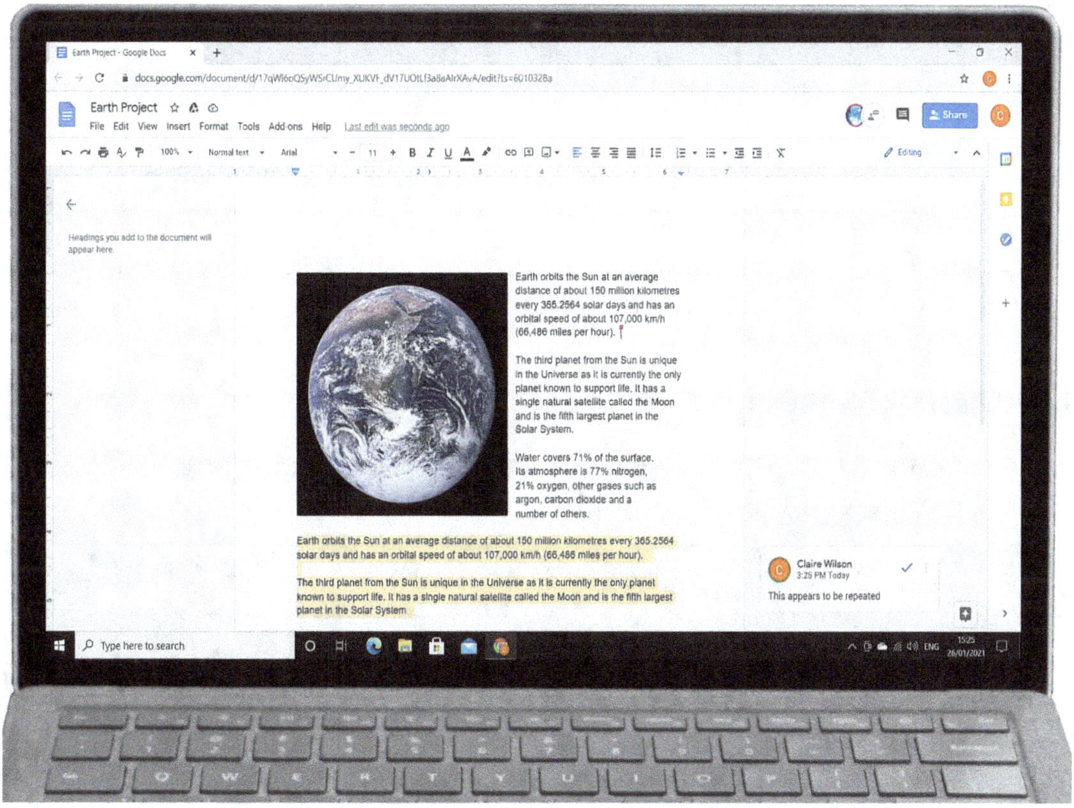

131

Chapter 6: Sharing & Collaboration

Editing Shared Documents

All the user's you've shared the document with can work on it together.

Making Edits

When you're working on a shared document, you'll see each person's edits marked with their username.

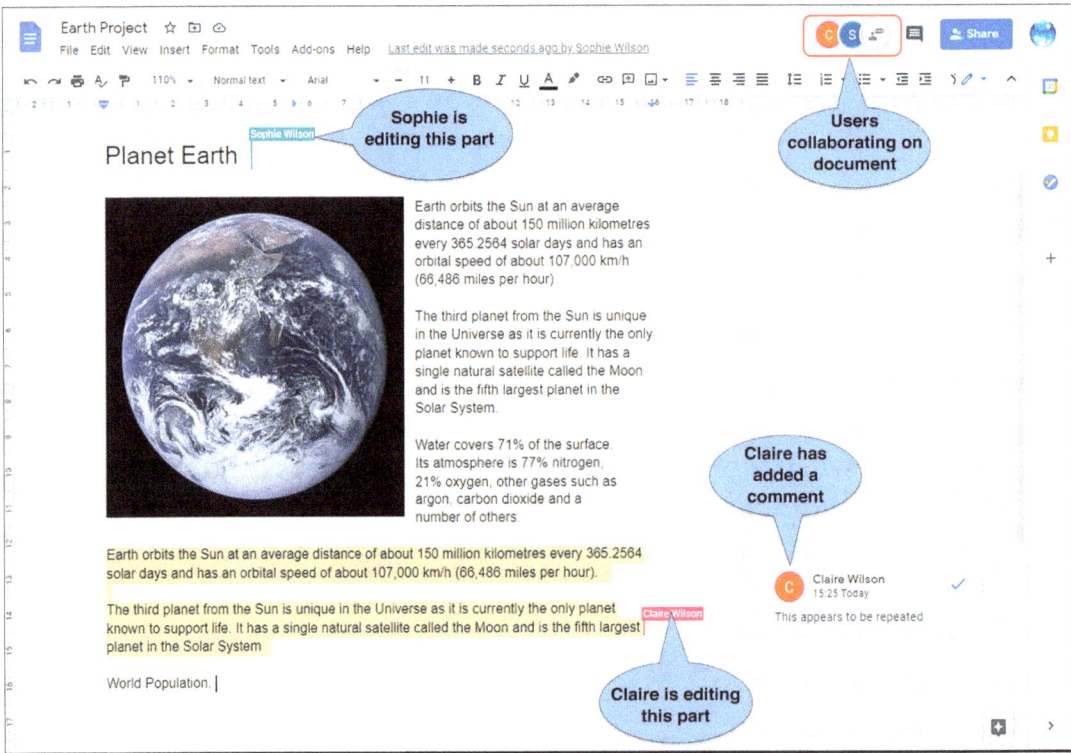

You can edit the document as normal, and see everyone else's contributions - they can see the same.

Chatting with Other Collaborators

You can chat to the other users working on your document. To do this, click the chat icon on the top right.

Chapter 6: Sharing & Collaboration

Use the chat window on the right hand side, enter your message in the field at the bottom right.

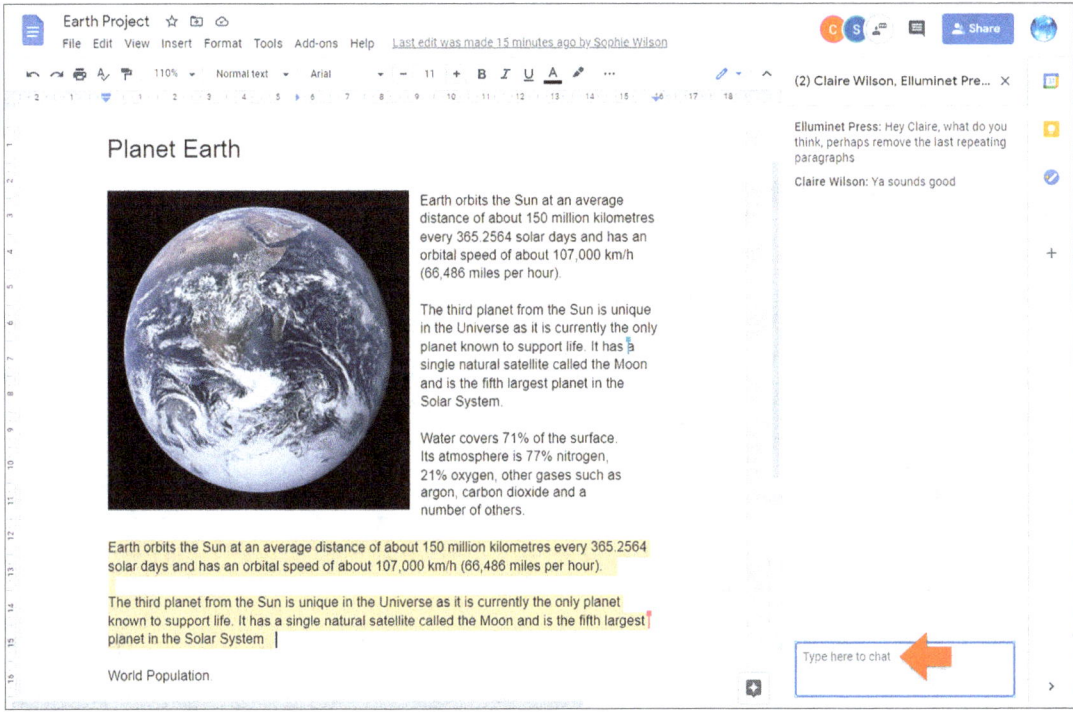

Making Comments

You can also comment on any part of the document. To do this, select the part of the text, then click the blue '+' comment icon that appears on the right hand side.

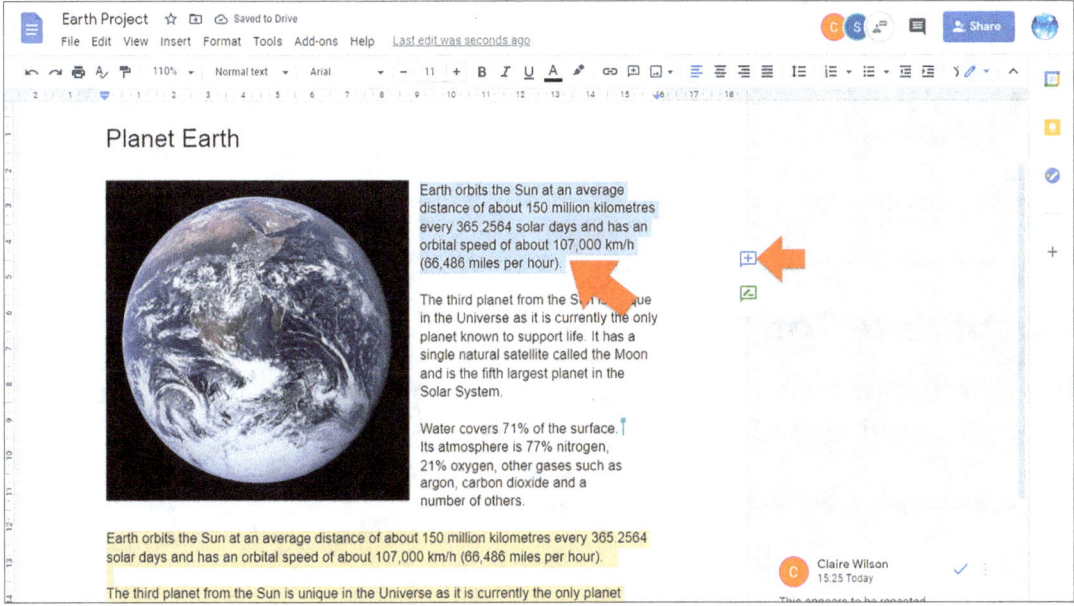

133

Chapter 6: Sharing & Collaboration

Enter your comment in the field on the right hand side. Click 'comment' to post your comment.

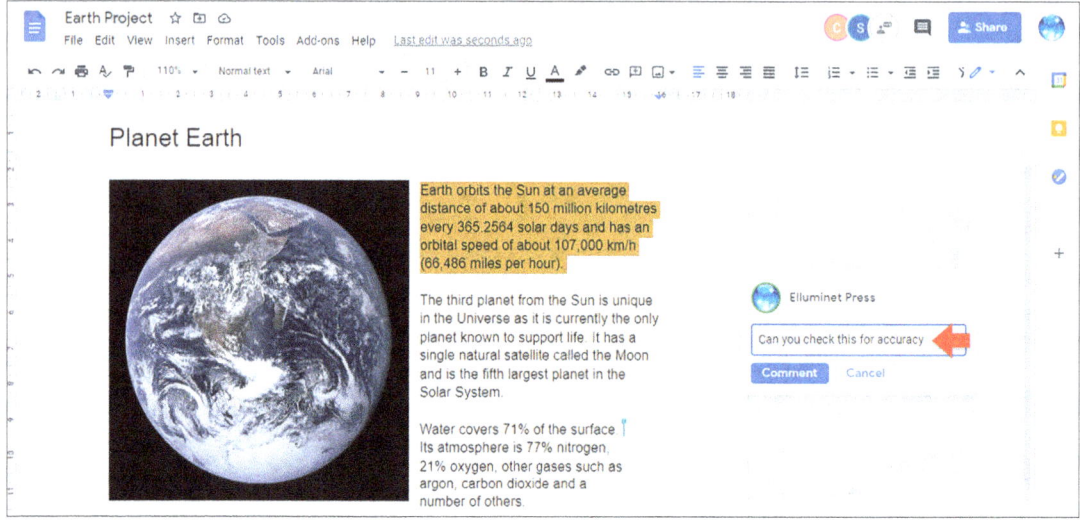

Reply to Comment

If you want to reply to a comment, click on it in the side bar on the right hand side.

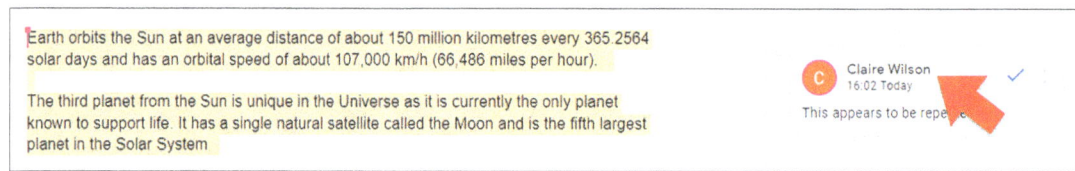

Enter your comment in the text field, then click 'reply' to post.

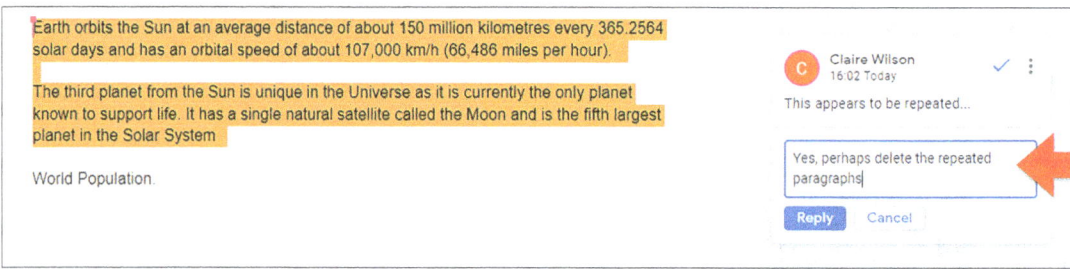

Resolve a Comment

If you're happy the comment has been resolved, click the tick icon on the right hand side of the comment box.

Chapter 6: Sharing & Collaboration

Making Suggestions

This feature works like Microsoft Word's track changes function, where you can see the changes made by other users. The suggestion feature allows you to make changes to the Doc that other users can then accept or reject the changes.

To start, you'll need to go into 'suggesting' mode. To do this, click the 'edit mode' icon on the top right. Select 'suggesting' from the drop down menu.

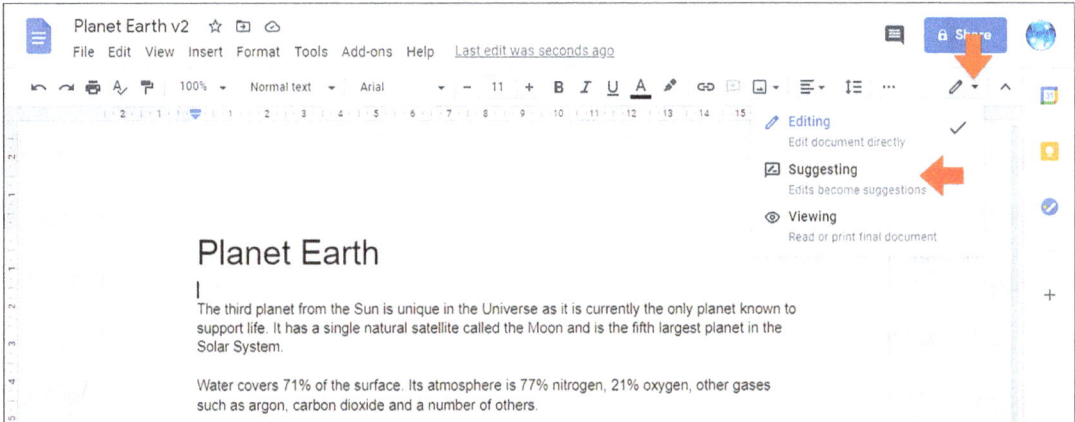

Now make your suggestions. For example, I'm going to suggest a different layout for the second paragraph in the example above.

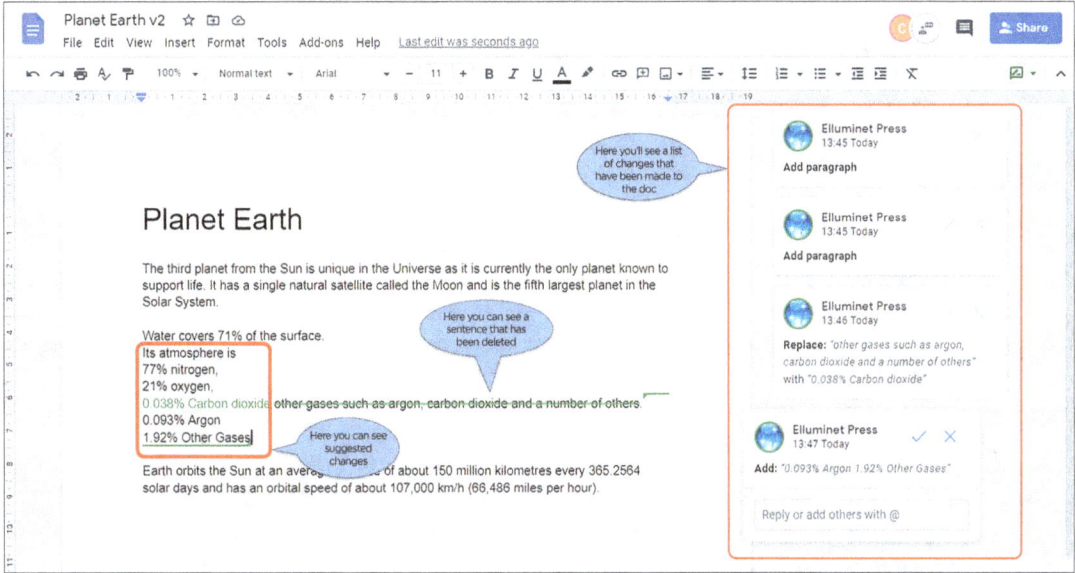

Everything a user types in under suggesting mode, appears in green text with a corresponding comment box on the right hand panel, that allows users with 'editor' share permissions to accept, reject or reply to the suggestion.

Chapter 6: Sharing & Collaboration

To comment on a suggestion, click on it in the right hand panel, then type your comment into the text field.

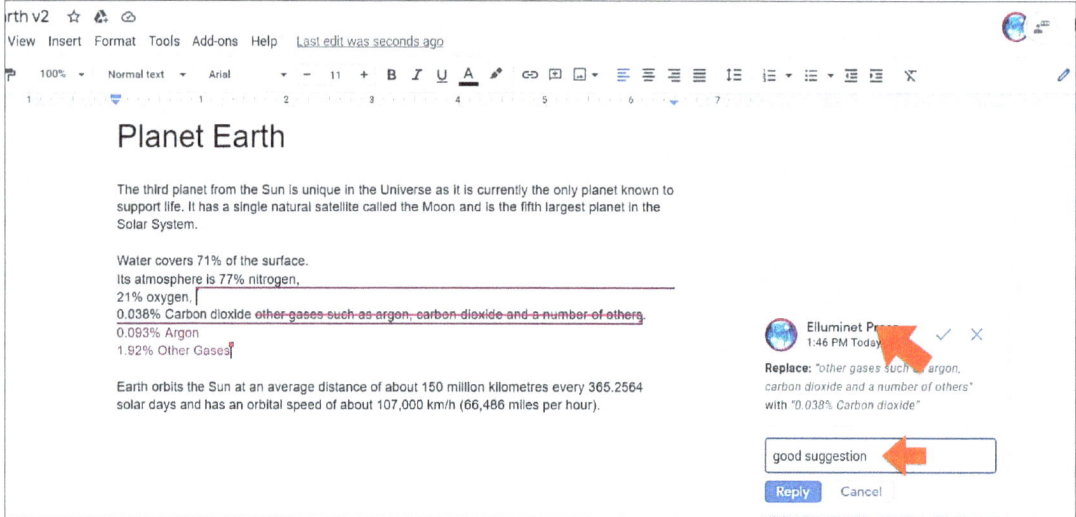

To accept the suggestion, click on the 'tick' icon on the comment box in the right hand panel.

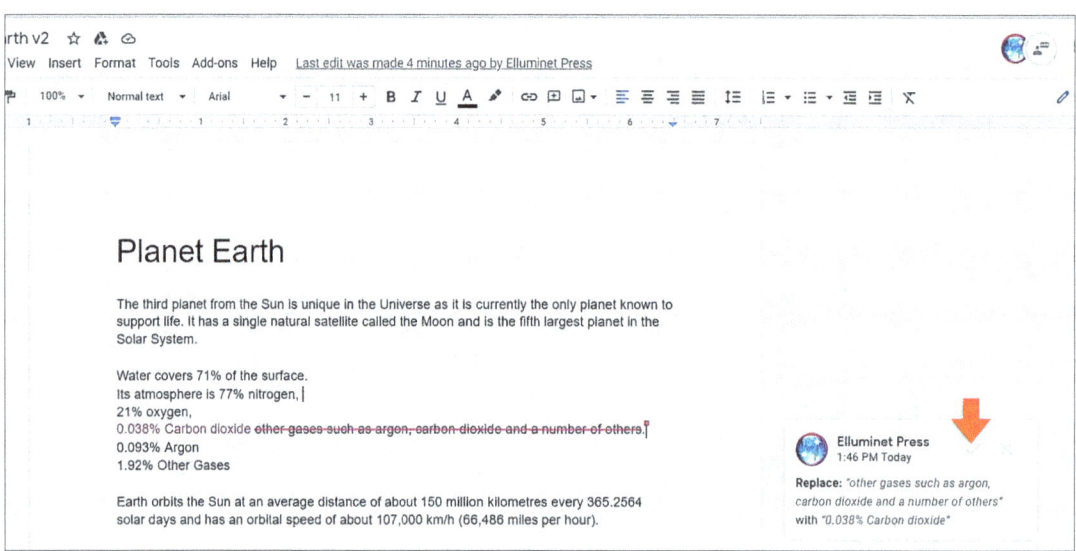

To reject a suggestion click the 'x' icon.

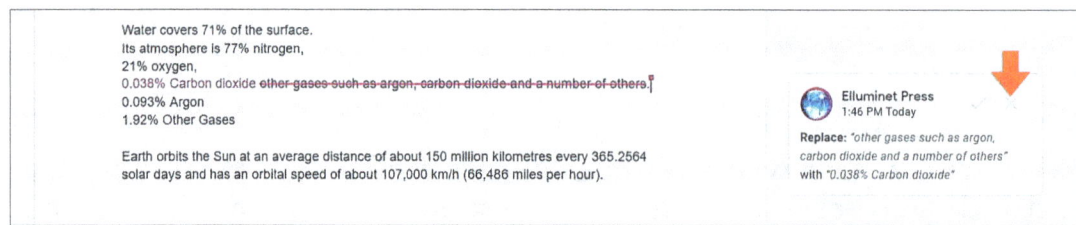

This will remove the suggestion and return to the original text.

Chapter 6: Sharing & Collaboration

Sharing a Link

You can share a link with someone who may or may not even have a Google account. To do this open the document you want to share, then click the 'share' icon on the top right.

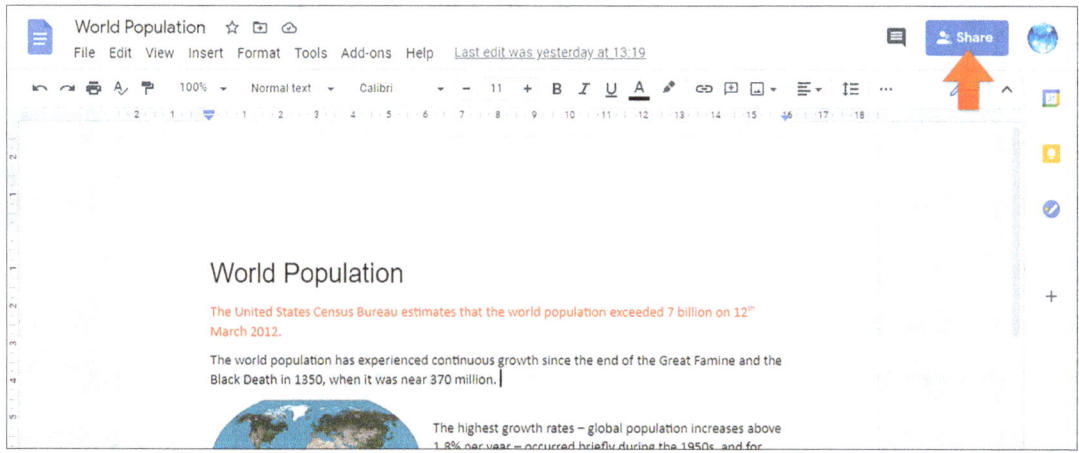

Sharing a Link with Anyone

Sharing a link with anyone means as it's name suggests, anyone who has the link can view the document. This is not the most secure way to share a file with someone, so don't use it to share documents with sensitive information.

Click 'change to anyone with link' in the bottom section.

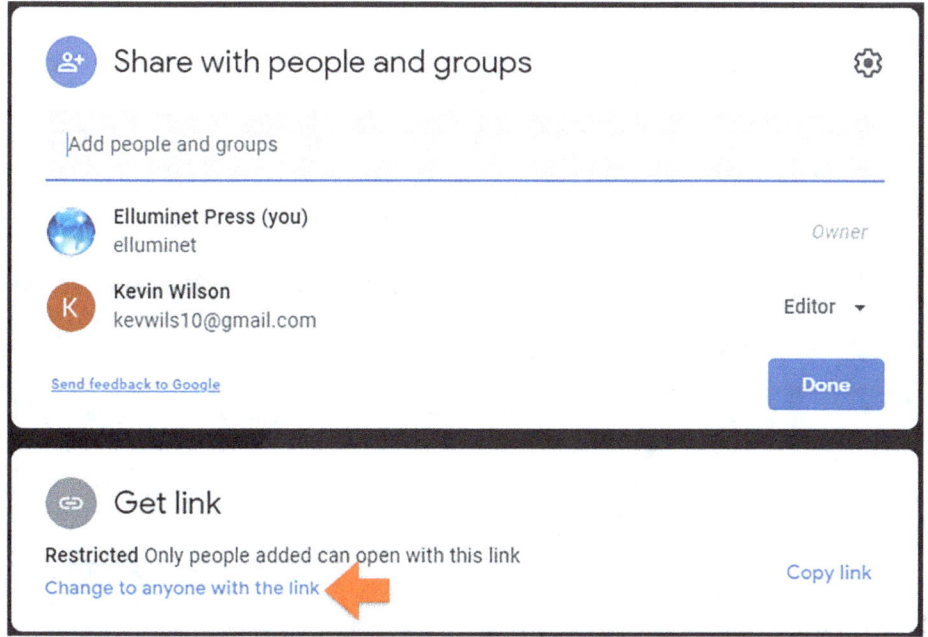

137

Chapter 6: Sharing & Collaboration

Google Docs will generate a link for you.

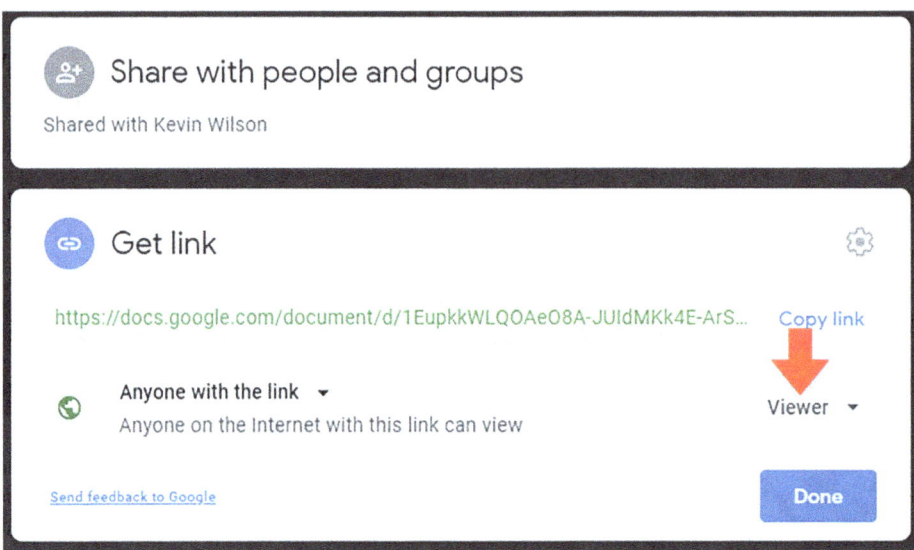

Set the 'view' permissions. Click on the 'viewer' drop down box, then select an option. If you want the person to just view the document, select 'viewer'. If you want the person to be able to edit the document, select 'editor'.

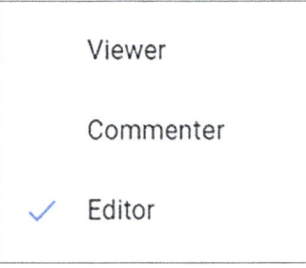

Click 'copy' to copy the link to your clipboard.

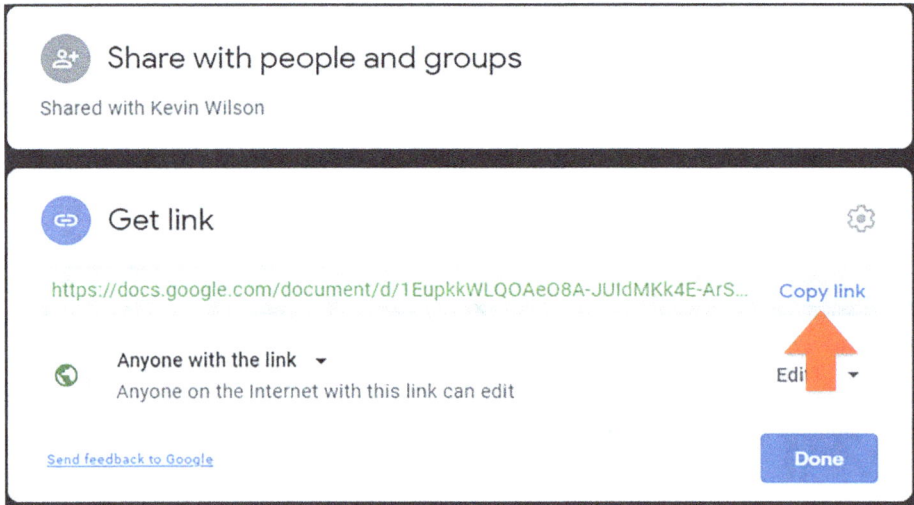

Chapter 6: Sharing & Collaboration

Paste the link into an email or message to send to the person you want to share with. Type a message, then press CTRL - V on your keyboard to paste in the link.

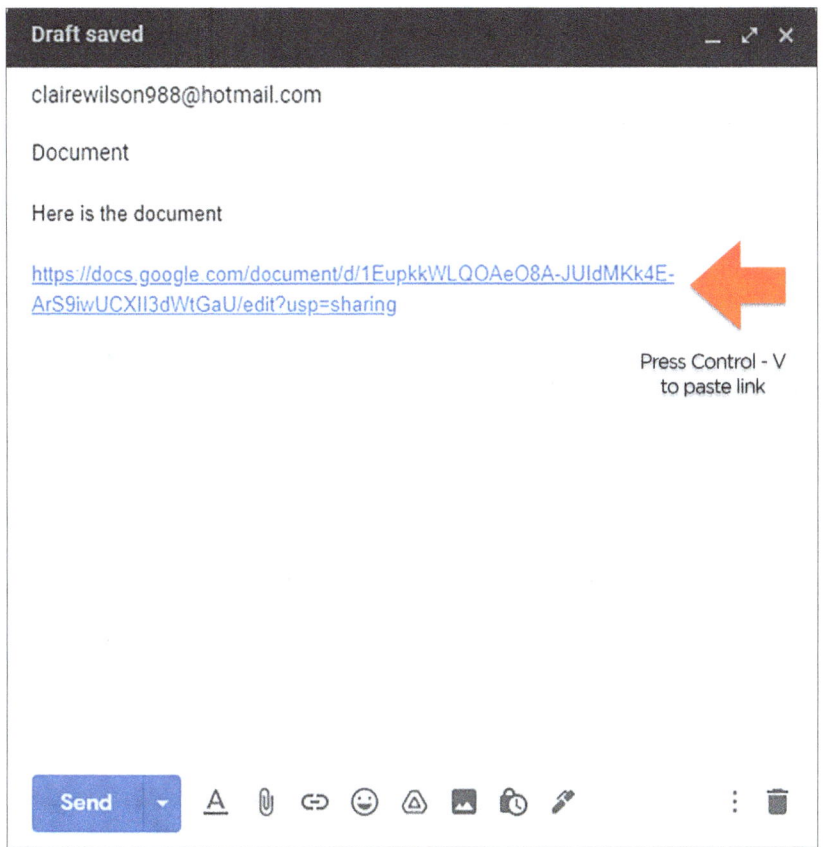

Click 'send' when you're done.

Restricted Links

To generate a link to send to people you've shared a document with, click the 'share' icon on the top right.

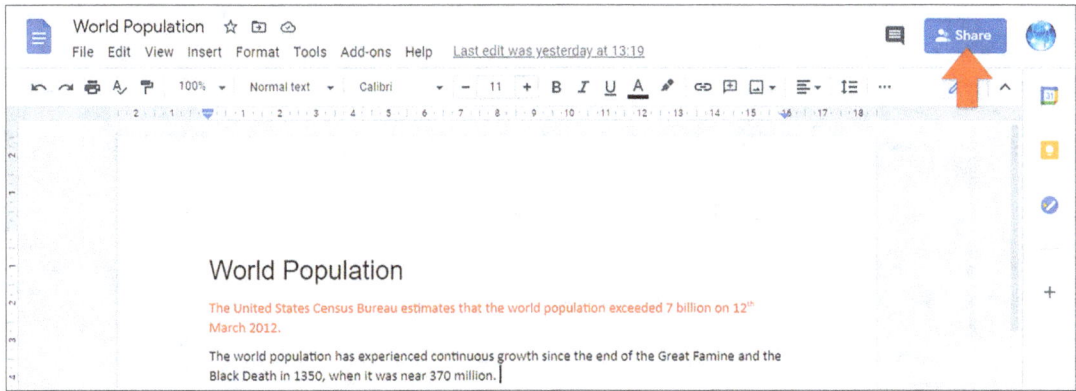

139

Chapter 6: Sharing & Collaboration

You'll see a list of people along the top the document has been shared with. Click 'change' in the bottom section.

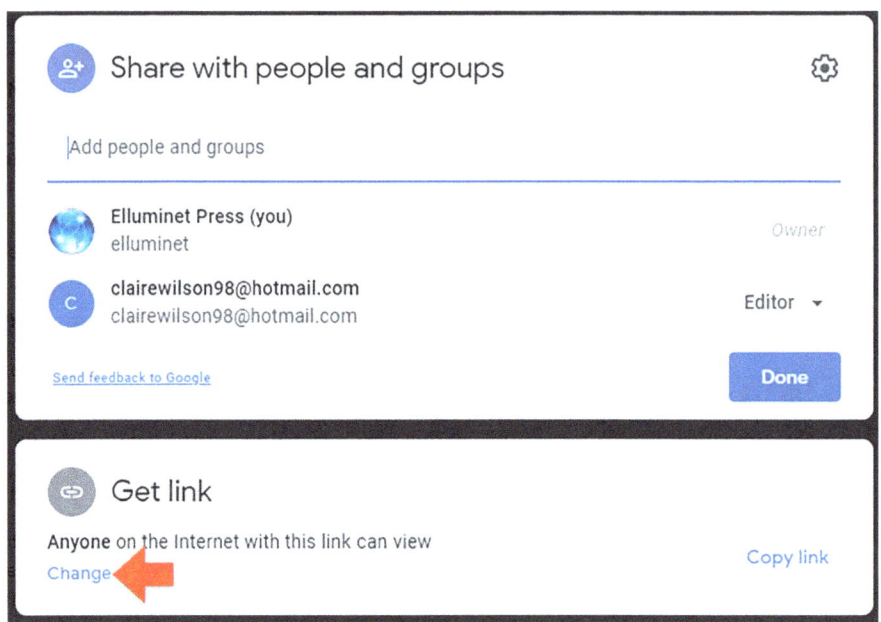

From here, click 'anyone with a link' and change it to 'restricted'.

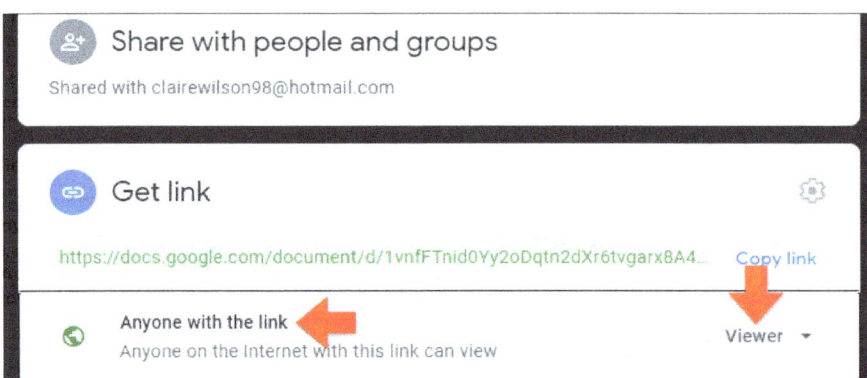

If you want to invite the person to edit the document, select the drop down box on the right, change from 'viewer' to 'editor'.

Click 'copy link' on the right hand side, then click 'done'. Paste the link into an email or message.

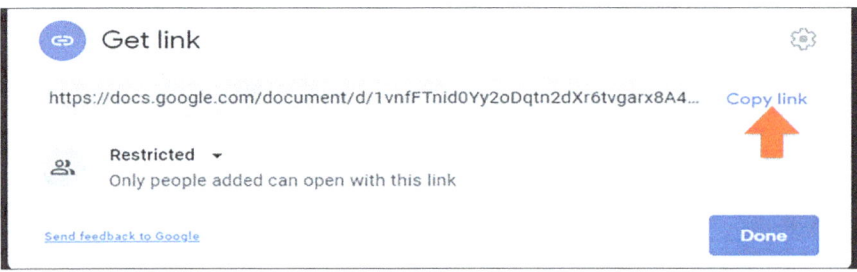

Chapter 6: Sharing & Collaboration

People without Google Accounts

Sharing a link publicly might not be the best option. If the person doesn't have a Google Account, you can still share the file with them. To do this, open the file then click the 'share' icon on the top right.

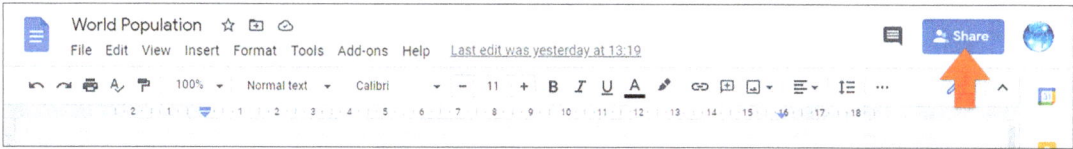

Enter the person's email address in the top field and press enter on your keyboard.

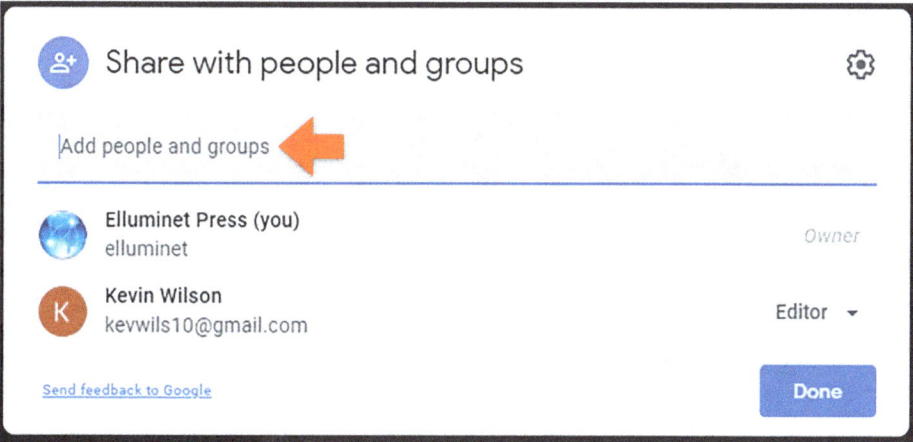

Add a message, then select the permission from the drop down box on the right hand side. Set it to 'editor' if you want this person to be able to edit the document.

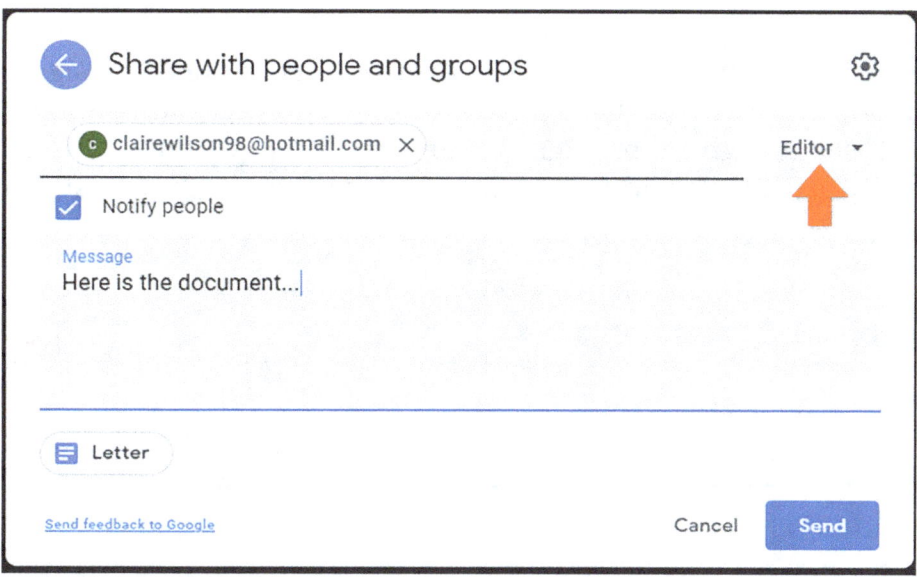

Chapter 6: Sharing & Collaboration

Click 'send', then select 'share anyway' if prompted.

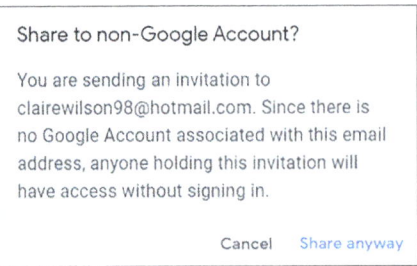

When the other person checks their email, they'll receive an invitation. To view the document, click 'open in docs'.

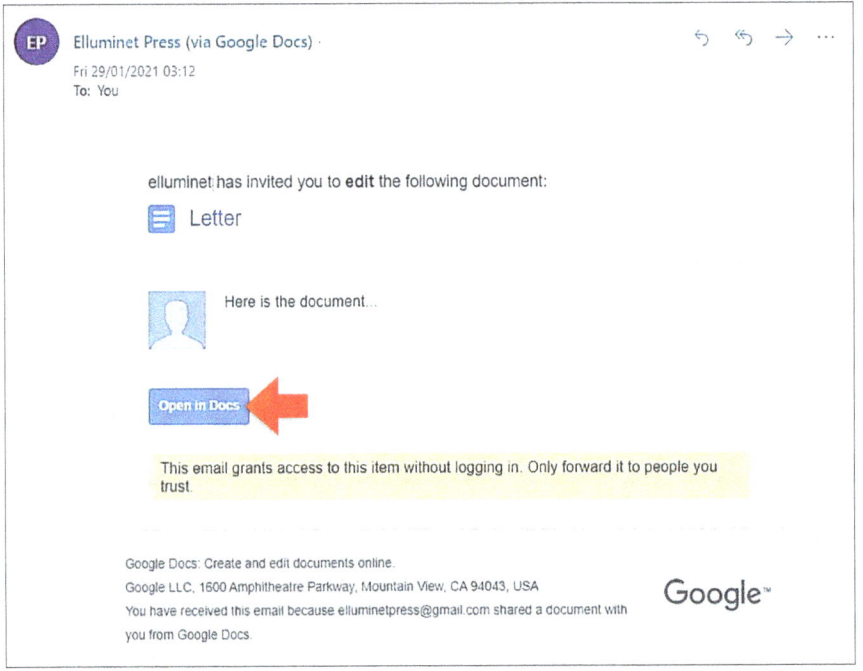

If the person doesn't have a Google Account, they'll need to sign up for one before they can edit the file. When the other person opens the file, they will see a 'sign in' or 'sign up' link on the top right of the screen. To sign up, click 'sign up to edit' and follow the on-screen instructions.

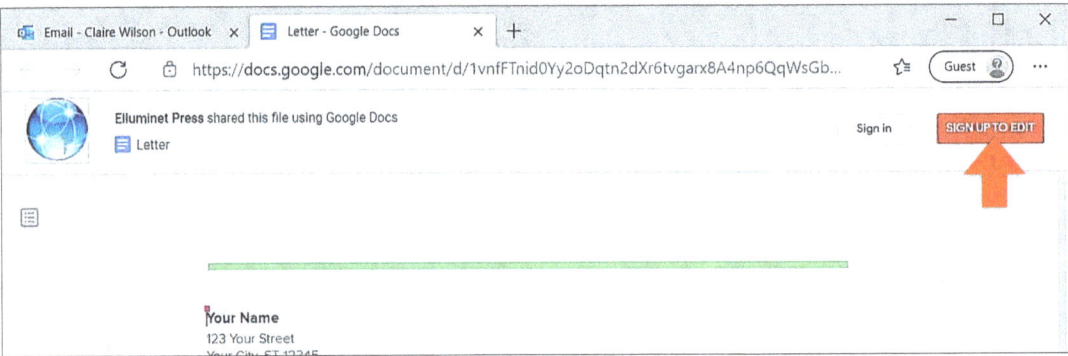

Chapter 6: Sharing & Collaboration

Stop Sharing a File

To stop sharing a file, first open it, then click the 'share' icon on the top right.

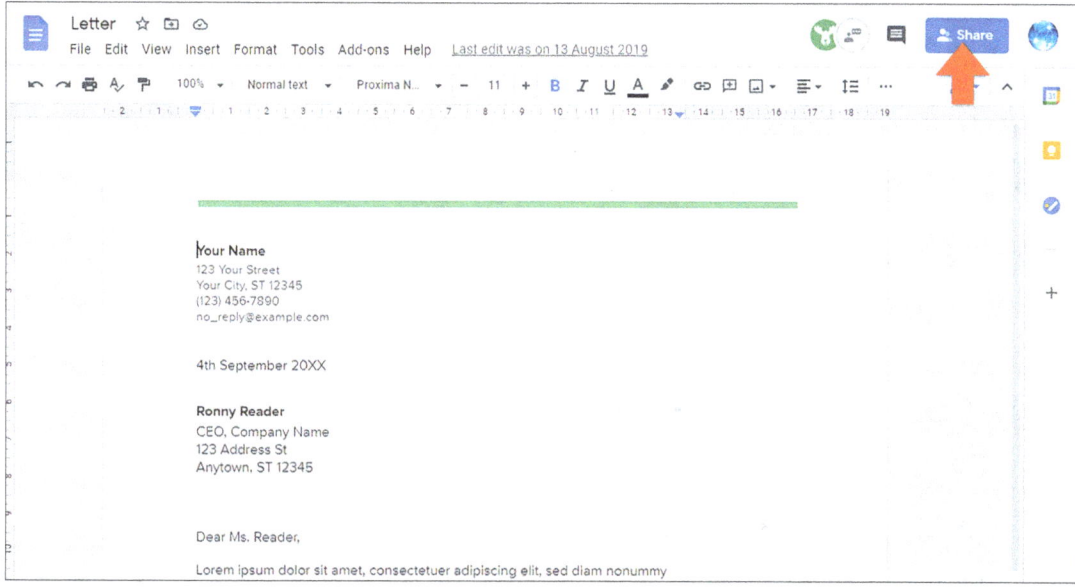

From the 'share with people and groups' section, click the drop down box next to the person you want to remove.

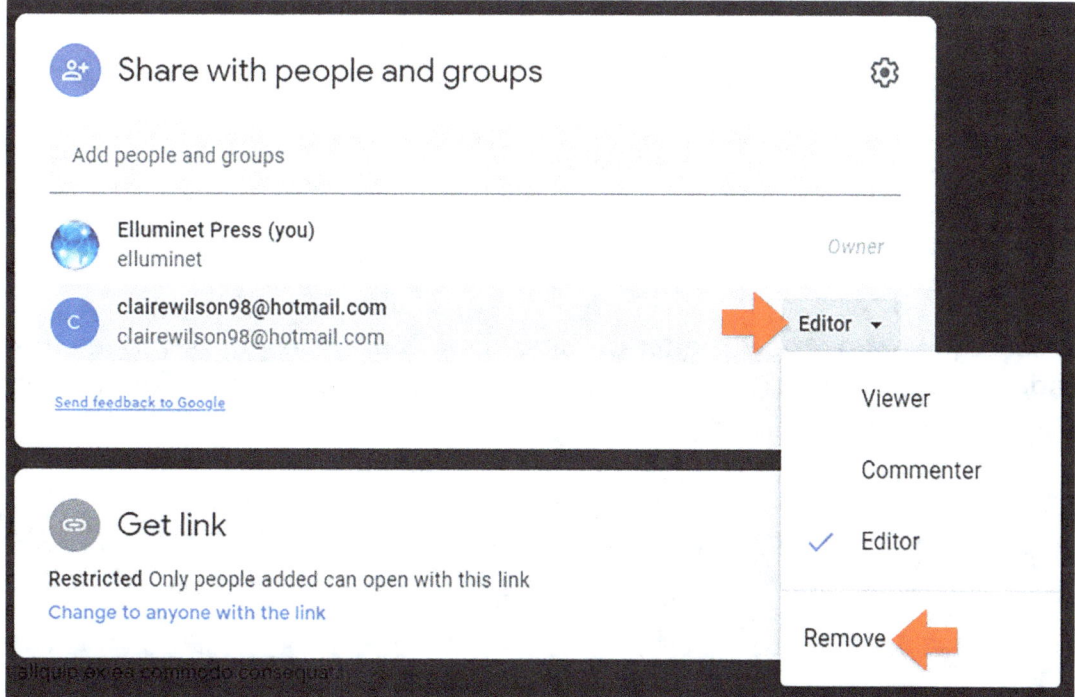

Select 'remove' from the drop down menu. Click 'save' when you're done.

Chapter 6: Sharing & Collaboration

Integrated eSignatures

Google Docs allows users to apply eSignatures directly to documents, making it ideal for contracts, agreements, and acknowledgments that need to be signed without having to leave the document environment or using external applications. Users can insert signature fields, send documents for signing via email, and track the status of signature requests in real time.

Integrated eSignatures are only available to users with Google Workspace subscriptions, such as Workspace Individual, Business Standard, Business Plus, and Enterprise editions. Free personal Google Accounts do not support this feature.

Adding an eSignature

Open the document that needs to be signed, or create a new one

In the Tools menu, select eSignature.

You will see a side panel open up on the right. Click the top dropdown box which is labeled "Insert fields for", you will see Signer one.

If you need to add more signer names, click "Manage signers", then click "add another signer". You should also give them meaningful names. Click "save" when you're done.

Chapter 6: Sharing & Collaboration

Next, click in the document where you want the signature field to appear. For example, in my publishing contract, I want the publisher signature field under 'publisher'.

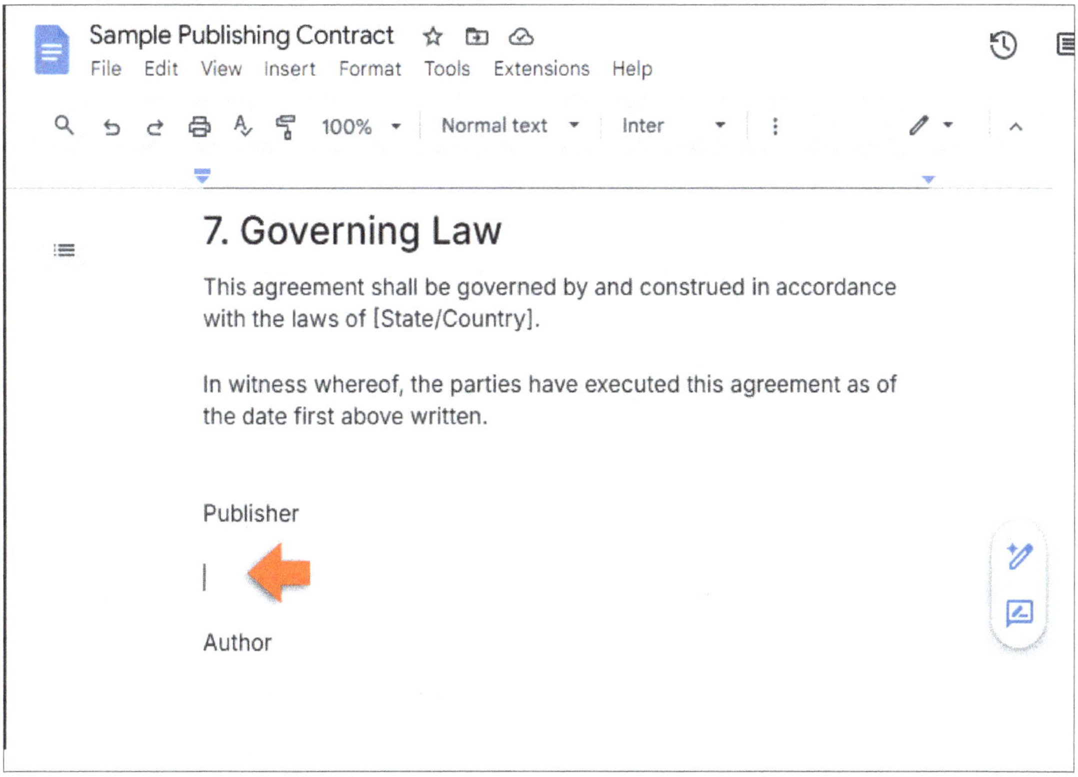

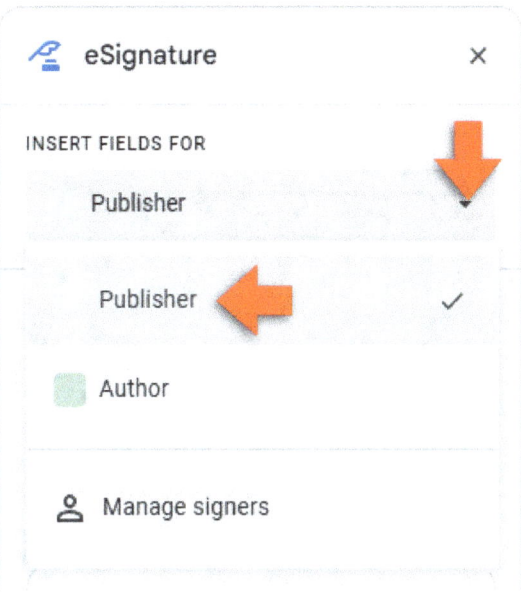

From the eSignature panel on the right, in the "insert fields for" drop down, select the signature for the party you want to add. In this case its my publisher signature.

145

Chapter 6: Sharing & Collaboration

Then select "signature". You'll see a signature field appear in your document.

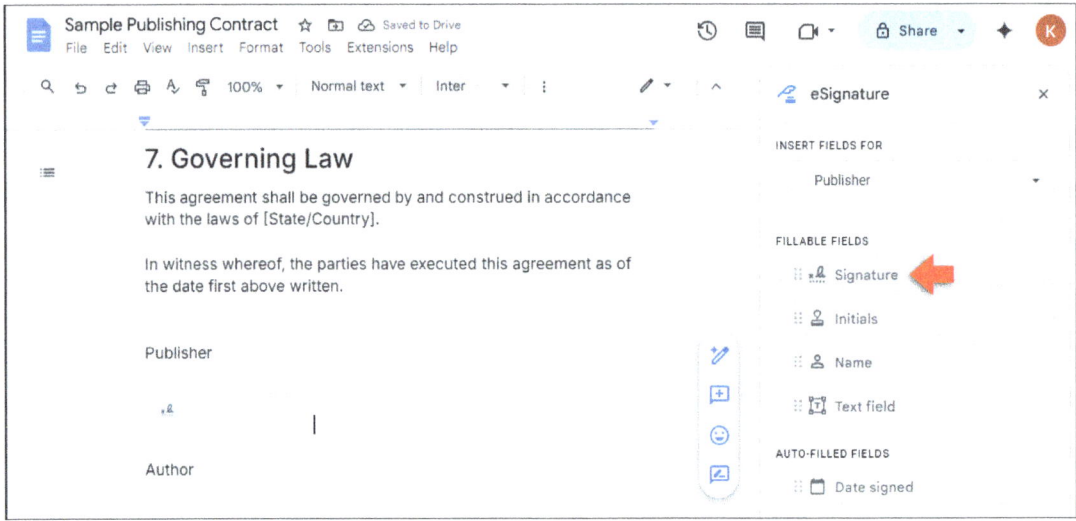

Do the same for any other signers you have, if you have more than one.

You can also add Initials — the signer will add their initials (optional, e.g., bottom of each page).

Name — the signer will type their full name (optional).

Text field — the signer can enter other information (e.g., job title, address).

Date signed — automatically captures the date when the signer completes the document.

Once you're done, click "request eSignature".

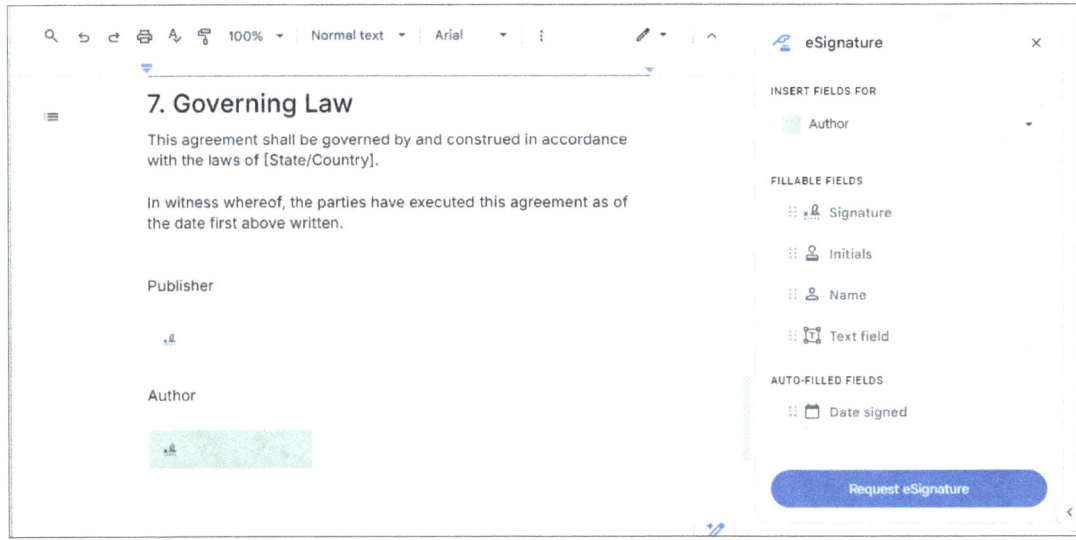

Chapter 6: Sharing & Collaboration

Fill in the email addresses of all parties that need to sign. Then click 'request 'eSignature'.

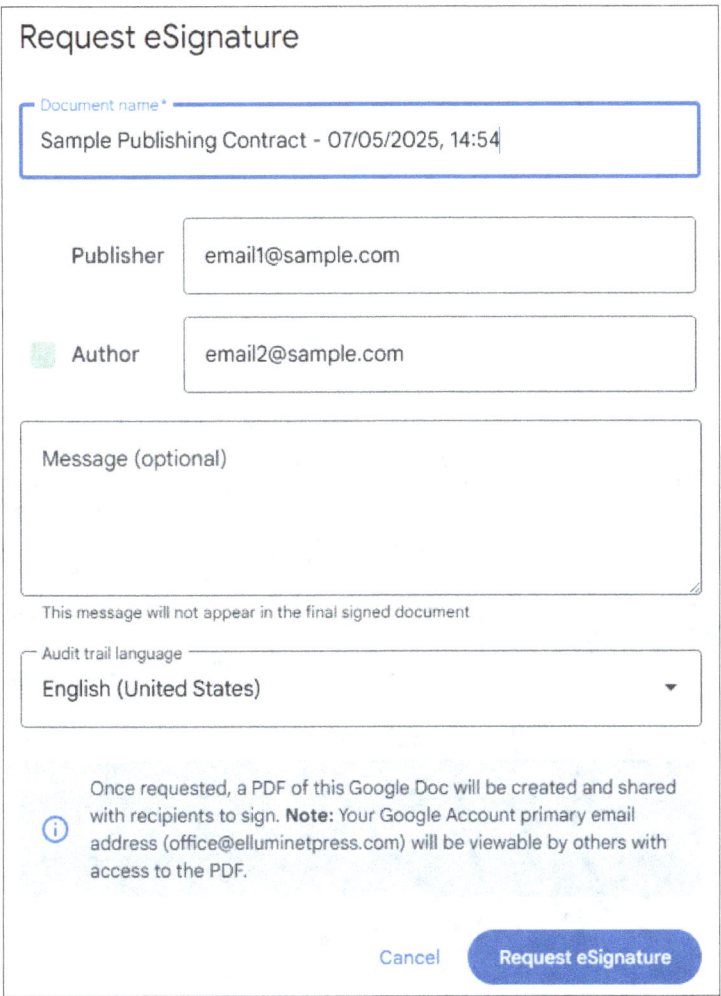

Signing a Document

To sign a document, open the email, then click on 'open'.

147

Chapter 6: Sharing & Collaboration

Click on the signature field in the document

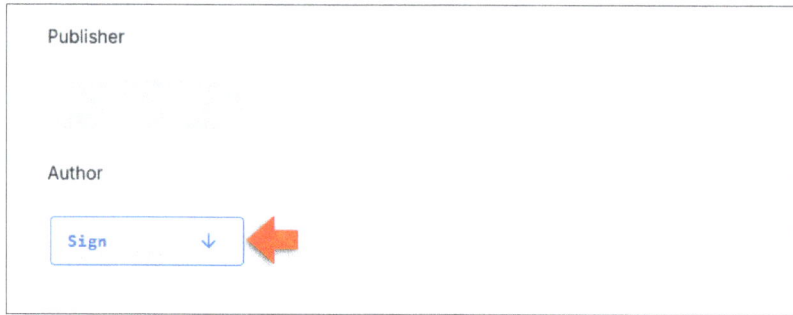

Fill in the details.

Click 'mark as complete' along the top of the screen.

Document Approvals

The Document Approvals feature in Google Docs provides a built-in workflow for reviewing and approving documents. Rather than relying on email exchanges or informal comments, users can request approvals directly within a document, track pending approvals, and view final decisions in a centralized, organized manner.

Chapter 6: Sharing & Collaboration

This is particularly useful for teams that require structured review processes for reports, proposals, contracts, or other critical documents.

Document Approvals are part of Google Workspace's advanced collaboration tools and are available to users on supported paid Workspace plans. This feature is not accessible through free Google Accounts.

Let's say you're a Marketing Manager preparing a proposal titled "Q3 Marketing Strategy Plan". Before the proposal can be finalized and shared with clients or executives, it must go through an internal review and approval process by your department head and legal team. To initiate an Approval Request, click File then select Approvals. In the right-hand panel, click Make a request.

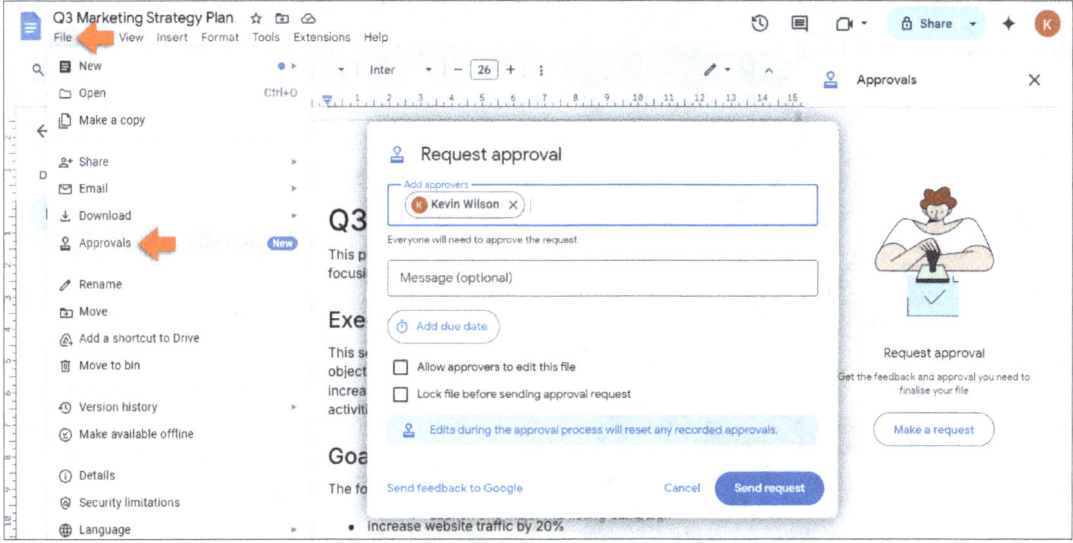

In the 'request approval' dialog box, add one or more approvers by entering their email addresses. You can also set a due date and add a message explaining the request. Click 'send request' when you're done.

Approvers will see a banner above the document when they open it.

To approve a document, click "Approve" on the right-hand side of the banner. Click "view details" to see the list of approvers, their decision statuses, any comments they've made, the requester's information, and the approval timeline.

7 Managing Documents

In this section, we'll take a look at how to save and open documents, convert them to other formats, and how to print them out if you need a hard copy.

We'll also take a look at page and print setup, print margins, and how to scale printouts to paper sizes.

- Opening Documents
- Uploading Documents
- Downloading & Converting Documents
- Printing Documents
- Email as Attachment
- Document Translation
- Define & Lookup
- Spelling & Grammar
- Add Ons

Have a look at the video resources section. Open your web browser and navigate to the following website.

elluminetpress.com/ managing-googledocs

Chapter 7: Managing Documents

Opening Documents

If you're already working on a document, you can open another using the 'file' menu. Just select 'open'.

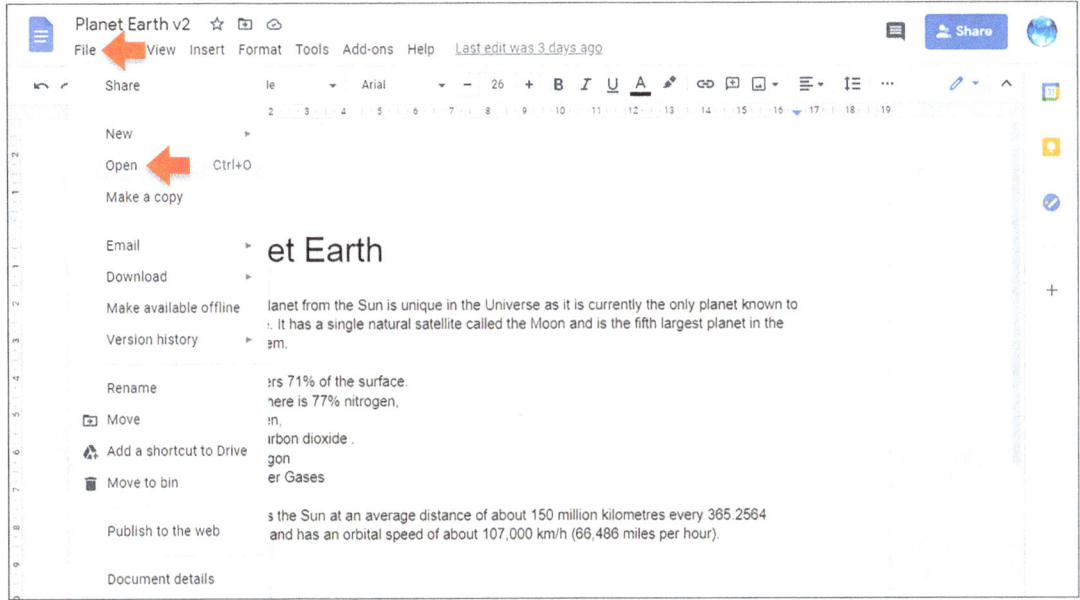

From the 'open' dialog box, navigate to 'My Drive', then select the document you want to open.

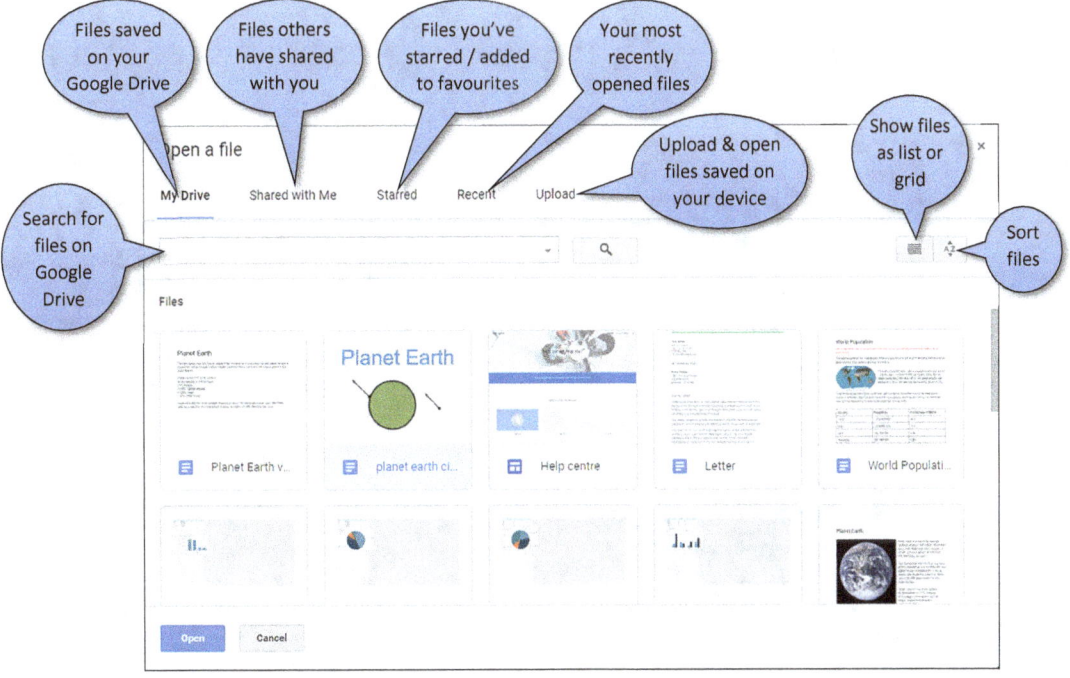

Click 'open' on the bottom left of the dialog box.

Chapter 7: Managing Documents

If you're opening a document from the home screen, click the 'file picker' icon on the right hand side of the screen.

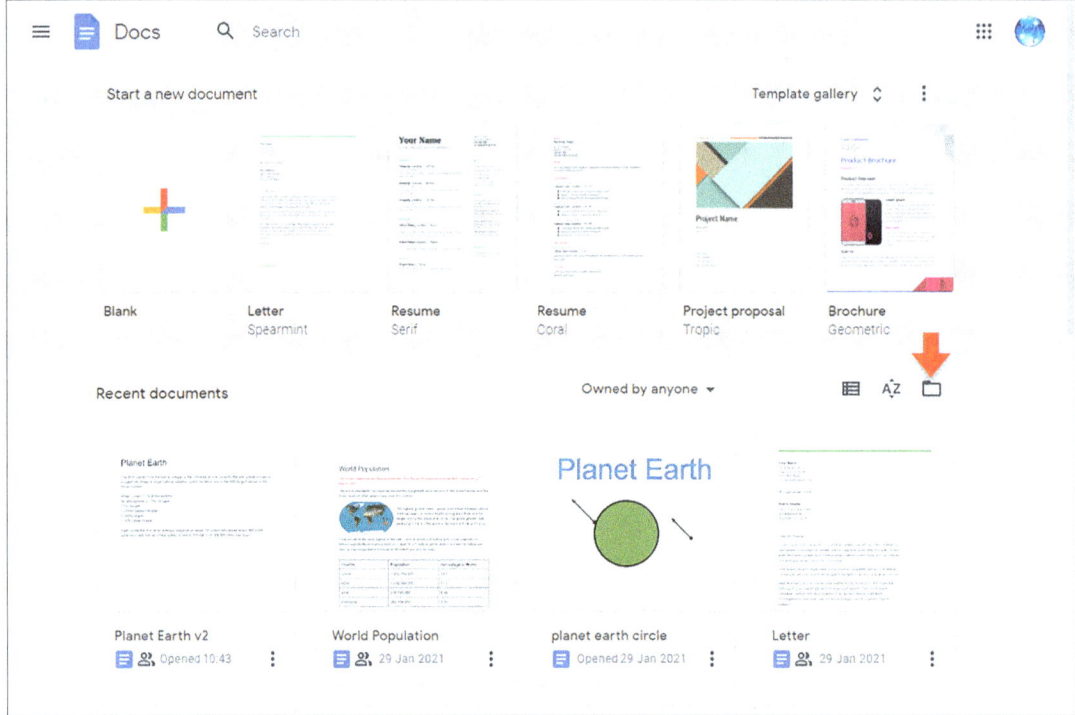

Select the 'My Drive' tab, then click on a file to open.

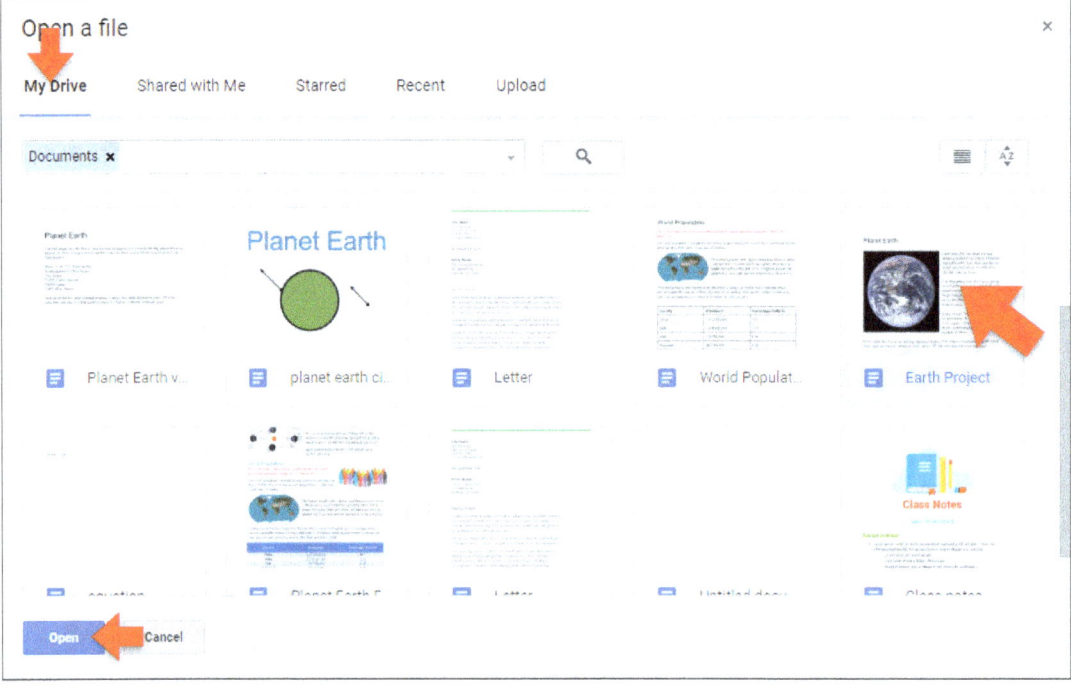

Click 'open' when you're done.

Chapter 7: Managing Documents

Uploading Documents

If you have a document saved on your PC, Mac or Laptop, you can upload it

To upload a document, click on the 'file picker' icon on the right hand side of the home screen.

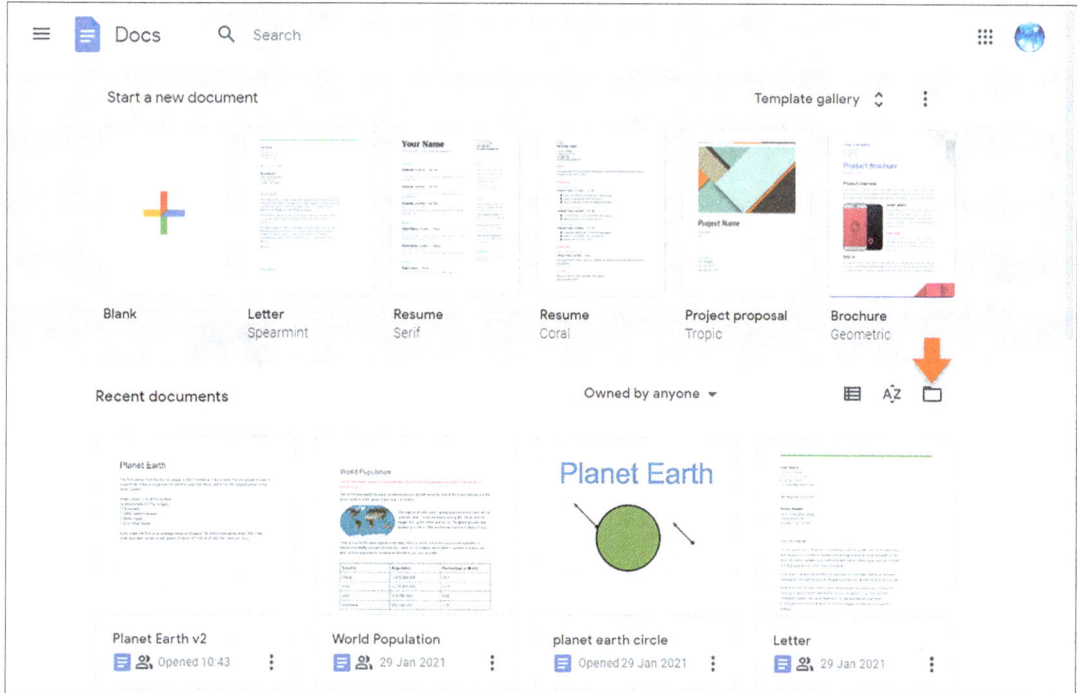

Select the 'upload' tab, then click 'select a file from your device', or 'browse'.

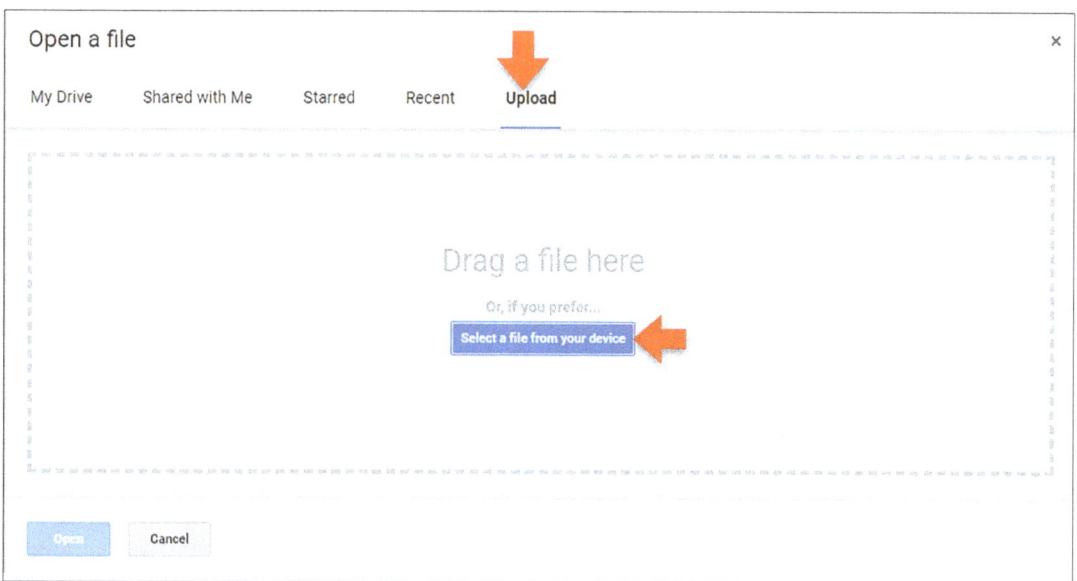

Chapter 7: Managing Documents

Select a document. As we're uploading to Google Docs, you should upload a microsoft word document (.doc or .docx), text file (.txt), or a rich text file (.rtf).

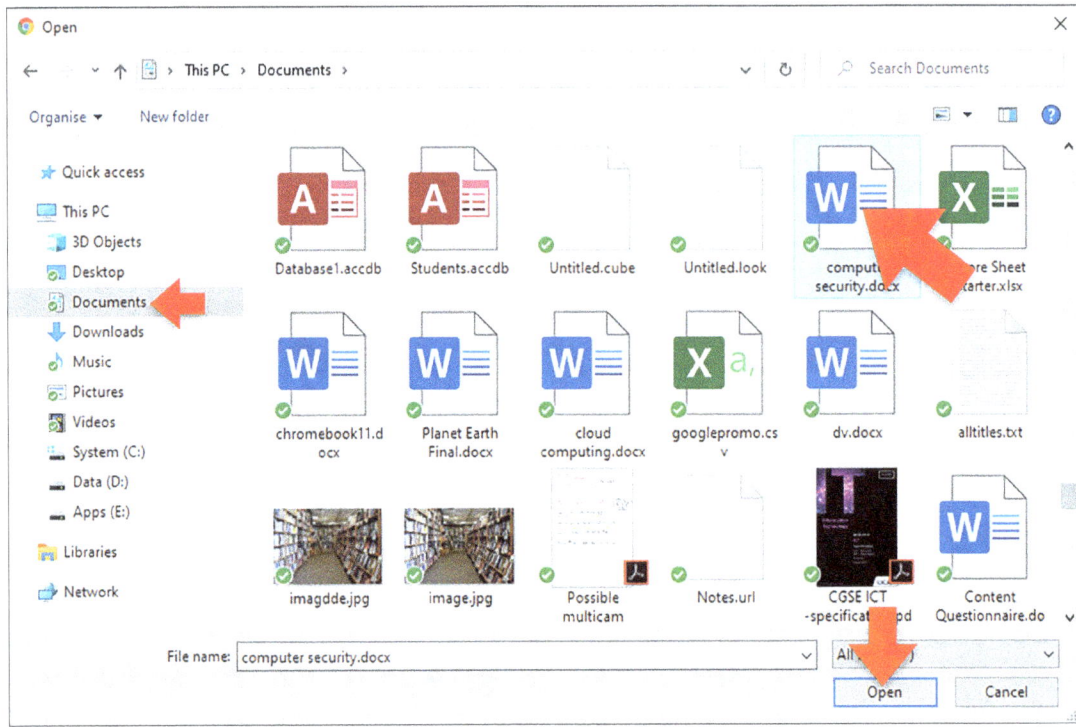

If you've uploaded a Microsoft word document, Google Docs will convert it for you.

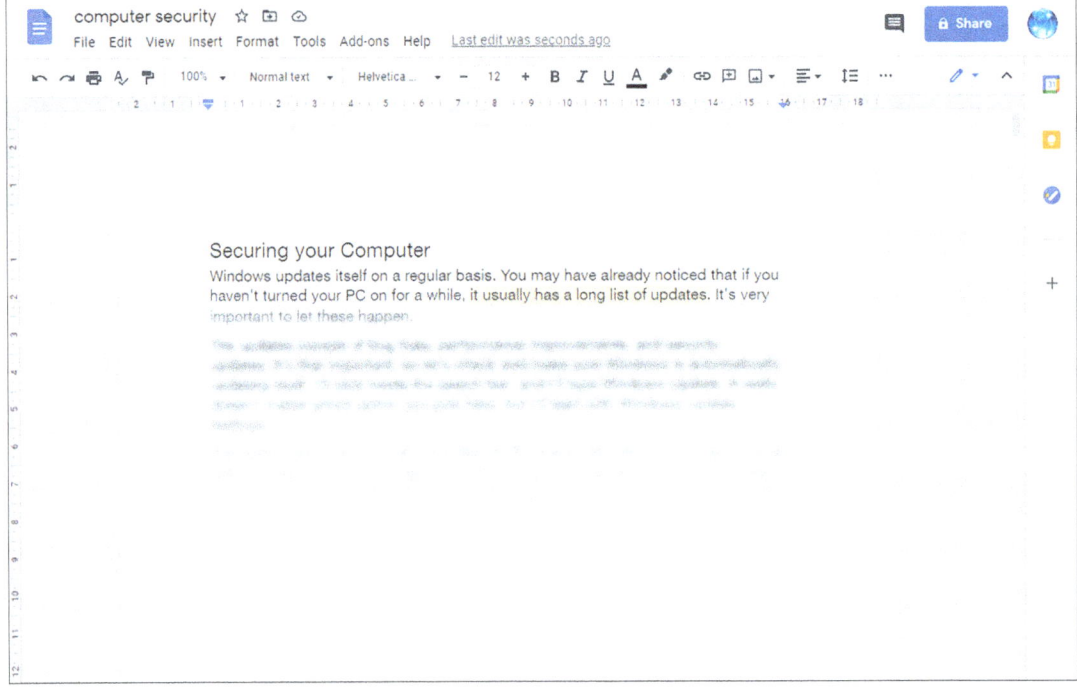

Chapter 7: Managing Documents

Downloading & Converting Documents

If you need to save your document for Microsoft Word, or a PDF, you can do this using the 'document download' feature. This is useful if you want to send someone the document who uses Microsoft Word, or if you need to send a report to someone as a PDF.

First open the document you want to convert and download. Select the 'file' menu, then go down to 'download'.

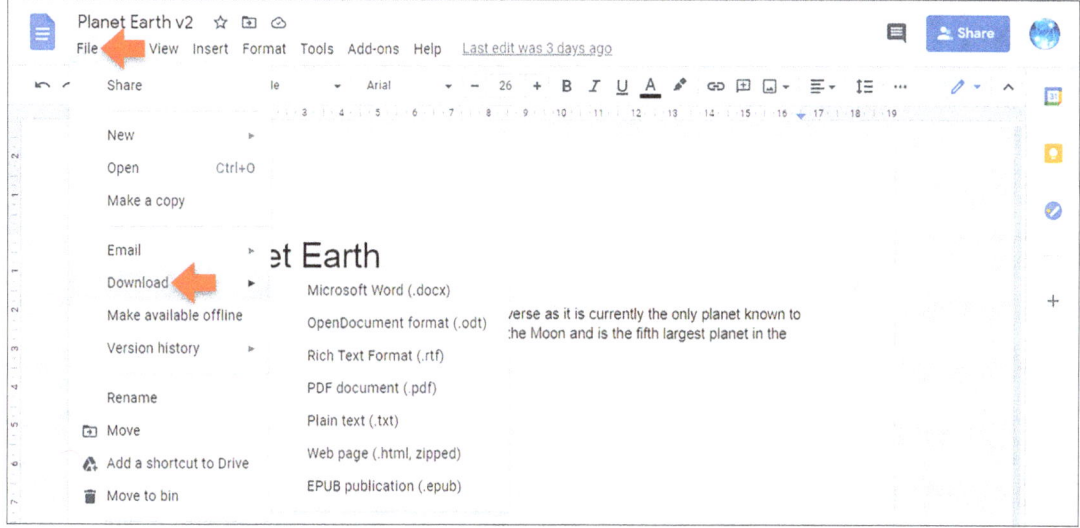

Select the format you want from the slideout menu.

- Use 'microsoft word' if you want to convert and download the document as a word document.
- Use 'opendocument format' if you want the document to be compatible with various word processors, such as Word Perfect, Apache OpenOffice or LibreOffice.
- Use 'rich text format' if you want maximum compatibility with other word processors. RTF is a universal document format and is compatible with most word-processing packages.
- Use 'PDF document' if you want to send a read-only version of the document such as a sales report to someone else.
- Use 'web page' if you want to convert the document to an HTML document for a website.
- Use 'epub publication' if you are writing an ebook and want to read the document on e-readers such as kindle, google books, nook and other e-book readers.

In this example, I'm going to export this document as a PDF.

Chapter 7: Managing Documents

Navigate to the folder on your PC, laptop or mac; give the document a name. Here, in the example below, I'm saving this document into my 'documents' folder.

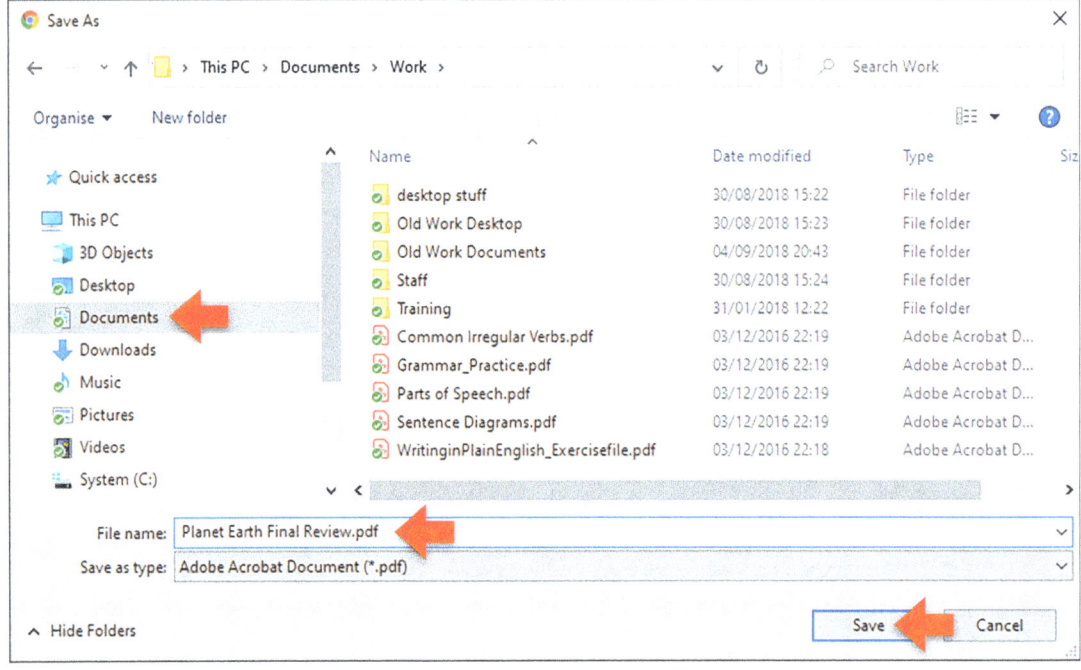

Click 'save'.

Printing Documents

Once you're finished writing your documents, you might need to print them. To do this, make sure your printer is connected and online.

Page Setup

If you need to change the page orientation, paper size, page margins, or page colour, you can do that here. Once you have a document open, go to the file menu, on the top left. Select 'print setup'.

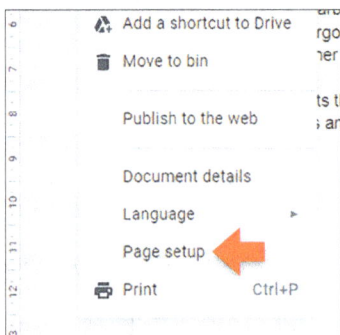

Chapter 7: Managing Documents

From here, you can change the page orientation: landscape or portrait. You can change the paper size: select A4, letter, legal, etc

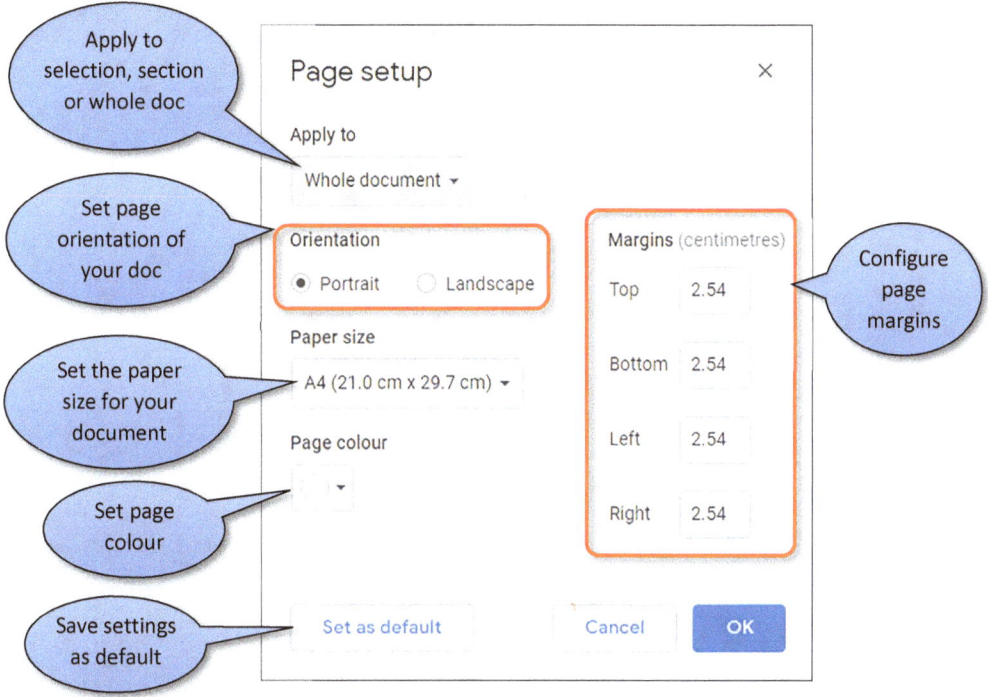

You can set the margins for your document and choose a page colour.

Click the drop down box under 'apply to'. Here, you can select what part of your document you want to apply the page setup settings to.

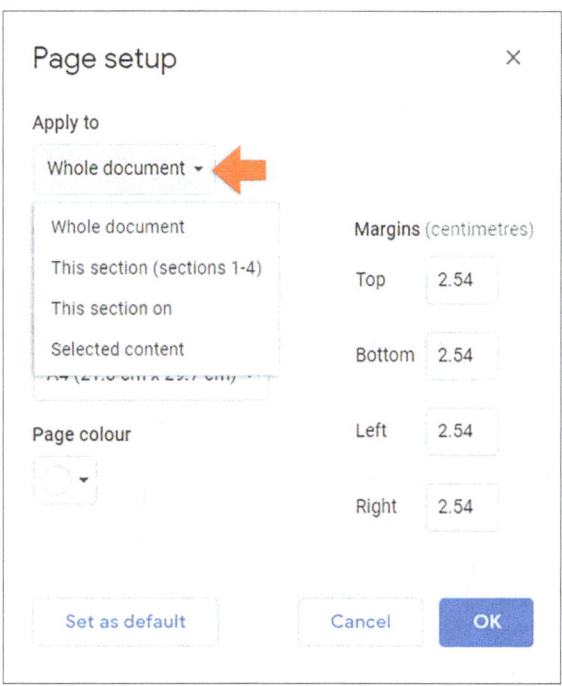

157

Chapter 7: Managing Documents

Use the 'apply to' setting at the top of the dialog box to apply these settings to a section of your doc if you've split your document using section breaks.

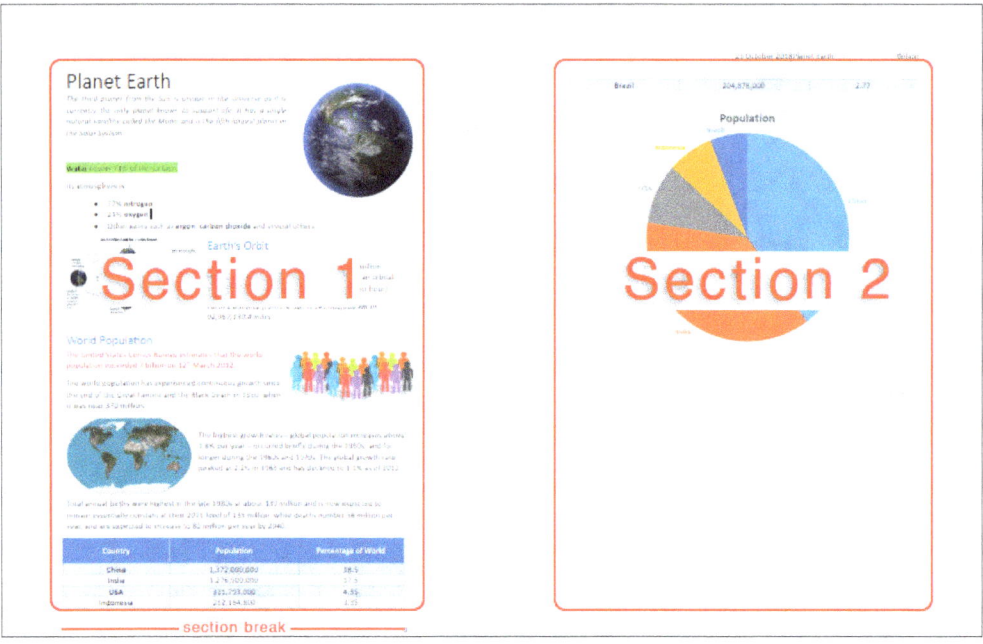

Or if you've selected part of your document - highlighted the text with your mouse.

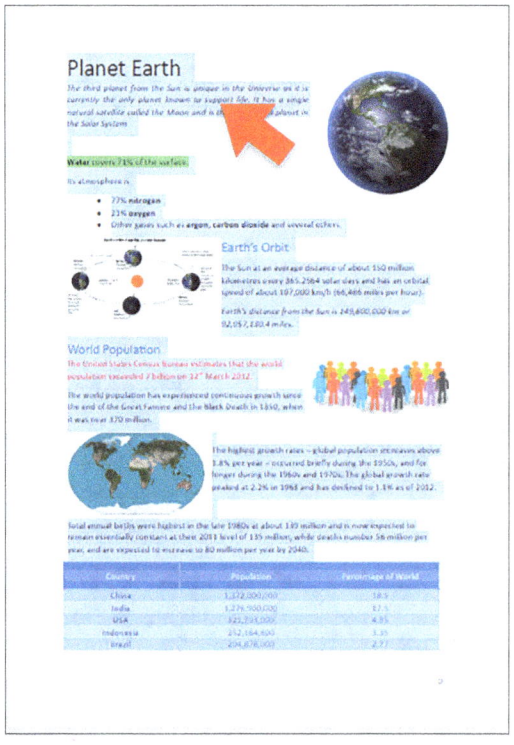

Or the whole document...

Chapter 7: Managing Documents

Print

To print your document, click the 'file' menu on the top left, then select 'print' from the drop down menu.

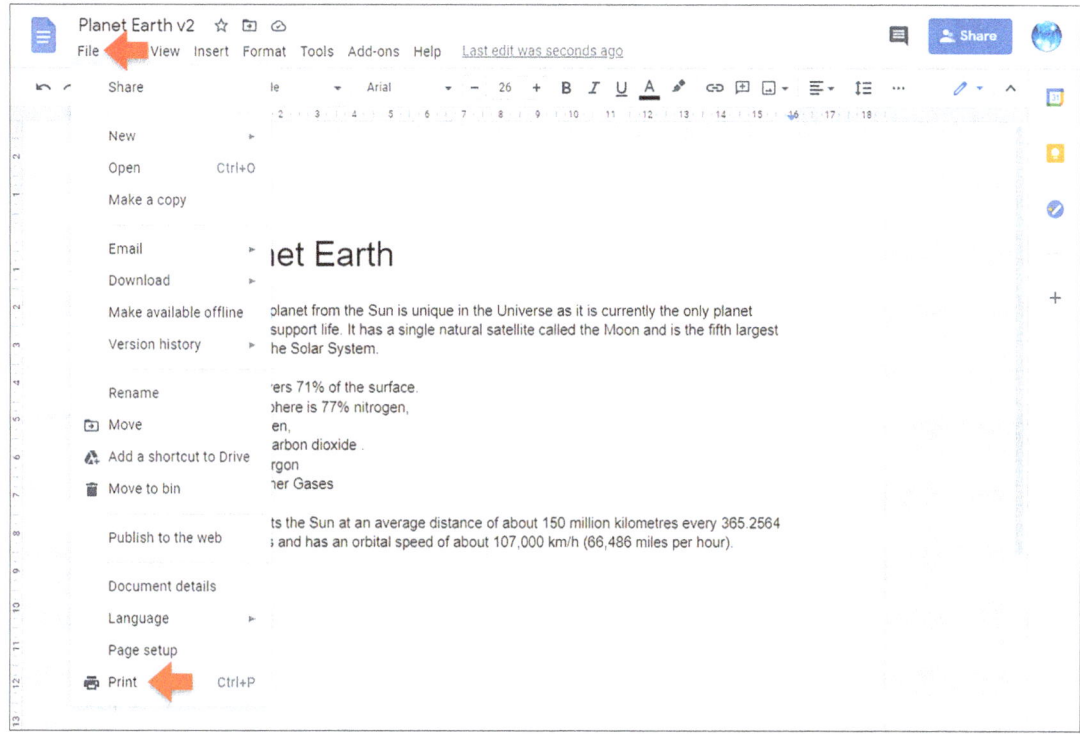

From the dialog box that appears, select your printer from the 'destination' drop down selection box.

In the 'pages' field, set it to 'all' to print all pages in your document. If you only want to print certain pages, select 'customised' from the drop down selection box, then type in the page numbers of the pages you want to print. In this example, I'm going to print pages 1 and 4.

Set how many copies of the document you want, and whether you want to print the document in full colour, or just black and white.

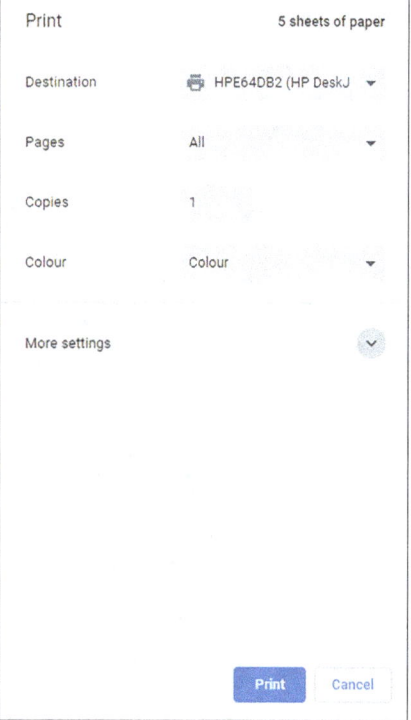

159

Chapter 7: Managing Documents

Click 'more settings'. Here, you can change the paper size (A4, letter, legal, etc) using the 'paper size' field.

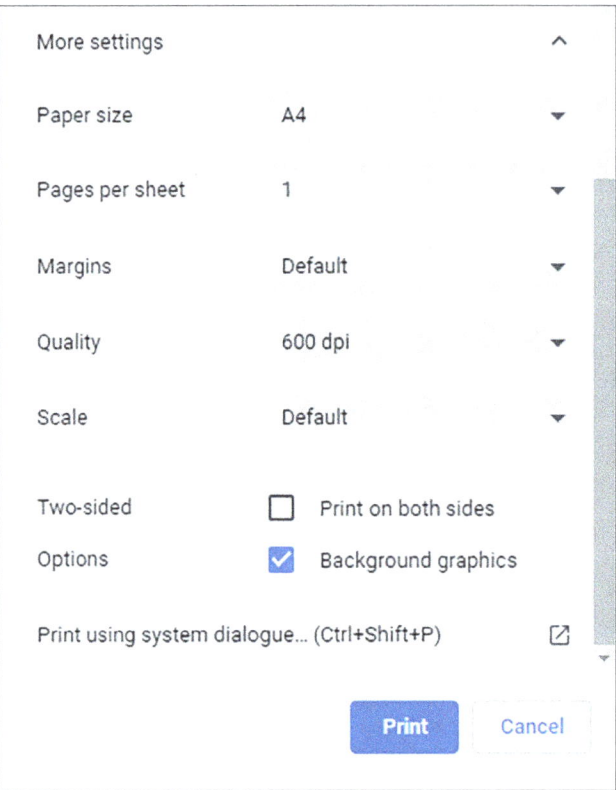

You can change the number of pages per sheet. So for example, if you wanted to put two pages on one sheet to save paper...

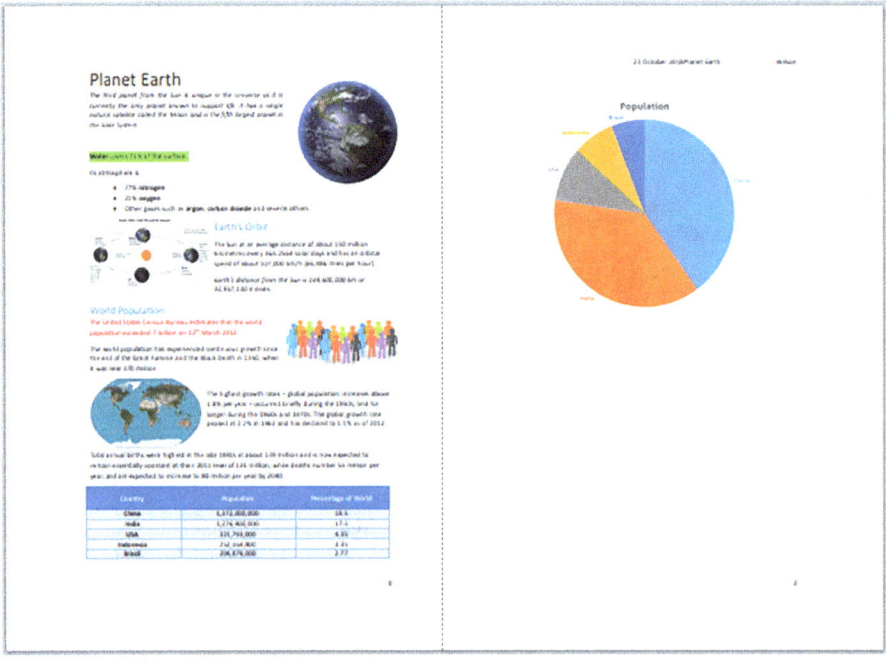

Chapter 7: Managing Documents

Using the 'margins' selection box, you can set your margins to 'none', 'minimum', or 'custom'. Select 'none' or 'minimum' to reduce the margins to their smallest.

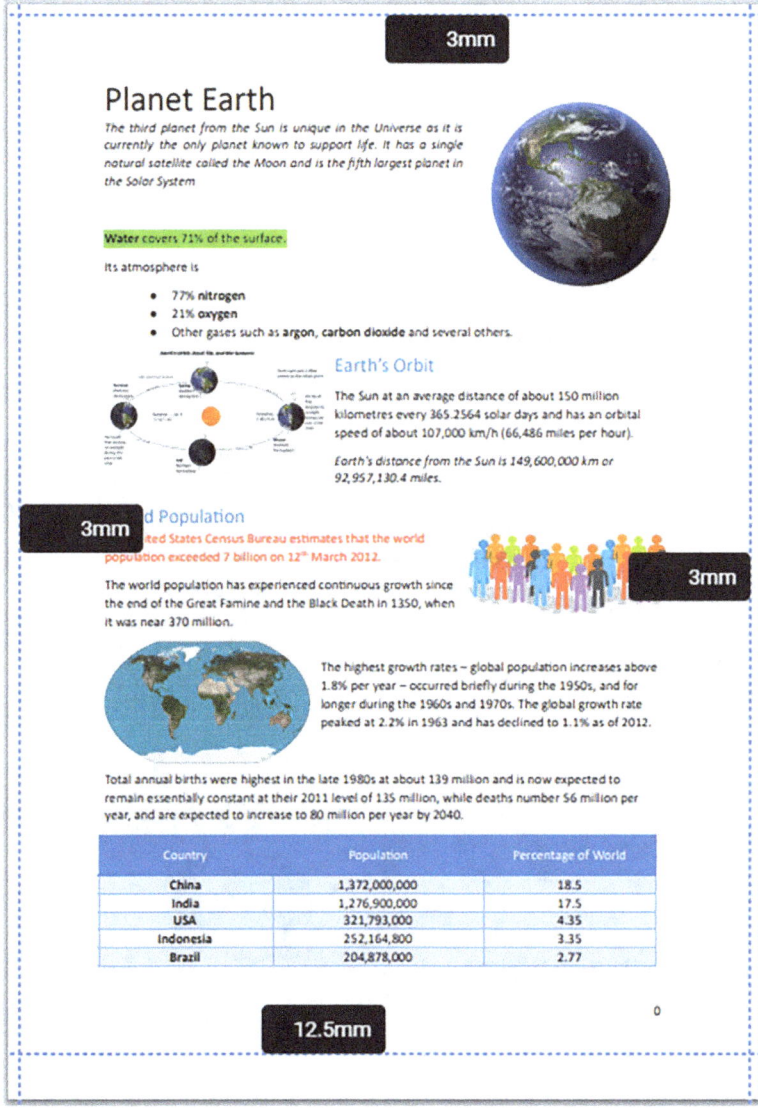

If you select 'custom', you can type in the margins. To do this, click in the margin measurement on the print preview on the left hand side of the window, then enter a new measurement. For example, below I've changed the bottom margin to 3mm.

Chapter 7: Managing Documents

Use the 'quality' selection box to set the quality of your print.

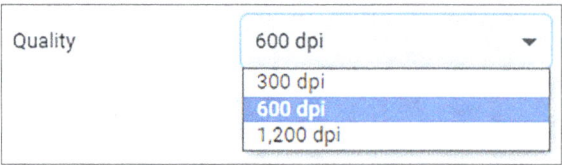

If you're printing a final copy then select a higher quality such as 600dpi or 1200dpi. However, if you're printing a quick draft and don't full quality then select 300dpi.

Using the 'scale' selection box, you can reduce or enlarge the size of a document to fit the page. Enter a percentage, eg 50% for half the size, or 125% to increase the size by 25%.

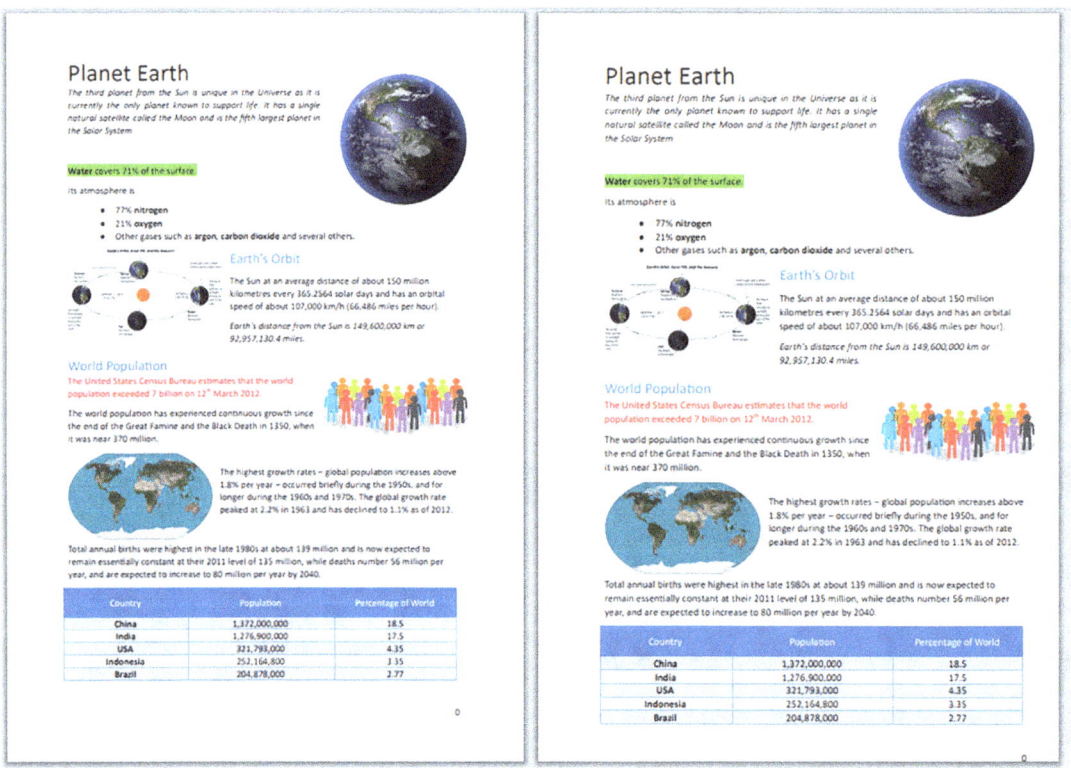

Use the 'two sided printing' option to print double sided if your printer supports this feature.

Use 'print headers and footers' to keep or remove the headers and footers if there are any on your document

'Print background graphics' doesn't apply to google docs. This is used for printing web pages that include backgrounds that you many or may not want to print.

Finally, click 'print' when you're done.

Chapter 7: Managing Documents

Email as Attachment

You can email your document in a variety of formats such as PDF, Word, HTML, plain text and rich text.

To do this, click on the 'file' menu, go down to 'email', then select 'email this file' from the slideout menu.

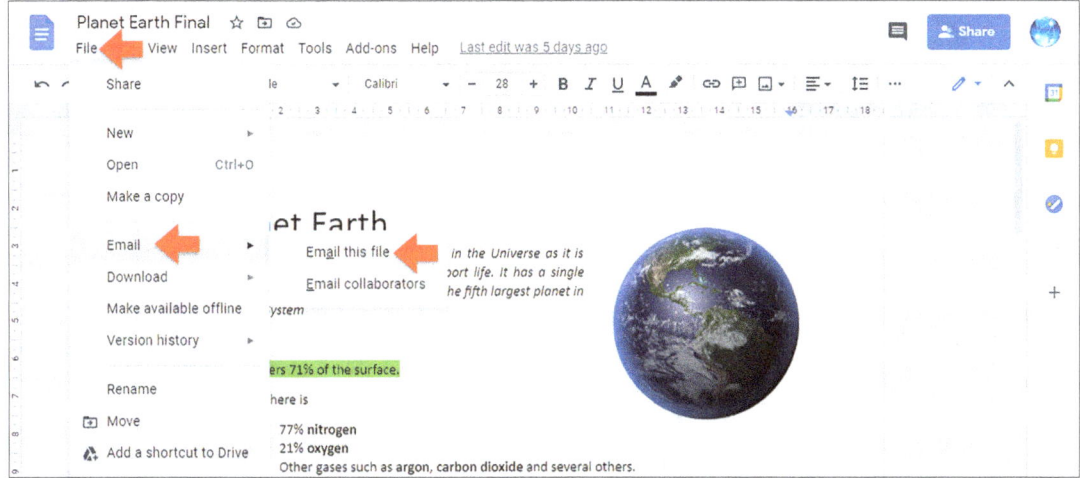

Enter the person's email address in the field at the top, add a message.

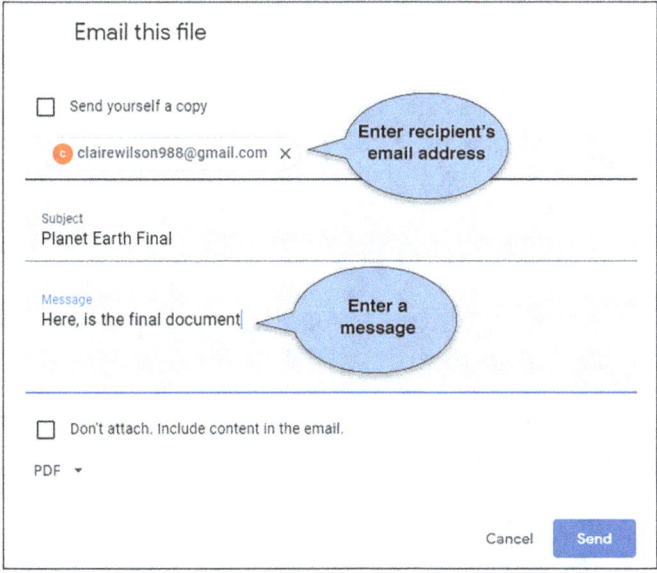

Tick "send yourself a copy" if you want to receive a copy of the email with the document attached.

Tick "Don't attach. Include content in the email" if you want to send the document as part of the email message rather than attaching it to the end.

163

Chapter 7: Managing Documents

Select the format using the drop down box on the bottom left.

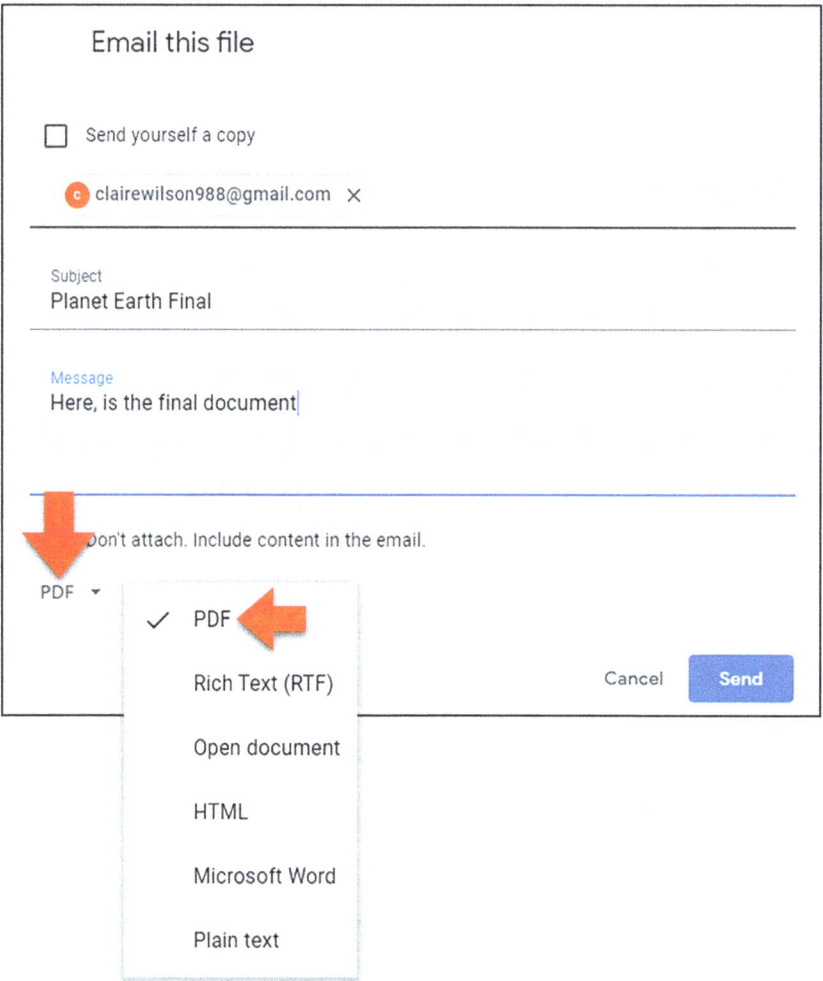

Here, you can select the format you want to send.

- PDF is useful for portability across different platforms, however the recipient won't be able to edit a PDF.

- Rich text or open document is good for compatibility between other word processors such as open and libre office.

- HTML which is useful if you want to publish your document on a website

- Microsoft word if your recipient users Microsoft Office.

- Plain text is useful if you just need the text with no formatting or images.

Select your format, then click 'send'.

Chapter 7: Managing Documents

Document Translation

You can translate a document into another language. While the translation is generally good enough to be understood, it's important to recognise that the translation is not perfect.

To translate a document, open the 'tools' menu, then select 'translate document'.

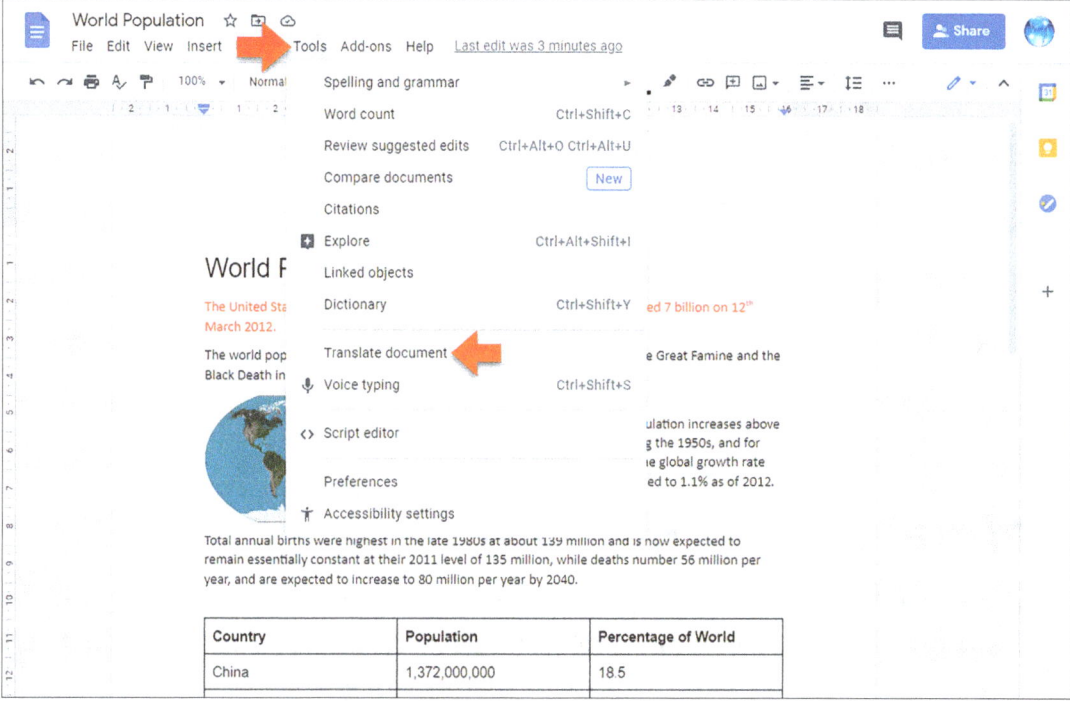

Give the document a name, then select the language you want to translate the document into, eg spanish.

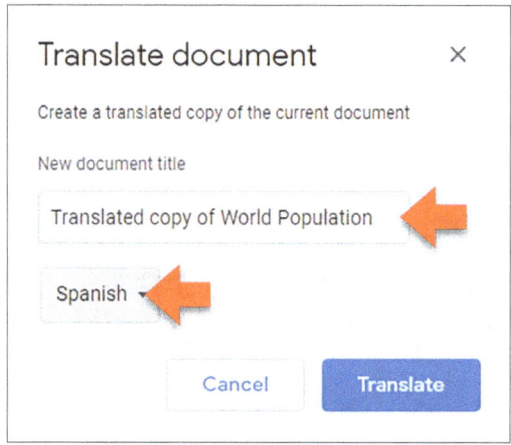

Click 'translate'.

Chapter 7: Managing Documents

Once the translation is complete, Google Docs will create a new document for your translation

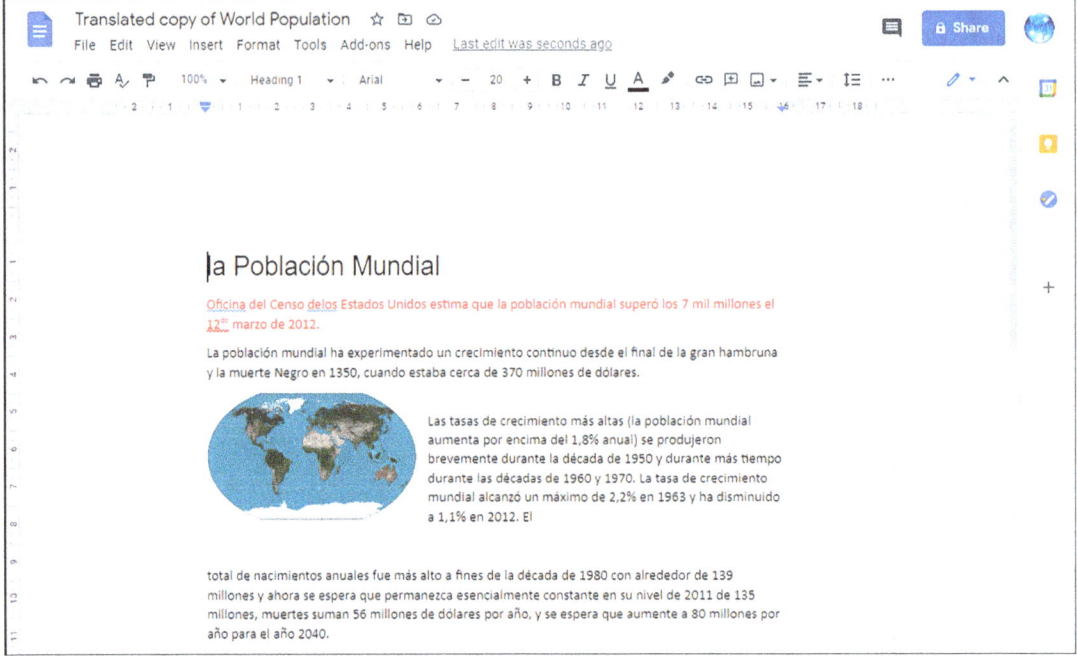

Define & Lookup

You can quickly find a definition or lookup a word in your document using the built in dictionary and Google search features. To do this, highlight a word or phrase, then right click on the selection.

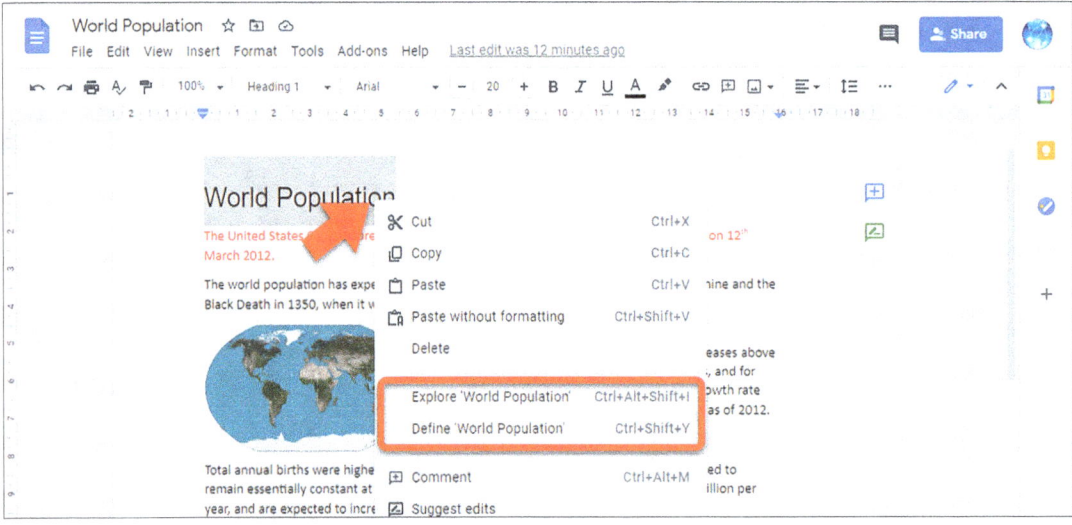

Select 'explore...' to do a Google search for the phrase, or select 'define...' to look it up in the dictionary.

Chapter 7: Managing Documents

Here, I've used 'lookup' to look up the word 'population'

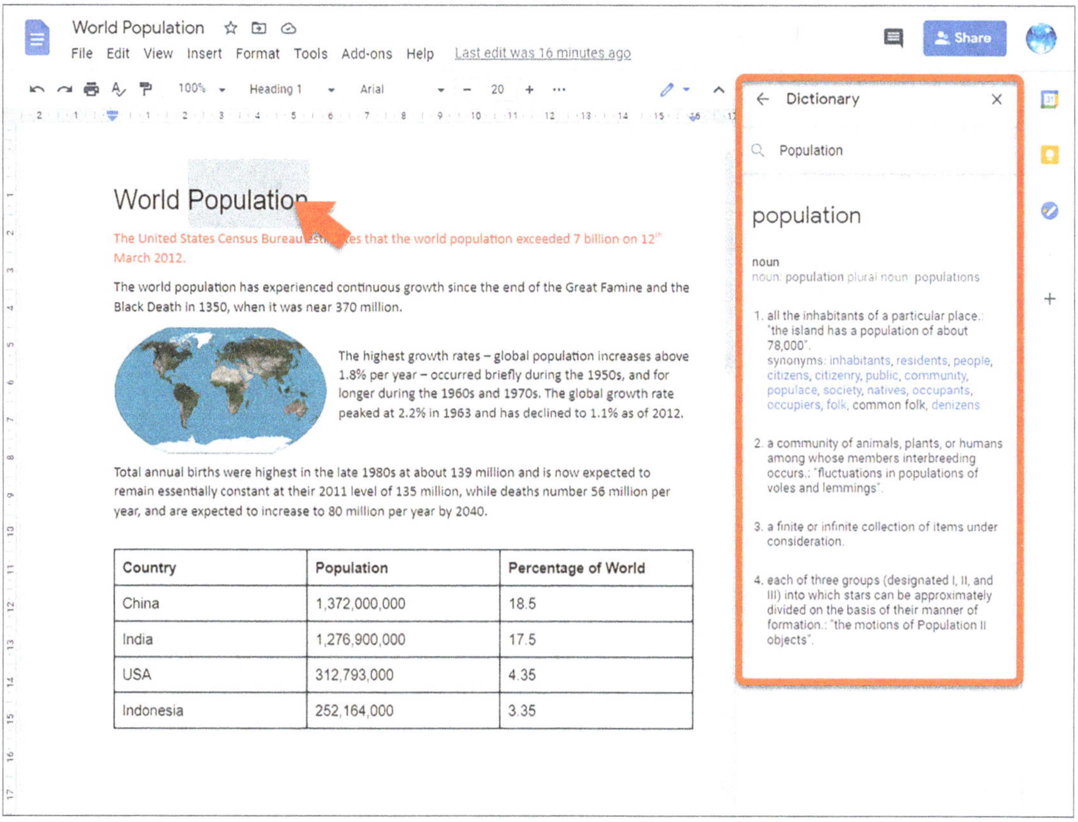

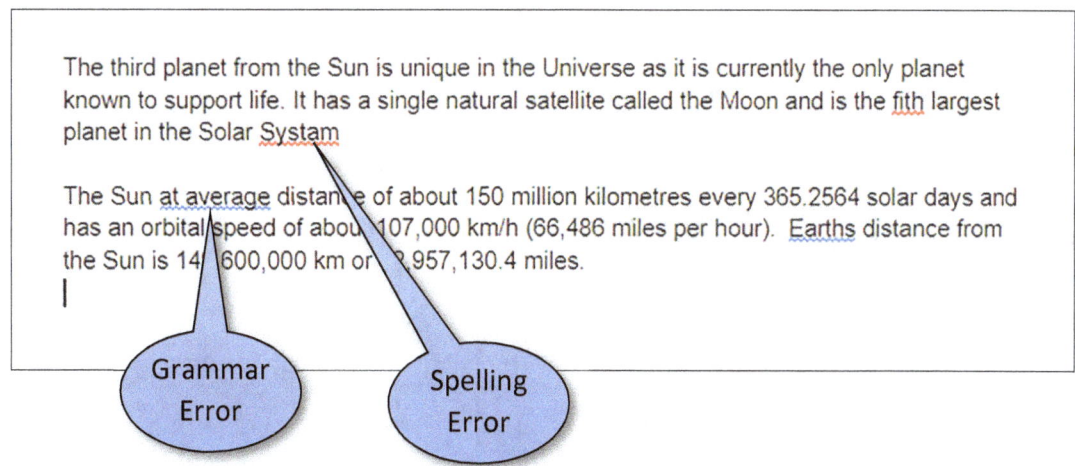

Spelling & Grammar

Google Docs automatically checks your spelling and grammar as you type. Any spelling errors are underlined in red, and grammatical errors are underlined in blue. Here, in the document below, you'll notice a couple of spelling and grammatical errors.

Chapter 7: Managing Documents

Right click on the errors to see corrections or suggestions. In the example below, click on the spelling error "systam". You'll see Google Docs spell check show you a suggestion. If the suggestion is correct, click on it to correct the error.

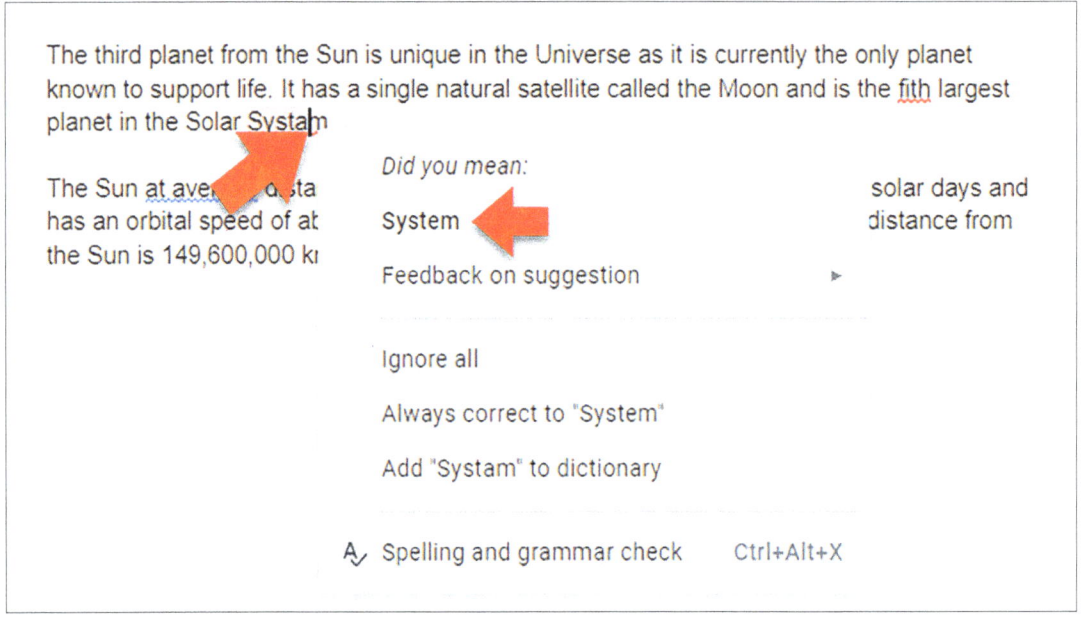

If this happens to be a common error you make with this particular spelling, select 'always correct to…'. This will automatically make the correction for you. If the error happens to be a person's name or some term you know is spelled correctly, then click 'add to dictionary'.

To run a spell & grammar check, open the 'tools' menu, select 'spelling and grammar'.

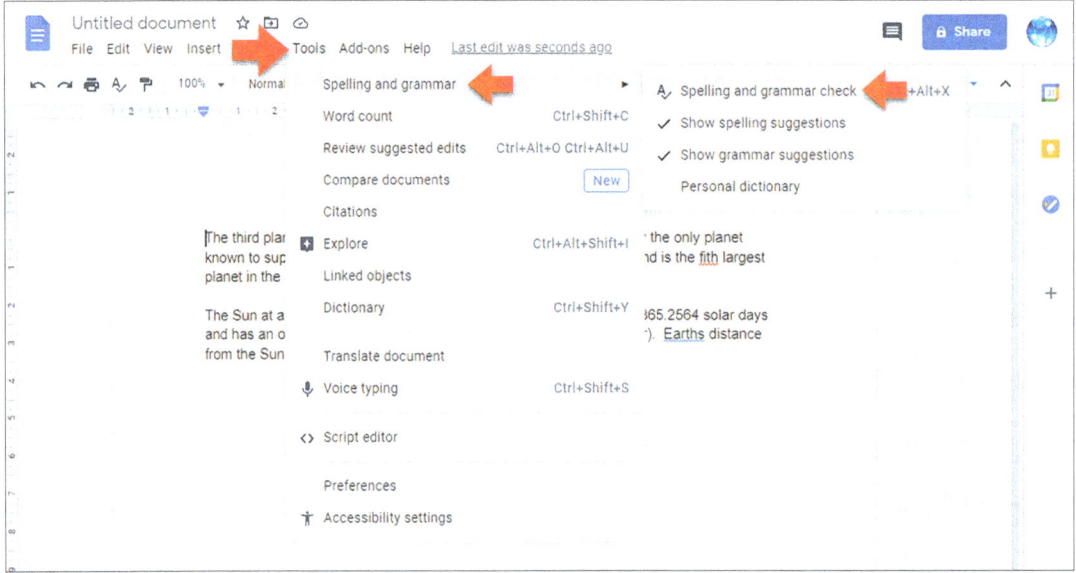

Chapter 7: Managing Documents

Use the left and right arrows on the top right of the 'spelling and grammar' dialog box to run through the flagged errors. Click 'accept' to correct the spelling, or 'ignore' to ignore it.

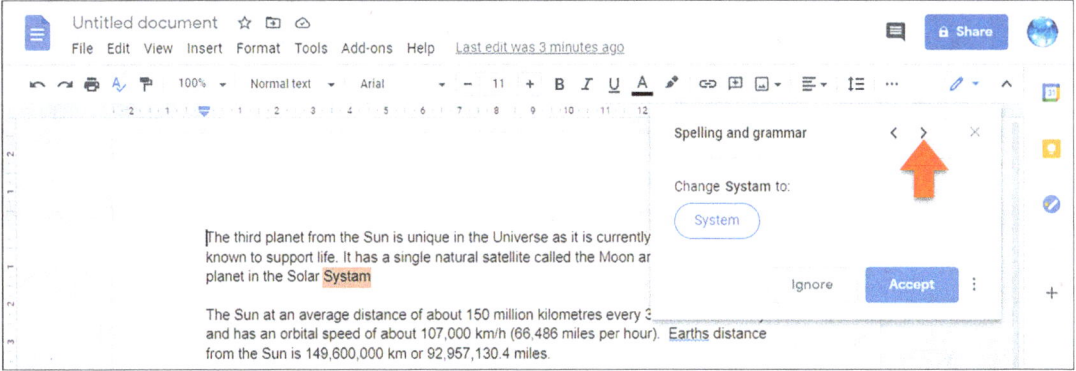

If you need to add words to your personal dictionary, open the 'tools' menu, go down to 'spelling and grammar', then select 'personal dictionary'

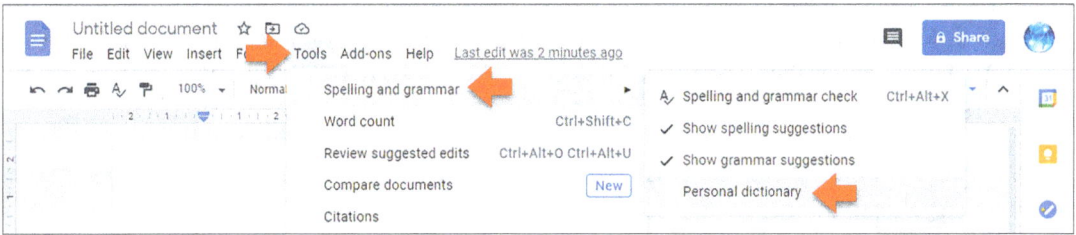

Here, you can add custom words. Type in word, click 'add'.

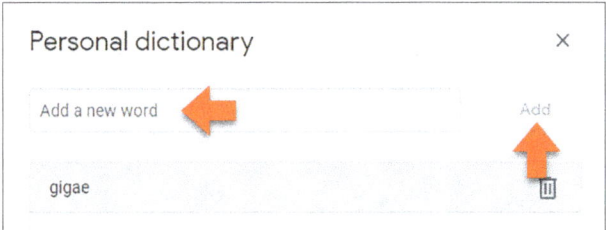

To remove a word, select the word in the list, click the trash icon.

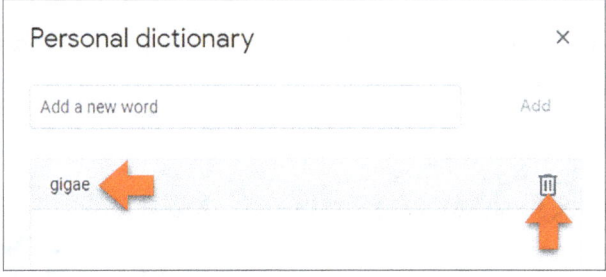

Click 'ok'.

Chapter 7: Managing Documents

AI Writing Tools

Google Docs is increasingly integrating artificial intelligence (AI) to enhance user productivity and document quality. These AI-driven features offer a range of functionalities, from improving writing clarity and suggesting stylistic changes to automating content generation and summarizing large amounts of text.

With anything that is generated, do not blindly accept it all; use your judgment to ensure the it fits your intended meaning, and make sure facts are correct.

Help Me Write

The "Help Me Write" feature is designed to generate text based on natural language prompts, that can be inserted, revised, or further customized. Initially introduced to Google Workspace users with business, enterprise, and education accounts , as well as select participants in Google's Workspace Labs program. Access to this feature is generally unavailable for personal Google accounts, although a small number of personal users who joined early access programs may still have it.

First, open a Blank document, or an existing one where you want to use AI writing assistance

Look for the "Help Me Write" button on the right hand side of the document.

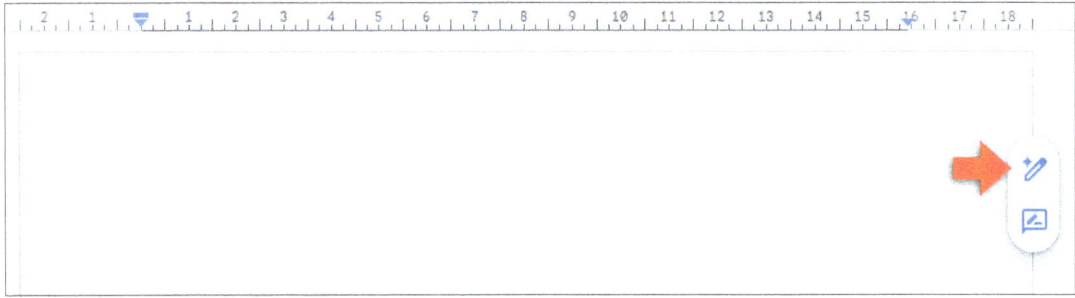

This will open an input box. Type a clear, specific description of what you want to generate.

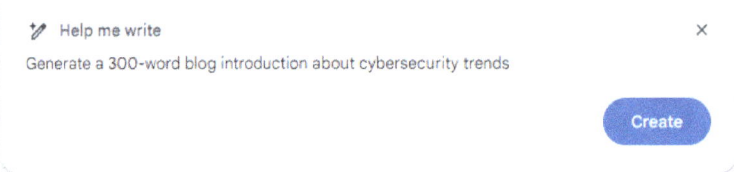

Chapter 7: Managing Documents

For example, you could type:

- "Write a professional email requesting feedback on a project."
- "Generate a 300-word blog introduction about cybersecurity trends."
- "Summarize this paragraph."

Once the content is generated, you'll see a preview in the dialog box. Click "insert" to insert the content into your document. Before you do this, you can also go through and edit the text, or you can ask the AI to make edits using the "refine with prompt" field at the bottom.

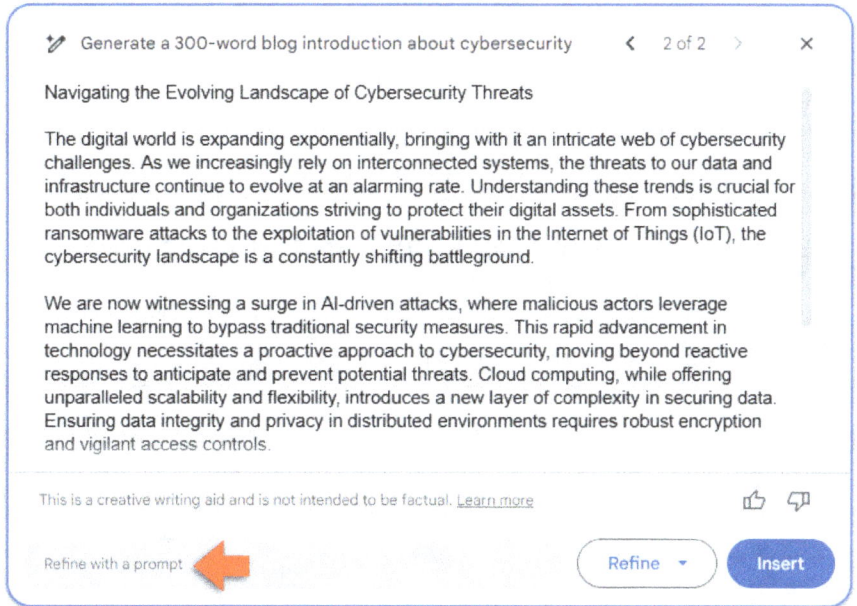

You can click the "Refine" button on the bottom right, and select from options to modify the content automatically.

Shorten reduces the length of the text, making it more concise and eliminating unnecessary words; **Elaborate** adds more detail and depth to expand the content; **More formal** adjusts the tone to be more professional and polished; **More casual** makes the tone more relaxed, conversational, and informal; **Bulletise** restructures the content into bullet points for easier scanning 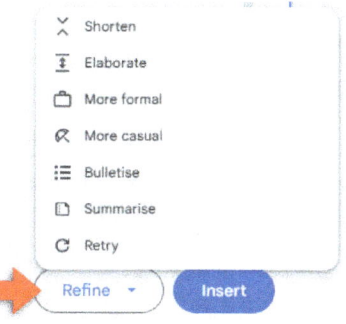 and clarity; **Summarise** condenses the content into a shorter summary capturing the main ideas; and **Retry** generates a completely new alternative version of the text.

171

Chapter 7: Managing Documents

Add-ons

You can expand Google Doc's functionality with add-ons. These add ons are developed mostly by third party developers. You'll find add-ons for adding Merge Mail, LucidChart Diagrams for creating flowcharts, and other diagrams, as well as MathType for writing and formatting mathematical equations.

Install

To install an add-on, open the 'extensions' menu, then select 'add-ons', then click 'get add-ons.

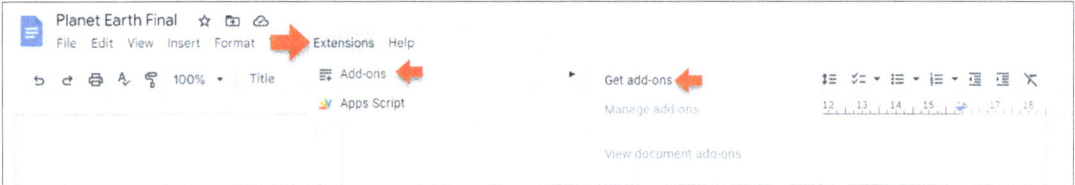

Use the search bar along the top to find an add-on you want to install. For example I'm going to search for MathType

Or click on the hamburger icon on the top left, then select a category to browse through.

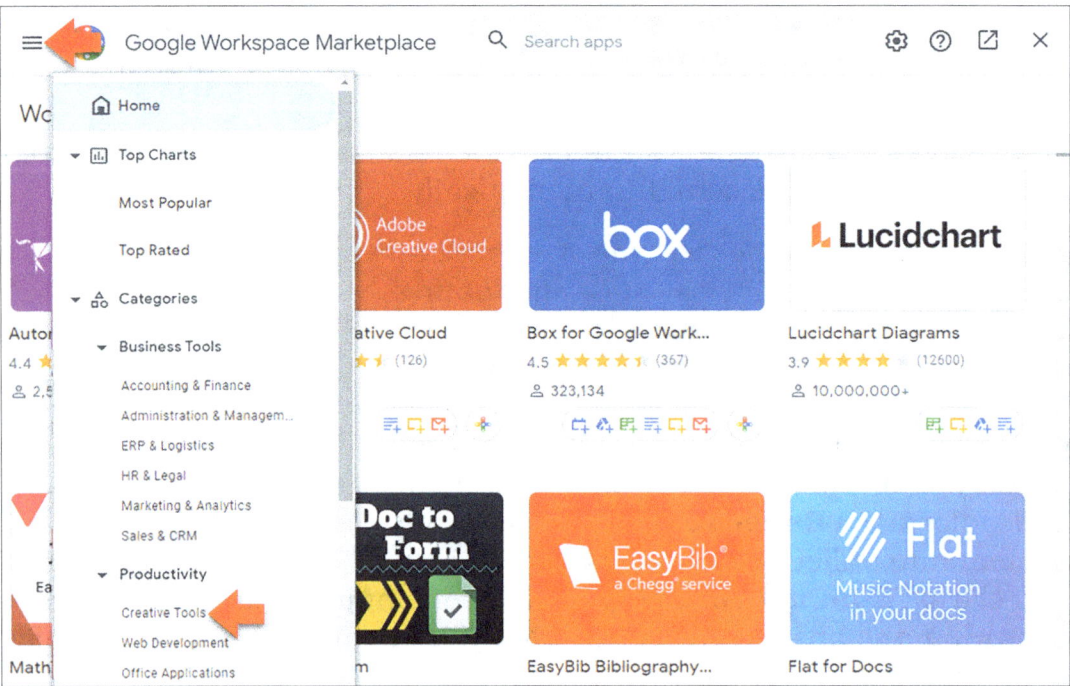

Chapter 7: Managing Documents

From the search results, select the add-on to install.

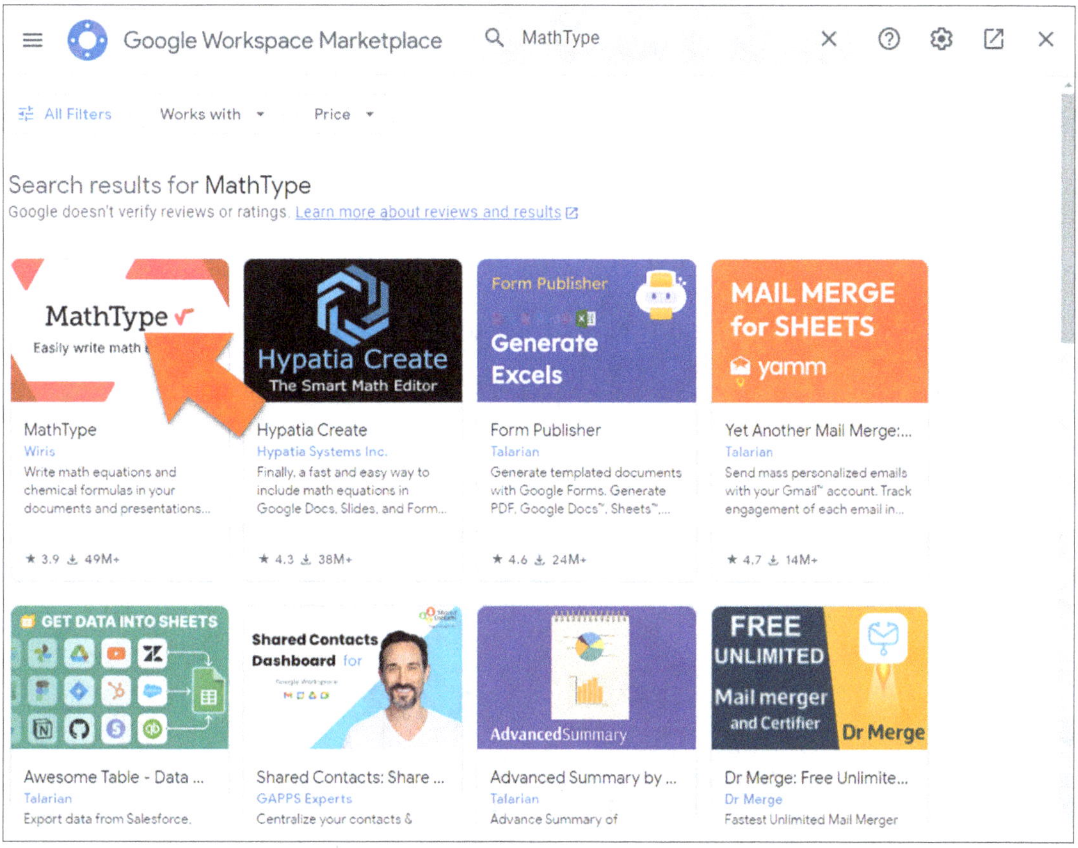

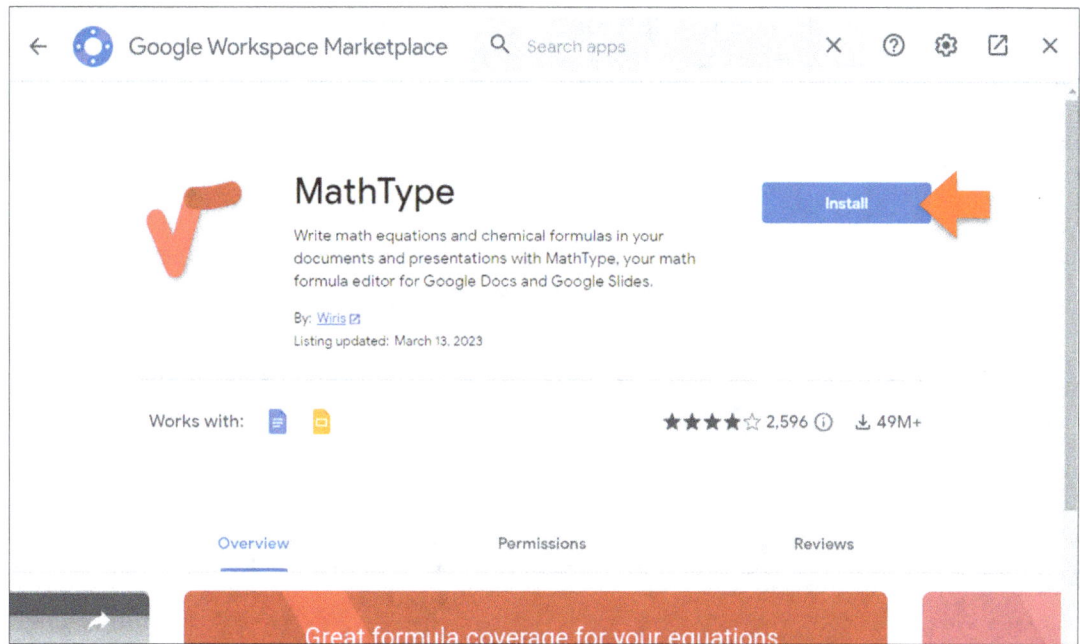

Click 'install' on the summary page. Then click 'continue' on the confirmation prompt.

Chapter 7: Managing Documents

Click 'continue', choose your Google Account, then click 'allow'.

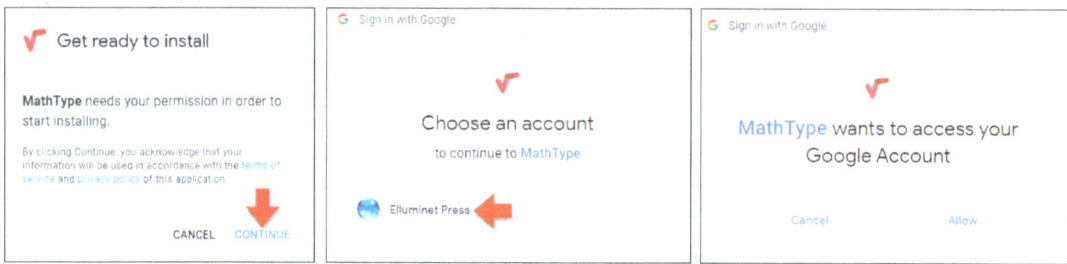

You'll find the add-on appear in the 'extensions' menu.

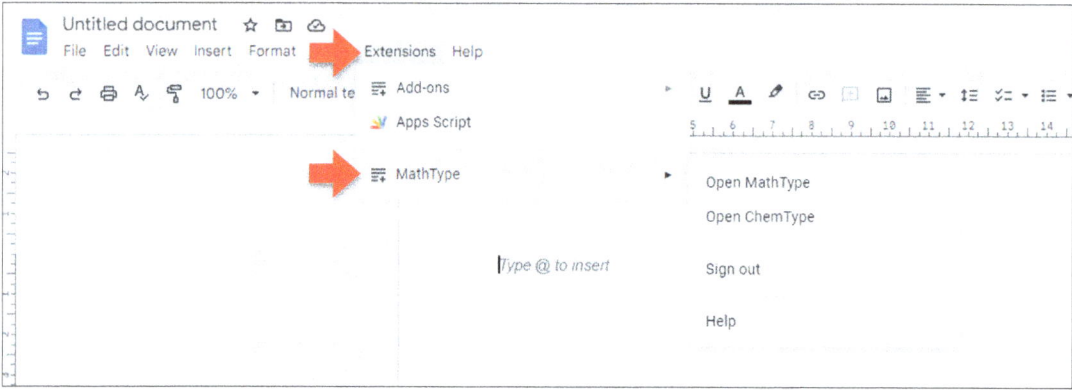

Some add-ons don't appear in the extensions menu. For example LucidChart doesn't appear. To use these types of add-ons, you'll need to open Google Drive. To do this, navigate to the following site:

`drive.google.com`

Click the '+' icon on the top left hand corner to create a new document.

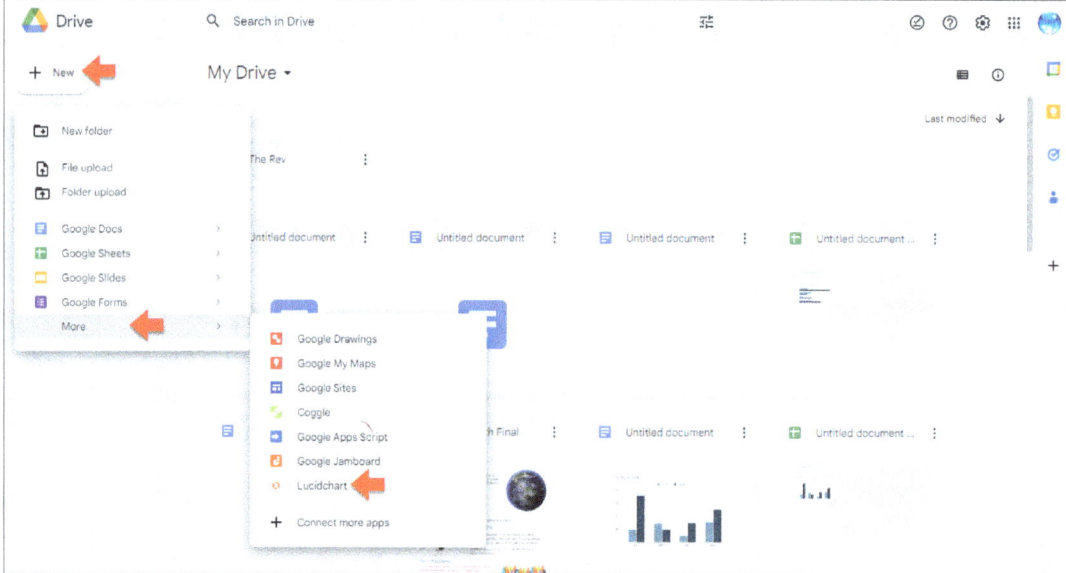

Chapter 7: Managing Documents

Manage Add-ons

To manage your add-ons, open the 'extensions' menu then select 'add-ons'. From the slideout menu, select 'manage add-ons'.

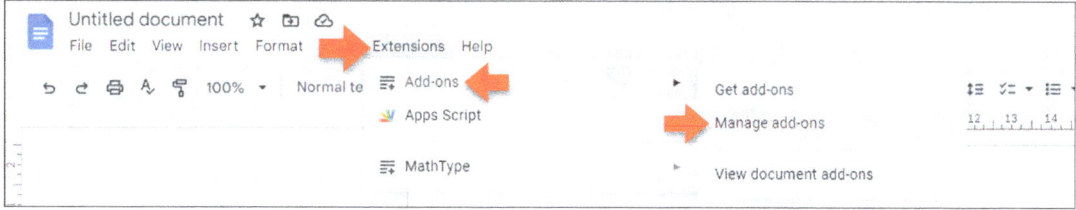

Here, you'll see all the add-ons you've installed. Click the three dots icon on the top right of the addon thumbnail to uninstall.

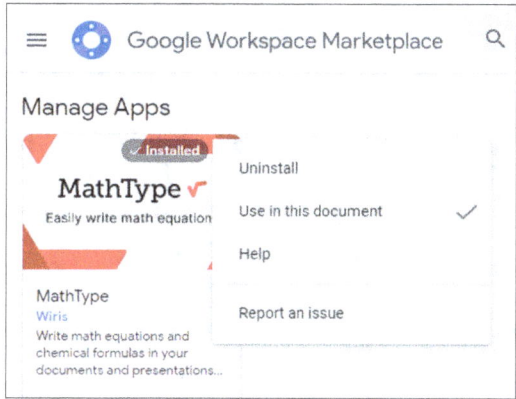

Useful Add-ons

There are many useful add-ons for Google Docs that can help enhance productivity and streamline workflow.

Grammarly is an add-on that checks your writing for grammatical errors, spelling mistakes, and style issues. It offers suggestions for corrections and can help improve the clarity and readability of your document.

DocHub is a PDF editing and signing tool that lets you annotate, highlight, and edit PDF files directly in Google Docs. It's useful for anyone who works with PDFs on a regular basis.

Coggle is an add-on that allows you to create and edit mind maps directly within Google Docs. It's a helpful tool for brainstorming and organizing ideas.

DocuSign is an add-on that allows you to sign and send documents for signature directly from Google Docs. It's useful for anyone who needs to sign and send documents quickly and securely.

Using Tablets

You can use Google Docs on a tablet or phone. You can download the app for an iPhone/iPad, or for an android phone or tablet.

In this section, we'll take a look at how to get started with Google Docs on a tablet using the app.

We'll go through downloading and installing the app on your tablet, then take a look at some basics on how to open documents, format text, add tables and images.

- Download Google Docs
- Getting Started
- Formatting Text
- Paragraph Formatting
- Insert Images
- Resize Image
- Insert Table
- Insert Row
- Insert Column
- Format your Table

Chapter 8: Using Tablets

Download Google Docs

To download the Google Docs app, open the Google Play Store on an android device, or the App Store on an iPhone/iPad. In this demo, I will be using an iPad.

Open the Apps Store, then search for google docs. Tap 'get' to install.

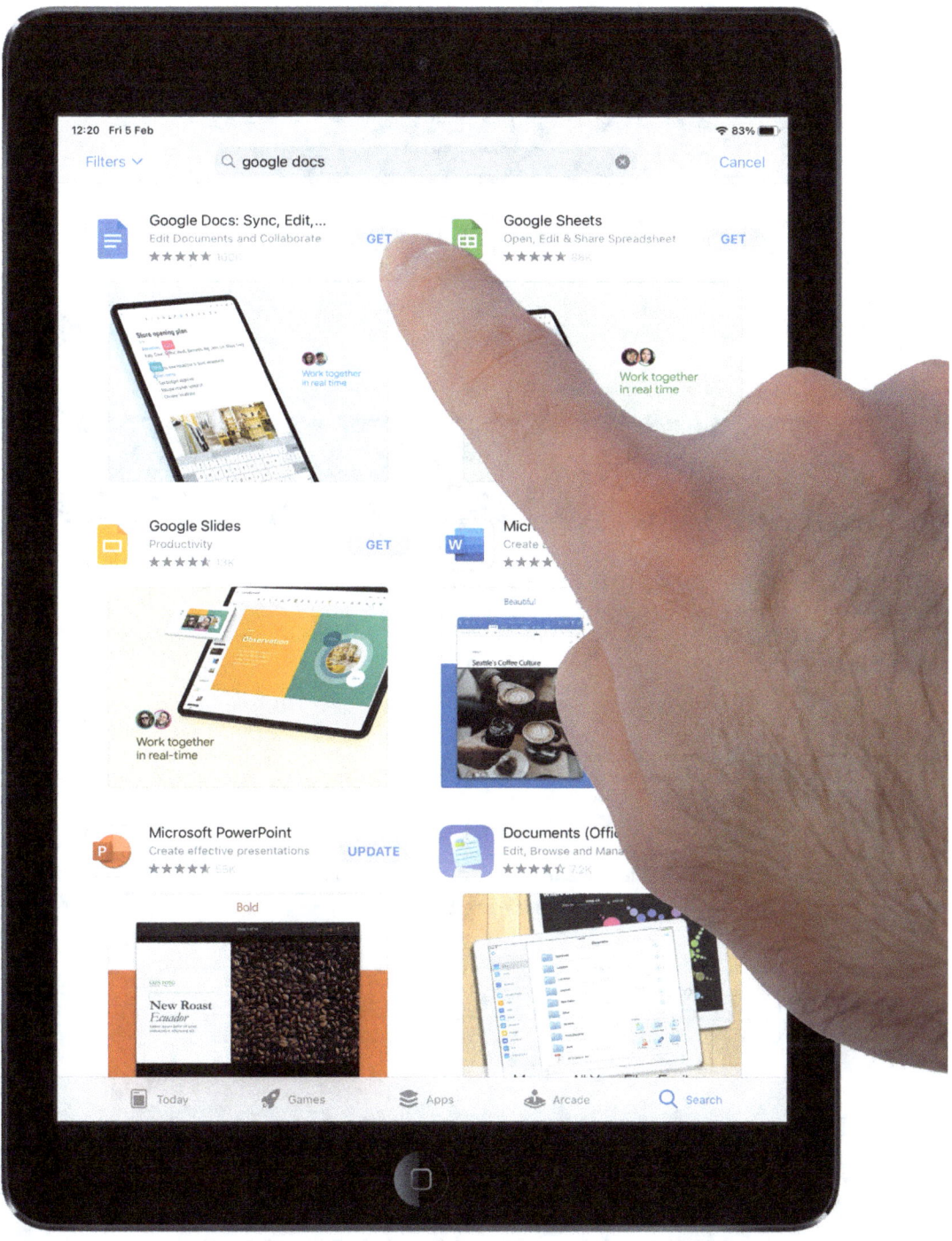

Chapter 8: Using Tablets

Getting Started

Once Google Docs has installed itself, you'll find the icon on your home screen. Tap on it to launch the app.

The first time you run the app, you'll need to sign in with your Google Account. To do this, tap the 'sign in' icon on the bottom left.

Enter your Google Account email address and password.

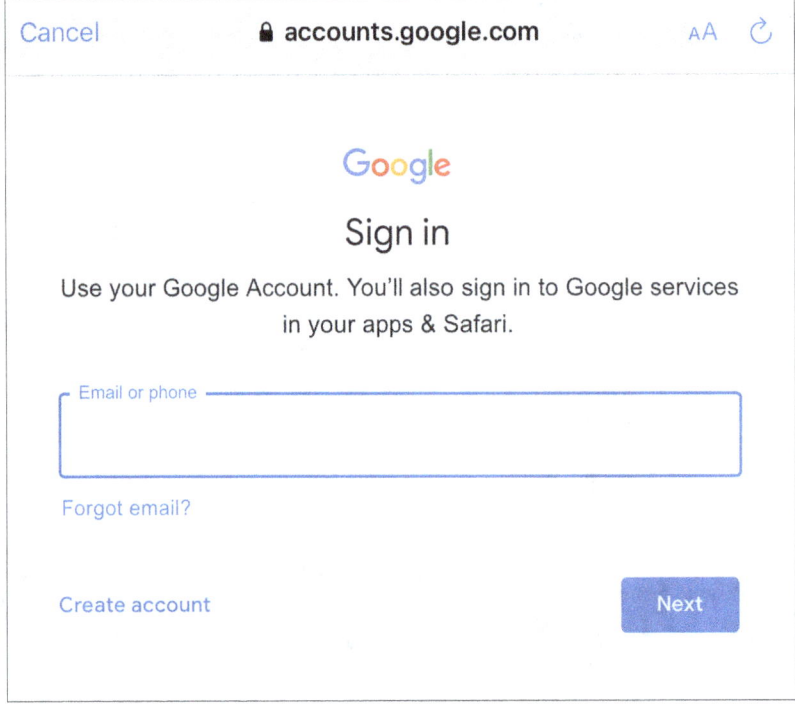

Chapter 8: Using Tablets

You'll land on the Google Docs home screen. Let's take a look around. Along the top you'll see an icon to open the sidebar, a search field, file selection field, and your profile icon on the right to change your Google Account Settings.

- Sidebar, settings, google drive, shared etc
- Search for documents in Google Docs
- Open a file on Google Drive or one shared with you
- Recently opened documents listed here
- Doc options: share, save as word, link, print etc
- Tap on document to open
- Open new blank document

Select a document from the recently used list, or click the plus icon on the bottom right, then select 'new document' from the popup to open a blank document. In this example, I'm going to open a blank document.

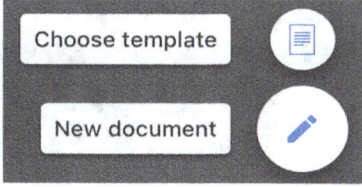

179

Chapter 8: Using Tablets

Give the document a meaningful name, then tap 'create'.

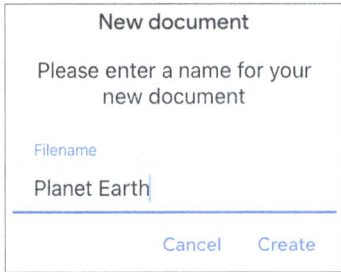

Once you've opened your document, you'll land on the editing screen.

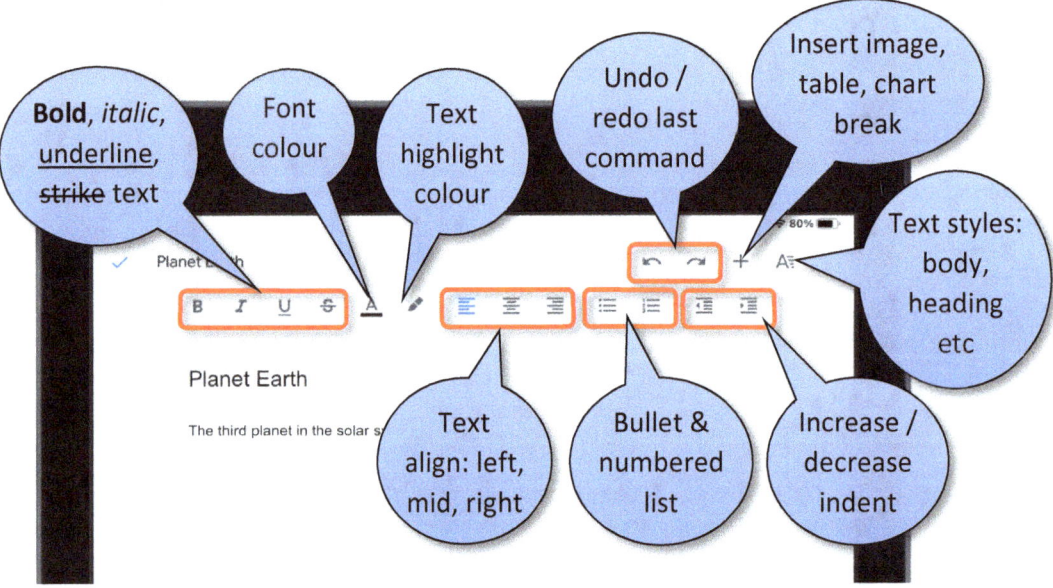

At the bottom of the screen, you'll see your on screen keyboard.

Chapter 8: Using Tablets

Formatting Text

To format text first open your document, then tap the 'edit' icon on the bottom right of the screen.

Next you need to select the text you want to format. To do this, double-tap on the location in the document you want to format. You'll see a blue marker appear on the text.

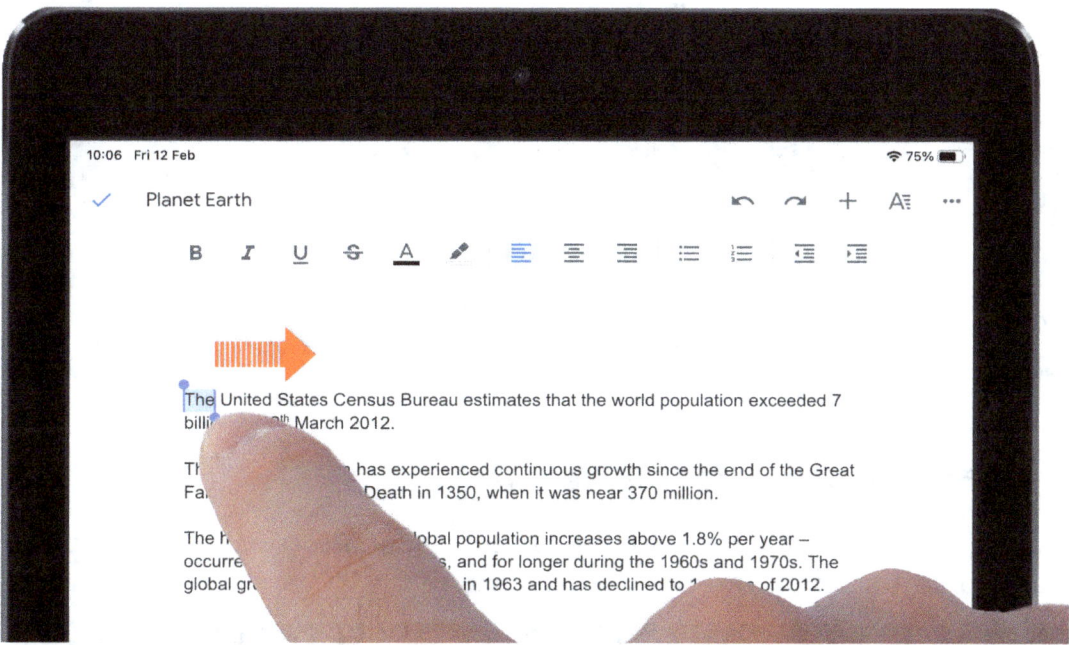

Use your finger to move the blue markers so they highlight the text you want.

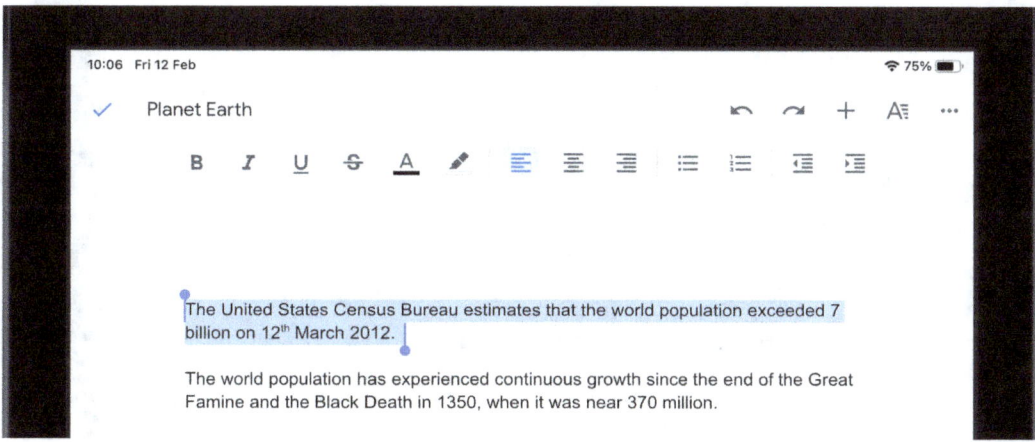

181

Chapter 8: Using Tablets

Tap the format icon on the top right. From the drop down menu select the 'text' tab. Here, you can select **bold**, *italic*, <u>underlined</u>, ~~striketext~~, superscript and subscript. Underneath you can change the text style, font typeface, font size, and text colour. Just tap on the option you want to apply to your selected text.

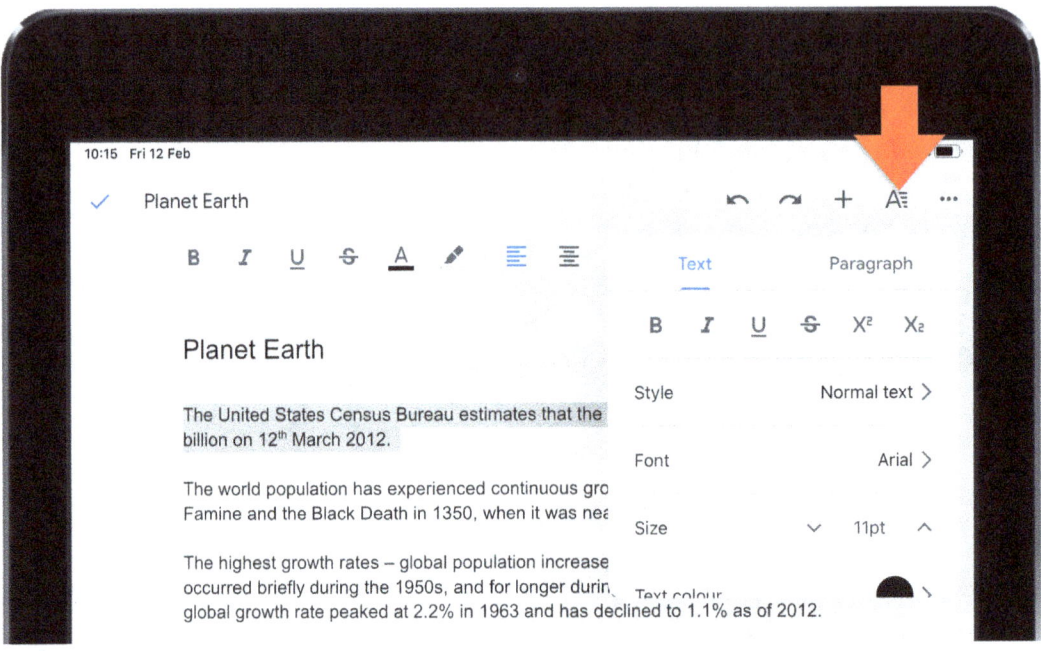

Paragraph Formatting

To align text, set indents, or adjust line spacing, select the text you want to adjust, then tap the format icon.

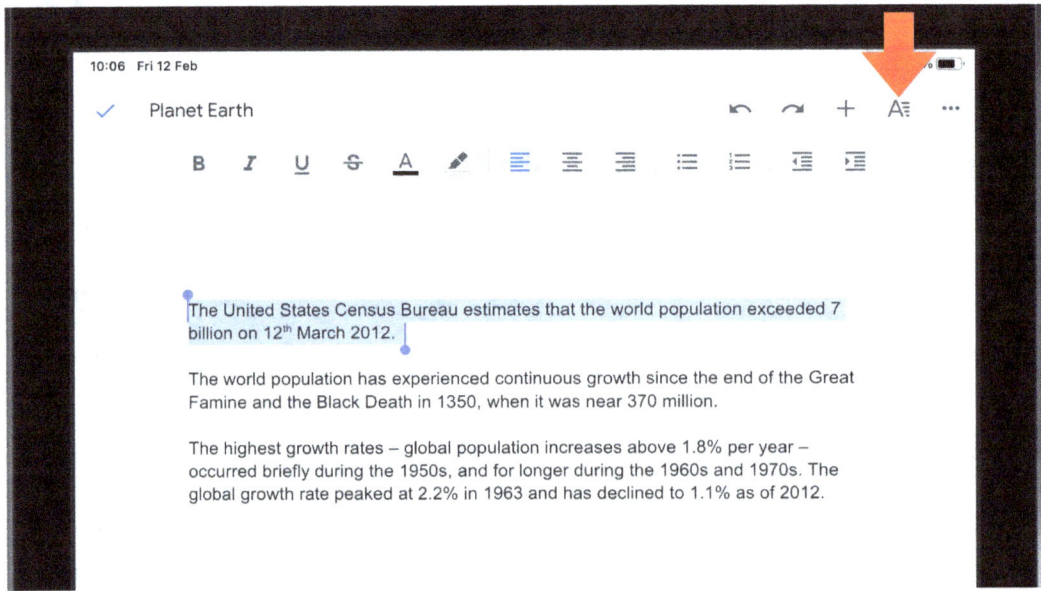

Chapter 8: Using Tablets

Select the 'paragraph' tab on the top of the drop down dialog box. Here, you can adjust the text alignment (left, centre, right, full). You can increase or decrease line indents, you can create numbered and non-numbered lists, and adjust the line spacing.

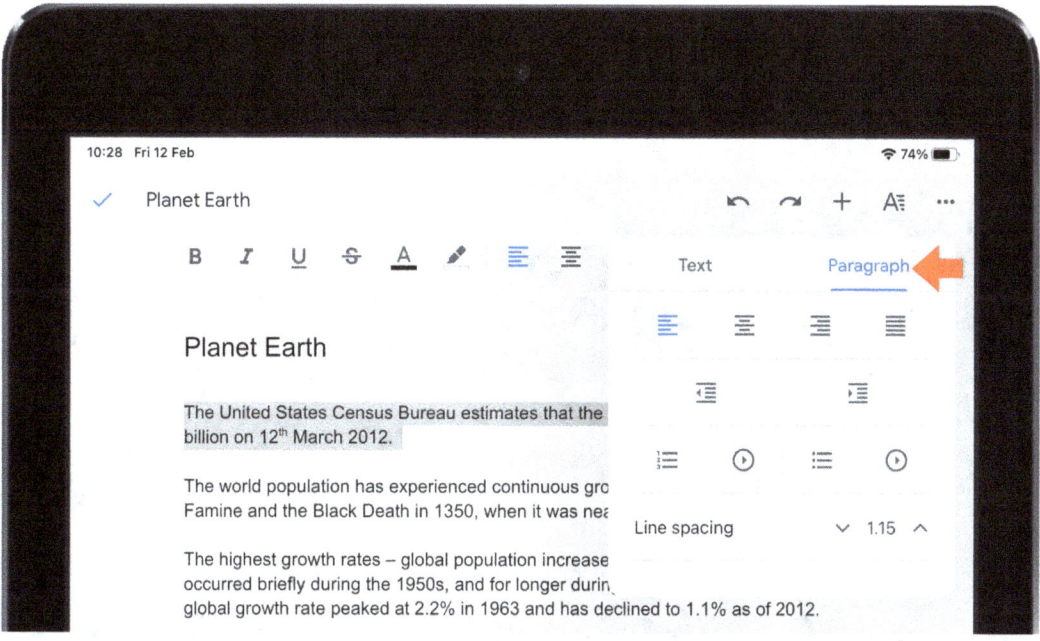

Insert Images

You can insert images saved in your photos on your tablet or directly from your camera. To do this, tap the line in your document where you want the image to appear. Tap the 'plus' icon on the top right, then select 'image' from the drop down menu.

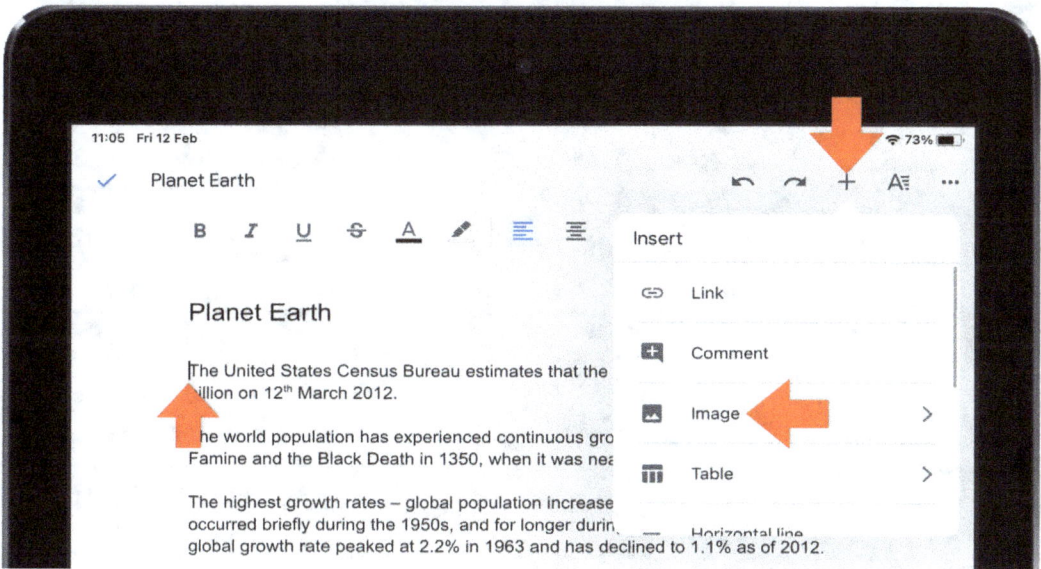

Chapter 8: Using Tablets

Select 'from photos' to select an image from your photo albums, or select 'from camera' to take one with your tablet's on-board camera.

Select an image to insert...

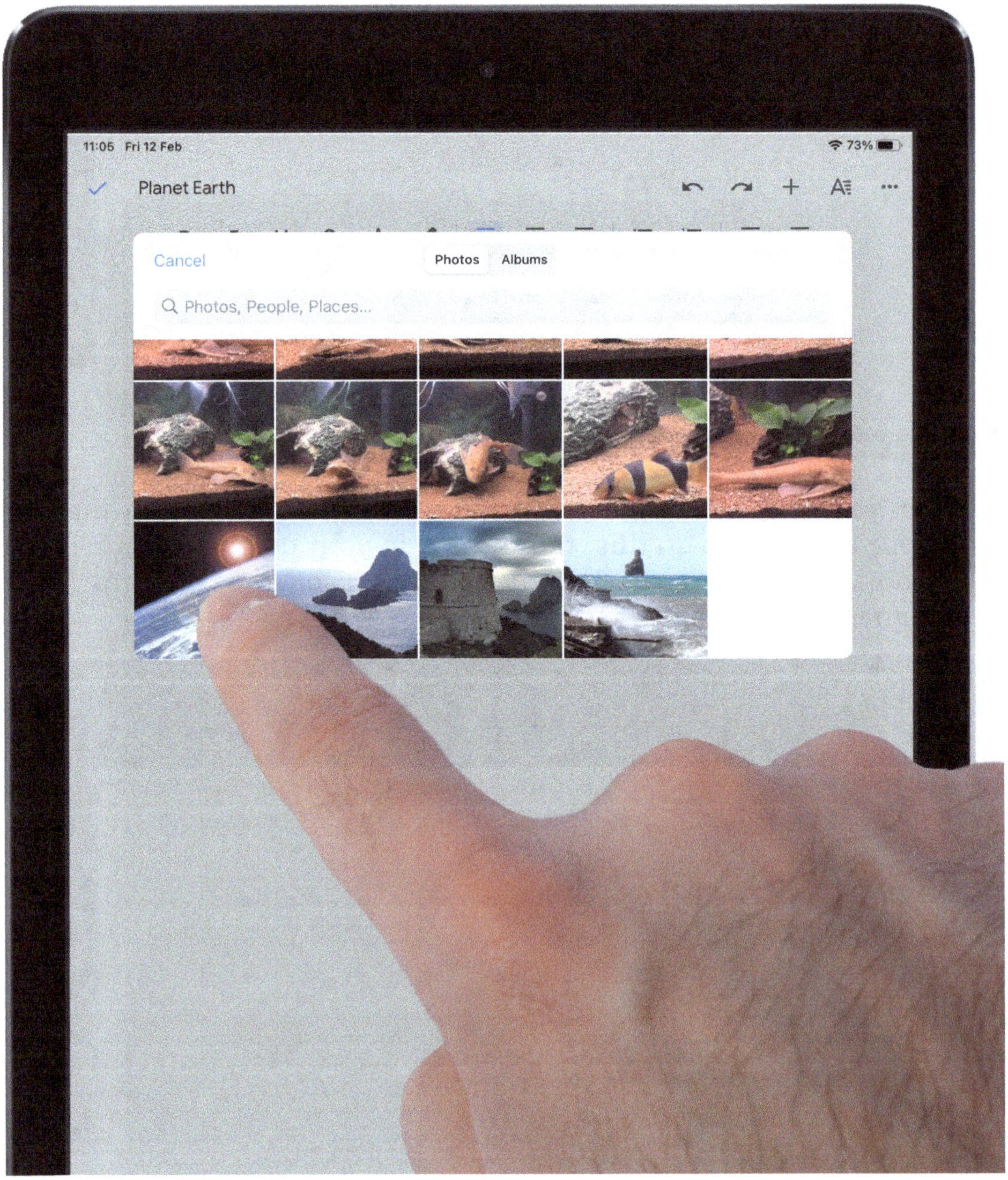

Chapter 8: Using Tablets

Resize Image

To resize an image, select it in your document. You'll notice a border appear around the image with resize handles appear

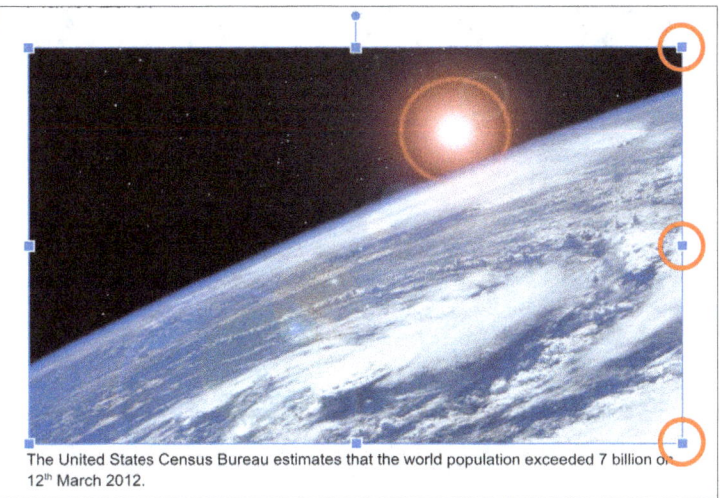

Tap and drag these handles to resize.

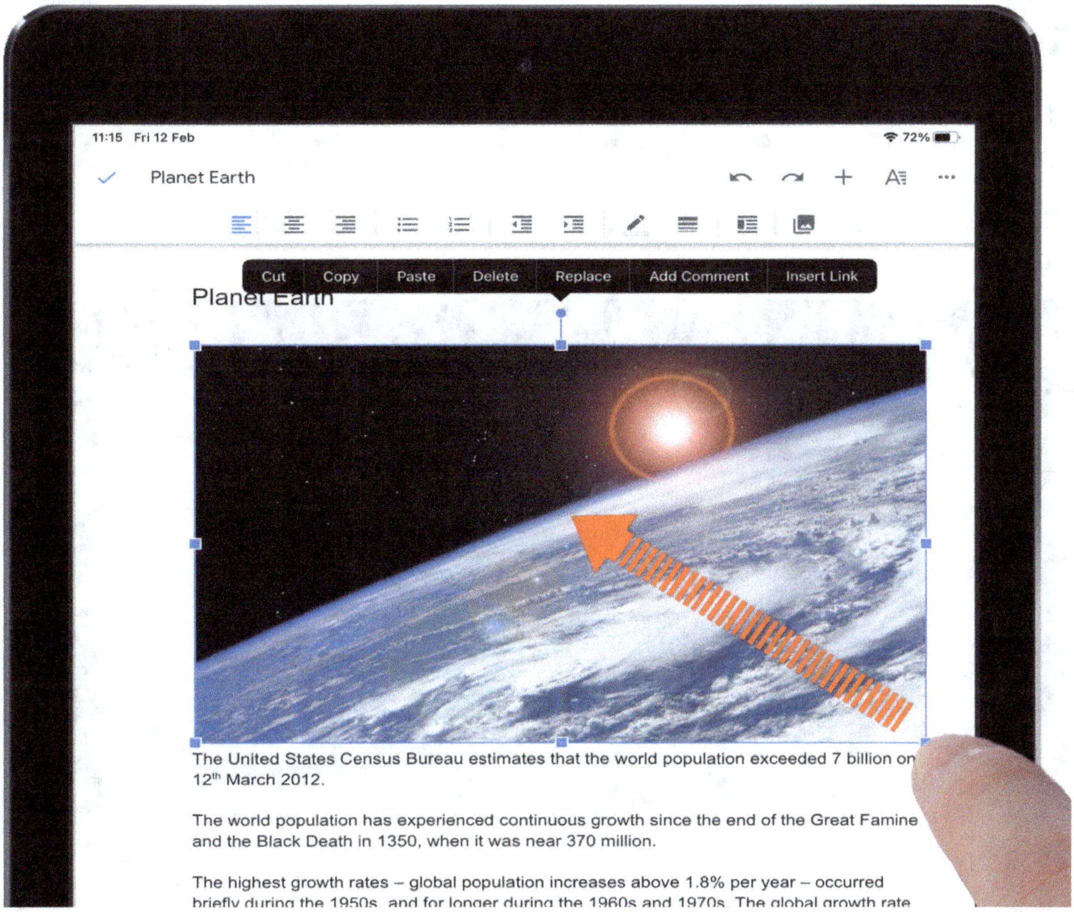

Chapter 8: Using Tablets

Insert Table

Tap the location in your document where you'd like the table to appear. Then tap the 'plus' icon on the top right of the screen.

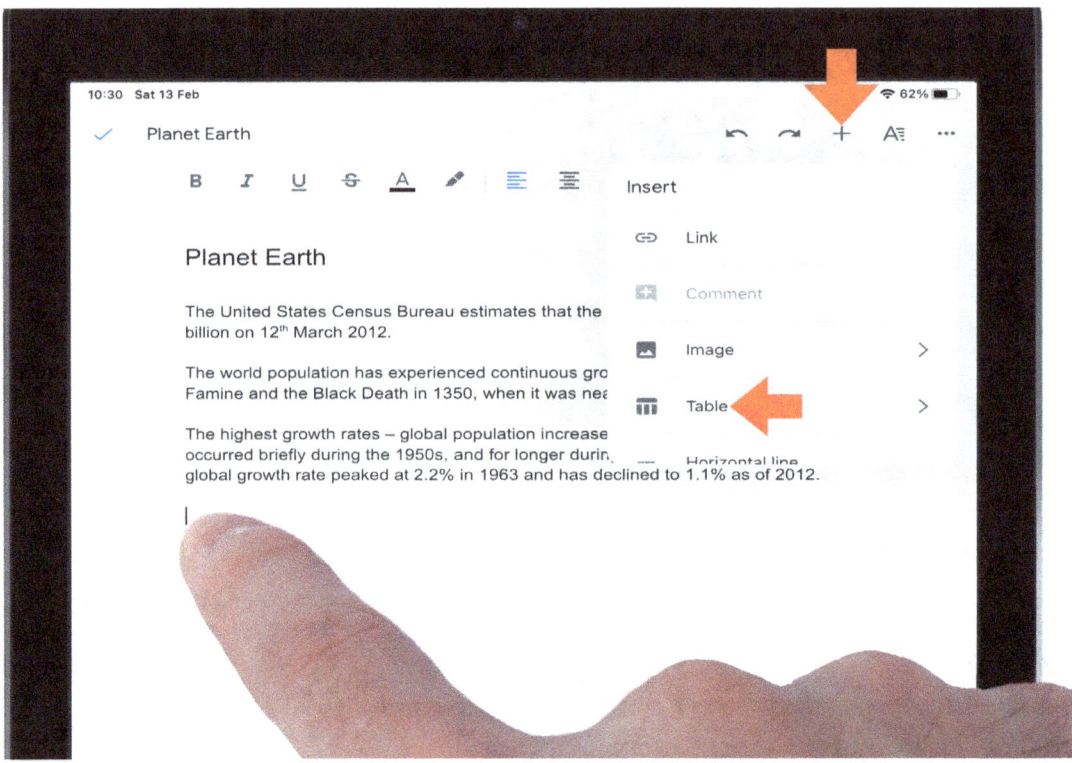

Choose the number of rows and columns you want in your table, then tap 'insert table'.

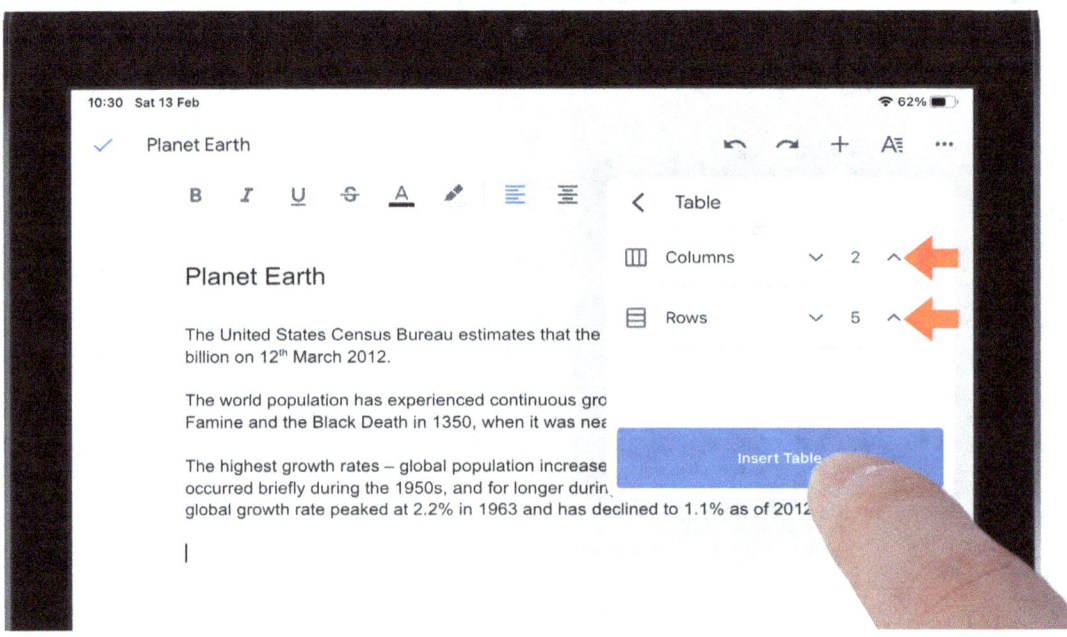

Chapter 8: Using Tablets

Insert Row

In our table, lets add a row between 'india' and 'USA'. To do this, tap in the row 'india' is in.

Country	Population	Percentage of World
China	1,372,000,000	18.5
India	1,276,900,000	17.5
USA	312,793,000	4.35
Indonesia	252,164,000	3.35

Tap the 'format' icon on the top right, then select the 'table' tab. Select 'row below'

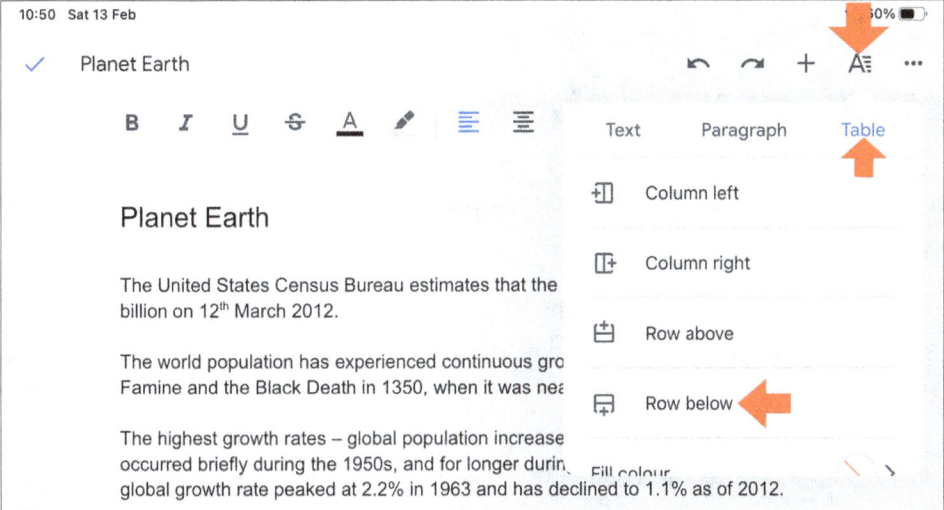

Insert Column

In our table, lets add a column between 'population' and 'percentage of world'. To do this, tap in the column 'percentage of world' is in.

Country	Population	Percentage of World
China	1,372,000,000	18.5
India	1,276,900,000	17.5
USA	312,793,000	4.35
Indonesia	252,164,000	3.35

187

Chapter 8: Using Tablets

Tap the 'format' icon on the top right, then select the 'table' tab. Select 'column left'

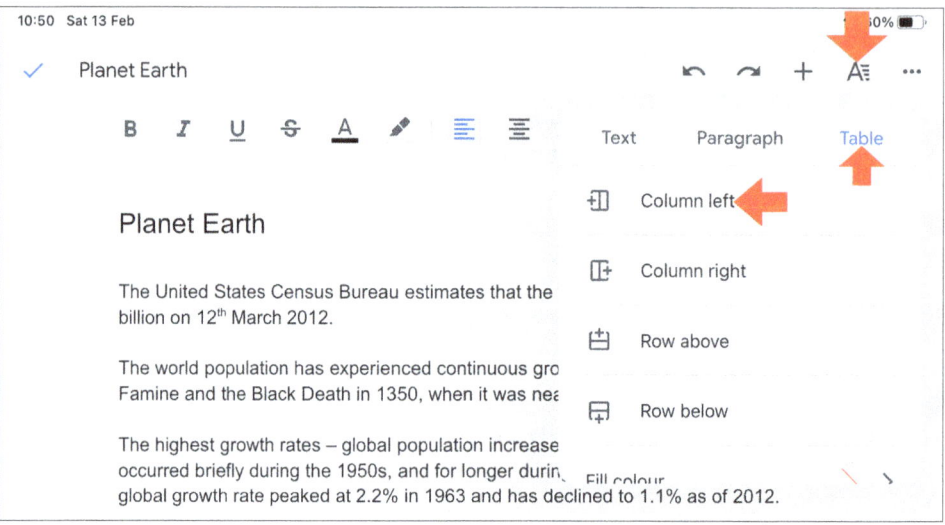

Format your Table

First select the cells you want to format. To do this tap on the first cell, you'll see a blue border appear with two dots either side. These are called resize handles.

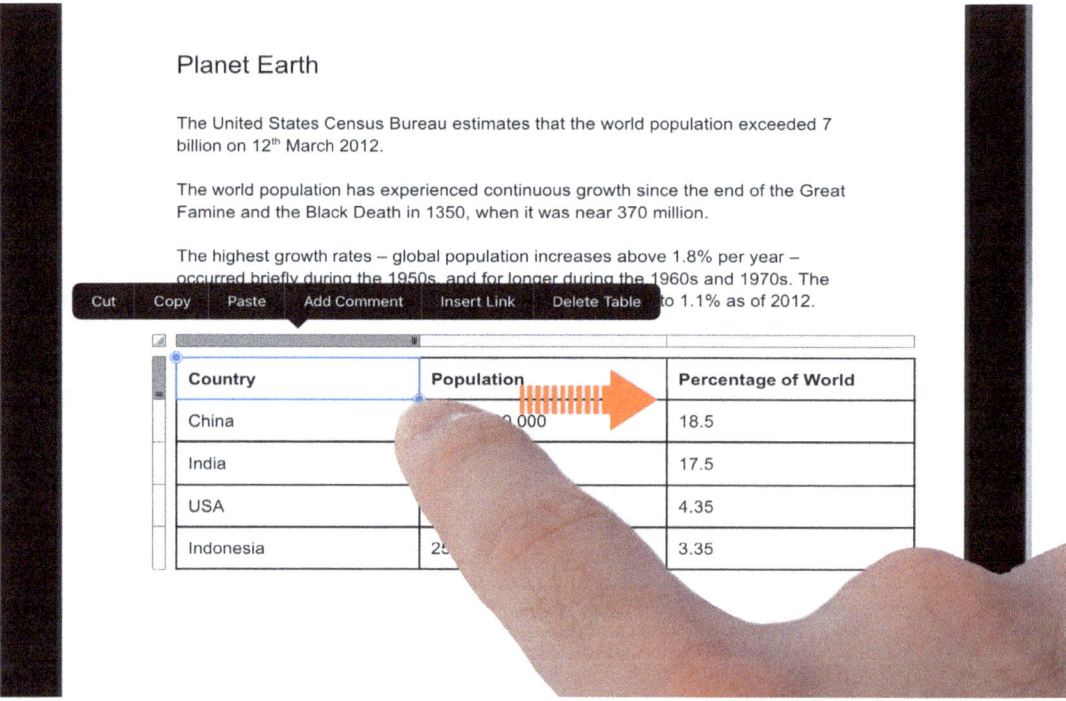

Tap and drag these handles to select the cells you want.

188

Chapter 8: Using Tablets

Tap the 'format' icon on the top right, then select the 'table' tab.

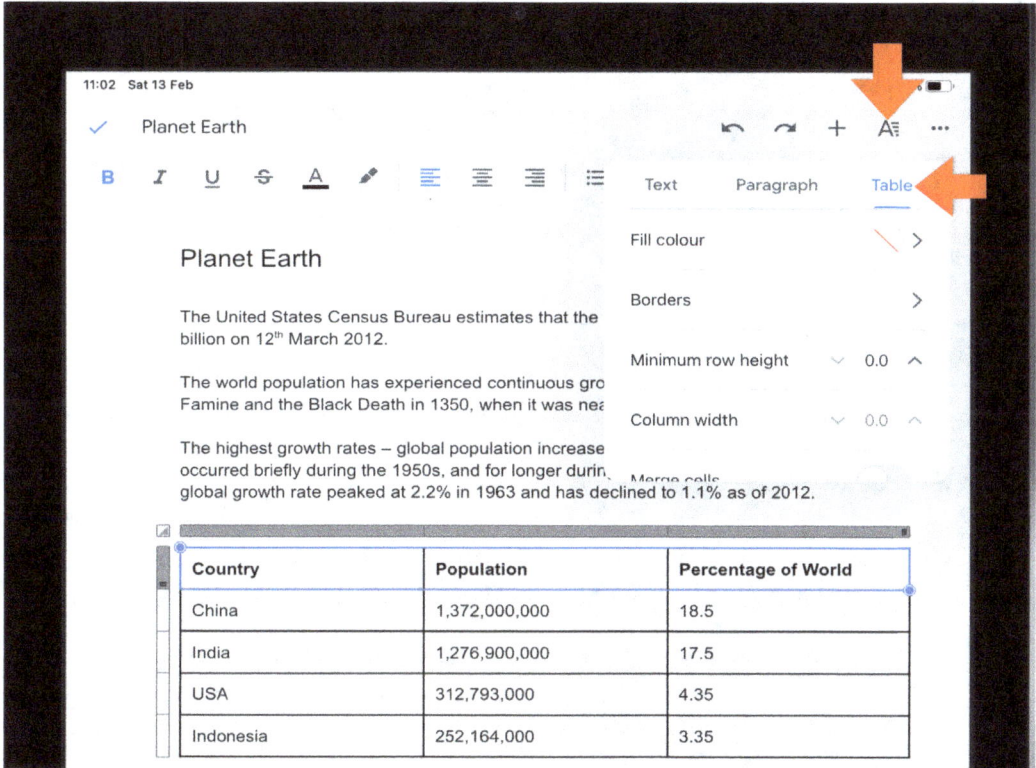

Here, you can change your fill colour, borders, row height and column width.

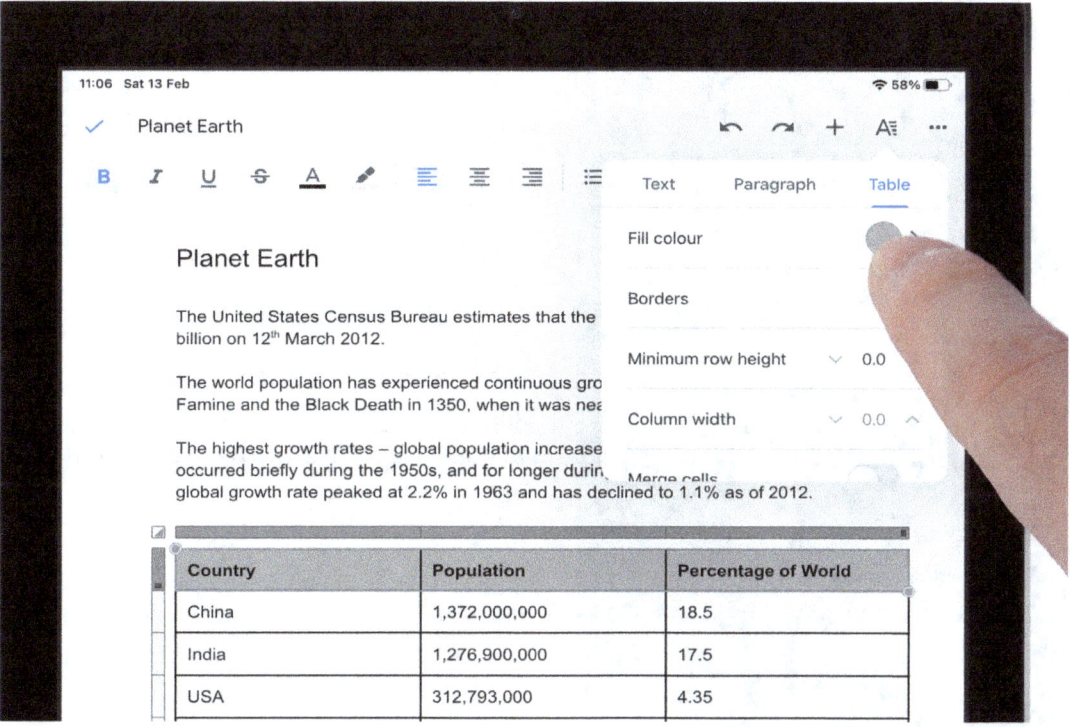

9

Using Google Drive

Google Drive is a cloud storage and synchronization service developed by Google that allows users to store files and synchronize them across multiple devices including Windows, Mac, and chromebook, as well as Android and iPad/iPhone.

You get 15 GB of space on your Drive for free but you can subscribe to various storage plans to suit your needs.

- Opening Google Drive
- On the Web
- The App
- Getting Around Google Drive
- Sync Files with your Computer
- Google Drive for Desktop
- Backup and Sync

Have a look at the video resources section. Open your web browser and navigate to the following website.

elluminetpress.com/
google-drive

Chapter 9: Using Google Drive

Opening Google Drive

Once you've created your Google Account, you can access Google Drive in any web browser (ideally chrome), or from the Google Drive App if you're using a tablet or phone

On the Web

To access Google Drive on the web, open your web browser, then navigate to the following website.

`drive.google.com`

The App

If you're using Google Drive on a tablet or phone, open the app store then download Google Drive if you haven't already done so.

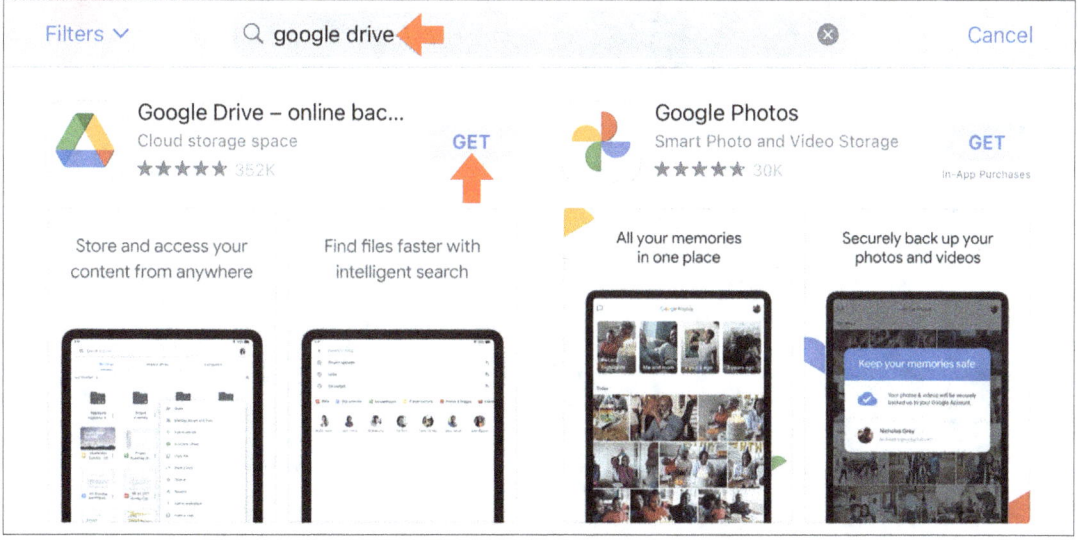

You'll find the Google Drive app on your home screen.

Just tap on the icon to start the app

191

Chapter 9: Using Google Drive

Getting Around Google Drive

Once you sign into Google Drive using your web browser, you'll land on the home screen. Let's take a look. Down the left hand side panel you'll see some options.

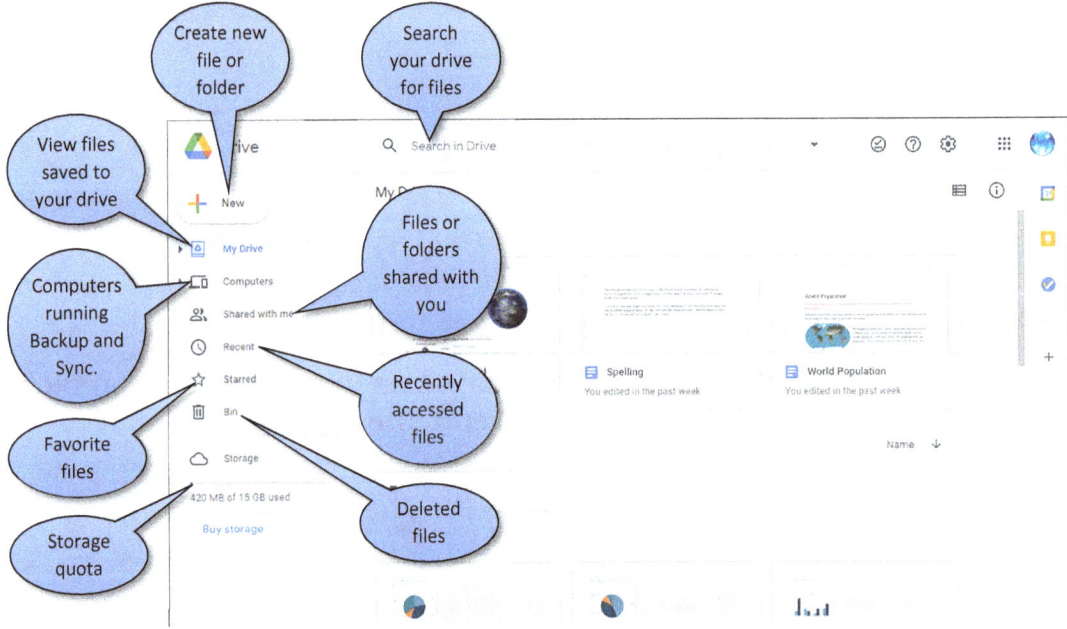

In the main screen, you'll see your 'my drive' view with a list of all the files and folders you've saved to your drive.

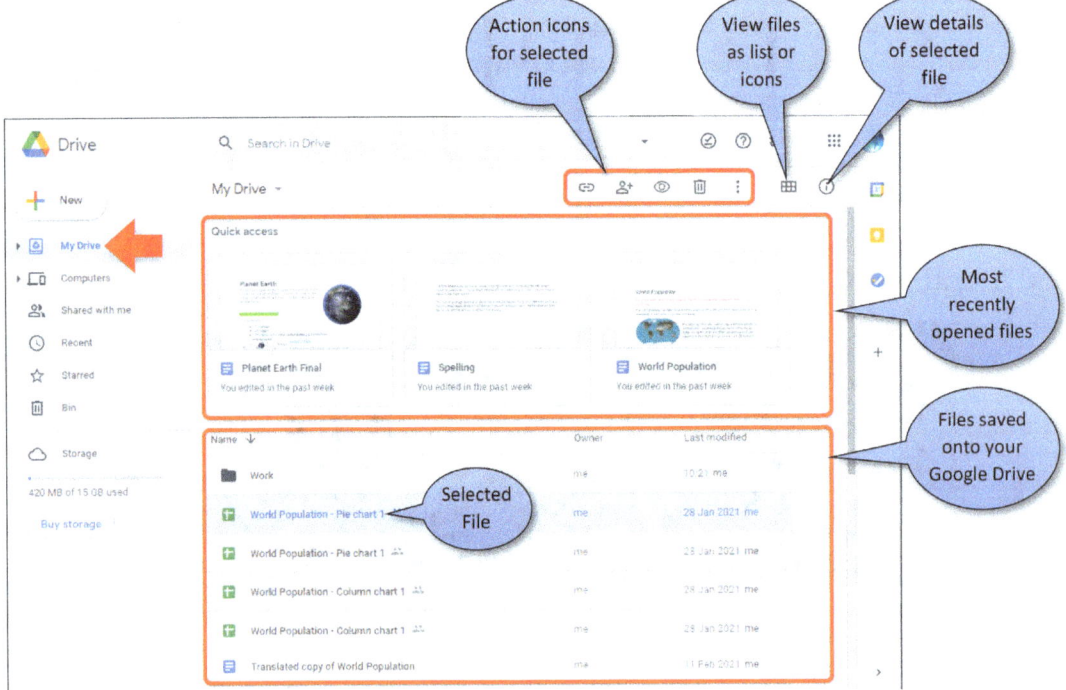

192

Chapter 9: Using Google Drive

If you select a file, you'll see an icon panel appear on the top right. Here, you can create a shareable link, share the file, preview the file or delete the file.

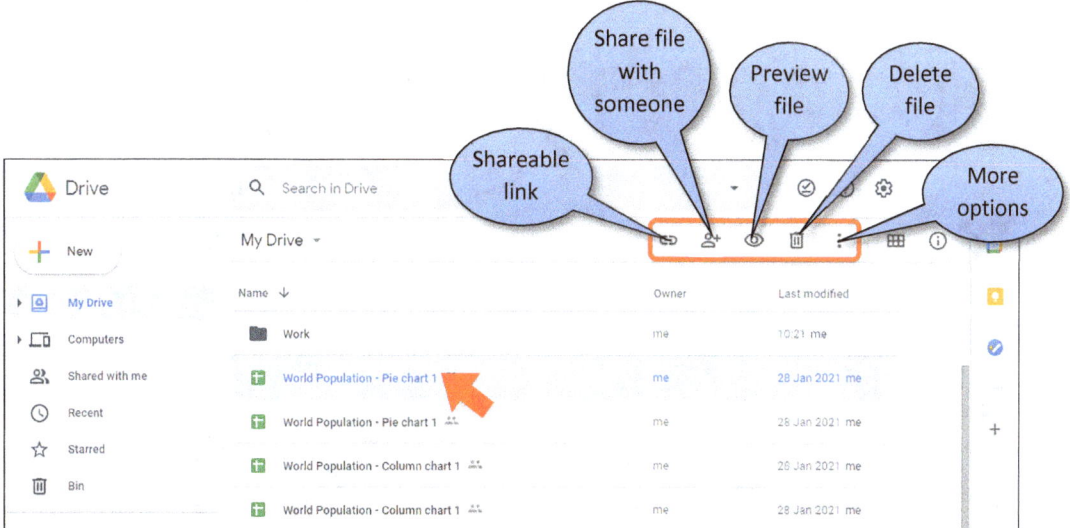

Select the 'more options' icon and you can open the selected file with another app, add a shortcut to your drive sidebar, move the file to another folder, make the file available offline, rename the file, view the file's details, make a copy and download the file for use in another application such as Word, Excel, etc.

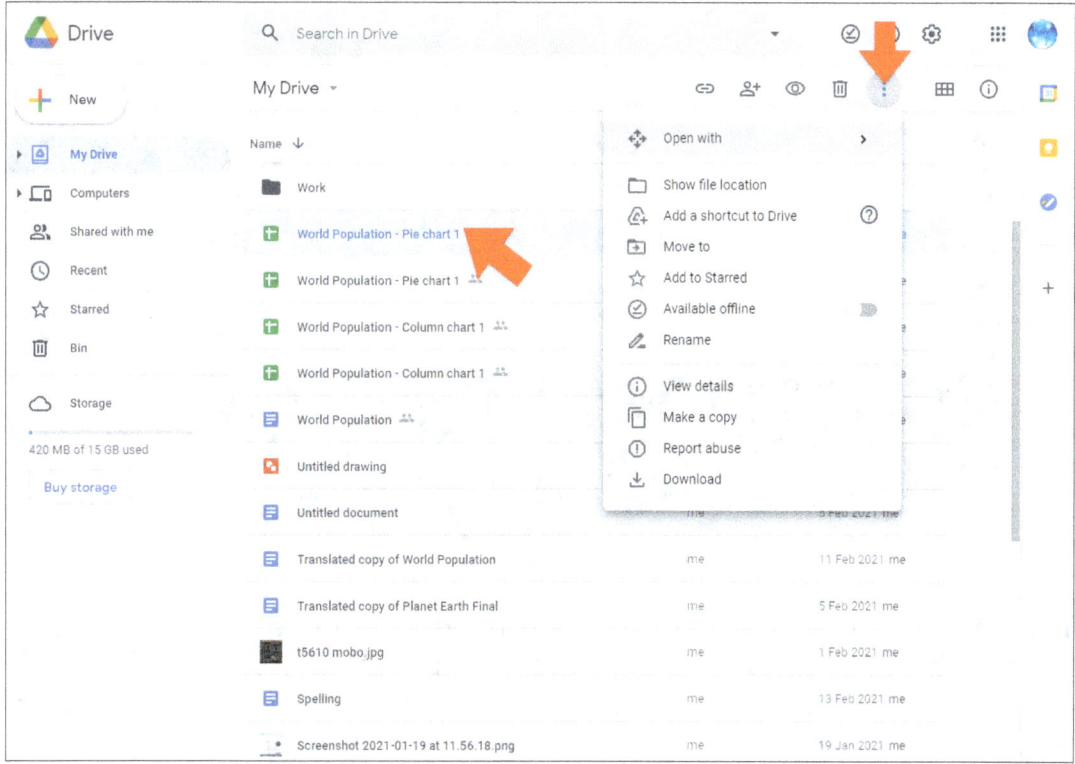

Chapter 9: Using Google Drive

If you're using the app on your phone or tablet, things look a little different. To see all your files and folders, tap the 'files' icon on the right hand side of the icon panel along the bottom of the screen. View your files as icons as shown below - tap the 'view as' icon on the top right.

Tap on a file to open it up. Tap the three dots icon on the bottom right of each thumbnail icon to view actions you can take on that file, such as share a link, rename, view details, or delete. Tap the large plus icon on the bottom right to create a new folder or file.

194

Chapter 9: Using Google Drive

Sync Files with your Computer

You can sync files with your PC, chromebook, mac, phone or tablet.

To sync files between your computers and Google Drive, you'll need to download and install the Google Drive for Desktop or Backup and Sync utility. To do this open your web browser and navigate to the following website.

www.google.com/drive/download

Google Drive for Desktop

Google Drive for desktop (formerly known as Drive File Stream) is best suited for organisations using Google Drive or Team Drive to share files amongst multiple users working in collaboration. You can't use this version with individual Google Accounts.

Backup and Sync

Backup and Sync is the consumer version of the utility and is aimed at home and individual users.

Chapter 9: Using Google Drive

To install backup and sync, scroll down the installation web page to the 'individual' section. Click 'download'.

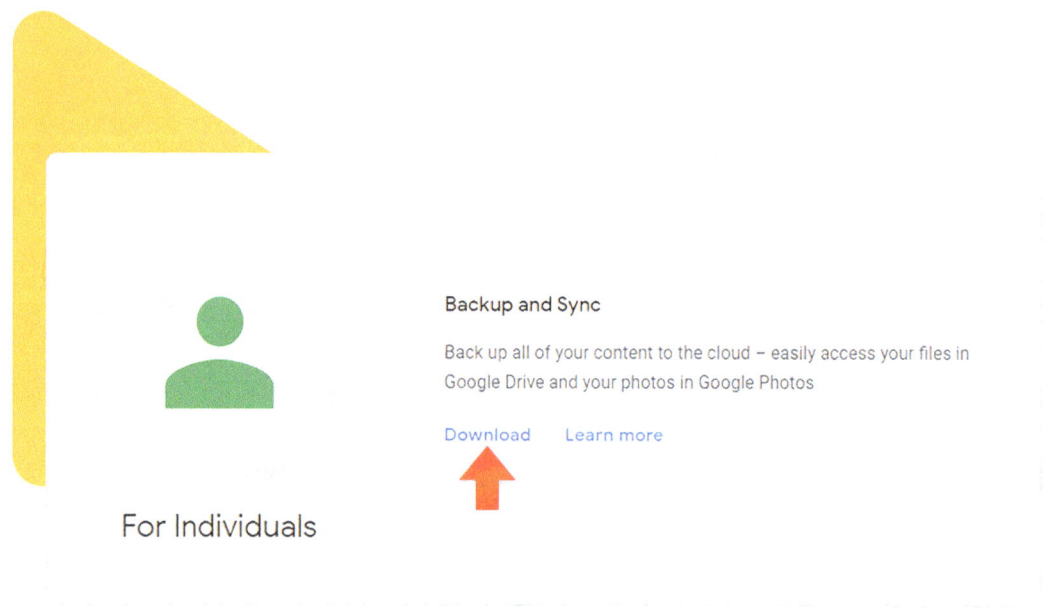

Click the download on the bottom left of your screen to begin. If you don't see a prompt, you'll find the utility in your downloads folder.

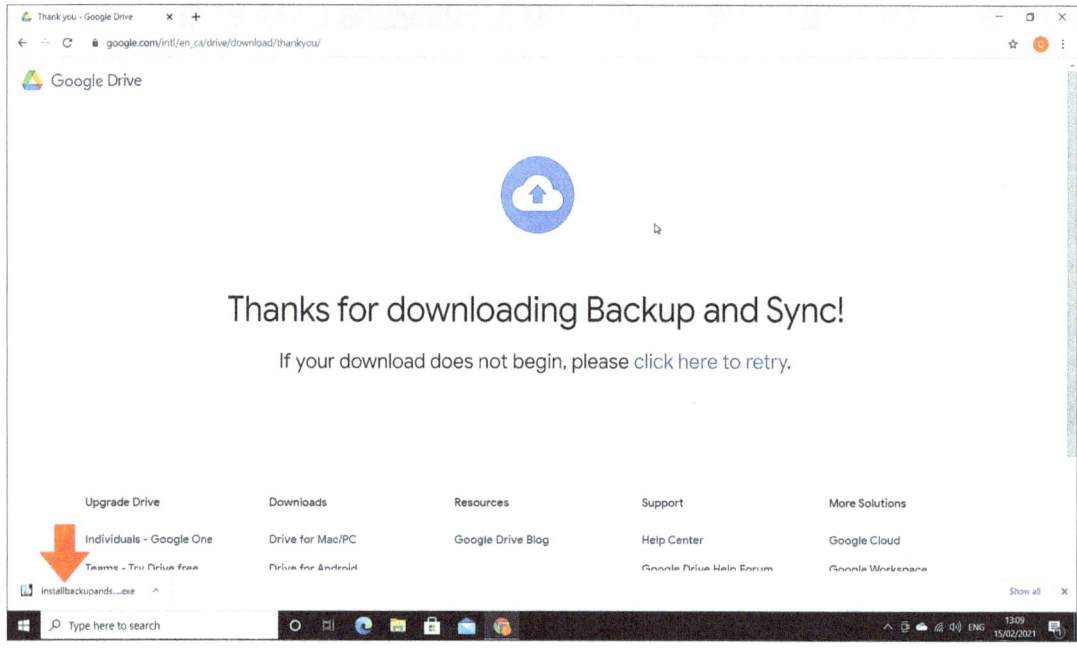

Follow the prompts on the screen to begin the setup.

The utility will download and install on your computer. After a few seconds, you'll see the install wizard appear.

Chapter 9: Using Google Drive

Click 'get started'

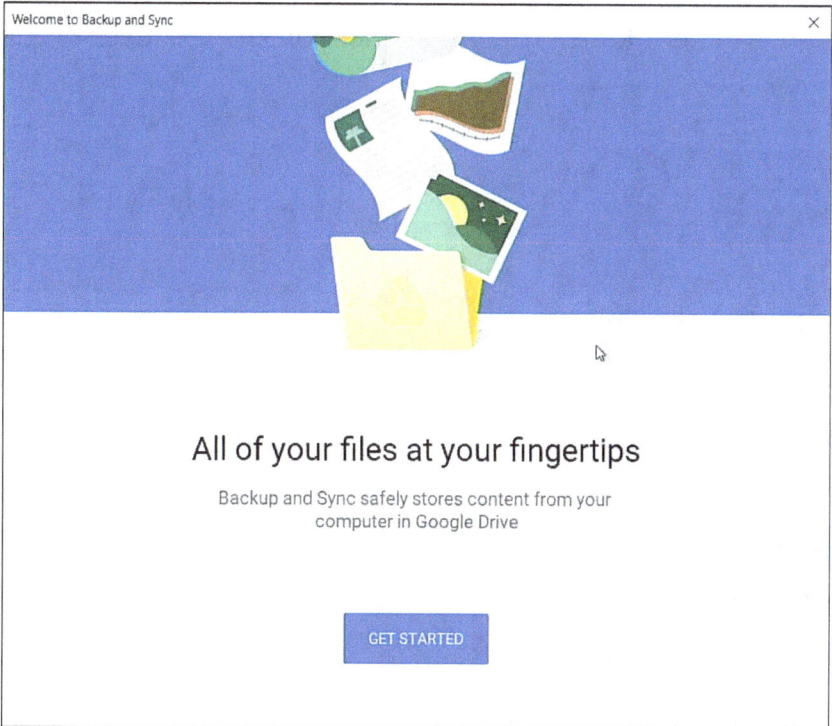

Sign in with your Google Account email address and password.

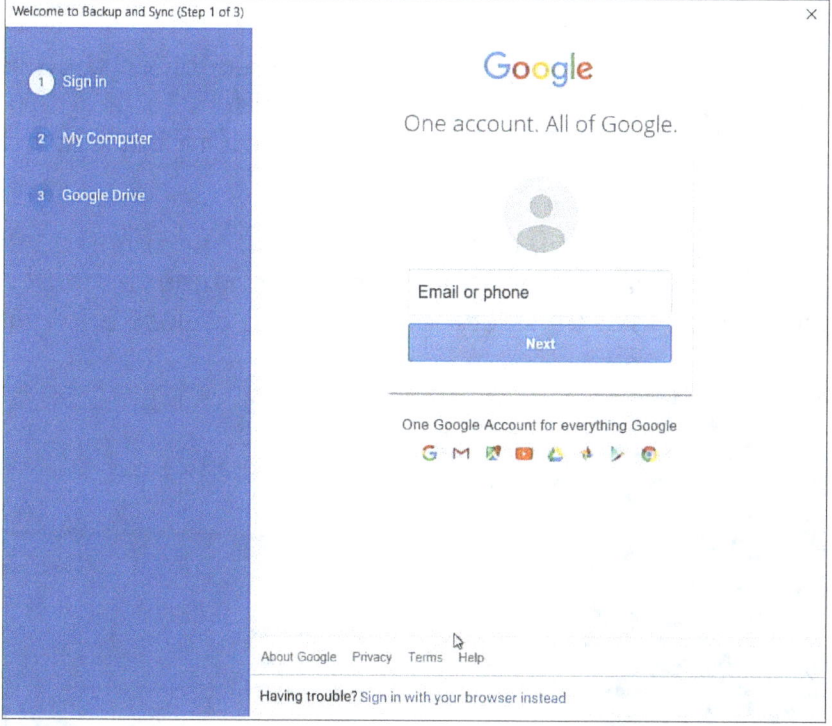

Click 'next'.

Chapter 9: Using Google Drive

Select any folders on your computer you want to backup to Google Drive. This could be your documents folder, pictures, or any folder you save files to. These folders appear in the 'computers' section on Google Drive.

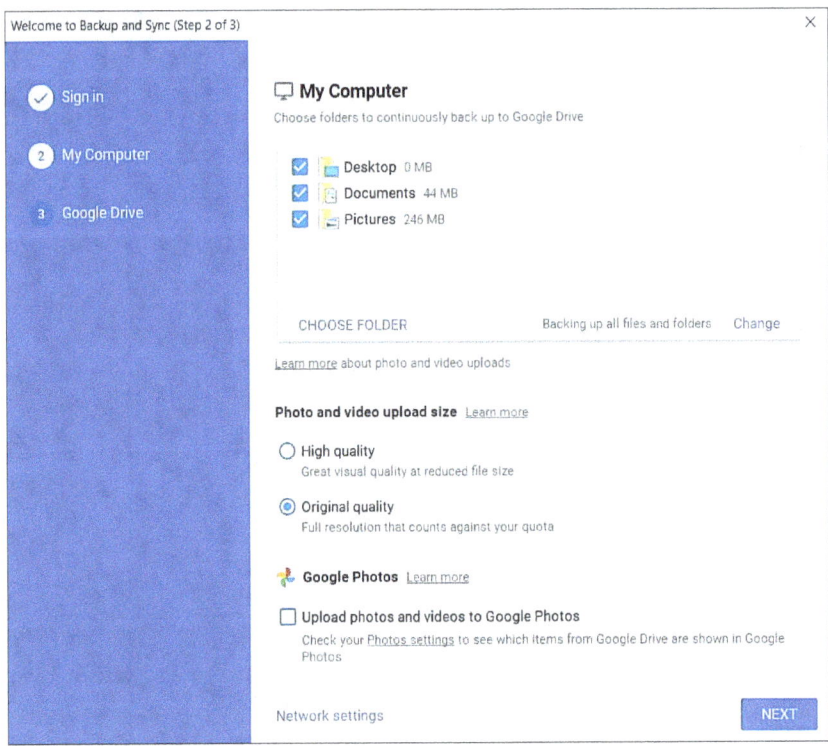

If any folders you use don't appear, click 'choose folder' then select the folder to add. You don't have to select any folders to backup and you can untick all the suggestions if you don't want to backup files. Click 'next'.

Select 'sync my drive to this computer'. Most of the time you can leave this in the default location, but if you need to change the folder or drive Google Drive syncs files to, select 'change' then choose a folder.

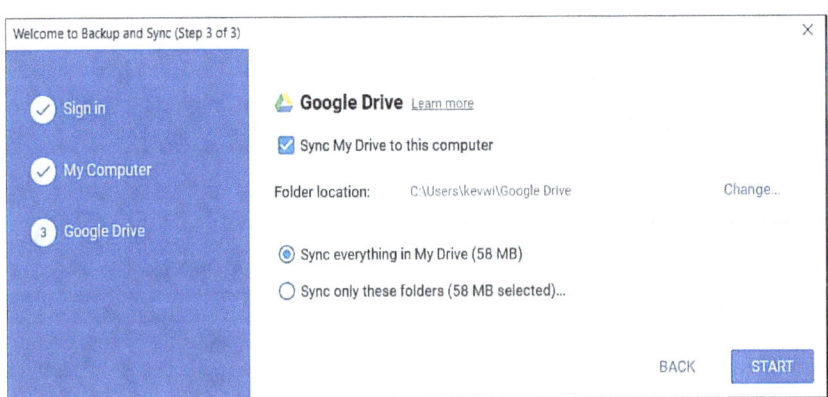

Select 'sync everything in my drive', then click 'start'.

Chapter 9: Using Google Drive

You'll notice some icons appear on your desktop, these are shortcut icons to Google Drive, Docs, Sheets, etc.

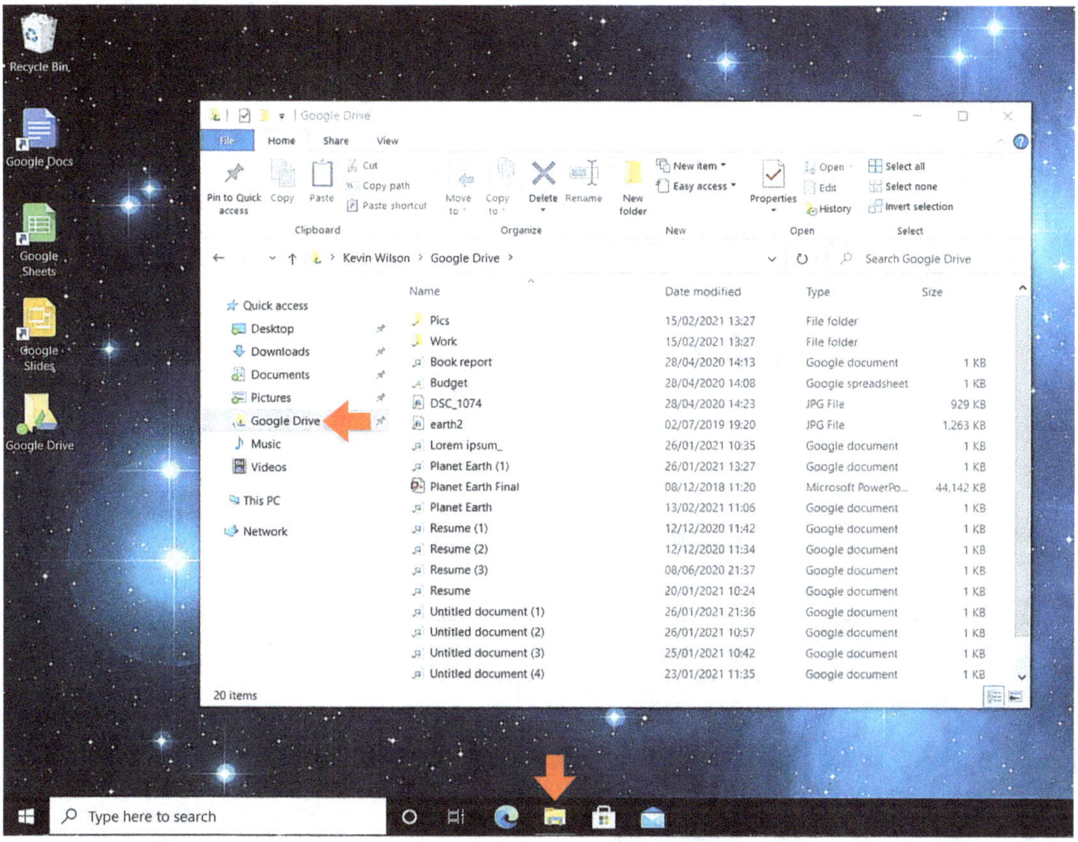

You'll also find the Google Drive folder in File Explorer. This is where you should save new files that you want to sync across to Google Drive and be available on all your devices.

You'll also see the backup and sync utility in the system area on the bottom right of the screen. Here you can view recently synced files as well as change settings.

The icons along the top of the window allow you to view Google Drive folder in File Explorer, open Google Drive in a web browser, open Google Photos.

The three dots icon on the top right, will reveal a drop down menu, where you can change settings, pause sync, or change account.

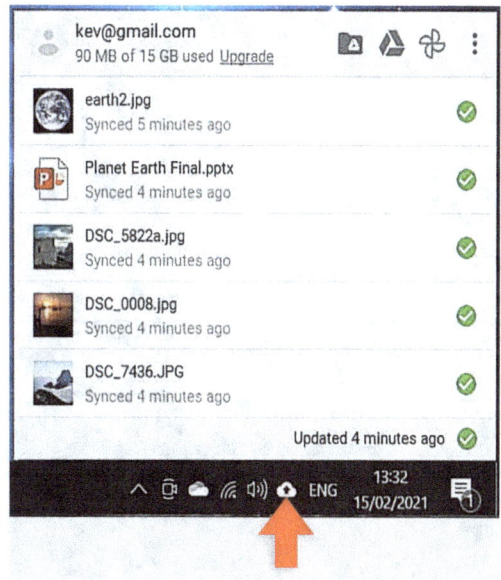

199

Resources

To help you understand the procedures and concepts explored in this book, we have developed some video resources and app demos for you to use, as you work through the book.

To find the resources, open your web browser and navigate to the following website

elluminetpress.com/google-docs

At the beginning of each chapter, you'll find a website that contains the resources for that chapter.

Appendix A: Resources

File Resources

To save the files into your OneDrive documents folder, right click on the icons above and select 'save target as' (or 'save link as', on some browsers). In the dialog box that appears, select 'OneDrive', click the 'Documents' folder, then click 'save'.

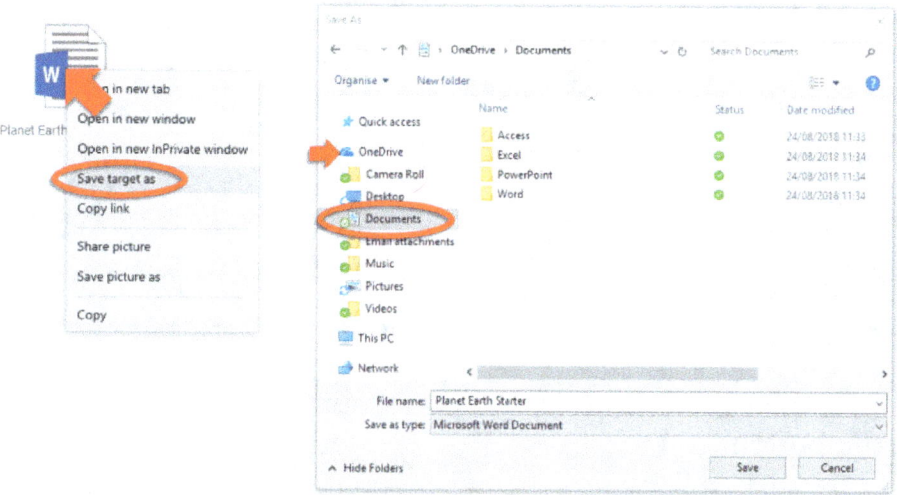

Upload a document to your Google Drive. Click on the 'file picker' icon on the right hand side of the home screen.

Select the 'upload' tab, then click 'select a file from your device', or 'browse'.

Select a document you want to upload from the ones you downloaded from the website.

Google Docs will convert it for you.

201

Appendix A: Resources

Video Resources

The video resources are grouped into sections for each chapter in the book. Click the thumbnail link to open the section.

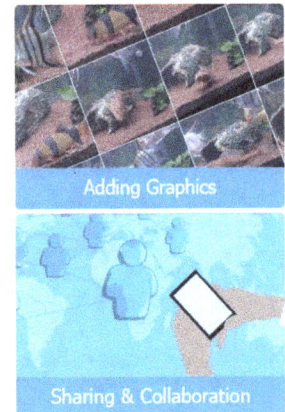

When you open the link to the video resources, you'll see a thumbnail list at the bottom.

Click on the thumbnail for the particular video you want to watch. Most videos are between 30 and 60 seconds outlining the procedure, others are a bit longer.

202

Appendix A: Resources

When the video is playing, hover your mouse over the video and you'll see some controls...

Let's take a look at the video controls. On the left hand side:

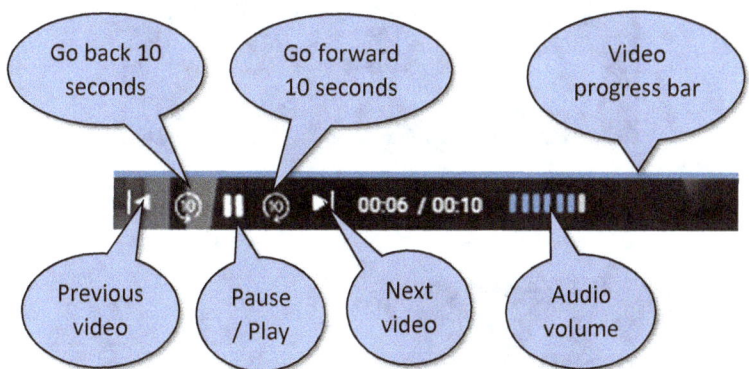

On the right hand side:

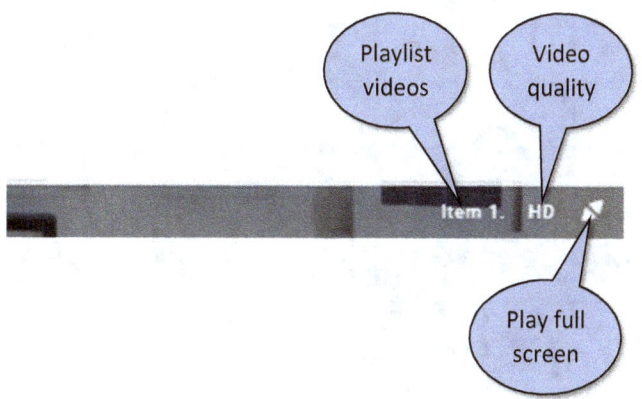

203

Appendix A: Resources

Scanning the Codes

At the beginning of each chapter, you'll a QR code you can scan with your phone to access additional resources, files and videos.

iPhone

To scan the code with your iPhone/iPad, open the camera app.

Frame the code in the middle of the screen. Tap on the website popup at the top.

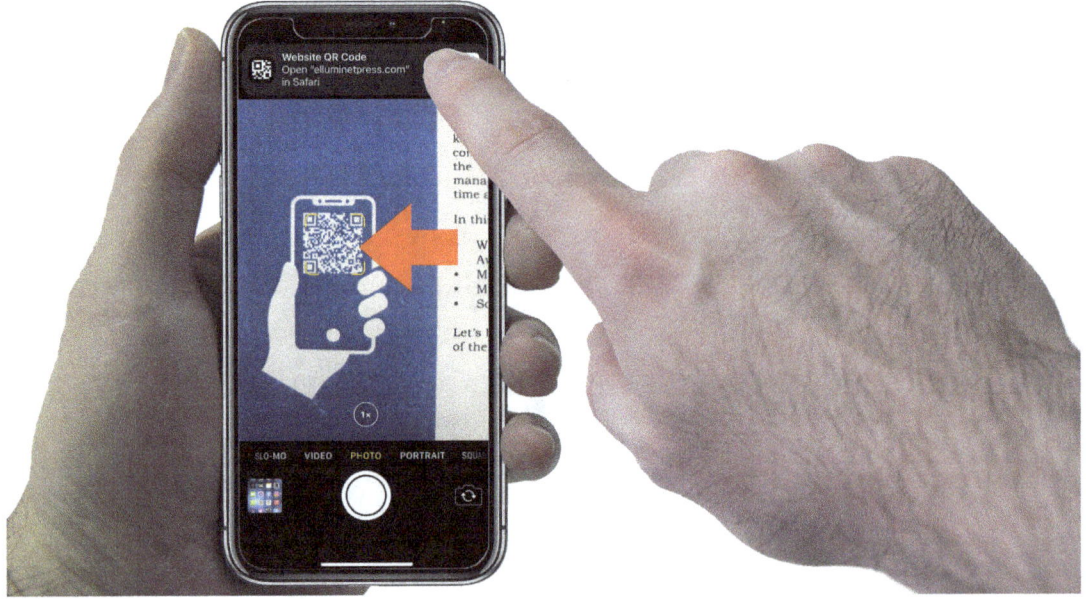

Appendix A: Resources

Android

To scan the code with your phone or tablet, open the camera app.

Frame the code in the middle of the screen. Tap on the website popup at the top.

If it doesn't scan, turn on 'Scan QR codes'. To do this, tap the settings icon on the top left. Turn on 'scan QR codes'.

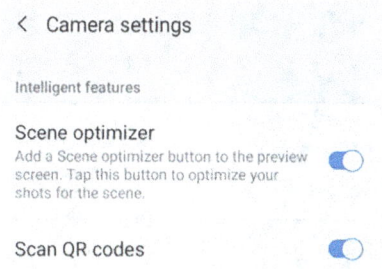

If the setting isn't there, you'll need to download a QR Code scanner. Open the Google Play Store, then search for "QR Code Scanner".

205

Index

A
Add Ons - 172
   Install - 172
   Manage - 175
   Useful Add-ons - 175
AI Tools - 170
Align Text - 32
app - 176
Approvals - 148
artificial intelligence - 170
Attachment - 163
Automatic Document Generation - 78

B
Backup and Sync - 195
Bold - 46
Breaks - 61
Bulletise - 171
Bullet List - 53

C
Case - 51
Center Align - 32
Charts - 119
   Axis Title - 123
   Background Colour - 123
   Border Colour - 123
   Customise - 121
   Data - 124
   Download & Publish - 127

Index

    Effects - 123
    Gridlines - 126
    Horizontal Axis - 125
    Title - 123
    Vertical Axis - 125
Checklists - 76
Chrome - 24
Collaboration - 128
    Accepting the Invitation to Collaborate - 131
    Chatting with Other Collaborators - 132
    Commenter - 130
    Comments - 133
        Making - 133
        Reply - 134
        Resolve - 134
    Editor - 130
    Making Edits - 132
    People without Google Accounts - 141
    Sharing a Document - 129
    Sharing a Link - 137
        Restricted Links - 139
        Sharing a Link with Anyone - 137
    Stop Sharing a File - 143
    Suggestions - 135
    Viewer - 130
Columns - 68
Contents Pages - 69
Converting Documents - 155
    ePub - 155
    HTML - 155
    Microsoft Word - 155
    PDF - 155
    RTF - 155
Copy & Paste - 43
Cropping Images - 91
Cut & Paste - 41

D

Define - 166
Dictate Text - 28
Document Approvals - 148

Index

Document Tabs - 72
Download Chart - 127
Download Google Drive - 191
Download Google Drive App - 191
Downloading Documents - 155
   ePub - 155
   HTML - 155
   PDF - 155
   RTF - 155
   Word - 155
Drawings - 95
   Images - 100
   Shapes - 97
Drive File Stream - 195

E

Elaborate - 171
Email as Attachment - 163
   HTML - 164
   PDF - 164
   Plain Text - 164
   RTF - 164
   Word - 164
Emojis - 71
Equations - 58
eSignatures - 144
Export as Another Format - 155

F

File Stream - 195
First Line Indent - 33
Font Color - 49
Font Size - 49
Footers - 63
Footnotes - 67
Formatting Text - 181

G

Gemini - 16, 102
Generating Images with AI - 102

Google Account - 15, 19
   Creating - 19
Google Chrome - 24
Google Docs App - 177
Google Drive - 191
Google Drive App - 191
Google Drive for Desktop - 195
Google Gemini - 16
Google One - 17
Google Workspace - 15
Grammar - 167

H

Hanging Indent - 34
Headers - 63
Help me create - 78
Help Me Write - 170
Hidden Characters - 55
Highlighting Text - 48
Hyper-links - 57

I

Images - 81
   Camera on Laptop - 86
   Camera on Tablet/Phone - 87
   Cropping Images - 91
   From Google Drive - 81
   Google Photos - 82
   Insert Images on iPad - 183
   Resize Image on iPad - 185
   Resize Images - 89
   Rotate an Image - 90
   Upload from PC - 83
   Web Search - 84
   Wrap Text around Images - 93
Indenting a Line - 33
Indents - 33
   Customize indents - 36
   First Line - 33
   Hanging Indent - 33, 34
   Line Indent - 33

Index

Inserting Footers - 64
Inserting Headers - 63
iPad - 176
iPhone - 176
Italic - 46

J
Justification - 32

L
Left Align - 32
Line Spacing - 40
Lists - 53
Lookup - 166
Lowercase - 51

M
Menus - 22
Microsoft Edge - 24

N
New Document - 27
Numbered Lists - 53

O
Opening Documents - 151

P
Padding - 111
Page Breaks - 61
Paragraph Formatting - 182
Paragraph Spacing - 39
Paste without Formatting - 45
PDF - 155
Photos - 81
Printing - 156
   Margins - 161
    Page Setup - 156
    Paper Size - 160
    Print - 159
    Quality - 162

Index

    Scaling - 162
Publish Chart - 127

R

Refine - 171
Resize Images - 89
Resources - 200
Right Align - 32
Rotate an Image - 90
Ruler - 36
Rulers - 23

S

Section Breaks - 61
Selecting Text - 31
Sharing - 128
Sharing a Document - 129
Shorten - 171
Signature - 144
Sign In - 20
Signing a Document - 147
Smart Canvas - 73
    Smart Checklists - 76
    Smart Chips - 73
    Smart Tables - 77
    Smart Templates - 75
Smart Chips - 73
Spelling - 167
    Corrections - 168
    Suggestions - 168
Start Screen - 21
Styles - 52
Subscript - 47
Summarise - 171
Superscript - 47
Symbols - 54
Sync - 195
Sync Files with your Computer - 195

T

Tables - 77, 105

    Borders - 109
    Cell Alignment - 112
    Cell Color - 107
    Cell Padding - 111
    Column Width - 114
    Delete Column - 118
    Delete Row - 118
    Format Table on iPad - 188
    Insert Column - 117
    Insert Column on iPad - 187
    Inserting Tables - 105
    Insert Row - 115
    Insert Row on iPad - 187
    Insert Table on iPad - 186
    Merge Cells - 113
    Row Height - 114
    Split Cells - 113
    Text Formatting - 107
Tablets - 176
Tabs - 37
Template - 27
Templates - 75
Text Align - 32
Text Color - 49
Text Size - 49
Text Wrap - 93
Titlecase - 51
Toolbars - 22
Translation - 165

U

Underlined - 46
Uploading Documents - 153
Uppercase - 51

V

Voice Commands - 30
Voice Dictation - 28

W

WordArt - 96

Workspace - 15
Wrap Text - 93

SOMETHING NOT COVERED?

We want to create the best possible resources to help you learn and get things done, so if we've missed anything out, then please get in touch using the links below and let us know. Thanks.

   office@elluminetpress.com

 elluminetpress.com/feedback

www.ingramcontent.com/pod-product-compliance
Lightning Source LLC
Chambersburg PA
CBHW051404070526
44584CB00023B/3285